Gentrification in a Global Context

Gentrification in a Global Context brings together fresh theoretical and empirical work on gentrification in the context of increasing changes and pressures focused on neighbourhoods in cities across the globe. Processes of class colonisation in the deprived locales of cities across the world now appear commonplace with the consequences often being a series of secondary social problems which have included the dislocation of the urban poor and a growing community conflict over local territories.

This book provides a balanced re-assessment of a subject that has deeply divided commentators, policy-makers and community activists. While gentrification has appeared to physically improve neighbourhoods and has been linked to the wider economic development of cities it has also forced out existing residents leading to fundamental questions about the social cost of urban revitalisation. Gentrification in a broad range of countries across the globe is presented with authors both re-considering well-trodden debates as well as new primary research.

The causes and consequences of upward neighbourhood trajectories require a new contextualisation in the face of globalising economic shifts, neo-liberal urban policies, the need to promote re-development in de-industrial cities and the continuing growth of professional class fractions in many new national economies. The authors in this volume provide critical reflections on this much discussed phenomenon that give new light and energy to a contested form of urban change which continues to challenge observers.

Aimed at undergraduates, academics and those with an interest in urban affairs and injustices more generally, this book is designed to be an integrated introduction as well as contemporary survey of gentrification with an expansive set of geographical reference points. A truly global collection comprises contributions from the USA, UK, Canada, Australia, Japan, Eastern and Southern Europe, Turkey, Brazil, Germany, and Poland among others.

Rowland Atkinson is a lecturer in the Department of Urban Studies, University of Glasgow. **Gary Bridge** is senior lecturer at the Centre for Urban Studies, School for Policy Studies, University of Bristol.

D0061066

Housing and society series

Edited by Ray Forrest
School for Policy Studies, University of Bristol

This series aims to situate housing within its wider social, political and economic context at both national and international level. In doing so it will draw on the full range of social science disciplines and on mainstream debate on the nature of contemporary social change. The books are intended to appeal to an international academic audience as well as to practitioners and policymakers – to be theoretically informed and policy relevant.

Housing and Social Change
East–West perspectives
Edited by Ray Forrest and James Lee

Urban Poverty, Housing and Social Change in China
Ya Ping Wang

Gentrification in a Global Context
The new urban colonialism
Edited by Rowland Atkinson and Gary Bridge

Forthcoming
Housing and Social Policy
Edited by Peter Somerville and Nigel Sprigings

Managing Social Housing
David Mullins, Barbara Reid and Richard Walker

Housing Structures
Shaping the space of twenty-first century living
Bridget Franklin

Gentrification in a Global Context

The new urban colonialism

Edited by Rowland Atkinson
and Gary Bridge

Taylor & Francis Group

LONDON AND NEW YORK

First published 2005
by Routledge
2 Park Square, Milton Park, Abingdon, Oxon OX14 4RN

Simultaneously published in the USA and Canada
by Routledge
270 Madison Ave, New York, NY 10016

Routledge is an imprint of the Taylor & Francis Group

Typeset in Times and Frutiger by
HWA Text and Data Management, Tunbridge Wells
Printed and bound in Great Britain by
TJ International Ltd, Padstow, Cornwall

British Library Cataloguing in Publication Data
A catalogue record for this book is available from the British Library

Library of Congress Cataloging in Publication Data
A catalog record for this book has been requested

ISBN 0–415–32950–7 (hbk)
ISBN 0–415–32951–5 (pbk)

Contents

Contents

Contributors

Rowland Atkinson is a lecturer in the Department of Urban Studies at the University of Glasgow. He has maintained a strong interest in gentrification since completing his doctorate on gentrification and displacement in Greater London. He has written on issues relating to urban public space, neighbourhood change, social inequalities and affluent spaces.

Matthias Bernt studied Political Sciences at Freie Universität of Berlin and wrote his dissertation on the changing urban renewal politics of Berlin. Since 2001 he has worked as a Researcher in the Department for Urban and Environmental Sociology at the UFZ – Centre for Environmental Research Leipzig-Halle. His main fields of interest are governance and urban renewal. He has been active in tenants' organizations and neighbourhood initiatives in East Berlin for several years.

Gary Bridge is Senior Lecturer in the Urban Research Centre, School for Policy Studies, University of Bristol. His publications include *A Companion to the City* (Blackwell 2000) and *The Blackwell City Reader* (2002) both co-edited with Sophie Watson, and *Reason in the City of Difference: Pragmatism, Communicative Action and Contemporary Urbanism* (Routledge 2004).

Eric Clark is a professor in the Department of Geography, University of Lund. His research has considered the limits of the empirical application of economic theories relating to the processes underpinning gentrification activity. More recently he has focused his interests on the human geography, biogeographic and evolutionary components of island existence. His current work draws again on the importance of gentrification processes and on metaphors in multicultural cities for socially equitable development.

Paul Dutton is Senior Lecturer in Housing and Urban Studies and the Director of the Centre for Research in Applied Community Studies at Bradford College.

He has published work on gentrification and his research interests also include housing and urban policy, housing markets and socio/economic restructuring.

Yoshihiro Fujitsuka is Associate Professor of Geography in the Faculty of Education at Kochi University. His teaching and empirical research concerns economic restructuring, inner city problems, gentrification and urban revitalisation. He has been Chairperson of the Kochi City Planning Committee.

Daniel J. Hammel teaches in the Department of Geography-Geology and the Stevenson Center for Community and Economic Development at Illinois State University. His research explores the effect of market and policy forces on the American inner city.

Andrej Holm, Humboldt University of Berlin, Dipl.Sowi (Social Sciences); 1998–2001 Research Fellow at the DFG (German Research Foundation) on 'Prenzlauer Berg – Housing Modernisation and Urban Renewal under Changing Conditions'; 2001–3 graduate student in Urban Sociology at the Humboldt University of Berlin ('Restructuring the Space and Social Power in Urban Renewal Areas'). He has been active in tenants' organizations and neighbourhood initiatives in East Berlin for several years.

Tolga Islam is a PhD Student in the Department of Urban and Regional Planning at Yildiz Technical University, Istanbul. He has studied the gentrification process in the Galata neighbourhood of Istanbul in his masters thesis and has presented a number of papers about the gentrification processes taking place in Istanbul.

Jerome Krase is Emeritus and Murray Koppelman Professor at Brooklyn College, CUNY and was an activist-scholar in NYC neighbourhoods. He publishes and lectures on 'visual/spatial semiotics' in the US and abroad. Published works include *Self and Community in the City* (University Press of America 1982), *Ethnicity and Machine Politics* (University Press of America 1992), *Italian Americans in a Multicultural Society* (Forum Italicum 1994) and *Ethnic Communities in New York City* (2004).

P. Manuel Martínez Monje is Associate Professor of Social Inequality and Exclusion at the University of the Basque Country. His current research focuses on the links between urban poverty, spatial exclusion and urban development in advanced capitalist societies.

Petros Petsimeris is Professor at the University of Paris I. He is an urban geographer and has conducted extensive in-depth research on gentrification and micro-social processes in cities in southern Europe. His work has often focused on the experiences of residents in declining areas as well as that of minority ethnic groups in the major cities of Italy, Greece, France and Spain.

Silvana Rubino is Professor at the Department of History of the Universidade Estadual de Campinas (State University of Campinas), São Paulo. Her fields of research and articles are about the politics of cultural heritage, intellectual history in Brazil, musems and modern architecture, and gentrification of areas landmarked as historical. She has published in periodicals such as *Revista o Patrimônio Histórico e Artístico Nacional*, *Revista da USP*, among others. Now she is conducting an inventory of historical building in Campinas and a research about the first working-class neighbourhood of the same town.

Kate Shaw is an activist for cultural diversity and low-income housing in the city. She has a masters degree in Urban Planning and is completing a PhD on the politics of protecting places in the Faculty of Architecture, Building and Planning at the University of Melbourne.

Wendy Shaw is interested in manifestations of post-colonial whiteness in cities. Her research explores the theoretical debates about urbanism, cosmo-politanism and the complex realities of postcolonial urban life. Current projects include 'A postcolonial palimpsest of Honolulu', a study of emergent apartment landscapes and several collaborations in indigenous geographies.

Tom Slater is Lecturer in Urban Studies at the University of Bristol. He has research interests on a range of inner-city topics, especially gentrification, segregation, the politics of neighbourhood change, community organising and urban social movements.

Darren P. Smith is a Senior Lecturer in Human Geography at the University of Brighton. His research interests focus on processes of urban and rural transformations, particularly studentification and gentrification, which are tied to emerging cultural consumption practices and lifestyles, migration and new family forms.

Luděk Sýkora is Associate Professor at the Department of Social Geography and Regional Development, Faculty of Science, Charles University of Prague. His research focuses on urban restructuring in post-communist cities, impacts of globalisation on urban transformation, real estate development, housing and housing policy, urban strategic and physical planning in East Central Europe.

Lorenzo Vicario is Associate Professor of Urban Sociology at the University of the Basque Country. His main research interests include urban regeneration, spatial segregation and gentrification. His current research focuses on urban regeneration strategies and state-led gentrification in Spanish cities.

Elvin K. Wyly teaches at the Department of Geography at the University of British Columbia. His research focuses on the interaction of market processes and public policy in the production of inequality in US cities.

Acknowledgements

The editors and publishers wish to acknowledge with gratitutde the following for permission to reproduce previously published material. Figure 2.1: copyright © Andrea Mohin/The New York Times, reproduced by permission. Figures 2.2 and 2.3: photographs by Dan Hammel. Figure 3.1: enRoute magazine. Figure 3.2: photograph by Kertu Kurist. Figures 7.2 and 7.2 data from STERN. Figure 8.1: Atatürk Library of Istanbul Metropolitan Municipality. Figures 9.1–9.3: Population Census of Japan. Figure 9.4: Japanese National Tax Agency. Figures 13.1–13.4: source OPCS Census 1981, 1991.

1 Introduction

Rowland Atkinson and Gary Bridge

Globalisation and the new urban colonialism

Gentrification is now global. It is no longer confined to western cities. Processes of neighbourhood change and colonisation represented by an increasing concentration of the new middle classes can be found in Shanghai as well as Sydney, or Seattle. Nor is it now limited to the 'global' cities, the focus of much of the gentrification debate to date. It can now be found in new regional centres such as Leeds (United Kingdom) and Barcelona (Spain) as well as capital cities previously not associated with the process such as Moscow, Brussels and Berlin. All of this is to say nothing of the now rampant and almost exhaustive process of gentrification in cities like San Francisco, London, New York, and Melbourne. For some gentrification is now no longer even confined to cities, with examples of growing rural gentrification in the UK (Philips 1993; D. Smith 2003), or upstate New York.

The geographical spread of gentrification or 'gentrification generalised' as Neil Smith has recently called it (Smith 2002) raises questions about how much gentrification is a part of globalisation, involving, in this case, the growth of an international professional managerial class and the new or rehabilitated residential enclaves which they choose to colonise. To what extent is gentrification an important component for city governments of wider 'regeneration' strategies involving commercial or prestigious flagship arts of sporting facilities – what Monje and Vicario in this book call 'the Guggenheim effect' in the wake of Frank Gehry's museum in Bilbao? Alternatively how does the fact that gentrification has moved into very different urban contexts – rapidly urbanising, post-colonial, post communist, or communo/capitalist all overlaid by a diversity of cultural and religious forms – inflect, or indeed generate, a very different process? Is global gentrification hallmarked by its cultural, national or regional specificities?

A further set of questions is raised by these contextual details when pitched at the global scale. To what extent is gentrification a global phenomenon, with diverse causes and characteristics, or a phenomenon of globalisation, conceived as a process of capital expansion, uneven urban development and neighbourhood changes in 'new' cities? At the very least these questions raise a much wider research agenda than has often been presupposed by numerous local case studies at the neighbourhood and city scales in past years.

The current nature and extent of gentrification raises questions not just about its interrelations with globalisation but also its manifestation as a form of new urban colonialism. The geographical spread of gentrification over the last twenty years has been reminiscent of earlier waves of colonial and mercantile expansion, itself predicated on gaps in economic development at the national scale. It has moved into new countries and cities of the global 'south' but has also now cascaded down the urban hierarchies of regions within the urban north where it has been established for much longer. In short, gentrification appears to have migrated centrifugally from the metropoles of North America, Western Europe and Australasia. This has happened at the same time as market reform, greater market permeability and population migration have promoted internal changes in the economies of countries not previously associated with gentrification.

Contemporary gentrification has elements of colonialism as a cultural force in its privileging of whiteness, as well as the more class-based identities and preferences in urban living. In fact not only are the new middle-class gentrifiers predominantly white but the aesthetic and cultural aspects of the process assert a white Anglo appropriation of urban space and urban history.

The colonial aspects of gentrification are also evident through the universalising of certain forms of (de)regulation. There is the obvious spread of market discipline, such as the privatisation of housing markets in ex-communist countries for example. The neighbourhood transitions that result are accompanied, or indeed sometimes led by, an expansionist neo-liberalism in public policy that often accentuates the social divisions between gentrifiers and the displaced. As Hammel and Wyly argue in this book, these policies have resulted in a kind of neo-colonialism in the US context.

Gentrification in a global context also has the aspect of colonialism as the universalisation of forms of public administration. There is a trend towards urban governments around the world, of whatever particular political complexion, adopting gentrification as a form of urban regeneration policy broadly connected with an entrepreneurial style of urban governance (Harvey 1989a) and a focus on the middle classes as the new saviour of the city. As Neil Smith has argued, gentrification as urban policy has been tied to a whole range of 'revanchist' public policy measures (such as zero tolerance for the homeless in New York) that represents the elite re-taking the urban core (Smith 1996).

At the neighbourhood level itself poor and vulnerable residents often experience gentrification as a process of colonisation by the more privileged classes. Stories of personal housing dislocation and loss, distended social networks, 'improved' local services out of sync with local needs and displacement have always been the darker underbelly of a process which, for city boosters, has represented something of a saviour for post-industrial cities (Atkinson 2003b). Again Neil Smith (1996) has long argued that the symbolic and practical implications of the movement of the gentrification 'frontier' are profound and have had enormous implications for the fate and status of the colonised.

Those who come to occupy prestigious central city locations frequently have the characteristics of a colonial elite. They often live in exclusive residential enclaves and are supported by a domestic and local service class. Gentrifiers are employed in what Gouldner (1979) called 'new class' occupations, and are marked out by their cosmopolitanism. Indeed in many locations, especially in ex-communist European and east Asian countries, they often are western ex-patriots employed by transnational corporations to open up the markets of the newly emerging economies.

We suggest that debates emerging in gentrification research also capture the degree to which the 'colonial rule' of gentrification can be sustained in some of its outposts and at its margins. Twenty years ago Damaris Rose coined the term 'marginal gentrifier' to capture some of the variability of profiles and motives of those in the gentrification process (in her case poorer female lone parents) (Rose 1984). Now the sheer extent of gentrification raises questions about the gentrifier and neighbourhood types involved, especially away from the core cities and locations, calling for an expanded imagination and nuanced reading of the profile and contextual unravelling of the process. This has led to discussions about the emerging differences of provincial forms of gentrification and instances where the gentrification aesthetic has a weaker link to class identity (Dutton in this volume and Bridge 2003). In other words, the wider social, economic, political and cultural benchmarks within which gentrification has been interpreted have themselves shifted dramatically in a quarter of a century.

The range of these questions mark out the expanded terrain of this volume. It collects the writings of gentrification researchers from around the globe to assemble a comprehensive overview of its emerging forms and current conceptualisations. The book contains contributions from Australia, Canada, Japan, England, Spain, the Czech Republic, Turkey, Argentina, Germany, East European cities and the US. We include established scholars and voices that represent a new generation of gentrification researchers and which testify to the continued strength and relevance of gentrification research.

Forty years of gentrification research

The range of perspectives included in this volume is just the latest in a research area now entering its fifth decade. It is exactly forty years since the term 'gentrification' was coined by Ruth Glass in 1964. It is worth returning to Glass's original definition as a way of judging just what has happened to gentrification and gentrification research in the subsequent four decades:

> One by one, many of the working class quarters of London have been invaded by the middle classes, upper and lower. Shabby, modest mews and cottages – two rooms up and two down – have been taken over, when their leases have expired, and have become elegant, expensive residences. Large Victorian houses, downgraded in an earlier or recent period – which were used as lodging houses or were otherwise in multiple occupation – have been upgraded once again. Nowadays, many of these houses are being subdivided into costly flats or 'houselets' (in terms of the new real estate snob jargon). The current social status and value of such dwellings are frequently in inverse relation to their size, and in any case enormously inflated by comparison with previous levels in their neighbourhoods. Once this process of 'gentrification' starts in a district, it goes on rapidly until all or most of the original working class occupiers are displaced, and the whole social character of the district is changed.
>
> (Glass 1964: xviii–xix)

Since the time of Glass's article more than a thousand research papers, monographs, book chapters, government evaluations and reports have been written on the subject. Early developments were concerned essentially with an empirical mapping of the extent of the process in the larger western cities. Early definitions, like that of Glass, tended to focus on the residential housing market and the rehabilitation of existing properties. In the introduction to their landmark collection Smith and Williams defined gentrification as 'the rehabilitation of working-class and derelict housing and the consequent transformation of an area into a middle-class neighbourhood' (Smith and Williams 1986: 1). Since then the definition has been widened by some to include vacant land (usually in prior industrial use) and newly built designer neighbourhoods, as well as neighbourhoods of working-class housing suggesting a portability to the concept which has grown over time.

Where Glass's definition focused on 'sweat equity' gentrification, with the middle-class householder rehabilitating, or hiring a small builder to gentrify their dwelling, more recent discussions have included off-the-peg new-build developments, often beside water or in other landmark locations in the city. And most recently Smith has argued that gentrification has widened yet again to become a new form of neo-liberal urban policy (Smith 2002). Certainly the impacts of gentrification have been hotly disputed politically, with certain municipal governments, hungry for tax dollars, in the US and elsewhere, welcoming middle-class resettlement of the inner city. Alternatively a diversity of grassroots neighbourhood groups have opposed gentrification because of its effects in displacing the poor and the vulnerable (Marcuse 1989; Atkinson 2001a, 2001b; Slater 2002). Table 1.1 summarises some of the main neighbourhood impacts of gentrification.

Table 1.1 Summary of neighbourhood impacts of gentrification

Positive	Negative
	Displacement through rent/price increases
	Secondary psychological costs of displacement
Stabilisation of declining areas	Community resentment and conflict
Increased property values	Loss of affordable housing
	Unsustainable speculative property
Reduced vacancy rates	price increases
	Homelessness
Increased local fiscal revenues	Greater take of local spending through lobbying/articulacy
Encouragement and increased viability of further development	Commercial/industrial displacement
Reduction of suburban sprawl	Increased cost and changes to local services
	Displacement and housing demand pressures on surrounding poor areas
Increased social mix	Loss of social diversity (from socially disparate to rich ghettos)
Rehabilitation of property both with and without state sponsorship	Under-occupancy and population loss to gentrified areas

As the significance of this social/physical neighbourhood change was noted, the conceptual meaning of gentrification, its origins and characteristics became the subject of dispute. Early interpretations saw it as a 'back to the city' movement of middle-class suburbanites wanting better proximity to jobs and the kind of cultural and recreational infrastructure that were hard to find on city peripheries (Laska and Spain 1980). From a Marxist perspective Smith countered this with the assertion that gentrification was a 'movement of capital, not people'. For Smith gentrification was explained by the 'rent gap' which was the difference between the potential value of inner urban land (low – because of abandonment due to de-industrialisation and suburbanisation) and its potential value (if put to a higher and 'better' use). When the gap between actual and potential values was wide enough investors would discount the riskiness of inner urban land because of the greater opportunity for profit by re-investing on devalorised land and closing the rent gap. Gentrification was one way of closing the rent gap.

While the rent gap theory was set in a Marxist critique of global capitalism it focused on the relativities of land values between a city and its suburbs. At its widest, the explanation looks to an urban system within the nation-state. Equally, it is hard to imagine Ley's 'following the hippies' explanation of the urban liberal neighbourhood movements in waterside Vancouver accounting for the massive expansion of gentrification in 1980s London, which although involving an enlargement of the professional managerial class, was associated strongly with financial deregulation of the City of London (Big Bang). In earlier explanations of gentrification both 'capital' and 'culture' were very firmly located in a national context.

The early distinction between a back-to-the-city movement of capital or a back-to-the-city movement of people has persisted in the literature on gentrification in various guises (production/consumption, capital/culture, supply/demand, production of gentrifiable housing/production of gentrifiers, Marxist or liberal explanations). David Ley (1986, 1996) in his work on Canada has suggested how the bohemianism of a student generation following the hippy era fed the pro-urbanism of this generation as they entered new middle-class occupations. This lifestyle aesthetic informed their activism in neighbourhood preservation and the politics of a liveable city (Ley 1996). At the same time in the USA Neil Smith has argued that middle-class pro-urbanism has now been replaced by a desire for revenge on the poor and the socially marginal. This 'revanchism' has taken the form of middle classes re-occupying, forcibly in some cases, and re-appropriating the central core of the city through the operation of the property market, gentrification, and by other means, for example the use of the police and legal agencies.

Some authors have sought to encompass the insights of both capital and cultural explanations for gentrification. Sharon Zukin's (1982, 1995) work suggests how cultural innovation, particularly around the activities of artists, can at first attract and then in fact be displaced by commercial forms of gentrification – capital captures culture. Chris Hamnett (1994b) has argued that neither culture nor capital arguments are particularly germane and points to the expansion of professional occupational sectors in key cities, of which gentrification is a residential manifestation. Loretta Lees (2000) suggests that the complex geography of gentrification means that both culture and capital explanations have a part to play. More recently there have been some attempts to reconcile culture and capital arguments by using the work of Pierre Bourdieu to look at gentrification as a manifestation of cultural capital (Butler 2003; Butler and Robson 2001; Bridge 2001a, 2001b).

At the same time as we might chart this move from description to explanation there have been numerous case studies which have looked at particular neighbourhood or city examples of the process. However, on the whole there has been more theory and less observation in recent times with perhaps not enough work to connect the two and engage with pragmatic policy responses to gentrification. This is highlighted by the use of urban pioneer terminology in the UK urban renaissance documentation which sought to promote a new life for Britain's cities (Lees 2003c). Economic and local state institutions often seem strongly motivated by re-capturing the middle class in the central city as both a symbol of, and mechanism for, success. All of this only serves to maintain and sustain moves towards a gentrifying imperative in many cities.

The gentrified neighbourhood in a global context

Whatever the emphasis given to capital or culture we argue that gentrification today must be seen in the context of globalisation. Globalisation has become a complex term expressing conflicting conceptualisations of growing economic, political and cultural interchanges at the ultimate geographical scale. For Cable (1999) 'globalization has become a portmanteau term – of description, approval or abuse' (p. 2) while, for theorists like Giddens, globalisation represented a decoupling of space and time with knowledge and culture being shared around the globe in very short timespans (1990). For other writers globalisation has been expressed as a kind of re-articulation of state power (Brenner 1998) at supra and sub-state levels which have become increasingly significant.

The literature on globalisation has not been geared towards the level of the neighbourhood. However, in the context of neighbourhood changes like gentrification it would seem increasingly important to acknowledge that neighbourhood scales may be an important locus of concentrations of professionals and managerial groups in networks of dialogue and co-ordination of state and sub-state governance structures. In short, the neighbourhood has been under-recognised as the site of the reproduction of a wider set of power relations and contacts which operate at local, urban, regional, and international levels.

On the political left globalisation has been seen as an ideology of and for that of the political right, a justification for unilateral trading partnerships, persistent and widening inequalities and a pro-growth movement that has extended largely western economic hegemony at the expense of the global 'south'. The contested nature of the debate on globalisation should not be understated. Key questions remain over the role of the state, global economic actors and corporations and the relative impact on and involvement of the world's poor. However, our focus in this book here is less on the globalisation debate itself, but, rather, on the connections between processes of global social and economic change and upward changes at the neighbourhood scale.

Literature on the effects of globalisation has often focused on its impacts on poorer social groups generally and burgeoning international trade specifically.

Processes of global migration by social elites and population displacement of the poor have largely operated in separate social spheres with the former generally being unregulated and embraced while the latter has been seen as a distinctive and unwelcome fallout of regional conflicts. Even in the 'advanced' industrial west competition for foreign investment, financial services and the groups servicing these developments, have led away from welfare and social justice agendas in an attempt to remain competitive. The market has been portrayed as a natural reality. The effect in many cities has become increasingly apparent with labour market deregulation, neighbourhood revitalisation and welfare retrenchment leading to progressively ghettoised poverty isolated from work opportunities (Cross and Moore 2002; Friedrichs 2002).

At the crest of this wave of urban redevelopment and colonisation ride the gentrifiers who appear as both the emissaries of global capital flows as well as new-found victims of employment restructuring instigated some years back (Sennett 1998; Butler 2003). For Butler a key message is that gentrification itself may be understood as a response to the insecurities of rapid flows of global finance and identity. Sense of place has become a basis for the ontological security of professionals seeking the habitus of neighbourhood living with like-minded people.

The explanation offered by Smith's rent gap formulation (1979, 1996) now seems to underpin an expanded cognitive map of search and re-location activities of elite social fractions, be they political, cultural or economic. In a sense the decision to locate in Seattle is no longer a world apart from London in its amenity or ambience, even less its distance by jet. At another level in the professional and urban hierarchy this might be a choice between Athens and Auckland, Madrid and Mumbai. International services, ICT linkages, increasing urban homogeneity of services and 'feel', as well as rapid travel, mean that many more 'new' neighbourhoods exist insulated from local poverty, wider systemic inequalities and public squalor (Graham and Marvin 2001).

Gentrification appears as a facet of the global forces acting on rapidly urbanising cities in the south and on post-communist cities where the impacts are particularly complex. In cities of the south massive in-migration from the countryside in search of work and strong in situ fertility combines with restrictions in the supply of land, because of private ownership, which has resulted in unprecedented levels of unemployment, inadequate shelter and homelessness. At the same time the communications and financial services sectors have expanded in many of these cities, resulting in a larger professional managerial class. In residential terms this has resulted in a reinforcement and expansion of colonial patterns of neighbourhood segregation with many elites retreating into gated communities, or leaving the city for luxury residential developments in ex-urban locations.

Foreign Direct Investment has been moving away from the west for the last decade. This measure of relative expansion of trans-national corporations and globalisation has been growing particularly quickly in Eastern Europe and developing countries since 1992, though the asset base of these companies often remains largely in the West and other developed economies. In Eastern Europe and post-communist cities social divisions have increased in a housing market that is at once commodifying property relations and subject to the repatriation of property to pre-communist owners. The particular configuration of these forces led to city by city and neighbourhood differences in the extent and impact of gentrification, as Luděk Sýkora points out in this volume.

A further element of gentrification, as an aspect of globalising tendencies, has been neighbourhood-to-neighbourhood connections between geographically dispersed locations. This has already been suggested in the connections between the residential destinations of the cosmopolitan professional managerial class but there is the other side of the global city represented by social networks of recruitment and migration of low-paid personal service workers who, for instance, clean the offices and apartments of the professional elite (Sassen 2000b). The transnational migration and sustained identities of unskilled service workers tie disparate neighbourhoods together in ways explored by Jerry Krase in his chapter in this volume.

Nevertheless we should be both receptive and critical to the idea that gentrifiers float somehow weightlessly in their residential choices. The economic forces that drive residential mobility are often tempered by the gravitational forces of social networks, kin and friendship ties, as well as national background and heritage. However, networks of elites and cosmopolitan professional managerial classes present challenges in terms of understanding their culture, lifestyle and social cohesion. This cosmopolitan class has skills that now transfer anywhere and can be argued to possess 'decontextualised cultural capital' (Hannerz 1996: 108) that allow portable social resources to be deployed in new contexts. This ability to transfer professional skills has created a super-mobile fraction that consider their identities in a global context (Rofe 2003) while professional and managerial groups more embedded in national and neighbourhood contexts perhaps aspire to these kinds of networked and boundless identities.

Cosmopolitan elites in exclusive residential enclaves may have stronger ties to similar neighbourhoods in other global cities than to the city that surrounds them (Sassen 2000a, 2000b, 1998; Rofe 2003). They live in the neighbourhood equivalent of a city-state. Increasing rapidity of information flows, financial transactions, population migration and travel have all helped to connect people, institutions and states in ways that have had profound consequences not just for societies but also the cities and neighbourhoods of cities. In short, there is an increasing sense that what is happening at a global scale is being articulated in small urban areas, transmitted by key social groups who have selectively grown as a result of a shift towards personal, financial and information services and boosted by both free and selective trading at the global scale. In this sense, it is no coincidence that cities like New York, Tokyo and London were at the vanguard of gentrification activity linked to a space of flows of information and finance (Graham and Marvin 2001; Hamnett 2003a; Castells 1996). Like Merton's foot-loose 'cosmopolitans' (1957) gentrifiers form a residential class who share an identity shaped by locational preferences, stage in the lifecycle, occupation and a social network that crosses national boundaries.

As well as the gap in land values between city and suburb there are now relativities that inform investment decisions on specific neighbourhoods at a global scale. Whether it be Battery Park City, New York, or Chelsea Harbour and Islington, London, or Darling harbour, Sydney or the smaller scale versions in numerous other cities, investment opportunities are now driven by super-profits on highly valued locations, rather than by comparisons with devalorised land: a kind of global 'rent gap'. These investments in luxury residential developments are made by transnational corporations and involve architects with international reputations. Neil Smith's point is that this model of urban reinvestment is driving much more modest projects sponsored by national urban policy in the form of versions of 'urban renaissance'.

Figure 1.1 considers the critical processes underpinning the transformations we have been discussing at significant spatial scales. These processes may be conceived as drivers of local neighbourhood change with diverse outcomes as well as intrinsic processes of globalisation.

The global forces consist of communications technology that creates a 'space of flows' (Castells 1996) between certain key locations in a global context. It consists of a transnational set of elite gentrifiers both following and being created by the expansion of financial services in certain key cities and the real estate investment that exploits these changes in the labour market. These changes have

Global	National	City	Neighbourhood
• Migration of the rich and educated	• Policies on inward investment ⇨	• City administration: ⇨	
• Global governance and trade policy rules	• Migration of the poor	– Receptiveness/ subsidy of investment	• Gentrification
• Financial markets	• Welfare infrastructure	– Labour regulations	• Ghettoized poverty
• Communications and travel (ICT and transport infrastructure)	• Property rights and legislation	– Fiscal autonomy	
	• Relative scale of middle class	• Local infrastructure – amenity environment quality of life	

1.1 Spatial scales of global transformation and forces shaping neighbourhood change

been particularly concentrated in the major global cities (such as London, New York, San Francisco and Tokyo) and the newly emerging global cities, such as Shanghai, but they also impact on many large cities in regional settings. The effects of these changes are also felt lower down the urban hierarchy as suitable neighbourhoods have been 'filled up' in leading cities so that gentrification has been pushed to other areas hitherto not considered. In addition to this cascade effect (Hamnett 2003a) a much wider range of city types and locations are feeling the impact of international trade.

As we pass to the national level interest rate levels impact on the amount of activity in the residential market but also the degree of overseas investment in that market. The degree to which nations are placing themselves (or are able to place themselves) as tertiary or quarternary specialists in a global marketplace impacts on the size and prominence of the professional managerial class *vis-à-vis* the working class and other economic groups. National legal frameworks for property ownership are also important. This has taken a particular prominence in post-communist cities where ownership is being transferred or is subject to dispute. It is also significant in many cites of the global south where the high levels of private land ownership severely restrict the ability of municipal governments to obtain land for social or affordable housing development.

At the city level the overall labour market mix will determine the degree to which gentrification is manifest in the urban form. Even with continued suburbanisation pockets of gentrification are visible even where the total number of professional managerial workers is quite modest. The reasons for this may vary widely, from utilitarian consideration of accessibility to city centre jobs to aesthetic and lifestyle choices. In cities where there has been a significant historical shift from manufacturing to service sector employment (of both high and low skills) the impacts of gentrification in terms of displacement of working-class and poorer residents are likely to be greatest. In some rapidly growing cities of the south, such as São Paulo or Beijing, both service sector and manufacturing employment are growing apace with the bifurcated effects in terms of social residential divides of wealth and poverty. The existing tenure structure of a country also has an impact. In countries where renting has been the norm (such as the Netherlands or Eastern European countries) the impacts of gentrification have hitherto been more restricted but now provide a weaker set of property relations through which gentrification has easily cut a swathe.

Related to levels of de-industrialisation (or absence of industrialisation) and the size of the city is the overall quality of life in different cities. Access to open space, to leisure and cultural facilities and the general liveability and manageability of the particular urban environment has been significant in attracting gentrifiers, as Ley (1996) and others noted some years ago. The quality of life in the city is now seen by many city governments as a key element to sell the city to prospective middle-class residents, to lure them back from the suburbs. This last point is related to the idea of urban government as entrepreneur, rather than manager, a change noted by David Harvey fifteen years ago (Harvey 1989a).

The place marketing of cities (Kearns and Philo 1993) and other forms of civic boosterism and growth coalitions (Logan and Molotch 1987) has become more evident as cities increasingly compete with each other for inward-investment. With Florida's (2003) popular argument that city competitiveness is essentially linked to where bohemian, gay and professionals wish to locate, gentrification has been reconfirmed to city fathers as the route to economic success. The particular parts of the city that investors or gentrifiers head for are determined by their architectural desirability or symbolic value as a landmark location. Clearly neighbourhood distinctions in tenure mix are vital as well as the degree of disinvestments in the local housing stock, although the latter tend to be more important in the early stages of gentrification.

The factors outlined configure differently on different cities but all have had a part to play in the increasing incidence of both ghettoised poverty and gentrification in cities across the world. It is these connections, as well as differences within gentrification activity, in a global setting that the current volume seeks to capture. Through the range of contributions we hope to bring together perspectives and literatures on gentrification that have all too long existed apart.

The new urban colonialism: contributions to the volume

Gentrification has been discussed as a middle-class aesthetic of historic preservation, such as the Victoriana of Melbourne (Jager 1986) or Toronto (Ley 1996). In some cities this also relates to a postcolonial context. Wendy Shaw reveals how heritage designations and the gentrification aesthetic are a selective editing of history that writes out struggles for Aboriginal identity, as well as supplanting the working-class labour history of many inner city locales. For Shaw gentrification has become a celebration of whiteness and in its selective appropriation of history, a form of neo-colonialism that excludes competing legitimate voices in the history of many neighbourhoods now experiencing sudden upward social trajectories.

The colonial resonances of gentrification and the role of heritage designations is a strong theme of Silvana Rubino's analysis of gentrification in several Brazilian cities. This is brought out strongly in the tensions over the proposal to build a branch of the Guggenheim museum in Rio, an initiative that was seen by many as a symbolic form of neo-colonialism. For Rubino gentrification is a curious blend of revitalisation and commodification that is played out against the background of squalor in the 'favellas' where poverty is rife and yet concealed from the lives of affluent gentrifiers and city administrations with global aspirations.

Wyly and Hammel link gentrification to globalisation in the neo-liberal politics of US cities where the market has been deemed the primary method of allocation and reasoning behind many policy actions. Gentrification in this neo-liberal regime is ever more extreme, buffering the districts of elite gentrifiers by violently removing all traces of the poor and homeless. This builds out from Smith's (1996) idea that gentrification represents a vengeful urban policy predicated on the need to attract global inward investment by securing the elite social groups who act as its functionaries. Using a range of empirical measures Wyly and Hammel map this frontier of gentrification and revanchism across the US urban system pointing out the environments of super-affluence against the ever-harsher surveillance and control of the poor and the vulnerable. This intensification of gentrification activity appears as an extension of colonial logic with cities embracing the tried and tested revanchist policies of cities like New York where a kind of frontier spirit has taken hold (Smith 1992a).

For Slater, city policies in Canada connect with Wyly and Hammel's notions of an extended revanchist urbanism. Slater sees longstanding concerns with diversity and social balance in neighbourhoods supplanted by moves towards gentrification even while it is being presented as a form of diversity in its own right. As Slater emphasises, gentrification has become a kind of diversity that is valued by gentrifiers and city administrations in ways that either seek to or, by default, exclude the voices of a growing urban poor.

The opening up of new emerging housing markets to these pressures of neo-liberal capitalism is one development captured by gentrification research in the last decade or so since the collapse of communism in Eastern Europe. In his chapter on gentrification in post-communist cities Ludek Sykora questions Neil Smith's assertion that gentrification is well advanced in Budapest. Sykora suggests a much more variable picture for Budapest and a range of East European urban centres. Local conditions are important, especially the pathways to privatisation (restitution vs individual flat sales). The global context is writ large in these cities with the presence of ex-patriots employed by the growing number of western companies, as well as the growing indigenous middle class and a general glossing over the fate of those displaced.

In their detailed investigation of changes in the Prenzlauer Berg district of former East Berlin, Matthias Bernt and Andrej Holm show how local rent control laws protect certain properties from conversion and result in a scattering of gentrified and non-gentrified rental units. Local government subsidies rather than rent gap profits are the key incentive to landlords and it remains to be seen the degree to which the rental market eventually collapses wholesale as, for example Hamnett and Randolph demonstrated for the flat break-up market in London thirty years ago. The degree to which districts like Prenzlauer Berg in post-communist cities take a different path is an open question.

The dynamics of gentrification in the more traditional territories of western cities is also open to question in the sense that the expansion of post (mid-1990s) recession gentrification has spread down the urban hierarchy and the degree to which the experience in regional cities increasingly mimics that of the metropolis. Paul Dutton finds that the provincial situation might be captured by a core-periphery model with the footloose global gentrifiers occupying the new-build neighbourhoods in the urban core in contrast to the more piecemeal efforts, via sweat equity, of professionals with more local connections to the city of Leeds. In the context of house price growth in regional centres now exceeding that of the hot spot of England's south-east region gentrification appears to be leading a debate on the future of regional cities which is re-setting notions about which cities might be considered desirable for professional and managerial households.

The degree to which gentrification is observed in a range of cities, and its possible future trajectory might be linked, especially in the UK case, to the existence of large numbers of students in the urban core, as Darren Smith argues in his chapter. If higher education is one prerequisite for membership of the new middle class (Ley 1996) then its acquisition combined with central city living might act as a recruitment centre for future gentrifiers. Gentrification in this sense is a process of socialisation into a colonising class prepared to tolerate inner city living in return for later investment rewards. In addition, a range of socio-spatial effects are being felt with the conversion of former commercial and other properties for student accommodation and the increased presence of students in more traditional neighbourhoods due to rising student numbers. These changes are having a similar effect to gentrification both in terms of the transfer of ownership from working-class to middle-class owners (in this case owners for investment) and the displacement of working-class residents from central city neighbourhoods through changes in local price and rental structures as well as a sense of no longer feeling at home in these newly colonised spaces.

In her assessment of gentrification in a range of countries and her focus on the case study of St Kilda's in Melbourne, Kate Shaw examines the factors that can give local efforts to stem the tide of gentrification some efficacy. These efforts might appear small scale and fragmented but are all the more important in what she calls third-wave gentrification in which urban policy has moved from passive to active support of the process. For Shaw local government provides the central spatial focus around which gentrified colonisation might be usefully challenged to provide more socially equitable outcomes.

Inter-neighbourhood linkages at a global scale are very much at the heart of Jerry Krase's account of the particular manifestations of gentrification in a Brooklyn neighbourhood and in Krakow, Poland. Krase demonstrates how certain aesthetic practices take similar aspects in the originating and destination locations. This connection of aesthetic practice and international migration highlights the global character of gentrification in these areas, standing testament to a diverse but coherent gentrification aesthetic and process of ethnic colonisation itself threatened with being supplanted by local gentrification.

Contrasts in the form that gentrification takes are evident from Fujitsuka's account of gentrification in Kyoto, Japan. Here we find a large number of new build condominiums and a strong presence of gentrifiers with children that present contrasts to the early stages of the process in western cities. In a country where strong land ownership rights have blended with a desire for the 'new', large swathes of architectural urban heritage have been lost. In this context gentrification has taken forms of both the rescuing of older urban neighbourhoods as well as condominium new-build which step away from the type of neighbourhood changes often associated with 'typical' patterns of gentrification in the West.

Tolga Islam looks at the gentrification in Istanbul (Turkey), highlighting the role of redevelopment, rural forms and commercial aspects in a country which has been largely neglected in the literature but which is likely to figure ever more prominently with entry to the European Union in prospect. Here he finds constraints on mortgage finance interacting with a new desire to live centrally among an arts-based local intelligentsia who wish to live in a wider global context of social diversity and relative tolerance. Islam examines the process of gentrification in both rural and urban locations showing the range of types and stages through which different cities and neighbourhoods have progressed in relation to differing local state involvement with a growing value set against traditional nineteenth-century housing.

Petros Petsimeris looks at the dynamics of gentrification in a range of southern European cities and points to the significance and particularities of architectural and physical form in understanding the intensity and extent of gentrification here. In an analysis of changes in cities within Spain, Italy and Greece he argues that these places are increasingly characterised by the appropriation of central city areas which were long considered to be places of dilapidation and lacking status as places of fashion and lifestyle. Now these cities have rapidly appreciating property values and questions emerge over a second wave of the removal of the poor in ways that mirror renaissance efforts at the redevelopment of these cities hundreds of years ago.

Finally, Eric Clark concludes this volume with a provocative view of the characteristics of gentrification and its proliferation. For Clark it is important to move beyond an orthodoxy in which gentrification is seen to be too chaotic or complex to be reduced to a concept able to bridge temporal and spatial boundaries. Clark asks observers to consider an 'elastic yet targeted concept' which will allow discussion and a subsequent focus on social problems rather than continued theoretical debates.

Conclusion: distance neutralised, place emphasised – gentrification in a global context

The central message of this book is that gentrification provides a vital debate around which the analysis of globalisation, international migration, and neighbourhood change are increasingly attached. Gentrification has moved very much from being a process in which analysis has often been couched within city and neighbourhood contexts to one in which global tendril connections can be found between many cities and neighbourhoods. We have tried to suggest that this new urban colonialism is occuring in a range of differentiated ways in diverse cities. In particular we have drawn attention to the importance of globalisation as a neo-liberal force which has transformed local policies towards attracting professional and elite groups just as it has swelled the ranks of a local and international class fraction who are mobile at the city and international scales. All of this has been facilitated by new information and transport technologies in tandem with urban policies supporting the displacement of non-owning residents in the name of achieving economic development.

As gentrification has become generalised so it has become intensified in its originating neighbourhoods, many of which have now moved into stellar price brackets and now resemble established elite enclaves rather than the ascetic pioneer gentrifier spirit of the 1960s and 1970s. This has led to a cascade effect down an international and regional set of urban hierarchies in which the saturation of investment motives in gentrified cities like New York and London have pushed towards neighbourhood changes in new regional nodes. At the same time the global 'south' has experienced massive expansion of inward investment with the functionaries of these economic advances moving to colonise disinvested central city neighbourhoods in cities like Shanghai and Sao Paolo.

The map of gentrification activity has unfurled to include rural settlements, previously derelict land and suburban new-build with the central hallmark of the process focusing on a tracking of the colonisation of new spaces by the middle classes (Atkinson 2003b). Just as gentrification appeared to contradict the urban theories of invasion and succession (Smith and Williams 1986a) of the early twentieth century, so now gentrification has evolved into an adaptable and often meaner beast capable of taking advantage of new opportunities at the global scale to pin-point and bear down on strategic neighbourhood locations.

The movement of capital and people act as driving forces for neighbourhood changes in the form of gentrification as well as the more regularly commented on ghettoisation of poverty. In this sense an analysis of the movement of the middle classes is very much bound up with an attempt to explain patterns of wider poverty and segregation. Policies designed to bring gentrification have concentrated poverty and engendered displacement either in the name of market freedom and personal choice or in more direct ways through vengeful policies which have attacked the land tenure and human rights of those least able to articulate resistance to the process. However, this is to miss the diversity of impacts of gentrification at different spatial scales and in different city and national contexts. It remains important for policy-makers and academics to try and understand how equitable development can be achieved without the stark problems associated with unchecked gentrification, itself symptomatic of a middle-class and self-serving process of investment. In short, gentrification as a process of investment and movement by the wealthy may have modified or positive effects in cities characterised by strong welfare regimes, enhanced property rights and mediation, and low competition for housing resources.

In this global context of neighbourhood change centrality can no longer be understood as the CBD or the world cities themselves. A spatial expansion of gentrification activity attests to a growing network of lifestyle identities and cognitive maps in which new centres of economic and cultural life are being identified by the middle classes in novel regional, rural, suburban and provincial city contexts. It is now possible to live in New York and feel genuinely close to Tokyo, for example, with ICT facilitating human bonds as well as the economic processes that drive these locational decisions. Underlying this gentrification is a set of common processes, linked in part at the global scale but also explained locally by policy interventions or non-interventions and facilitated by changing class structures, economic restructuring and public policy more widely.

Gentrification continues to divide commentators at the same time as more people are involved in the process, both as gentrifiers, intermediaries, poorer local residents and analysts. Gentrification may be constituted of black and white, gay and straight, urban/suburban and rural forms but, most importantly, the view of a process linked only to the west is now firmly out of date. If gentrification is, as we assert, about following the neighbourhood level migration of the upper socio-economic groups then this allows a clarity of focus at the same time as embracing a wider set of neighbourhood changes that still present frontiers for research and social action.

In many ways gentrification might usefully be conceived as a nexus within which tensions between the destination and welfare of global middle-class social fractions and an embedded urban poor are increasingly connected. This adds a new urgency and relevance to the study of gentrification as a lens through which wider urban inequalities might be understood but one which should be applied to a much broader range of places than have hitherto been explored.

2 Mapping neo-liberal American urbanism[1]

Elvin K. Wyly and Daniel J. Hammel

Starbucks, Wal-Mart, and the benevolent king

We are in the midst of a remarkable renaissance of interest in gentrification. As in the 1970s and 1980s, the transforming inner city is taken as a crucible of broader economic and cultural change. As in a previous generation, the scholarly literature is rich with impressive contributions to theory, method, policy, and politics (Hackworth 2001, 2002a, 2002b; Hamnett 2002; Lambert and Boddy 2002; Lees 2000; Ley 2002; Ley *et al*. 2002; Newman 2003; Slater 2002; N. Smith 2002). And, as in the past, it is hard to walk through a city neighbourhood or read the newspaper without encountering a flood of vivid illustrations of these theories in the urban landscape, in contingent intersections of culture and capital, transformation and tension. Not long ago, a Starbucks opened a few blocks from Cabrini-Green, a public housing project now almost completely surrounded by reinvestment north of downtown Chicago. In New Orleans, the supermarket chain Wal-Mart, the nation's largest employer, is at the centre of an effort to redevelop land for retail businesses on the former site of a public housing project. The plan has provoked intense local opposition, including a lawsuit on behalf of displaced project tenants, in a confrontation that one reporter dubs 'A Streetcar Named No Thanks' (Hays 2003).

The imagery is even more colourful in New York. Soho and the Village tamed, developers and art galleries are moving into Loho (a swath of the Lower East Side between East Houston and Canal) in pursuit of 'the underground's underground, a radical alternative to most alternatives you can name', while newly-renovated studios rent for US$3,000 a month (Hamilton 2000; Cotter 2002: B29). Others venture farther out on the 'trendy frontier', north to the new jazz and comedy clubs of SoHa (South of Harlem, the area above West 96th) or 'Eastward Ho!' into Bushwick, Brooklyn (Barnes 2000; Pogrebin 2002). Meanwhile, in the old industrial lands down under the Manhattan Bridge overpass (Dumbo), Bob Vila finds the perfect dilapidated brownstone to renovate on his nationally-televised home improvement show; he walks through the old building with his son, and they laugh at the handiwork left behind by squatters – sheet rock partitions, an improvised bathroom, spare windows … 'A real penthouse'. Vila jokes that the squatters' work 'gives you an indication about how desirable this part of New York is' (Cardwell 2003: A18).

Vila discovered the building through a connection to its owner, David C. Walentas, a local developer who 'may be the only person to have put a New York City neighbourhood on the residential map himself' with well-timed building purchases, loft conversions, strategic benevolence to arts groups, and a payment of $90,000 to persuade the Metropolitan Transit Authority to re-route a bus line (Hellman 2002: D1). Walentas endured twenty years of false starts and failed deals in what he calls his 'Stalingrad phase', before the plan came together in the last few years with new commercial tenants, loft conversions, and million-dollar condos. Now the artists who lived in his buildings through the Stalingrad years are being forced out by doubled or tripled lease rates. When he appears at a sound check before a David Bowie concert in the neighbourhood, Walentas is chided by the Director of Arts for the performance space. 'It must be interesting to handpick your whole neighbourhood', she says. 'But you can do it, David, because you're the king of Dumbo' (Hellman 2002: D5). 'I'm the mayor', he replies, adding, 'Well, maybe the benevolent king' (ibid.). In a lengthy *New York Times* profile, Walentas is photographed with his wife Jane in their spacious loft in the top floor of Dumbo's centerpiece 1915 building. David and Jane are standing in front of a bookcase, and one of the volumes on the shelf is a biography of another benevolent king of New York: Robert A. Caro's *The Power Broker*.

What is the new face of American gentrification? Are Starbucks and Wal-Mart the new urban pioneers, working with city and federal officials to spur a 'renaissance' by erasing the old welfare-state landscapes of the 1960s? Is David Walentas a reincarnated, privatized Robert Moses? Thirty years of change have made gentrification a durable but dynamic facet of American urban landscapes. In urban theory, however, long-running debates over causes and definitions have finally boiled over into frustration. Liz Bondi (1999: 255) suggests that we abandon the subject, because of 'its inability to open up new insights' and she wonders if 'it is time to allow it to disintegrate under the weight of these burdens'. Working to move beyond the old entrenched dichotomies, Tom Slater (2003: 6), asks:

> are we really to believe that Ley (1996) ignored the economy in his comprehensive account of the emergence of the post-industrial metropolis, or that Smith's (1996) compelling assessment of the emergence of the revanchist metropolis was divorced from the impact of cultural studies?

In an even more troubling trend, important questions of theory and policy are clouded by rather mundane, straightforward empirical issues. Carrying on a

2.1 David and Jane Walentas, in their loft in Dumbo (Down under the Manhattan Bridge overpass). David 'may be the only person to have put a New York City neighbourhood on the residential map himself' (Hellman, 2002: D1). (Copyright © Andrea Mohin/*The New York Times*. Reproduced by permission.)

tradition from the 1960s, for instance, many policy-oriented researchers are drawing sharp distinctions among physical types of reinvestment (classical 'invasion-succession', new construction on old industrial lands, loft conversion, etc.) to reconcile their ethical concerns over a rich menu of new government programmes to promote redevelopment, 'new markets', and income-mixing in the inner city. Many want to support these policies so long as they avoid what has wrongly been used as the litmus test of gentrification – direct, conflict-ridden displacement of existing working-class or poor residents. No matter its physical form, gentrification is fundamentally about the reconstruction of the inner city to serve middle- and upper-class interests. When it avoids direct displacement, the process usually involves middle-class or developer subsidies that cannot be seen in isolation from cutbacks in housing assistance to the poor and other attacks on the remnants of the welfare state.

What are the different types of reinvestment in the gentrifying American city? How unequal are these different places? What has changed in the 1990s? Are other cities seeing the same reactionary class politics and entrepreneurial vengeance portrayed in Mike Davis's Los Angeles and Neil Smith's New York? In this chapter we offer answers that are at once crassly empirical and theoretically relevant. Neo-liberal policies in housing, social policy, and public space have created a complex new urban landscape – but it is possible to map this urban hierarchy and a few of its consequences.

Mapping the new urban frontier

In the last ten years we have assembled a simple database of gentrified inner-city neighbourhoods in large US cities. Our methods involve a combination of fieldwork, archival research, and multivariate statistical analysis (for detailed explanations see Wyly and Hammel 1996 and Wyly and Hammel 1999). We strive for comparable, consistent, and conservative measures to identify neighbourhoods that (a) endured disinvestment a generation ago, and (b) have since undergone the changes that nearly all researchers would agree are worth studying under the label 'gentrification'. A key part of our fieldwork involves 'ground-truthing' the census data so often used to describe urban growth and change; after several years of investigation we are now able to offer some comparative evidence from twenty-three metropolitan areas (Figure 2.2). Our list includes a wide variety of cities – places where reinvestment boomed in the 1970s or even earlier, and others where rapid changes have appeared more recently.

These cities provide a cross-section of the considerable diversity of American urbanism in terms of morphology, economic function, and policy climate. Although large cities always evade simple categorisation, several classical urban genres are obvious: old-line Fordist manufacturing centres reshaped by a generation of deindustrialisation (Detroit, Milwaukee), dynamic centres for the co-ordination of global production and investment networks (Chicago, San Francisco, Silicon Valley), stable middle-tier regional financial centres (Indianapolis, the Twin Cities), and turbo-charged sunbelt growth centre (Atlanta, Dallas, Phoenix). These inter-urban contrasts shape the context for the meaning and significance of inner-city reinvestment. The local imprint of urban market processes and policy interventions is forged by trajectories of growth and decline, industrial change and labour laws, currents of low-wage immigration, and the form of restructured social welfare systems under conditions of federal devolution (Staeheli et al. 1997). Gentrification, then, is woven into a distinctive and multiply-scaled web of tensions highlighting variations in political process and the particular characteristics of the inner-city built environment. In Chicago, for instance, the public housing landscapes built in the 1950s and 1960s played a key role in the restructuring of federal assisted housing policy during the 1990s, by which time thirty years of gentrification had reconfigured substantial parts of the urban core. In Atlanta, the decision to host the 1996 Olympics created 'a new, formal version of the old downtown business elite' (Keating 2001: 147) that aggressively reshaped portions of the city's inner-

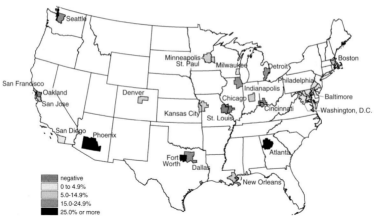

2.2 Population change in gentrified neighbourhoods, 1990–2000

Case study 2.1

The interaction of in-migration, displacement, and transitions in household composition inscribes complex variations in population growth. Yet almost all of the gentrified neighborhoods identified in our field surveys have enjoyed a remarkable resurgence in terms of their attractiveness to capital. Between 1993 and 2000, private, conventional mortgage capital to home buyers in these neighbourhoods expanded more than twice as fast as the suburban rate.

city African-American neighbourhoods at a time when hesitant gentrification finally began to gather momentum. In San Francisco, intensified and centralised housing market inflation has inflamed especially strong community antagonism to the growth-machine politics of inner-city real estate. And of course each city has a diverse range of gentrified districts, each positioned differently in relation to poverty, unemployment, and homelessness. Taken as a whole, our roster of gentrified neighbourhoods in two dozen cities can be seen as the anchor of a new urban system, based not so much on financial hierarchies, transport networks, or manufacturing linkages, but rather on the mixture of policies and inner-city landscapes distilled by current trends in globalisation and public policy.

A new urban system?

America's aggressive promotion of transnational corporate globalisation and a domestic recipe of privatised, market-oriented social policy have created a new, 'neo-liberal' urbanism – a network of urban processes shaped by a paradoxical, state-driven 'return to the original axioms of liberalism' in the tradition of eighteenth-century political economy (N. Smith 2002: 429). Deep public-private subsidies are given to demonstrate the efficiency of unregulated markets, while substantial funds are spent to demolish the redistributive infrastructure built from the 1930s to the 1960s. Measuring the imprint of these changes in specific neighbourhoods requires balancing the productive tensions among several literatures – not just critical social theory inquiry into questions of justice and difference (Harvey 2000; Merrifield and Swyngedouw 1997), but also the historical and positivist quantitative-revolution work on urban system development (Berry 1964, 1972; Pred 1977) and the richly-textured case studies of social and spatial relations in specific city neighbourhoods (Beauregard 1990; Bennett 1998; Hammel 1999b; Slater 2003; Ley 1981). We are certainly not the first to suggest such a synthesis. Don Mitchell (1997) offers the best example, in 'The annihilation of space by law: the roots and implications of anti-homeless laws in the United States'. Mitchell argues that the widely-cited realities and myths of accelerated capital mobility have forced cities into fundamentally new ways of trying to attract investment in a world where places seem to be rendered interchangeable by wage competition and race-to-the-bottom subsidies:

> … the ideology of globalization allows local officials, along with local business people and property owners, to argue that they have no choice but to prostrate themselves before the god Capital, offering not just tax and regulatory inducements, but also extravagant convention centers, downtown tourist amusements, up-market, gentrified restaurants and bar districts, and even occasional public investment in such amenities as museums, theaters, and concert halls … When capital is seen to have no *need* for any particular place, then cities do what they can to make themselves so attractive that capital … will *want* to locate there.
>
> (Mitchell 1997: 304, emphasis added)

The implication is clear. In classical theories of urban system development, cities fought through constant product innovation to reap the profits of locally-distinctive exports and to thus claw their way up the urban hierarchy. Now the competition is an innovative race to create an interesting and attractive – and *safe and sanitised* – playground for the professional elites employed by global capital.

> In city after city concerned with 'livability', with, in other words, making urban centers attractive to both footloose capital and to the footloose middle classes, politicians and managers have turned to … a legal remedy that seeks to cleanse the streets of those left behind by globalization and other secular changes in the economy by simply erasing the spaces in which they must live …'.
>
> (Mitchell 1997: 305)

Mitchell's qualitative inquiry yields a magisterial theoretical analysis drawn from philosophies of justice and conceptions of the public, along with a critical examination of court decisions and legislation. But this perspective also has important lessons for quantitative empirical studies of neighbourhood change. As urban politics has created the revanchist city – a vengeful world marked by 'a defense and reconstruction of the lines of identity privilege … in the context of rising economic insecurity' among the white, Anglo bourgeoisie (N. Smith 1997: 129) – we should expect to see a discernible regional geography in the backlash against the homeless, poor, and racialised minorities.

Part of this story can be captured in a simple comparison of the class character of gentrification and some of the more blatantly revanchist local policies documented by Mitchell (1997), N. Smith (1996, 1997) and Waldron (1991). Between 1993 and 2000, about 26,000 high-income households filed requests for loans to buy homes in gentrified neighbourhoods.[2] These inner-city elite are only a tiny fraction of wealthy buyers in the overall metropolitan housing market, but the new urban frontier accounts for a substantial share of those choosing the central city – more than a fifth in Chicago and Philadelphia, and half in Boston. To test whether elite gentrification worsens localised revanchist practices of discipline and surveillance, we turn to the extensive survey of homeless advocates and service providers conducted jointly by the National Law Centre on Homelessness and Poverty and the National Coalition for the Homeless (NCH/NLCHP 2002). We matched our case study cities to the report's Prohibited Conduct Chart, a depressing compendium of local ordinances codifying the kinds of principles and (often unconstitutional) legal mechanisms used to mask the state's failure to deal with homelessness. Here, we focus on ordinances involving curfews, or banning the following activities: spitting, urination and defecation in public; begging in public places; 'aggressive' panhandling; sleeping in public; camping in public; loitering, loafing, and vagrancy; and obstruction of sidewalks and public places.[3] As Mitchell points out, most of these activities are the kinds of things a homeless person simply *must do* in order to live – and yet this is precisely what inspires indignation and activism among the urban professional classes. Local authorities in any city usually move quickly against street people doing any of these things; but our reasoning is that the policies are formalised only under certain circumstances, and that gentrification is one of the processes that helps to broaden the base of support for explicit, city-wide 'quality of life' ordinances.

The criminalisation of homelessness has become a powerful form of travelling urban theory (Table 2.1). All but one of our cities have explicit ordinances against two or more of the specified activities; the sole exception (Chicago) ranks as one of the nation's 'meanest cities' for homeless people, on the basis of anti-homeless practices not captured in formal ordinances.[4] Six of the cities ban five of the specified activities, while one (Atlanta) bans six. The correlation of these ordinances with the strength of elite gentrification is rather weak, but still worth considering.

Table 2.1 Elite locational choice and revanchist municipal policy

	Share of affluent central-city buyers choosing gentrified neighbourhoods	Prohibited activities[†]									Ranked as 'meanest city'
		Minor curfew	Spitting	Urination or defecation	Begging	'Aggressive' panhandling	Sleeping	Camping	Loitering, loafing, or vagrancy	Obstruction of sidewalks or public places	
Boston	49.9%					×	×			×	
Philadelphia	23.9%	×	×			×				×	
Chicago	22.5%			×					×		2002
Milwaukee	18.8%					×			×	×	
Washington, DC	17.5%	×				×			×		
San Francisco	16.5%	×			×	×			×	×	1996, 2002
Seattle	14.8%			×		×				×	1996
Baltimore	13.3%		×	×		×				×	2002
Minneapolis-St. Paul*	11.7%	×		×	×				×	×	
St. Louis	9.7%	×				×			×	×	
Detroit	5.7%		×		×				×	×	
Cincinnati	4.9%					×					
Dallas	4.5%	×		×		×				×	
New Orleans	3.6%				×	×	×				
San Diego	3.5%				×	×	×			×	
Atlanta	3.4%	×	×	×		×		×		×	
Oakland	2.5%		×	×			×	×		×	
Denver	2.3%		×	×			×			×	
Kansas City**	1.1%	×	×		×	×				×	
Indianapolis	1.1%		×		×	×				×	
San Jose	0.6%	×							×	×	
Phoenix	0.1%	×		×		×	×	×		×	
Fort Worth	0.1%	×			×	×				×	

Notes

† Bans on begging, sleeping, camping, and loitering/loafing/vagrancy include only city-wide ordinances.

* Prohibited activities refer only to Minneapolis; St Paul not included in NCH/NLCHP survey.

** Prohibited activities refer only to Kansas City, MO; Kansas City, KS not included in NCH/NLCHP survey.

Of the cities ranked in the top ten according to elite reinvestment, seven also achieved top rank on local anti-homeless ordinances – defined here either as a 'meanest city' designation or banning five or more of the specified activities. By contrast, the bottom thirteen cities include only three meeting the same criteria: Atlanta, Oakland, and Indianapolis. The latter seems to reflect an unusually severe political backlash against the poor,[5] while Oakland's bans must be seen in the context of intense housing inflation and a race-to-the-bottom in anti-homeless policies throughout the Bay Area. The other anomaly is famous for an ordinance tailored to the imperatives of a low-density, auto-reliant built environment. In Atlanta, it is a crime to cut across or loiter in a parking lot unless you have lawfully parked your own car there; an estimated 18,000 people are cited annually for assorted quality of life infractions (NCH/NLCHP 2002: 15). Overall, then, if we set aside the residuals of Atlanta, Oakland, and Indianapolis, it is possible to discern a general pattern: gentrified enclaves claim a prominent place in elite housing markets where municipal policy incorporates provisions designed to cleanse the city of certain people and behaviours. Nevertheless, it is quite clear that revanchist policy is not limited to heavily-gentrified cities: there is enormous variation in the share of affluent buyers choosing the reinvested inner-city, while bans on a variety of human activities have diffused widely among many different kinds of cities.

Atop the revanchist hierarchy

Our data and methods make it hazardous to draw clear causal links in the emergence of the new neo-liberal American urbanism. But as a purely descriptive tool, the approach offers valuable insights into the kinds of places created by reinvestment, uneven metropolitan development, and interactions of city, state, and federal policy. If we were to update Berry's (1972) *City Classification Handbook* for the neo-liberal years of the 1990s, one way to begin is a standard multivariate numerical taxonomy. Consider a simple brew of contextual variables – measures of urban growth, housing affordability, segregation and inequality, the prevalence of anti-homeless ordinances – along with a few basic features of gentrified areas.[6] Our choice of variables is certainly open to critique, and some of these measures are at the centre of tempestuous debates over epistemology, methodology, policy, and politics. But the results of a simple cluster analysis do offer a systematic, empirical way to analyse one element of the revanchist city (Table 2.2).[7] Boston, San José, and Detroit each stand out as distinctive centres in classes by themselves, shaped by uniquely extreme configurations of elite gentrification, housing inflation, or new development in close proximity to the gated communities for the poor (correctional facilities) portrayed by Harvey (2000: 155). San Diego, San Francisco, and Seattle are marked by extreme housing affordability problems and fairly strong gentrification compared with other western cities, suggesting perhaps a unique Pacific coast brand of neighbourhood exclusivity. In the well-established enclaves

Table 2.2 A classification of the gentrified urban system

Interpretation	Pacific exclusion	Disciplined decentralisation	Elite revanchist cities		Latino segregation		Gated communities for the poor	
	San Diego San Francisco Seattle	Atlanta Baltimore Cincinnati Milwaukee New Orleans St Louis	Boston	Chicago Philadelphia Washington	San Jose	Dallas Denver Kansas City Oakland Phoenix	Indianapolis Minneapolis-St Paul	Detroit
Variable								
				Mean values				
Ratio of central city to metropolitan population growth, 1990–2000	0.7	-1.2	0.5	-0.4	1.2	0.5	-0.1	-1.8
Number of prohibited activities, 2000–1	3	3	3	2	2	2.8	3.5	3
Ratio of 'underclass' population to resident professional workforce, 1990	0.2	0.8	0.4	0.6	0.2	0.4	0.4	1.7
African-American share of population 2000	9.1	54.8	27.7	47.7	4.1	22.8	21.8	82.8
Hispanic share of population 2000	14.9	4.1	14.4	14.1	30.2	26.5	5.8	5.0
Black–white dissimilarity index, 2000	57.3	70.6	66.4	79.5	38.0	60.3	56.1	72.8
Hispanic–white dissimilarity index 2000	48.1	42.2	51.1	60.9	51.9	57.2	43.5	60.0
Housing wage for 2-bedroom apartment, metro, 2001 (US$)	22.9	12.2	18.8	15.4	30.6	15.9	12.1	12.8
Share of elite city buyers choosing gentrified neighborhoods, 1993–2000	11.6	9.0	49.9	21.3	0.6	2.1	6.4	5.7
White–black mortgage loan denial ratio in gentrified neighbourhoods, 1993–2000	1.8	2.3	1.8	2.6	3.6	2.2	2.2	3.2
Share of gentrified neighbourhood population in correctional institutions, 2000	1.3	0.5	0.7	0.1	0.1	0.0	4.4	14.6
Share of gentrified neighbourhood population homeless, 1990	1.8	1.1	0.7	1.3	0.3	0.3	2.1	0.1

of Chicago, Philadelphia, and Washington, elite reinvestment falls short of Boston, but in the context of similarly sharp divisions of race and class. In other cities segregation is similarly pronounced, but metropolitan expansion dilutes otherwise important inner-city changes to produce what might best be called disciplined decentralisation in Atlanta, Baltimore, Cincinnati, Milwaukee, New Orleans, St Louis. And the classification clearly highlights the racialised contours of the new urban frontier in cities segregated along white/black lines or anglo/latino divisions: note the divergent shares of African Americans and Latinos in cities of disciplined decentralisation versus those designated as Latino segregation.

Anti-homeless ordinances have proliferated across all of these categories. As Atkinson (2003a) has shown for the English case, urban policy entails an intricate and highly contextual fabric, with various 'strands of revanchism' woven into governance structures at various scales. Gentrification is loosely correlated with one strand – explicit anti-homeless laws – but most of the variation among cities comes from the broader urban context in which reinvestment and revanchism have emerged.

A taxonomy of neighbourhood inequality

Inter-city comparisons tell only part of the story. Can we identify systematic contrasts *within* and *among* cities in the kinds of inequalities inscribed by reinvestment? Answering this question is empirically simple (but methodologically provocative) if we harness the methods of the target-marketing industry. We matched our field surveys to the Neighbourhood Change Database developed by the Urban Institute (Geolytics 2003), which provides a limited set of variables for 1970 through 2000 for constant neighbourhood boundaries. We extracted a set of housing and population measures to highlight changes in inequality during the 1990s.[8] Then we used a standard factorial-ecology approach to eliminate multicollinearity and define six composite dimensions of neighbourhood restructuring (Table 2.3).[9] Another multivariate numerical taxonomy (using the rotated component scores) gives us a dozen distinct types among the 352 tracts identified in our field investigations (Table 2.4).[10]

In the target-marketing industry, of course, this kind of analysis is premised on consumption, market potential, and the commodification of place – distilled into catchy labels like 'money and brains', 'bohemian mix', or 'single-city blues' (a few categories in the consumer segmentation products offered by Claritas, Inc.). But this act of geographical objectification can also be used strategically to highlight the inequalities and dilemmas of gentrification. Our analysis highlights five main types of places inscribed by reinvestment, and seven smaller categories with unique, extreme configurations (Table 2.4). Almost two-fifths of neighbourhoods in our study are dominated by dynamic retail and residential districts popular among young, mostly white renters (vanilla playgrounds). Another quarter are the classic

Table 2.3 Principal components analysis of gentrified neighbourhoods, 1990–2000

Intepretation	Loadings on (varimax) rotated components					
	I African-American segregation	*II* Development	*III* Housing tenure	*IV* Institutions	*V* Latino segregation	*VI* Polarisation
Variable						
Change in housing units, 1990–2000		0.88				
Change in population, 1990–2000		0.79				
Non-Hispanic African-American, 1990	0.94					
Hispanic, 1990					0.94	−0.41
Group quarters, 1990		0.52		0.58		
Correctional institutions, 1990				0.91		
Homeless population, 1990		0.80				
Poverty rate, 1990		0.51				
White per capita income, 1989 dollars						0.74
White–black ratio of per capita income, 1989						0.68
Home-ownership, 1990	0.51					
Vacancy rate, 1990		0.61	0.86			
Non-Hispanic African-American, 2000	0.95					
Hispanic, 2000					0.95	
Group quarters, 2000				0.68		
Correctional institutions, 2000				0.92		
White married couples without children, 2000	−0.54		0.63			
Home-ownership, 2000			0.97			
White renters, 2000			−0.93			
Black renters, 2000	0.95					
Vacancy rate, 2000						
Percentage of total variance	20.1	17.2	14.7	10.7	8.1	6.9

Notes:
1 All variables are percentages unless otherwise indicated.
2 Loadings −0.40 to +0.40 not shown.

Table 2.4 A market segmentation of gentrified inequalities (a) Main clusters

	Vanilla playgrounds	Gold Coast enclaves	Racialised redevelopment	Precarious diversity	Latino frontier
Sample neighbourhoods	Capitol Hill, Denver Printer's Row, Chicago Wrigleyville, Chicago Western Addition, San Francisco	Capitol Hill, Washington DC Society Hill, Philadelphia Summit Hill, St Paul Back Bay, Boston	Bolton Hill, Baltimore Shaw, Washington DC Downtown, Detroit Corryville, Cincinnati	Eads Park, St Louis Grant Park, Atlanta North Oakland Black Pearl, New Orleans	Naglee Park, San José Lower Greenville, Dallas Lincoln Park, Denver Mission District, San Francisco
Cluster number	9	1			
Number of tracts	137	94	46	24	24
			Unweighted mean values		
Change in housing units, 1990–2000	10	12	14	2.4	9.2
Change in population, 1990–2000	15	13	17	2.0	10
Homeless population, 1990	2.0	0.29	1.3	0.41	0.64
Poverty rate, 1990	19	12	34	20	28
White per capita income, 1983 (dollars)	21,526	33,168	20,883	23,373	15,810
White–black ratio of per capita income, 1989	1.8	2.3	2.7	2.3	1.8
Non-Hispanic African-American, 2000	13	9.0	55	55	9.0
Hispanic, 2000	8.4	6.2	6.8	3.8	43
Group quarters, 1990	7.0	3.6	5.9	2.4	2.7
Correctional institutions, 2000	0.10	0.27	0.85	0.31	0.04
Home-ownership, 2000	17	42	21	49	23
White renters, 2000	81	56	70	43	72
Vacancy rate, 2000	7.3	7.3	12	8.9	7.1

Note: All figures are percentages except white per capita income and white–black income ratio.

Table 2.4 A market segmentation of gentrified inequalities (b) Outliers / Small clusters (continued)

Neighbourhoods	Loft lightning	Central citadels	Cells and apartments	Downtown sweep	Yuppies in training	Elite polarisation
	West Loop Gate, Chicago	Downtown, Minneapolis; Downtown, Indianapolis	Renaissance centre/ Greektown, Detroit; SoMa, San Francisco; Horton Plaza, San diego	Greektown, Chicago; Grand Ave, E1, Chicago; Downtown, Philadelphia; Downtown, Washington	Longwood Medical/ Academic area, Boston; University, Boston; Georgetown, Washington; Hyde Park, Chicago	Central City New Orleans; Mount Adams, Cincinnati; Belltown, Seattle; Downtown Dallas
Cluster number	4	7	2	8	11	6
Number of tracts	1	2	3	4	11	5
	Unweighted mean values					
Change in housing units, 1990–2000	610	8.6	32	225	8.6	101
Change in population, 1990–2000	684	77	23	108	15	89
Homeless population, 1990	34	0.0	11	46	1.0	1.2
Poverty rate, 1990	39	12	24	53	29	30
White per capita income, 1989 dollars	30,670	45,358	20,222	10,053	10,103	54,377
White–black ratio of per capita income, 1989	0.55	3.6	1.7	2.0	1.2	15
Non-Hispanic African-American, 2000	7.7	33	40	20	13	22
Hispanic, 2000	5.0	3.1	15	5.5	7.8	6.1
Group quarters, 1990	0.0	44	59	22	61	3.0
Correctional institutions, 2000	0.0	35	51	0.0	0.0	0.0
Home-ownership, 2000	88	26	17	44	26	22
White renters, 2000	11	74	80	51	73	75
Vacancy rate, 2000	21	13	12	16	6.9	14

Note: All figures are percentages except white per capita income and white–black income ratio.

gold-coast enclaves, such as Washington's Capitol Hill, Philadelphia's Society Hill and Boston's Back Bay. A generation of reinvestment has thoroughly reshaped vanilla playground and gold coast neighbourhoods, so in most of these places there is no longer much concern over displacement of the poor, who were pushed out years ago; current tensions typically involve competitive struggles among various gentrifiers (Hackworth 2002a, 2002b). The older, familiar lines of class conflict have moved deeper into the inner city. In about one-seventh of all neighbourhoods, gentrification is best understood as racialised redevelopment, with greatly magnified race-class inequalities in African American communities (Figure 2.3). In another group of neighbourhoods these changes are buffered and delayed by comparatively high rates of black homeownership, sustaining what is often an uneasy and precarious community diversity. Reinvestment and class transformation are marked by inequalities in historically Latino neighbourhoods in about 7 per cent of the cases.

But it is in the exceptional neighbourhoods, marked by extreme and dynamic social-statistical profiles, where revanchist neo-liberalism inscribes the most vivid urban ecologies. In one place (the near west side of Chicago) centralised housing demand has turbocharged a lightning-paced redevelopment of a latter-day zone in transition, replacing a mixed area of small wholesalers, suppliers, and old apartment houses with a suddenly-trendy 'West Loop Gate' of lofts, condo towers and an upscale entertainment corridor. In a handful of other neighbourhoods, downtown reinvestment coincides with county jails and other correctional facilities, creating wealthy central citadels or more modest retail districts of jail cells and mid-tier apartment developments – juxtapositions that provide a reminder that the creation or defence of attractive middle-class living spaces is never entirely unrelated to the infrastructures of discipline required to protect (some) people from deindustrialisation, poverty, discrimination, homelessness, and other externalities of contemporary neo-liberal globalisation (Gilmore 2002). A similar but converse process is underway in 'downtown sweep' places, where homeless shelters, SROs, and dilapidated homes are replaced by new apartments and downtown office or retail districts. In some cases the affordable housing and social services are relocated with no net loss, but in the last decade this outcome has become quite rare. Elsewhere, reinvestment is tied to elite colleges and universities, many of them either private or dealing with government mandates to respond to short-term market imperatives (we designate these neighbourhoods as training grounds for yuppies). In a few places reinvestment has created truly extraordinary cases of elite polarisation of wealth, poverty, and displacement (Figure 2.4).

Each of these categories, and indeed each place, deserves the kind of politically and geographically intimate analysis of Atkinson (2003a), or Beauregard (1990), Bennett (1998), Ley (1981), or Slater (2003). But even our superficial sketch of the comparative outlines of inner-city transformation is illuminating. Moreover, this neighbourhood analysis is closely linked to the metropolitan view provided

2.3 We all know the term for this trend

Case study 2.2

Gentrifying neighbourhoods in Cincinnati are on the front lines between poverty and reinvestment, and local variants of neoliberal urban redevelopment shaped the context in which policing practices led to a violent uprising in April 2001. Genesis Redevelopment, Inc. is across the street from the Laurel Homes, the city's oldest public housing project and a landmark of the West End; our quantitative analysis identifies the neighbourhood as an instance of racialised redevelopment (see Table 2.4). Genesis began receiving federal funds through city government agencies in 1991 to redevelop 130 homes. Eight years and US$800,000 later they had rehabbed their own offices and eleven homes, some belonging to board members. The scandal reached all the way to the city council (Anglen and Curnutte 2000; Osborne 2000; Korte 2001). Meanwhile, the Laurel Homes were targeted in a federally-funded redevelopment plan (HOPE VI, 'Housing Opportunities for People Everywhere') that facilitates the gentrification of severely distressed inner-city projects where local reinvestment boosts demand for market-rate units. The Laurel and adjoining Lincoln Court Homes are being upgraded to include 835 mixed-income rental units and 250 for-sale homes (Community Builders 2002). A former middle-school teacher whose students lived in the complex recalls telling them that 'inner city communities like the West End and Over-the-Rhine are not valued by the city planners until a trend occurs, which brings the young, upwardly mobile, and professional back to the inner city as residents. We all know the term for this trend: it's called "gentrification"' (Mincey 2001). Even the disinvested Over-the-Rhine neighbourhood, the epicentre of the 2001 uprising, has seen incipient signs of gentrification.

Population has continued to decline and abandoned buildings still mar the landscape, but displacement of long-time residents was cited as one of the background conditions that shaped local reactions to the police shooting of an unarmed teenager, Timothy Thomas. Policing and law involve an explicit spatiality, however, to discipline the neighbourhood. The area was the focus of a unique city ordinance that allowed police to ban suspected drug users from a 'drug exclusion zone' (Lazare 2001). The ordinance was eventually overturned in federal court, but in five years of enforcement, police used the law to ban more than 300 people, some of them residents (Grieco, Hills and Modic 2001: A1). One homeless man accumulated about a year of jail time through his repeated returns to the area for food and shelter. The law also swept up a grandmother arrested on charges of marijuana trafficking; although her case was thrown out of court, the banishment from the drug-free zone remained, preventing her from walking her grandchildren to school. Police now lament the loss of the ordinance: one official says, 'It worked, and they took it away' (ibid.) Over-the-Rhine has become a vivid example of contemporary neo-liberal inequalities, 'a neighbourhood where farmers sell mushrooms for $160 a pound at the Findlay Market within sight of drug dealers peddling their own herbs' (ibid.).

earlier (Table 2.2). Chicago and San Francisco, both distinguished by particularly strict anti-homeless regimes, have the largest and most diverse mix of gentrified neighbourhoods. Elite revanchist cities tend to the extremes, with over-representation of gold coast enclaves and racial redevelopment or downtown sweep neighbourhoods (while in Boston elite university districts compete with gold coast environments). In cities of disciplined decentralisation, we find fewer gold coasts, but more areas of racialised redevelopment and precarious diversity. Not surprisingly, Latino-segregated cities have more Latino frontier gentrified areas, but several also have a mix of gold coast enclaves and vanilla playgrounds.

Conclusions

A decade ago, the onset of recession prompted speculation that gentrification was dead. The subsequent boom proved once again that gentrification endures as an empirically limited but theoretically indispensable reflection of contemporary urbanisation. The continued vitality of high-end housing submarkets amidst the low interest rates in the recession of 2001–3 provides another signal of the closer integration of neighbourhoods and capital markets. Gentrification has been woven more tightly together with capital market processes, public sector privatisation,

2.4 From freedmen's town to Mars

Case study 2.3

Following the Civil War, freedmen's towns developed in many Texas cities as places where former slaves could live in relative safety, albeit horrendous squalor. In Dallas and Houston, these areas evolved into poor but vibrant centres for black culture and business, and after the 1920s they were often compared to Manhattan's Harlem. Recent gentrification pressures have wrought substantial changes in these communities. In the State-Thomas area of Dallas, most evidence of the history of African-American settlement has been obliterated, and most of the residents who lived there before 1990 are long gone. Many of the (mostly white) gentrifiers moving in during the late 1980s feared overdevelopment and the loss of the area's historic character, and thus worked closely with the city planning office to draft detailed guidelines and restrictions. A historian who worked on the guidelines reported measuring setbacks on Manhattan's Upper West Side, and the planning office borrowed heavily from similar plans in Seattle and Toronto (Griffin 2002). Yet much of the neighbourhood resembles an eerie attempt to recreate Philadelphia's Society Hill at a larger architectural scale. For its part the city made State-Thomas its first tax increment financing district in 1989, pouring in US$18 million in public infrastructure subsidies to leverage a remarkable quarter-billion of private investment (City of Dallas 2001). The development shown here (Drexel Court) is one of the few that did *not* involve direct public funds. Our quantitative analysis identifies this neigh-bourhood as an instance of elite polarisation (see Table 2.4). The scale and pace of change have stunned recent arrivals and long-time observers alike. One 96-year-old lifetime resident said 'It feels like I woke up one morning on Mars' (Griffin 2002).

globalised city competition, welfare and workfare policies, and all other parts of the fabric of neo-liberal urban governance. More than ever before, gentrification is incorporated into public policy – used either as a justification to obey market forces and private-sector entrepreneurialism, or as a tool to direct market processes in the hopes of restructuring urban landscapes in a slightly more benevolent fashion. Trumpeted under the friendly banners of regeneration, renewal, or revitalisation, many of these placebo policies fail in their boosterish goals: a solid consensus among mainstream economists and policy analysts holds that targeted revitalisation strategies, ranging all the way from tax credits to tax increment financing to enterprise zones, have only marginal impacts on the overall structure of land markets shaped by ongoing metropolitan decentralisation forces. But gentrification policy can have substantial effects at the neighbourhood scale, and when it does succeed in leveraging private capital it worsens housing affordability in ways that increase the demands on the remnants of the redistributive local state; waiting lists for housing vouchers (allocated at the federal level but administered by local authorities) have grown so long that some agencies have closed their list to avoid giving false hope (Carson 2003). In any event, the most durable result of gentrification may be its effect on new priorities in the formulation of urban policy. Inner-city land use decisions come to rely on considerations of middle-class market demand; gentrification underwrites new configurations of highest and best use, reallocations of neighbourhood public services, and realignments of police practices and public space regulation. The inherited landscapes and potential expansion of gentrification are now critical considerations in many domains of urban policy. To be sure, the word (which wealthy urbanites clearly understand as an epithet) almost never appears in the official discourse of renewal, revitalisation, and market optimism. But the interests and priorities of gentrifiers are a foundational element of the post-industrial city as growth machine (Molotch 1976). And even when gentrifiers have genuinely inclusive intentions, their income and consumption decisions accelerate local market pressures that interact with urban policy in a climate of social-welfare austerity, economic discipline, and a consistent preference for spatial mechanisms that avoid questioning underlying societal inequalities (Mitchell 1997). In short, the triumph of neo-liberalism has altered the context and consequences of gentrification, creating new inequalities and locally-distinctive strands of revanchism (Atkinson 2003a). But if local variations do matter, the underlying dilemma remains the same. The gentry want nice, attractive cities free of homeless people begging, sleeping, urinating, defecating in public – *living* in public – and in today's political climate, wealthy urbanites are increasingly willing to support policies that criminalise the activities that homeless people must do in order to live.

Our effort to map the diverse strands of American neo-liberal urbanism is a deliberate methodological provocation that carries serious risks. As in the world-cities literature, the approach is 'poised somewhere on a conceptual and

epistemological borderland where positivism, structuralism, and essentialism meet'
(M. P. Smith 1999: 119). The approach is built on the shaky foundations of
partitional thinking. The choice of variables defines the mathematical space that
is then mechanistically partitioned, so the process 'reminds one of a lunatic hacking
apart a pumpkin with a broadaxe' only to be astonished that 'no matter what
clustering routine is applied, points close together in the space (pumpkin) will
often appear in the same groups (pieces hacked apart)' (Gould 1999: 298). But
that is the point. America's history of gentrification in the 1960s and 1970s has
been reconstructed in tune with the transformation from managerialism to urban
entrepreneurialism (Harvey 1989a), and with the shift from roll-back deregulation
to roll-out neo-liberal innovation (Peck and Tickell 2002). The complexities of
place in the American inner city have been distilled into the rigid simplicity of the
market, creating in the language of policy an 'objectified and essentialized reality,
a "thing" operating outside the social construction of meaning' (M. P. Smith 1999:
119). One way to context, undermine, and reconstruct this objectification is to
define a taxonomic space that reveals the context of cities shaped by distinctive
configurations of neo-liberal housing and social policy, federal–local relations,
intersections of capital investment and disinvestment, and regional geographies
of homelessness and racial-ethnic inequality. Our sketch of a revanchist urban
hierarchy is a primitive first step towards understanding contemporary gentrification in its new political-economic context – and also to mapping alternative
urban futures.

Notes

1 Acknowledgments: we are grateful to the editors for helpful comments and criticisms on an
   earlier version of this manuscript. We are also indebted to Tom Slater, Winifred Curran, David
   Ley, and Vern Wyly for valuable discussions and comments on previous drafts. The usual
   disclaimer that the usual disclaimer applies, applies (Lake 2002).
2 We used mortgage disclosure data (FFIEC 1994–2001) to identify the top tenth of the distribution
   of inflation-adjusted incomes reported by all home purchase applicants in our twenty-three
   metropolitan areas. Cutoffs for the 90th percentile range from US$100,000 in St Louis (in
   2000 dollars) to US$231,000 in San Francisco.
3 Many municipalities have established ordinances banning one or more of these activities only
   in specified districts. To maintain the most conservative approach, our tabulations are restricted
   to *citywide* ordinances banning the specified activities.
4 In Chicago, 'police are using old, vague ordinances and charging people with vagrancy, begging,
   loitering, etc. ... The City has also closed and even destroyed many transient hotels as part of
   conscious gentrification plans to recreate neighbourhoods. ... Sweeps of homeless individuals
   are conducted whenever there are major events in the downtown area' (NCH/NLCHP 2002:
   133–4).
5 Six years ago, Indianapolis went so far as to ban the homeless from voting, before advocates
   managed to convince the state legislature to pass a law reaffirming voting rights. One homeless
   shelter requires those admitted to undress and don prison-style orange jumpsuits (NCH/NLCHP
   2002: 135).

6 Unless otherwise noted in Table 2.2, all measures are calculated for central cities. The prohibited activities measure excludes curfew and spitting ordinances. The housing wage variable measures the hourly pay required for a full-time worker to afford the fair market rent for a two-bedroom apartment in each metropolitan area.

7 Our taxonomy was developed using the FASTCLUS procedure in SAS, a non-hierarchical, iterative disjoint clustering procedure that minimises within-group Euclidian distances based on orthogonal, standardised quantitative measures. The overall R-squared (measuring how well variables can be predicted from clusters) is 0.68; the ratio of between-cluster to within-cluster variance $[R^2/(1 - R^2)]$ is encouragingly high (above 2) for most variables, with the notable exception of prohibited activities (0.42). The low value for this indicator persists through dozens of alternative specifications with a variety of other variables, indicating that these types of ordinances have proliferated across many kinds of cities.

8 The detailed long-form sample data for 2000 are not yet available in this dataset, so we are limited to the basic measures in the full-count census of the entire population.

9 The factor model is fairly robust, with the six-component solution accounting for 78 percent of the variance in the original 21 measures. More than half of the original variables achieve communalities over 0.80, and only three fall short of 0.60.

10 The overall R-squared is 0.68. The ratio of between- to within-cluster variance is over 2.0 for all components except III (housing tenure, with a ratio of 1.16) and VI (polarisation, 1.25).

3 Gentrification in Canada's cities

From social mix to 'social tectonics'

Tom Slater

'Canada's coolest neighbourhoods'

Suffering from insomnia on a red-eye flight from Los Angeles to Toronto, I thumbed through Air Canada's monthly magazine, *enRoute*, and happened upon an article entitled 'Canada's Coolest Neighbourhoods'. Criteria for entry in the top ten of coolness, selected by 'a panel of 38 prominent Canadians' (p. 37) were set out as follows:

> When today's archetypal young graphic designer leaves home, he [sic] is looking for something different than what his parents may have sought. Often, he will look for a 'young' place inhabited by his peers. He will seek out a 'fun' place, where he can indulge in his favourite leisure activities. But most of all, he will look for an area that makes him feel distinct and at home at the same time, a neighbourhood that reflects his tastes – a place that is cool (p. 37).

If we dispense with the amusingly arbitrary association of graphic designers with coolness, the striking feature of the list is the fact that every neighbourhood on it has experienced or is experiencing gentrification. In addition, arguably the two most famous gentrified neighbourhoods in Canada occupy the top two slots (see Figure 3.1).

While we should not read too much into the adjudication of an anonymous panel of prominent Canadians in a far from prominent publication, the outcome of Air Canada's survey demonstrates the extent to which gentrification in Canada (and indeed every major advanced capitalist country) has become, in the words of David Ley (2003), 'not a sideshow in the city, but a major component of the urban imaginary' (p. 2527). It is nothing new to see the association of 'gentrification'

1 Queen Street West, Toronto
2 Le Plateau Mont-Royal, Montreal
3 Vieux-Montreal, Montreal
4 West-End, Vancouver
5 Little Italy, Toronto
6 Old Strathcona, Edmonton
7 The Exchange District, Winnipeg
8 Lower Water Street, Halifax
9 Inglewood, Calgary
10 Le Vieux-Québec, Québec City

3.1 The top ten 'coolest neighbourhoods' in Canada

with 'cool', nor is it new in Canadian contexts to see positive accounts of gentrification like that exhibited in *enRoute*. What is new is the sheer extent to which gentrification is recognised, promoted and celebrated; etched into the public imagination and championed as the process which creates spaces for lavish middle-class consumption and a wider 'liveability' in the city.

A number of major theoretical statements on gentrification have emerged from research undertaken in Canadian cities (e.g. Ley 1981, 1986, 1996; Bourne 1993a, 1993b; Caulfield 1989, 1994; Rose 1984, 1996), so the time seems right to offer a review of earlier work and present the findings of recent research to show the 'changing state of gentrification' (see Hackworth and Smith 2001) in Canadian cities, and open up avenues for further inquiry. This chapter adopts a wide-angle lens to document the changing nature of gentrification in Canadian cities, and attempts to demonstrate how the 'emancipatory' potential for 'social mixing' through gentrification, identified in journalistic, political and academic circles, is showing signs of eroding and becoming the potential for something very different, a process of 'social tectonics' (Robson and Butler 2001). The meanings of 'social mix' and 'social tectonics' will be clarified in due course, but the changes in the context of Canada's cities are here attributed to the recent union of neo-liberal urban policy and gentrification.

The first part of this chapter is an abbreviated treatment of a literature that is significant in its size and geographical scope, the second part draws on an empirical investigation conducted in gentrifying South Parkdale, Toronto, to provide an illustration of the neighbourhood effects of what I have elsewhere called 'municipally-managed gentrification' (see Slater 2004a, 2004b). However, it is important to recognise that the role of policy in facilitating gentrification in Canadian cities is not new. As Ley (1996) argued, 'policy initiatives in Canadian cities after 1968 or so have proven propitious for gentrification, even though in most cases this has been an unintended consequence' (p. 52). But in the twenty-first century, hand-in-hand with the global diffusion of neo-liberalism, the emerging situation is that gentrification is now the *intended* consequence of numerous policy initiatives (as other chapters in this volume point out). Increasing municipal involvement in the process of gentrification is something that has been noted recently in major Canadian cities (De Sousa 2002; Sommers and Blomley 2002; Smith and Derksen 2002; H. Smith 2003; Ley 2003; Rose 2003), and my purpose is to use the case-study of South Parkdale alongside other recent research to make some tentative general points about the implications of policy-led gentrification.

Emancipatory social mixing: reform-era gentrification in Canadian cities

Gentrification is a process now so firmly established in Canadian cities that it is hard to find neighbourhoods in central city areas from Vancouver to Halifax that have not experienced either wholesale or sporadic gentrification of some form. The rapid pace of urban restructuring since the 1970s makes it all the more remarkable, in retrospect, that it took some time for 'gentrification', a British term, to enter the lexicon of Canadian urban discourse, both public and academic – not until the 1980s did it become the generic label for class transformation in Canadian neighbourhoods. The term 'whitepainting' was used when the process first emerged in Toronto in the mid-1960s, and was a reference to the gentrifiers' penchant for painting the exterior of their house white (Dynes, 1974; Aitkenhead *et al.* 1975; Rebizant *et al.* 1976). At the same time, the process was frequently labelled in other cities with socially innocent terms such as 'rehabilitation', 'townhousing' and 'sandblasting', and gentrification was restricted to a select few neighbourhoods in the largest cities

The process accelerated across Canada in the 1970s during what has become known as the 'reform era' of Canadian urban politics (see Harris 1987). Three scholars in particular, Jon Caulfield, David Ley and Damaris Rose, have provided detailed accounts of gentrification in this era; Ley's covering the six largest Canadian cities, Caulfield's focusing on what happened in Toronto, Rose's on the changing face of Montreal. A summary of their work is necessary in order to gain a historical perspective on gentrification in urban Canada.

For Caulfield (1994), 1970s and 1980s gentrification in Toronto was a very deliberate middle-class rejection of the oppressive conformity of suburbia, modernist planning, and mass market principles. In his words, it was

> a rupture in dominant canons of urban meaning and a cluster of social practices, carried out in the context of everyday life, oriented toward reconstituting the meanings of old city neighbourhoods towards an alternative urban future (p. 109).

Gentrification was portrayed as a highly critical middle-class reaction (what he termed a 'critical social practice') to the city's postwar modernist development – a concerted effort to create this 'alternative urban future'. Toronto's expanding middle-class intelligentsia was instrumental in the reorientation of Toronto's identity away from suburbia and the Fordist ethos back towards the central city and the emerging post-Fordist society. For the best part of two decades, Toronto's gentrification was in every sense a deliberate operation of resistance to everything that characterised urban development in the 1960s, and thus a practice 'eluding the domination of social and cultural structures and constituting new conditions for experience' (Caulfield 1989: 624). In his interviews with the gentrifiers of Toronto, Caulfield observed that their affection for Toronto's old city neighbour-hoods was rooted in their desire to escape the mundane, banal routines that characterised suburbia. Heavily influenced by Walter Benjamin, Roland Barthes, Jonathan Raban and Marcel Rioux, he argued the following:

> Old city places offer difference and freedom, privacy and fantasy, possibilities for carnival … These are not just matters of philosophical abstraction but, in a carnival sense, … the city is the place of our meeting with the other (ibid.: 625).

This issue of 'the place of our meeting with the other' will be taken up later on; here it is necessary to register that Caulfield's point was that gentrification could not be separated from reform-era middle-class resistance to political and structural domination.

A similar argument emerges from the work of David Ley in his long-running investigations into gentrification in Canadian cities. It would be foolhardy to attempt to summarise all his work in the space available, so my focus here is on Ley's coverage of the intertwining of gentrification and reform-era urban politics.[1] Post-1968, many centrally-located neighbourhoods in urban Canada saw their social and economic status elevated as the central city became the perceived and lived arena for counter-cultural awareness, tolerance, diversity and liberation. This occurred in the context of a laissez-faire state, a rapidly changing industrial and occupational structure (where 'hippies became yuppies', as Ley so tellingly put it, in the shift towards a post-industrial society), welfare retrenchment, a real estate and new construction boom, the advent of postmodern niche-marketing and conspicuous consumption (Ley and Mills 1993), and the aestheticisation and commodification of art and artistic lifestyles (Ley 2003). In the 1970s, neighbour-hoods such as Yorkville and The Annex in Toronto, Kitsilano and Fairview Slopes in Vancouver, Le Plateau Mont-Royal in Montreal, and indeed a number of entries on the list in Figure 3.1, became hotbeds of 'hippie' reaction against political conservatism, modernist planning and suburban ideologies (Ley 1996).

Suspicious of the empirical applicability of arguments from the United States which alluded to a conservative 'adversarial politics' among middle-class gentrifiers, Ley (1994) provided evidence from electoral returns in the three largest Canadian cities (Toronto, Montreal and Vancouver) to demonstrate that the principal gentrifying districts in each city in fact contained an electorate which predominantly sided with more liberal 'reform politics'. Reform politics exhibited

> closer management of growth and development, improved public services, notably housing and transportation, more open government with various degrees of neighbourhood empowerment, and greater attention to such amenity issues as heritage, public open space, and cultural and leisure facilities (pp. 59–60).

In all three cities under scrutiny there was 'no significant tendency overall for social upgrading in the city centre to be associated with [adversarial] conservative politics' (p. 70). In *The New Middle Class and the Remaking of the Central City* (1996), Ley exposed the power of the legacy of the counter-cultural youth movements of the late 1960s, arguing that their 'values diffused and evolved among receptive and much larger segments of the professional middle class' (p. 210). The professional middle class were a group which saw unprecedented expansion in the 1970s and 1980s (see also Hamnett 1991; Rose 1996), and for Ley, their collective disdain for the monotony of suburbia, for the mass organisation and repetition of postwar Fordism and its crushing of individualism and difference (and entire neighbourhoods, through freeway construction) could not be divorced from the explanation of gentrification. 'Consecutive waves of the new middle class' viewed the central city as 'a credential, a mark of distinction in the constitution of an identity separate from the constellation of place and identity shaped by the suburbs' (p. 211), and using both quantitative measures and qualitative accounts, Ley demonstrated that gentrification was the outcome in city after city across Canada (see also Ley and Mills 1986; Cybriwsky, Ley and Western 1986).

In Caulfield's work, and to a lesser extent Ley's, we find an endorsement of Damaris Rose's concept of the 'marginal gentrifier', first outlined in a paper published in 1984. This concept emerged from – and was later bolstered by (e.g. Rose and Le Bourdais 1986; Rose 1989) – research in Montreal, and refers to the fact that marginally-employed professionals, prominent among whom were women, single parents and receiving moderate incomes, were attracted to central city neighbourhoods due to the range of support services they offered – which were unavailable in the suburbs. For example, the worry of precarious employment could be eased by networking and holding more than one job; and by minimising space-time constraints, lone female parents could combine paid and unpaid (domestic) labour with greater ease than in suburban locations. Most relevant to this discussion, the concept of the marginal gentrifier was very much influenced by the major societal changes that took place in the reform era:

> [S]ome of the changes which are usually subsumed within the concept 'gentrification' can bring into existing neighbourhoods intrusions of alternative ways of living, which would never be tolerated if they were not being intro-duced by 'middle-class' and 'professional' people in the first instance (p. 68).

Rose concluded her article by calling for an approach to gentrification which explored 'the actual processes through which those groups we now subsume under the category "gentrifiers" are produced and reproduced' (p. 69). Crucially, she argued that such an approach 'may help us clarify what constitute progressive types of intervention and to identify "oppositional spaces" within the non-commodified sphere of daily life, where such interventions may be tried out' (p. 69). While the political undercurrent of this approach was subject to some trenchant criticism from Marxist scholars (see Smith 1987), Rose's work, like Ley's and Caulfield's, is a very clear lens through which we can see the causes of earlier rounds of gentrification in Canadian cities. Their work should not be interpreted as narrowly cultural, theorising the production of gentrifiers at the expense of other concerns, but rather as a collective of penetrating scholarship which captured the major social, economic and cultural shifts taking place in urban Canada following the major political upheavals of 1968 and the birth of reactionary, counter-cultural middle-class sensibilities.

The emancipatory discourse on gentrification is not something that can or should be easily disentangled from the issues of social mixing and social diversity in gentrifying neighbourhoods. It is Rose who has engaged with these issues in most depth as part of her continued interest in the gentrification of Montreal, particularly where that city stands *vis-à-vis* broad theoretical statements in the study of gentrification. In a critique of 'stage models' of the process, she argued that:

> it is not inevitable, even in advanced tertiary cities, that all neighbourhoods where a 'beachhead' of 'first wave gentrifiers' is established will ultimately be caught up in an irreversible dynamic largely driven by major real estate interests and leading to their transformation into homogenous yuppie preserves ... (1996: 153).

Rose points to the fact that many gentrified and gentrifying districts in Montreal in fact exhibit social diversity: '[e]ven at the scale of a city block, rare are the instances where a new social homogeneity has taken hold' (p. 157). This is because, first, the legacy of the city-building process created a very diverse residential morphology at a micro-scale, second, because small pockets of social housing were dotted throughout gentrifying neighbourhoods, and third, 'there were not

enough wealthy potential gentrifiers and the city's [1980s] economy was too weak
... to unleash a dynamic of wholesale transformation of the most "professionalized"
neighbourhoods' (p. 161). In this context, Rose concluded that different social
groups are brought together by gentrification, and seem to be staying together,
making social diversity 'an issue to be reckoned with rather than dismissed in
gentrification theory' (p. 161).

I will discuss Rose's most recent work in the conclusion to this chapter, but at
this stage it is worth pointing out that 'social mix' has a long history in Canadian
urban planning (one which pre-dates gentrification) and underpinned by nineteenth-
century utopiansim and normative principles on neighbourhood 'health', often
drawn up in contrast to ghettoisation in the United States (Harris 1993; Dansereau
et al. 1997). Any discussion of the emancipatory discourse on gentrification in
Canada must take into account the oppositional discourse from which it draws
most power. Canadian city images of liveability, freedom, tolerance, cross-class
interaction, diversity, mixing and conviviality are almost always articulated and
legitimised in contrast to gentrification in the United States, which, as portrayed
in an even larger literature, has been associated with controversy, resistance, unease,
'dirtiness' and 'revanchism' (Smith 1996). A discourse is rarely constructed without
reference to its 'other',[2] as Lees and Demeritt (1998) have pointed out comparing
American and Canadian city discourses:

> images of decay ... and images of civility are not simply contrasting; they are
> mutually constitutive. As a binary opposition, the meaning of one depends on
> the other (p. 335).

Yet the emancipatory discourse is also a product of its time (the reform-era,
and the era of rapidly-widening employment horizons, life course and housing
choices for middle-class women). Its power could well dwindle as gentrification
in Canada changes, and the next section of this chapter provides an illustration of
the influence of neo-liberal urban policy in producing a new situation which is far
from emancipatory.

Neo-liberal social tectonics: the case of South Parkdale

> The specific impact of gentrification on Toronto tenants is to exacerbate the
> tightness of the rental market by causing the withdrawal of generally cheap
> accommodation from this market.
>
> (Filion 1991: 563)

In two papers which could now be described as infamous, Larry Bourne (1993a,
1993b) questioned the longevity of gentrification in Canada (and elsewhere). Based
on evidence from Canadian cities, he argued that a 'demise' of gentrification would
lead to a 'post-gentrification era' because

the supply of potential young gentrifiers will be significantly smaller, given the passing of the baby-boom into middle-age, the declining rate of new household formation, and the general aging of the population. The expanding cohort of potential young gentrifiers will not be sufficient to compensate for the rapid decline in the younger cohorts. At the same time, given widespread macro-economic restructuring, corporate down-sizing and a persistent recession, we might also expect slower rates of employment growth in the service sector and associated occupations.

(1993: 104–5)

While his work was rightly taken seriously, Bourne's declamatory predictions did not materialise, and his arguments were refuted regularly (Badcock 1993, 1995; Lees and Bondi 1995; Smith 1996; Ley 1996; Wyly and Hammel 1999; Smith and DeFilippis 1999; Hackworth 2001, 2002b). The language that replaced Bourne's post-gentrification thesis was that of a 'post-recession' era (from 1993 onwards) of *accelerated*, 'third wave' gentrification. Hackworth and Smith (2001) argue that this era differs from earlier gentrification in four ways. First, gentrification is expanding within and beyond the neighbourhoods it affected during earlier waves. Second, the real estate industry has restructured under globalisation, providing a platform for the involvement of larger developers in gentrification. Third, resistance to gentrification has declined due to continued working-class displacement from the inner city, and fourth, the state is now more involved in gentrification than in the 1980s 'second wave', which was largely market driven (see Mills 1988, for the case of Fairview Slopes, Vancouver). While it is very likely that there will be historical and geographical variances to these four points (something that Hackworth and Smith perhaps do not emphasise enough), I zoom in on the fourth category; specifically, increasing neo-liberal municipal government involvement in the process of gentrification. The following is a very condensed account of such involvement, drawn from research conducted in the neighbourhood of South Parkdale, Toronto.

South Parkdale is located in Toronto's west end (Figure 3.2), and has a history which is best described as turbulent. It emerged in the late 19th century as one of Toronto's first commuter suburbs, facilitated by the development of the railway and later the streetcar (Laycock and Myrvold 1991). Streets were laid out to facilitate resident access south to Lake Ontario, and north to Queen Street which became the main thoroughfare of commerce and trade, a condition unaltered today. In its early years it was considered 'one of Toronto's most desirable residential locations' (CTPB 1976: 7). Known informally as 'The Village by the Lake' (Laycock and Myrvold 1991), with fine Victorian and Edwardian terraces and some substantial mansions housing a largely elite and upper-middle class population, South Parkdale was for many years insulated from an era in Toronto

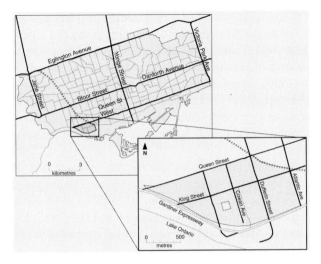

3.2 Queen Street

which Hiebert (1995) has described as 'a time of massive immigration, economic change and social ferment' (p. 55).

This insulation was removed when Toronto became a locus of experimental modernist planning in the 1950s (Caulfield 1994; Filion 1999). Expressways leading to suburban expansion were seen as signs of economic progress, legitimised by phraseology such as 'slum clearance' and 'urban renewal' (Kipfer and Keil 2002). While there was disinvestment from the neighbourhood after World War II (Whitzman 2003), South Parkdale's identity was forever changed when it found itself in the path of the construction of the Gardiner Expressway between 1955 and 1964. By 1959, South Parkdale was completely sliced off from Lake Ontario (Figure 3.2), its principal amenity. Over 170 houses were demolished, and entire streets erased from existence (Caulfield 1994: 33). A number of high-rise apartment buildings were constructed in the neighbourhood, with the City of Toronto hoping that those displaced by the Expressway construction would move in and remain in South Parkdale (CTPB 1976). This proved optimistic; the middle classes largely abandoned it in favour of other neighbourhoods and the suburbs. Throughout the 1960s and 1970s, substantial mansions and handsome terraces were demolished to make way for the high-rises; others were abandoned by owner occupiers and sold to absentee landlords or (dis)investment firms, who divided them into smaller apartments, and some properties remained vacant as the neighbourhood went into serious economic decline (Dunn 1974).

In the 1980s, South Parkdale was further affected by its proximity to the Queen Street Centre for Addiction and Mental Health, the largest psychiatric facility in Canada and 'a consistently vital resource' for Toronto's mentally ill (Court 2000).

In this decade, the Tory provincial government endorsed the deinstitutionalisation of psychiatric patients under the misnomer of 'community-based care' (Dear and Taylor 1982; Marshall 1982; Dear and Wolch 1987; Hall and Joseph 1988; Simmons 1990). Thousands of patients were discharged from the centre into South Parkdale in the early 1980s (Marshall 1982; Simmons 1990). Coupled with a major retraction in the welfare state, a consequence of a provincial fiscal crisis (Lemon 1993; Hasson and Ley 1994), deinstitutionalisation had profound and lasting effects on a neighbourhood already under stress from metropolitan restructuring and devalorisation.

Housing was neither plentiful nor adequate for the needs of discharged psychiatric patients, and by 1981, it was estimated that up to 1,200 lived in South Parkdale (Simmons 1990: 168), in a neighbourhood which by 1985 contained only 39 official 'group homes' for such patients (Joseph and Hall 1985: 150). A large majority thus had to find alternative means of accommodation. As the provincial government did not provide housing assistance to those discharged, patients gravitated to unofficial boarding homes, to rooming houses or the even smaller 'bachelorette' apartments in the single-family dwellings of the old South Parkdale. All of these housing types saw prolific (and usually illegal) conversion during the 1970s, resulting in one of the highest concentrations of low-income housing in Toronto. Home to such a large number of mentally unwell residents mostly left to their own devices, South Parkdale became beset by the social problems resulting from poverty, illness and institutional neglect. As Dear and Wolch (1987) put it, deinstitutionalisation in Ontario was 'a policy adopted with great enthusiasm, even though it was never properly articulated, systematically implemented, nor completely thought through' (p. 107).

South Parkdale has for a long time stood in stark contrast to most other neighbourhoods in central Toronto. Its reputation has proved highly resilient; a recent article in *The Globe and Mail* described it as 'a neighbourhood rife with poverty, drugs, and prostitution … no place for a child to grow up' (Philip 2000). However, while it might seem unlikely that gentrification could take place, it has experienced slow yet continuing middle-class resettlement since the mid-1980s, quickening in pace (though not yet rampant) since the mid-1990s. A neighbourhood that was so often an instigator of middle-class derision and fear attracted the middle-classes *precisely because* its insalubrious reputation kept property values down. As house prices rose elsewhere in Toronto in consecutive real estate booms, a growing segment of professional middle classes found a handsome, spacious and affordable Victorian and Edwardian architectural heritage on South Parkdale's broad, tree lined streets, with easy access to employment in downtown Toronto. Their expectations were that property values would eventually rise as the neighbourhood's profile rose, leading to handsome profits in years to come. There can be few better examples than the case of South Parkdale for the continued need for 'complementarity' in the explanation of gentrification (Clark 1992; Lees 1994);

a 'rent-gap' existed in tandem with the production of gentrifiers with tastes for a distinctive housing stock.

A major factor behind more recent gentrification has been South Parkdale's growing reputation as a community of artists. Artists have been shown to prime entire neighbourhoods for the real estate industry; the group rich in cultural capital who often pave the way for followers richer in economic capital (Podmore 1998; Bridge 2001b; Ley 2003). The South Parkdale section of Queen Street West represents the final stage of the Street's cultural (and socio-economic) transformation in a westerly direction from Spadina Avenue in the heart of Toronto. Artists have congregated in South Parkdale because studio and gallery rents are affordable, and because the 'edginess' of the neighbourhood serves to amplify the message of their 'cutting edge' art. Over 600 artists now live in the neighbourhood, and have the complete, uncritical support of the city, as was revealed to me by the City Councillor for the administrative ward which contains South Parkdale:

> Things are improving with the influx of the art galleries. This is the way we need to go, we need to open up the street to that sort of business. I was instrumental in that because I was on the board that helped to legalise live/ work spaces for artists who were living in poor conditions. So with Queen Street what is needed are speciality stores that will serve people in the neighbourhood and attract people from beyond it. It's not great at the moment, but it's getting there. We do need more pride from businesses on Queen Street, like cleaning up windows, storefronts, signs, that kind of thing.
>
> (City Councillor, interview, 2 April 2001)

Yet the resettlement of middle-class homeowners and tenants (who have been following the artists) has not been welcomed by the substantial number of low-income tenants in the neighbourhood, who are now threatened by displacement resulting from either the closure or deconversion of rooming houses and bachel-orette buildings. These are the cheapest forms of permanent rental accommodation currently available in Toronto, the last step before homelessness for the city's low-income population. Together with gentrification, a lack of profits for landlords, pressure from middle-class residents' associations (Lyons 2000), new zoning restrictions, and closure through illegality and poor safety standards, such dwellings have declined significantly across Toronto since the 1980s. This decline has been linked to the explosive growth of homelessness in the city (Filion 1991; Dear and Wolch 1993; Ley 1996; Layton 2000; Harris 2000; Peressini and McDonald 2000).

In December 1996, under pressure from middle-class residents concerned about the effects of low-income accommodation on adjacent property values, the City of Toronto passed a by-law that prohibited any rooming house/bachelorette development or conversion in South Parkdale, pending the outcome of an area study. The results were released in July 1997, in the form of proposals entitled

'Ward 2 Neighbourhood Revitalization' (CTUDS 1997). An examination of the document reveals what the City of Toronto viewed as the principal social problem of the area – the presence of single-person dwellings and their low-income occupants. The broad objective of the proposals was spelt out concisely and without disguising the intent:

> To stabilize a neighbourhood under stress and restore a healthy demographic balance, without dehousing of vulnerable populations.
>
> (CTUDS 1997:17, emphasis added)

The document repeatedly reminds its audience of an 'unhealthy' balance:

> [T]he area has gone from a stable neighbourhood, with a healthy mix of incomes and household types, to one with *a disproportionately large number of single occupancy accommodation* [sic].
>
> (ibid: 1, emphasis added)

> At the request of [the City] Councillor….[the] Land Use Committee requested the Commissioner of Planning and Development … to report back on *a strategy to encourage families to return to Ward 2*.
>
> (ibid.: 3, emphasis added)

> Limiting the number of units in future conversions to two will automatically ensure that at least one, and probably both the *units will be large enough for family occupancy*. The second rental unit, if provided as a rental unit, could *assist a young family in carrying a mortgage on their house*.
>
> (ibid.: 26–7, emphasis added)

It does not take a sophisticated decoding of this document to realise that an influx of families is seen as a way to unlock South Parkdale's 'revitalisation'. While the objective states that 'dehousing' of vulnerable populations would be avoided, it is not easy to see how this can be achieved because South Parkdale's most vulnerable are singles – the welfare-dependent, mentally ill and socially isolated. A defensible argument can be put forward that these proposals were not drawn up to improve the conditions for singles already in South Parkdale, but drawn up to reduce the percentage of singles in the neighbourhood, with middle-class families from other areas taking their place.

Following a boisterous anti-gentrification campaign by the Parkdale Common Front, a coalition of anti-poverty activist groups who united against new zoning and argued that the city's proposals were tantamount to 'social cleansing' (Lyons 1998; Kipfer and Keil 2002), the city went back to the drawing board. Responding to criticism that they had been exclusive of low-income interests in the neighbourhood, they invited members of all stakeholders to a series of meetings, in what became known as the 'Parkdale Conflict Resolution'. In October 1999, the outcome was published (CTUDS 1999a), and while quieter on the issue of attracting families, the 1996 by-law remained in place, and a team of planners and building inspectors, called the Parkdale Pilot Project (PPP), was formed to deal with the overcrowding, illegality and poor safety of many of the existing multi-unit dwellings; its manifesto is presented in Figure 3.3. The requirement for licensing eligibility most relevant to this discussion is that all units in a building must comply with the minimum unit size of 200 square feet (CTUDS 1999b: 14). A study undertaken in 1976 by the City of Toronto (CTPB 1976) revealed that many units are smaller than 200 square feet – since many remain unchanged since this study was undertaken, bringing buildings up to standard would almost certainly lead to the loss of smaller units, and to the displacement of tenants.

A representative of the PPP provided a revealing glimpse into the continued wish of the city to reduce the percentage of single-person housing:

> Generally accepted planning principles suggest that healthy neighbourhoods support a diversity of housing opportunities for families, couples and singles. There is a planning concern that by tipping the balance too much in favour of small, essentially single-person housing, that healthy diversity will be lost and the area will become ghettoised as more and more of the housing stock is abandoned by families and converted into bachelorettes and rooming houses. … So what we are doing now is bringing current conversions into the light, and banning all new ones.
>
> (Interview, 20 June 2001)

It is interesting how the very strong emphasis on family housing in earlier reports is now disguised with neo-liberal discourse such as 'a diversity of housing opportunities'. The City of Toronto is clearly using the laws on building safety and licensing to fulfil a broader objective, which is to re-balance the population of South Parkdale. The comments of the director of a drop-in centre for the homeless and mentally ill in the heart of South Parkdale lend credence to this:

> [T]he problem with the zoning legislation is that it was proposed in a neighbourhood with one of the largest, if not the largest, populations of psychiatric survivors in Canada, and the people living in rooming houses … have nowhere else to go. Admittedly there's also an obvious drive to encourage more families to live in Parkdale, as singles are seen as less sensitive to community issues, so the legislation was perhaps intended to make space for a family value ethic which Parkdale has not had since the before the Gardiner [Expressway].
>
> (Interview, 11 April 2001)

3.3 Parkdale Pilot Project

In recent years, responsibility for this drive to encourage the middle-class resettlement of South Parkdale has not only been in the hands of the municipal government, but indirectly with the provincial government.[3] The threats to South Parkdale's poor posed by gentrification were compounded by the more aggressively neo-liberal (1995–2003) Conservative provincial government (Keil 2000, 2002). In June 1998, their oddly named 'Tenant Protection Act' came into effect, the hallmark of which was the introduction of vacancy decontrol – the elimination of rent control on vacant units. When an apartment becomes vacant through 'natural turnover', the landlord may charge whatever they think they can make on the unit to a new tenant. Landlords are now less likely to negotiate if a low-income tenant falls into rent arrears, because the Act paves the way for them to attract middle-class tenants paying higher rents. This has 'reaked absolute havoc' on low-income tenants in South Parkdale, according to a legal worker working in housing issues at a non-profit legal aid clinic in the neighbourhood:

> In the past you could get your landlord to negotiate with you. Now the impetus is to get rid of you, totally, as they will pay off the arrears they lose when they get a richer tenant paying way more rent … The landlord has no reason, if they think they can get more for that unit, to forgive the people who are in arrears of rent.
>
> (Legal worker in South Parkdale, interview, 12 February 2001)

Layton's (2000) assessment of the Tenant Protection Act captures the problem:

> The ironically named Tenant Protection Act accomplished precisely the opposite result for tenants – exposing them to increased pressure by making evictions more profitable and easier to accomplish (p. 81).

Not only are there stories of threatened and actual displacement to be heard in South Parkdale (see Slater 2004b), there is also a contradiction between the two levels of government concerning the PPP. Following any mandatory maintenance/safety improvements ordered by the PPP inspectors, the landlord can still apply to the province for an 'above-guideline rent increase' allowed under the Tenant 'Protection' Act – so the costs of regularisation can be downloaded to the tenant. If the municipal government really is attempting to improve the existing housing stock 'without dehousing of vulnerable populations', their work may be undone by this loophole in the provincial government's tenancy legislation – achieving the desired rebalance of the 'unhealthy' demographics of South Parkdale.

To explain the social impacts of gentrification on South Parkdale, it is instructive to turn to the work of Robson and Butler (2001). Undertaking qualitative gentri-fication research in Brixton, London, they found that social relations

> might be characterized as 'tectonic'. That is to say, broadly, that relations between different social and ethnic groups in the area are of a parallel rather than integrative nature; people keep, by and large, to themselves. … Social groups or 'plates' overlap or run parallel to one another without much in the way of integrated experience in the area's social and cultural institutions. This does not make way for an especially cosy settlement, and many residents, middle class or otherwise, speak of palpable tensions (pp. 77–8).

The 'tectonic' social structure is reinforced by minimal class interaction and conflict. It is somewhat ironic that this structure of class isolation and absence of social capital exists in Brixton, a place which attracts gentrifiers because of its social heterogeneity and multiculturalism. As these authors explained in a companion essay, a tectonic social structure 'celebrates diversity in principle but leads to separate lives in practice' (Butler and Robson 2001a: 2157). This is precisely what is happening in South Parkdale, but it is policy-led. Social diversity is encouraged by neo-liberal urban policy which shows an alarming lack of attention to South Parkdale's complex historical geography. 'Social balance' under the guise of gentrification is being deliberately mapped onto one of the last outposts of low-income housing in central Toronto, and socially tectonic relationships are the outcome. Interviews conducted with incoming gentrifiers and extant non-gentrifiers in South Parkdale provided a sense of the *lack* of social mix between different social classes (see Slater 2004b). Lives are lived in parallel, under the auspices of what Peck and Tickell (2002) have called 'roll-out' neo-liberalism: the 1990s onwards fit of policy into the grooves laid down by market forces, in contrast to the 'rolling-back' of the state during earlier 1980s neo-liberalism. As Smith and Derksen (2002) have argued, 'where there is the residual welfare state, as in Canada, policies cosmetically ameliorate housing conditions without essentially altering the market or the trajectory of gentrification' (p. 68).

Conclusion

It is important to exercise caution when making general arguments about gentrification in Canada from particular cases, like that of South Parkdale in this chapter. However, there are wider signs that the shift toward relationships in gentrified neighbourhoods characterised by socially tectonic processes is by no means restricted to this neighbourhood or indeed this city. It would also seem that the nature of these social relationships is linked to an increased role played by public policy in the process itself. Recently published research from Vancouver's Downtown Eastside, a neighbourhood with a history even more turbulent than South Parkdale's, documents a municipally-managed 'Community Revitalisation Program' in conjunction with a 'Housing Plan'. The purpose here was to 'introduce into the neighbourhood a wider mix of housing types, tenures, households and socio-economic classes' (H. Smith 2003: 504). While the alleged intention of these policies is 'to ameliorate growing tensions between the area's newer and more established residents', there is every indication that socially tectonic relationships, rather then social mix, is the outcome as neo-liberal urban policy accentuates 'the clashing of upgrading and downgrading in the neighbourhood' (p. 505; see also Sommers and Blomley 2002). This 'clashing' could also serve as a powerful descriptive indicator of social polarisation under neo-liberal urban policy in South Parkdale.

In a recent study, Damaris Rose (2003) acknowledges that gentrification is 'a particularly "slippery" area of social mix discourse' (p. 1) and demonstrates the impact of recent municipal policies to encourage the movement of middle-income residents into Montreal's inner-city neighbourhoods.[4] Much of this is facilitated by new housing construction, 'instant gentrification', as Rose calls it, yet there has also been a municipal drive to provide social housing in the vicinity of middle-income developments, and vice versa. At the same time, reflecting the Canadian desire for social mix, there are policies designed to encourage the deconcentration of the poor into middle-income neighbourhoods. As Rose points out, 'it would be quite inappropriate to interpret the Montreal policies and programs as being part of a neo-liberal agenda' (p. 14); there are geographical variances in policy-led gentrification in Canada (Ley 1996). By interviewing professionals who moved into small-scale 'infill' condominiums (constructed by private developers on land often purchased from the City) in Montreal between 1995 and 1998, Rose gathered the views of gentrifiers on municipally-encouraged 'social mix'. Interestingly, a quarter of the forty-nine interviewees expressed some degree of 'NIMBY' sentiments with respect to the prospect of adjacent social housing; as one interviewee remarked:

> I don't want to find myself in a neighbourhood where you'll have confrontation and then there'll be big problems … social problems in the community.
>
> (Interviewee 645 quoted in Rose 2003: 22)

The apparent lack of a neo-liberal policy agenda at the municipal scale of government 'says nothing about the existence of a broader social climate influenced by neo-liberalism and individualism' (Rose, personal communication, 16 January 2004). There has, quite simply, been a neo-liberal revolution across Canada with a concerted attack on the much admired Canadian welfare state, massive cuts in federal funding of social services in the provinces (due to globalisation priorities and structural adjustment demands), provincial cutbacks and privatisation of social services, and the downloading of social responsibility to municipalities and the voluntary sector. The impacts are of course geographically uneven, with some regions/provinces/cities affected more than others but at the urban scale:

> [G]entrification, fuelled by a concerted and systematic partnership of public planning with public and private capital, has moved into the vacuum left by the end of liberal urban policy.
>
> (Smith and Derksen 2002: 67)

Social mix in urban settings remains the goal of urban planners, policy-makers, and middle-class residents. These goals need to understood in light of a continuing influence of reform-era emancipation and is, at first glance, an admirable intention.

However, such 'social mix' increasingly appears to be a shield under which gentrification is being actively promoted as a means of achieving a social mix which improves local tax bases rather than civic pride and disparate social interaction. It is this which appears to create additional problems. Gentrification as an emancipatory experience has only ever been portrayed as a middle-class experience that generally excludes the voices and experiences of other residents. The final outcome of these changes can only be anticipated. Nevertheless, these moves push towards an urban future in which the image of neighbourhood 'coolness' and social mix, projected by boosters of Canadian cities, sits uneasily with the apparent entrenchment of gentrification which has brought few benefits to low-income residents of many of these neighbourhoods.

Acknowledgements

I would like to thank Damaris Rose and David Ley for their very helpful comments and suggestions.

Notes

1 This is something of a neglected aspect of Ley's work, as many commentators have chosen to situate him as the cultural opposite to Neil Smith's economic explanations of the process, with the unfortunate effect of misrepresenting both scholars, overdrawing their perspectives, and sidelining issues of vital epistemological importance. If this irritating tendency ends, gentrification research will advance even further.
2 As an example, take Ley's (1996) telling caveat in his round-up of Canadian city gentrification: 'the geographical specificity of gentrification should caution us from making arguments that are too binding from evidence that is limited to the United States' (p. 352).
3 While provincial policies are not geared towards particular neighbourhoods, they have a significant influence on the ways in which Canadian urban spaces are lived and contested (Stoecker and Vakil 2000).
4 At the same time, reflecting the Canadian desire for social mix, there are policies designed to encourage the deconcentration of the poor into middle-income neighbourhoods.

4 Heritage and gentrification

Remembering 'the good old days' in postcolonial Sydney

Wendy Shaw

> This past doesn't just endure: it displays itself against the tawdry present which it also actively indicts.
>
> (Wright 1997: 106)

Introduction

The globalising metropolis of Sydney (Daly 1992; Baum 1997) is experiencing a renaissance at its centre. The Central Business District (CBD) is being rebuilt to accommodate its burgeoning status, and the old housing areas nearby, which were shunned through suburbanisation, are transforming as well. The graceful terraced houses of the inner city, with their nineteenth-century Victorian architecture, have become highly desirable. Building on this gentrification trend, former industrial areas are also changing with the conversion of warehouses and factories into apartment blocks. As in many other cities around the world, older built environments near the centre of the city of Sydney have become desirable housing areas with a sense of heritage.

The heritage landscapes of inner Sydney do, however, speak of a very specific history. It is where the history of white settlement, and its architectures, grand and humble, are celebrated. These architectural artefacts have become the desirable remnants, the *post*colonial heritage of colonial and neo-colonial pasts. The task of this chapter, then, is to recount the reinvention of the built legacy of white settlement *as* heritage, and to identify a capacity to forget and exclude other, less palatable aspects of the past, that lurk within this celebration of part of a nation's history. This chapter considers some of the motivations behind the creation and consumption of heritage, its selective designation, its expanding embrace, and its protection. It recounts some of the innovative ways that in Sydney, space, places and built artefacts are negotiated in the name of (white) heritage. Examples are drawn from

57

one of gentrification's 'final frontiers' (cf. Smith 1996), where a specifically designated Aboriginal place known as 'The Block' or Aboriginal Redfern (Anderson 1993a, 1993b) sits in increasing juxtaposition to the transforming city that surrounds it (Figure 4.1).

Although set in Sydney, Australia, a fundamental aim of this chapter is to build on existing considerations of the materiality of cultural processes that are integral to gentrification. David Ley (1980, 1986, 1994) has long advocated the need to consider aesthetics and taste to better understand gentrification and consumption practices. By asking questions about taste and consumption, links between culture and capital have been made, and the production of 'cultural capital', particularly at the local level of gentrification (Jager 1986; Zukin 1982, 1986, 1995; Jackson 1995). At a larger scale of analysis, globalising 'commodity cultures' (Featherstone 1990; King 1991; Ritzer 1993) are also recognisable across gentrification landscapes in cities around the world, as Jerry Krase suggests in this book.

As the introduction to this book argues, globalising consumption cultures have been linked to the emergence of a global society. This has been made possible by communications and mass media and accompanying discussions about global economics and the spread of generic forms of urbanism. In the context of wholesale urban redevelopments occurring in many cities, new fields of cultural consumption are being created. In Sydney's inner city, new commodity cultures are emerging in and through the repackaging of inner-urban residential landscapes for residential markets. These reveal globally familiar trends in the way city spaces are (re)made and consumed (Kearns and Philo 1993). One example is the reinvention of inner-urban housing as 'heritage' (cf. Hobsbawm and Ranger 1983). To understand the

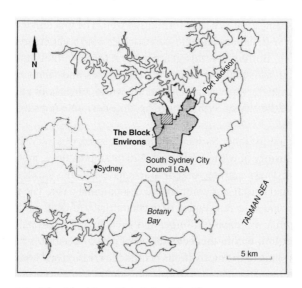

4.1 'The Block' or Aboriginal Redfern

relationships between commodity cultures and social processes, such as gentri-fication, explorations of the 'traffic in things' (Jackson 1999: 105) need to appreciate the production of meanings in, for example, (the promotions of) commodities. As Peter Jackson (1999: 105) remarked, 'such meanings are ... frequently coded in terms of various forms of social difference'.

Geographies of gentrification have long considered questions of 'difference' in relation to dominant groups. The focus on distinction by class has expanded, and questions about 'race' and ethnicity, gender and sexuality have been well documented (for example, Bondi 1999a and Lees 1999 on gender and Lauria and Knopp 1985 on gay gentrification). Shifting the emphasis, the production of normative values and spatialities are now considered (Lees 1996; Fincher and Jacobs 1998; Shaw 2000) and the burgeoning field of postcolonial studies (Jacobs 1996; Gelder and Jacobs 1998, and Gandhi 1998 in Australia, Spivak 1990 and Bhabha 1994) has added a distinctly new dimension to studies of urban trans-formation. In Australia, a postcolonial perspective brings history into contact with current Aboriginal dispossession and poverty.

In Australia segregation by ethnicity cannot be separated from processes that continue to privilege some and disadvantage already dispossessed others. At the heritage-gentrification nexus there are socio-cultural processes at work that privilege, and dispossess, and there are also nostalgic yearnings that are part of these processes. In Australia, such yearnings can rarely be separated from a colonial history. As desires for heritage develop and consolidate with gentrification, and become more inclusive of difference, migrant and indigenous heritages continue to remain outside the heritage orbit. These are not simply forgotten, they are actively denied through the production of specifically coded forms of heritage(s) that reinforce and consolidate already empowered groups. As Michael Jager (1986) quipped, Victoriana is a fetish of the middle classes. This chapter details some of the desires that push a cultural politics of heritage within the somewhat less traversed terrain of gentrification's postcolonial condition. To dissect the meanings within these yearnings for the *good old days*, and their very material effects, it has been useful to revisit some of the earlier insights, of Simmel (1903) and Wirth (1938), as new forms of urbanism, *ways of living*, emerge in re-imaged cities.

This chapter is divided into the following sections. The emergence of heritage impulses and the valorisation of select pasts, and objects associated with these pasts, follow a short overview of the gentrifying neighbourhood in which the Aboriginal community of The Block sits. The dynamism of heritage production in inner Sydney is then considered, in detail. From Victorian to industrial (facade) landscapes, to retro chic and heritage referencing in new buildings in inner Sydney, specific codes of desirability, taste and specific nostalgias determine what *does* and what *does not* constitute 'heritage'. The last section of this chapter considers preoccupations with (white) heritage in a postcolonial city.

Wendy Shaw

Gentrifying (post)colonial landscapes and urban indigeneity

The neighbourhoods that surround the Aboriginal place and community of The Block in inner Sydney are a rich field for studying heritage desires and gentrification. This area has transformed swiftly and dramatically into a desirable space, and identifications of 'heritage' are central to its newfound status. It is also a place with a history of struggle, which is continually reinscribed in the present. In the 1960s, the neighbourhood of Darlington, in which The Block now sits, was threatened with complete subsumption by the University of Sydney, which borders Darlington to the west. With half of Darlington lost during this battle, the relationship between the university and local residents continues to be uneasy. Then, in the 1970s, in another struggle over territory, a patch of Darlington became The Block (Anderson 1993a, 1993b). Colonisation had dispossessed the Gadigal/Eora people of this place as they were quickly and thoroughly exiled during the early days of British settlement (Reynolds 1996). Then, from the 1930s, when the earliest migrations (back) to what had become the city of Sydney began, urban settlement has also worked to displace Aboriginal people, in many ways. The recent onset of gentrification has meant a new set of responses to the existence of The Block. Now an extremely valuable site, it sits ripe for redevelopment with property developers moving in on all sides.

Meanwhile, the predominant script of The Block in popular imaginings is that it is 'chronically marginal' (Seth *et al.* 1998) and is spiralling into self-inflicted decline. The mostly non-Aboriginal gentrifiers are drawn to this previously avoided part of the city for heritage housing that is still, comparatively, reasonably priced, and marketed for its potential – it is an area 'on its way up'. As the heritage imaginary matures, and becomes part of the gentrification investment, heritage is formalised and in 1996, Darlington was listed as a 'heritage and conservation' area in South Sydney's Local Environment Plan. It is also listed on the Australian Heritage Commission's National Register.

In sharp contrast, the Victorian terraced houses on The Block are run-down, derelict or even razed to the ground and new arrivals to this 'heritage' area find that The Block does persist. Its high-profile street life and, at times, overt poverty, witnessed by all who traverse the area by car, by train, or on foot from the railway station – it is a high pedestrian traffic area because of its proximity to the university – also disrupts many widely held values about home, community, street life and neighbourhood. Yet, The Block is widely regarded to be more than just heritage-*less*. It flouts an emergent convention about the sanctity of Victoriana and is therefore *anti*-heritage. It is, perversely, a threat to investment in heritage.

Performing Sydney Heritage

> Certain places may be incorporated into sanctioned views of the national heritage while others may be seen as a threat to the national imaginary and are suppressed or obliterated.
>
> (Jacobs 1996: 35)

The British colonial past looms large in Australian heritage. The push of progress and redevelopment in Sydney, which began in the 1960s, catalysed a growing sense of preservation urgency by the 1970s. Then, in another burst of (re)development of swathes of former industrial areas in Pyrmont and Ultimo, fuelled by the 2000 Olympic games and increased demands for urban accommodation, Sydney's industrial built heritage was under threat. When fires ravaged several of the few large historic warehouses that were to be retained in Pyrmont, then a famous vista from the CBD to the iconic Sydney Opera House was to be obscured by the development of an apartment block dubbed 'the Toaster', anti-development and heritage preservation sentiments combined, and Sydney's 'heritage' became a *cause célèbre*. The 'heritage' landscapes that remain are more than precious; for some they are sacred (Taylor 1994). Of course, with scarcity, the cultural capital of heritage is also realised, and heritage buildings are increasingly expensive.

For many, conservation is a response to the mass destruction of modernist urban rebuilding but the motivations behind heritage impulses vary (Crang 1994). Historical societies and interest groups promote specific heritages of, for example, old churches or the homes of important historical figures. Real estate marketeers use the 'hard sell' of heritage in marketing campaigns and the 'heritage industry', more generally, engages in a range of heritage-related activities (Hewison 1987; Graham, Ashworth and Tunbridge 2000). The depth of popular feeling and enthusiasm for heritage in Australia, like elsewhere, has enabled the development of a 'cultural heritage movement' and professionals now advise on what should be kept and how to preserve what is left of just over 200 years of built environments.

Historian Ken Taylor (1994) has identified a number of factors that have influenced the emergence of the cultural heritage movement in Australia. These include responses to the former disinterest in history until the massive urban redevelopments of the 1960s and 1970s. A second influence was the resurgence of nationalism, in the 1970s. Third, the development of heritage management as a profession and public recognition of its potential, which was boosted in 1988 when governments opened their coffers in support of the Australian Bicentennial. The Australian Heritage Commission (AHC) and the AHC Act of 1975 and the Register of the National Estate and legislation have provided legitimacy for the protection of heritage. Tourism based on local history (Waitt and McGuirk 1996), and the recent rise of heritage awareness and protection, all point to a thriving heritage industry. Its marketability, or the profitability of nostalgia is not lost on big business either, and transnational corporations now occupy expensive historic buildings in downtown Sydney for the somewhat ironic function of selling American-style *fast food*. Residential property developers have also benefited through re-visioning old industrial areas into heritage-referenced 'warehouse' or loft apartments (Shaw 2000, 2001). In short, the heritage industry in Sydney is booming.

For Taylor (1994) the current nostalgia for the past in Australia is a search for identity and a reversal of the 'cultural cringe'. He described heritage as the 'ordinary sacred places ... [that] ... reflect our relationships with places that have meaning because either we, or our ancestors, have connections with them' (Taylor 1994: 27). As a former British colony, Australia is commonly regarded as lacking a recognisable, independent lengthy history upon which to build a national identity (Taylor 1994), regardless of its indigenous history. 'We' are therefore creating our own (heritage/identity), based on elements of connection that were imported in during the waves of 'migrations' that began a little more than 200 years ago.

Valorising select pasts as heritage

The designation of 'heritage' is not universal and the prospect of heritage preservation can provoke different responses, from a range of respondents. Reflecting on Lowenthal's contention, in 1979, that 'things worth saving need ... [to be] familiar or well loved', Shaw and Jones (1997: 3) have remarked that:

> Today the same place or building can be variously viewed as a homely landmark, a relic of imperial oppression and a tempting commercial opportunity.

In a well-documented example of a proposal to redevelop an old brewery site into a large commercial concern in Perth, Western Australia, the contest also included competition over heritage designations. Conflict arose between recognition of indigenous and non-indigenous 'heritages' (Mickler 1991; Muecke 1992; Jacobs 1996, Shaw and Jones 1997). In this example, the non-Aboriginal version of heritage was that the old brewery building should be preserved. The Aboriginal version was that the site was the home of a spiritual ancestor: the Waugal serpent (Jacobs 1996) and the building should be removed. Regardless of the struggle, the possibility of a compromise required that one heritage would dominate and the fate of the brewery site remained ultimately 'in white hands' (Shaw and Jones 1997: 154).

Because heritage is more than a reuse of the past (Graham *et al.* 2000), heritage impulses have raised suspicion. Lowenthal (1985) and Rosaldo (1989) have examined yearnings for the past as a form of power while Jager (1986) detailed the operation of class in heritage appreciation. As property developers know all too well, urban conservation can reuse history for the saleable purpose of social distinction (Thrift and Glennie 1993). In conceptualising nostalgia as a form of oppression, as a yearning for 'other' times and/or cultures, Rosaldo (1989: 108) has observed that:

> 'we' valorize innovation and then yearn for more stable worlds ... in any of its versions, imperialist nostalgia uses a pose of 'innocent yearning' both to capture people's imaginations and to conceal its complicity with often brutal domination.

This enables the dynamism and contemporary trajectory of British-based colonial European-ness and its inheritances. This heritage-dynamic, of ancient indigeneity and temporally fluid non-indigenous heritage, are played out at the 'birthplace' of colonial Australia, called 'The Rocks'.

Tony Bennett (1993) traced the selective preservation and restoration of the mostly residential 'heritage area' of The Rocks, just near Sydney Harbour Bridge. Since its 'restoration', The Rocks now represents an idealised and sanitised history of colonisation (Bennett 1993). The past has been (re)fabricated and cleansed of the marks that bear testimony to other, contradictory, aspects of the history of colonisation. 'The glittering façade ... functions as an institutional mode of forgetting' (Bennett 1993: 225). The new allegory is the ascent of 'a free, demo-cratic, multicultural citizenry' (Bennett 1993: 227) with Aboriginality referenced only in 'traditional artefacts', which can be purchased from a craft shop. For Bennett (1993: 228), the notable lack of an Aboriginal presence reinforces the commonly held belief, and hope, that 'European civilisation' has tamed 'the natural' in this location. This natural past has been overwritten by (non-Aboriginal) 'humanity', and the controversy of invasion lies silent beneath the rewritten layers.

Back on The Block, in Sydney, the Aboriginal presence is undeniably present. The Block community consists of many kinship groups from around the country, so there is no Waugal-like ancestral claim to this place, as with the Perth experience. Indigeneity cannot be relegated to a pre-colonial past as this Aboriginal place was fought for and *won* as part of an emergent 'black politics' in Australia. Yet, the dominant understandings of heritage that surround it remain fixed on built heritage: the houses, large and small, the factories and the warehouses, and the preservation of this form of heritage. The next section of this chapter traces Sydney's gentrification and some evolutionary phases that have led to such an exclusionary form of 'heritage'. Although selective heritage impulses are not unique to this location (Hewison 1987; Jacobs 1996), there are attributes that are specific to this particular postcolonial experience of gentrification and its preoccupation with eliding indigenous heritages.

Gentrification and Victorian architecture

> [the city is] a poem … which unfolds the signifier and it is this unfolding that ultimately the semiology of the city should try to grasp.
>
> (Barthes, cited in Short 1996: 390)

Because cities can be 'read', the 'systems of communications' can tell us 'who has power and how it is wielded' (Short 1996: 390). We now recognise the 'symbolic and representational realms (figurative and discursive) … in the constitution and mediation of social and material processes' (Jacobs 1993: 829), and that meaning is 'hidden' in, for example, architecture, or artefact (Crilley 1993). These hidden meanings can be also be 'read' (Barnes and Duncan 1992) and variously interpreted, and re-interpreted.

Different gentrification cycles (Redfern 1997) have registered different heritage or conservation impulses, and premiums, in Sydney. As the inner city has become increasingly attractive, the value of heritage has also increased. Bourdieu's (1984) notion of cultural, or symbolic capital considered the 'social uses of art and culture and the way that "tastes" function as markers of "class"' (Bourdieu in Jackson 1991: 220, see also Butler 1997). As gentrification cycles mature, the cultural capital in heritage becomes increasingly attractive and higher premiums are paid. As has happened elsewhere, those seeking cheap housing in inner Sydney, to buy and renovate or rent, are increasingly sidelined. Neil Smith (1987) has identified those who (can and will) pay a premium for heritage as 'second stage' or 'yuppie' gentrifiers. These gentrifiers are distinct from 'first stage' gentrifiers who buy into less desirable inner-city areas at low cost, when un-renovated or 'poorly' renovated houses, those that appealed only to a minority of people, are plentiful. Heritage and preservation issues may be of interest but ultimately, first stage buyers produce heritage capital simply through their efforts to save and restore the built fabric of terrace houses. First stage gentrifiers provide legitimacy for living in such housing, and then second stage gentrifiers move into areas with established heritage pedigrees.

Neighbourhoods adjacent to The Block were largely impervious to gentrification until the 1990s when the stocks of 'unimproved' (un-renovated) Victorian terrace houses were depleting elsewhere. Although the tardiness of Darlington's gentrification has been attributed to factors such as the mix of (long defunct) industry with housing, the presence of public housing, and the lack of retail services, a planning survey revealed the significance of 'the presence of ethnic and racial groups and … associated physical violence and social tension' (Cameron and Craig 1985: 29). In 1985, 16 per cent of terraced housing in the Darlington/Redfern area remained unimproved whereas in Paddington, the benchmark suburb for gentrification in Sydney, only 7 per cent remained so (Cameron and Craig 1985: 25). The scarcity of 'unimproved' housing stock indicates the advanced stage of the gentrification cycle in an area. By this stage, unimproved houses attract premiums and only those with the economic power to put economic necessity at a distance (Bourdieu 1984) can afford such distinction. In Sydney, real estate agents sell '*original* condition' and 'Victorian features'. Houses renovated in the *wrong* style, particularly those with a 'Mediterranean finish' (Howe 1994: 155) sit lower on the selling pecking order.

Like the occupation on The Block, Sydney's migrant experience of terrace house renovation is widely considered anti-heritage (Armstrong 1994; Lozanovksa 1994). Postwar migrants 'rescued the reputation of the terrace house as a place to live as well as restored its fabric' (Howe 1994: 155), just like first stage gentrifiers', but Greek migrants, and others, are blamed for defacing 'authentic' heritage. In Darlington, real estate agents associate Greekness with 'tasteless' renovation, and the replacement of decorative timber windows with ugly aluminium, and timber floors with concrete. Heritage, on the other hand, was associated with restoration of timber windows and floors. The modifications that migrants from southern Europe made to aging housing stock, to make them more liveable and culturally appropriate (Lozanovksa 1994), now constitute a deficit in heritage capital. The layer of history added by these migrants is therefore unwanted, and usually removed. Intact Victorian architectural features, without the hindrance of other layers of history/defacement, have become a priority for those who can afford them.

From grand to humble ...

By 1999, house prices in inner Sydney had risen substantially and premiums were paid for terrace houses in Darlington/Redfern, regardless of their condition. By this stage, any renovation (other than immaculate restoration) of houses had become a detractor to sales, and vendors found that they had over-capitalised. By late 1999, another trend, the conversion of small, sometimes three metres wide, terrace houses into 'urban living spaces' had also started. In Darlington, some were gutted, with the façades of these highly capitalised properties retained because of their heritage, and to meet heritage regulations (South Sydney Council Local Environment Plan 1996). This trend, where the sky seemed to be the limit on interiors, indicates that investors were confident enough to outlay large sums of capital on small land parcels, regardless of the area's insalubrious reputation. Additionally, retaining the heritage feature of the *interiors* of these houses, formerly inhabited by the working classes, is not nearly as important as what they can be turned into.

In Darlington, the rise of heritage significance of the smaller 'working class' houses is very recent, and associated with an emerging scarcity of larger housing stock. The former battlers, and the working-class roots of the area, are still celebrated in some ways. The (retired) high-profile (Labor) Mayor of South Sydney

City Council proudly promoted his 'working-class' heritage, and local newsletters, such as *Chippo Politics* and the council's *South Sydney Inner-city News*, carry on this tradition. The memory of the diminishing 'working classes' is part of the folkloric heritage (and cultural capital), and has helped to legitimise the appeal of smaller terraces, dubbed as 'workers' cottages'. Built heritage is consolidating through nostalgias that 'write-in' those histories that have hitherto been less important (Crang 1994). But as one resident noted, smaller houses are actually an 'ugly reminder of dirt floor basic housing … that was probably not very pleasant' (interview, 25 April, 1998). These 'ugly reminders' are prettied up on the outside, and inside, they are transformed. Their heritage value lies in their shell, and the occasional quaint attribute, such as a salvaged 'dunny' (brick shed housing original toilet), used as a small garden shed.

Heritage dreaming: industrial facadism, retro chic and new-build

In another turn in the gentrification trajectory, the industrial landscape of Chippendale (which borders The Block to the north), described as a 'dead space' in 1997 (North and Christie 1997) was reborn as Sydney's own version of SoHo (New York), by 2000 (Shaw 2001). Loft apartments filled old warehouses and factories and this formerly disregarded area is now an important 'industrial heritage' landscape.

Similar to some of the smaller workers' cottages, in this version of heritage a remnant, such as the shell of the old building, is kept (Figure 4.2a). In this façadism compromise (between retaining a whole 'heritage' building and complete replacement), which seems to indicate that a little bit of heritage is better than none at all (Figure 4.2b), it is the *purpose* of the factory, its business such as 'The Printery' and 'The Piano Factory', that is celebrated. This form of industrial heritage fetishises objects connected to the factory or warehouse, such as the bicycles or pianos once made within. Industrial architectures, and remnants of some of the larger industrial aspects of the interiors, such as large wooden or steel beams, and the occasional 'block and tackle' removed from its original position to take pride of place in an apartment lobby, are part of the promotional aspects used to sell the apartments within these structures.

The promotion of nostalgias for objects serves to partition the past. The heritage of the 'battlers' that occupied the interior as workers is not recalled. The class relations, the working conditions then and displacements now are easily truncated and buried in history and, therefore, more easily forgotten (Jenks 1981; Harvey 1990). For Rosaldo (1989), such partitioning has the capacity to allow, or even participate in the repetition of forgotten violences. For some of the older folk, who lament the loss of places such as 'Miss Muffett's jam-making factory', those 'dirt floor' days were actually *the good old days*, that are quickly being forgotten.

A

B

4.2 Façadism

Meanwhile, the 'consumption circuit' (Jager 1986: 87) of heritage continues to expand. From grand Victoriana, to the inclusion of small Victoriana and more recent factories and warehouses, two new players, 'retro chic' and 'new-build' faux-heritage, have gained status. Retro chic includes an appreciation of old things, objects that are, in Patrick Wright's (1997: 104) words, 'not-quite-antiques', but are nonetheless collectable. Definitions of heritage have expanded to include, for example, *Art Deco* architecture, and furnishings, and the more recent addition of 'retro-modern' style from the 1950s and 1960s (Collins 1995). Newtown, which adjoins Darlington to the south, has become *the* retro-modern and *objects d'art* centre of Sydney and is comparable with the concentration of more standard antique shops in Paddington and Woollahra (that specialise in 'top end' antiques). The emerging preference for retro-modern furnishings and items, particularly from the 1950s and 1960s, which are cheaper than Victoriana (antiques from the nineteenth century), signifies a diversity and distinctiveness of tastes (for objects of desire) that exist within gentrification cycles.

Amid the 'heritage' built environments of inner Sydney, heritage-referencing or faux heritage, has also gained currency. Although not heritage *per se*, these forms of 'neo-archaism' (Jager 1986: 88) are expressed in new developments and within some warehouse conversions. Heritage-references can be found in 'heritage' brickwork, cobbled laneways, stone gutters and faux Victorian housing and are preferred over non-heritage building designs in this part of Sydney (Figure 4.3).

As the meaning of 'heritage' continues to expand, to be rubbery and diverse, desires for *built* heritage, and its preservation are mainstreamed. Such desires prioritise the symbols of select pasts, of terraced houses and old industrial façades, over contemporary expressions of human diversity. In Darlington, resident action groups mobilise to fight developments that are regarded to be 'tasteless' (non-heritage referenced) and/or dedicated to housing *others*, such as students from abroad. Such NIMBY preoccupations, which tend to be dominated by self-interested protectionism (Dear 1992), assist in the disengagement from, and concerns about human diversity, yet it is 'diversity' that is part of the lexicon of expanded heritage designations. Threats to old architectural diversity are monitored and protected by 'the community'.

At the same time, desires to protect human diversity (such as the memory of those may have toiled behind the protected façade, the migrant others, or the Aboriginal community around the corner) are sidelined by concerns about *who* will occupy new developments. For example, students from overseas are clearly not wanted. A purpose-built development, that houses students attending a nearby university, has become the benchmark of undesirable 'tastelessness' for the area. The intertwining of heritage and taste percolate through the discourses of protest against such developments and these buildings now represent the benchmark for *anti*-heritage design. Darryl Crilley (1993) has identified how property developers promote diversity to enhance the appeal *of* developments rather than to appeal *to*

4.3 Faux-Victorian architecture

a diverse market. Homogeneity is concealed within the appearance of diversity, as expressed through, for example, heritage architecture. 'Diversity', in this case, is simply another consumable attribute for affluent tastes (cf. Hage 1998; Bourdieu 1984) and rather than appealing to a range of types of people, only those with the necessary attributes (such as cash, class and/or ethnicity) have membership in such a niche market.

The preoccupation with protecting symbols from the (neo-)colonial past(s), or allowing only those developments that are deemed tasteful to middle-class (white) sensibilities, has enacted an architecture of denial whereby human diversity is denied, as the expanding orbit of heritage designations continues on its trajectory of exclusion. The deeply embedded desires to preserve (colonial remnants) and protect (white space) have become an escape from everyday realities of a colonial aftermath that has produced, for example, overt Aboriginal poverty and dispossession just around the corner from a tasteful 'heritage' built environments. The notion of heritage, as it is popularly conceived and as governments have legislated generally, exhibits a certain consistency. Heritage remains commonly associated with old buildings and objects.

The unspoken heritage story around The Block is the history of colonialism, of encounters between Aboriginal and non-Aboriginal people. The heritage of The Block, its struggle for Aboriginal civil rights, is excluded from newer understandings regardless of its formal heritage status. There is no commemorative plaque, or acknowledgement that this site has finally been recognised as a site of *cultural* heritage. Heritage, as it is commonly conceived, is part of the unspoken definition of 'community', of belonging. For the area around The Block, heritage remains architectural/artefactual. Where people *are* considered, it is the elegant lives of those who could afford High Victoriana or, in a more recent working of heritage it is a partial legacy of (housing of) the working classes, that is collectively remembered (Boyer 1998). A yearning for 'more of the same' (pasts) is sometimes muffled in such imaginings (Bennett 1993: 235).

While Aboriginal people may be acknowledged as having heritage, such understandings are often tied to a non-urban, cultural and ethnic pre-colonial condition. The politics of the 'Black Capital' (The Block), of the unification of disparately dispossessed Aboriginal peoples, is continually written out of the evolving urban heritage imaginary. The non-Aboriginal, non-migrant gentrifier imaginings of heritage has excused itself from engagement with the urban histories of others.

Conclusion: escaping … (into the past)

In the neighbourhoods surrounding The Block, imaginaries of the past are being constructed to consolidate specific entitlements to place. In a somewhat contradictory way, they also envision escape from aspects of the everyday of that place.

Such escapes are engaged by looking to romanticised and select pasts, and by protecting those memories. For those living in New York style loft apartments, the harsher realities of 'the street' can be distanced through new urban lifestyles (Shaw 2001). Both strategies of escape produce *indifferences* to the here and now, through denial or elision of pasts that have contributed to current conditions, particularly with the expanding gap of inequity shown daily by the presence of The Block community. By denying encounters with indigenous peoples current local dispossessions and poverty are denied.

There is an imaginary of other times in inner Sydney, of vague and varying notions of *the good old days* that are indifferent to recalling those aspects of class and race relations that make the memories less palatable. Such imagined pasts, therefore, deny any repercussions of the past, in the gentrifying present. Only the partially remembered pasts, glorified through built heritage and specific objects, are brought forward into the present, celebrated and preserved. This renders all other local concerns, such as Aboriginal or other heritages of the inner city, as inconsequential. Heritage-making legitimises certain presences, in the present.

As Lowenthal (1985) has suggested, the past is like a foreign country. Escapist imaginaries are found in the fantasies that 'old stuff' can invoke. These fantasies go beyond the simple desires to recycle resources. The days before the social upheavals of civil rights movements and, in particular, the rise of indigenous politics in Australia in the 1960s, are remembered and glorified through artefacts of (white) heritage, be they considered to be tasteful or kitsch. History is truncated and compartmentalised yet unfolding through heritage production. The sanctioned discourses of heritage:

> ... erect ... a set of rigid, iconic, homogeneous, national categories which stereotypically define who belongs and who does not ...
>
> (Herzfeld in Rapport 1995: 645)

The categories are complex but are not difficult to identify. In the new residential, postmodern context of a globalising postcolonial city, the renewed interest in pre-modern, (neo)colonially encoded built formations has helped to embed a white identity politics that is manifested in representations of, and *by* 'heritage'.

This chapter has attempted to identify the evolution of an increasingly exclusionary nexus between gentrification and heritage designations. It has also considered the celebration of a history of white settlement embedded within the gentrification of inner Sydney, Australia as an example. As gentrification circuits mature, heritage impulses may expand to become more inclusive but only within specific parameters. In the Sydney example a process of reinvention, a time-line of what constitutes heritage, started with Victorian terrace houses. It then expanded to include industrial landscapes and now includes retro-chic and faux heritage.

Migrants, and their efforts to preserve and utilise crumbling housing stocks, the labours of the 'working classes', and the emergent 'black politics' of the 1970s, through the formalisation of an urban Aboriginal community, remain outside the heritage imaginary that is evolving with gentrification. In this place-based example, preoccupation with historical designations have proved to be a useful way to deny the current realities of class relations. Because Aboriginal people and associated places have been disengaged from the recent past, they are rendered as museum-like objects, or disregarded altogether in the current wave of inner city gentri-fication.

In what may seem to be increasingly pluralistic city spaces (Kearns and Philo 1993), specific exclusionary politics are increasingly associated with gentrification. The remembrance of specific versions of history in cities around the world, brings with it the capacity for malevolent escapism, strategies for retreat from the realities of everyday life including poverty and dispossession. This chapter has documented the reproduction, packaging and consumption of select histories as heritage that are less formalised than the more recognisable heritage theme parks, such as Sydney's oldest point of settlement: The Rocks. Although the specifically (neo)colonial heritages produced in Sydney are unique, gentrification, everywhere, has the capacity to forge selective remembrances that assist in the maintenance and consolidation of increasingly exclusive territories, gained in the recent past and the present, and this trend seems set to continue as heritage orbits expand at a global scale within gentrifying cities.

5 'Studentification': the gentrification factory?

Darren P. Smith

> … gentrification has been broadly defined to embrace several processes which are also known by other names in the literature.
>
> (Van Weesep 1994: 80)

The conceptual terrain of gentrification has been constantly debated, particularly since Beauregard's (1986) landmark discussion of the 'chaos and complexity of gentrification'. There is now an extensive literature which has teased out the varied myths and meanings (e.g. Mills 1993; Ley 1996; Bridge 2001a), and explored the diverse representations and differences (e.g. Lees 1996; Hamnett 2000) of gentrification. This work problematises the taken-for-granted ways in which the term has been historically tied to different processes of urban revitalisation, and seeks to sophisticate understandings of the complexity of gentrification in a wider variety of spatial contexts.

It has recently been suggested that the term gentrification is a neologism. Indeed, it is claimed that the conceptual power of gentrification is weakened as the boundaries are extended to encapsulate new forms of revitalisation, such as (post-recession) 'financification' (Lees 2002), 'Londonisation' (Dutton 2003), and 'greentrification' (D. Smith and Phillips 2001; D. Smith 2002a). At the same time, such pluralistic uses of the term gentrification herald a wider consensus that: 'it makes no sense to try and separate it [gentrification] out conceptually from the broader transformation known as revitalisation' (Badcock 2001: 1560). In this respect, there would appear to be a growing synonymy between gentrification and revitalisation within academic discourses (N. Smith and Williams 1986; N. Smith 1996). Arguably, there are many conceptual weaknesses and merits associated with this perspective of gentrification as a capacious concept; although it is not the aim here to tease out the advantages and disadvantages in this chapter.

This chapter hooks up to the debate of the meaning of gentrification, and takes inspiration from recent calls for scholars of gentrification to be cautious and (self)reflexive when utilising the term gentrification (Lees 1999). Without doubt, this critical stance will have important bearings for theorisations of the causes and consequences, as well as the varied dynamics and trajectories, of nascent expressions of gentrification. In light of this scenario, this chapter focuses on a newly emerging process of urban change termed 'studentification', which underpins the formation of 'student ghettos'. The term 'ghetto' is utilised here to emphasise the residential 'concentration' of higher education (HE) students in distinct enclaves of university towns.

The discussion is divided into three main parts. The following section outlines a definition of studentification, and considers the conceptual overlaps between studentification and gentrification. The second part unravels the components of studentification, focusing on the production of studentifiers and studentified housing, as well as teasing out the spatiality, tenurial and migration specifics, and cultural-consumption facets of studentification. The third part contends that the social and cultural spaces of studentified locations provide a 'training ground' for potential gentrifiers, and that studentification represents a 'factory for gentri-fication'. The discussion is informed by empirical findings from recent exami-nations of studentification in the north (Leeds, West Yorkshire) and south-east (Brighton, East Sussex) of England.

The conceptual meaning of studentification

Studentification engenders the distinct social, cultural, economic and physical transformations within university towns, which are associated with the seasonal, in-migration of HE students. At a conceptual level, processes of studentification connote urban changes which are tied to the recommodification of 'single-family' or the repackaging of existing private rented housing, by small-scale institutional actors (e.g. property owners, investors and developers) to produce and supply houses in multiple occupation (HMO)[1] for HE students.

In a similar vein to gentrification in the 1980s and 1990s, the dramatic trans-formations associated with studentification have captured the interest of the national media. The term was listed in the top 100 new words of 2002 (BBC 2002), and has permeated into numerous national media articles. Examples that pin down some of the more emotive effects of studentification include:

> In the past three years, more than 8,500 families have left. Last year 1,600 houses were converted to house students. Home prices have risen by 50 per cent, knocking first-time buyers out of the market. Schools fear closure because of a shortage of children in the area. Because students move on, there is an electoral roll-over of 52% a year in Headingley, compared with an average 8% in other Leeds wards.
>
> (Chrisafis, 2000)

Pubs have been converted to theme bars, which often shut during the summer months when students have returned to their homes. Fast-food takeaways and off-licences selling cheap alcohol dominate the shopping streets. Schools have seen their class sizes plummet as families move out of the area ... House prices have also rocketed as landlords have created a property boom and now people wishing to move house but stay in the area have found themselves priced out of the market.

(Harris and McVeigh 2002)

The remarkable coverage of student ghettos within media discourses is not surprising, particularly given the visibility and rate at which studentification has proceeded in the urban landscape. Indeed, these contemporary urban geographies are manifest in the majority of English university towns, such as Birmingham (Collinson 2001), Nottingham (Midgley 2002), and Leeds (McCarthy 2003) creating social and political concern, with community organisations, private sector institutions and policy-makers debating the causes and effects of studentification in many locations. In this sense, studentification can be seen to represent a trenchant restructuring of urban space and politics.

Despite this significant profile, there have been limited academic studies of studentification. In the English context, the processes which underpin the formation of student ghettos have been of passing concern within wider studies of: student's cultural consumption orientations in Bristol and Newcastle (Chatterton 2000; Chatterton and Hollands 2002), relations between student and local communities in Sunderland (Kenyon 1997), and the institutional supply of student accommodation (Rugg *et al.* 2000). To date, there has been no conceptualisation of studentification under the wider rubric of gentrification; the key focus of this chapter.

This is unfortunate given the many parallels between the social, cultural and economic effects of gentrification and studentification. Such similarities are well exemplified in the definition of studentification (see Warde 1991, for an equivalent definition of gentrification), outlined below. It is important to stress here that the definition conflates the common signifiers of studentification; although empirical evidence suggests that studentification unfolds in different ways, and takes different forms in different contexts (for example, see Van Weesep 1994, for a similar discussion of gentrification). In line with gentrification and other contemporary processes of change studentification has four different dimensions:

Economic: studentification involves the revalorisation and inflation of property prices, which is tied to the recommodification of single-family housing or a repackaging of private rented housing to supply HMO for HE students. This restructuring of the housing stock gives rise to a tenure profile which is dominated by private rented, and decreasing levels of owner-occupation.

Social: the replacement or displacement of a group of established permanent residents with a transient, generally young and single, middle-class social grouping; entailing new patterns of social concentration and segregation.

Cultural: the gathering together of young persons with a putatively shared culture and lifestyle, and consumption practices linked to certain types of retail and service infrastructure.

Physical: associated with an initial upgrading of the external physical environment as properties are converted to HMO. This can subsequently lead to a downgrading of the physical environment, depending on the local context.

At the level of process, studentification does not indicate the varied trajectories and complexities of gentrification (see Warde 1991). Rather, processes of studentification are aligned to forms of gentrification which are instigated by small-scale institutional agents, or to borrow Ley's (1996) term 'organic entrepreneurs'. In this sense, it is the small-scale property owners and investors who recognise an opportunity for profit-maximisation, primarily in locations within close proximity to university campuses, that can be viewed as the 'pioneers' of studentification; although a relatively small number of HE students will have often ventured into the location beforehand (see below). It follows, therefore, that studentification can be viewed as a material capital-led process, albeit involving significantly lower levels of material capital when compared to the large-scale, capital intensive private sector redevelopment of waterfronts and city centres (e.g. loft living).

Moreover, when contextualised within wider understandings of gentrification, studentification does not express the cultural capital-led process of gentrification, whereby 'economic capital becomes more significant than cultural capital as gentrification proceeds' (Bridge 2001b: 92); a representation associated with process-related commonalities of the 'classical' stage-model of gentrification (see Ley 1996). The following sections now tease out the key components of student-ification within a theoretical framework of gentrification.

Studentifiers: the consumers of studentification?

Pinning down the studentifiers of studentification is not straightforward. Indeed, clarification of this conundrum exposes some marked temporal and production-based differences between the prototypical inhabitants of gentrified housing and studentified housing (namely the HMO). First, by contrast to traditional represent-ations of gentrifiers (i.e. residents with relatively 'mid- to long-term' residential attachment to the gentrified location), HE students that reside in HMOs are predominantly inhabitants only for the duration of the academic year or their period of study. Hence, if studentification is conceptualised as an expression of gentrification, this raises questions about the residential status and the conceptual meaning of a gentrifier. Second, HE students do not usually undertake any production-based activities, or participate in the recommodification of 'single-family' housing to HMO.

From a production-consumption perspective it would appear that studentifiers are comparable with later waves of gentrifiers, who predominantly consume 'ready-made' gentrified commodities that are produced and supplied by 'professional developers' (see N. Smith 1979). The key difference here, however, is that the latter groups of gentrifiers are often owner-occupiers, and utilise high levels of economic capital to buy into and 'capture' the cultural capital of gentrification (Bridge 2001b). At the same time, there are prominent economic-related similarities between studentifiers and early phase (marginal) pioneer gentrifiers (see Smith's 1979, discussion of 'occupier developers' for fuller discussion), given their comparable low levels of economic capital, constrained position within the housing market and quasi-participation in the labour market (Rose 1984). In this respect, studentifiers are similar to artists and other creative-workers, and may be viewed as the ground-breakers for gentrification activity in some contexts (Bowler and McBurney 1991).

Despite these similarities and differences HE students do not fit neatly into ideas of gentrifiers being: 'the necessary agents and beneficiaries of the gentrification process' (Beauregard 1986: 41). Instead, it may be more appropriate to consider the institutional actors (i.e. property investors, landlords) that convert and control or own HMO as the 'studentifiers', rather than the HE students. This issue clearly has significant resonance with earlier conceptual debates over which producer-consumer groups could most usefully be defined as gentrifiers (Hamnett 1991, 1992; N. Smith 1992).

Putting this definitional issue aside, there is some value within the context of this chapter to consider HE students as the 'studentifiers' – given it is this social and cultural grouping which ultimately consumes the accommodation within HMO. It is also the demand from HE students for this type of accommodation which, in part, forms the sub-housing market within university towns for short-term rental accommodation in HMO. Clearly, HE students are not the passive recipients of the studentification process, and their agency, expressed in their decision-making and search processes for HMO, is pivotal to the dynamics of the processes of change (see below).

The production of potential studentifiers

According to Hamnett (2000: 187), 'if gentrification theory has a centrepiece it must rest on the conditions for the production of potential gentrifiers'. Taking this approach, the production of potential studentifiers is clearly rooted in the social, economic and political forces which are reshaping advanced capitalist societies (see N. Smith 1996), and the deeper social, cultural and economic restructuring of society (Butler 1997). In line with long-standing theorisations of the production of gentrifiers (e.g. Ley 1980, 1996), it can be argued that the promotion of HE (and thus the increase of HE students) is bound-up with reproduction of post-industrial service-based socio-economies, and the dramatic rise in the total number and percentage of the labour force with higher educational credentials (Hamnett 2000).

The enhanced participation in higher education is an established and ongoing agenda across post-industrial nations, and this is linked to the professionalisation of the occupational and employment structures in metropolitan and global cities (Hamnett 1994a). In the English context, this societal trend is borne out by the recent White Paper *The Future of Higher Education* which proclaims: 'In a fast-changing and increasingly competitive world, the role of higher education (is essential] in equipping the labour force with appropriate and relevant skills, in stimulating innovation and supporting productivity' (Department for Education and Skills 2003: 10). Indeed, one of the key rationales for the expansion of HE is based on a forecast that 80 per cent of new jobs between 1999–2010 will be in higher level occupations; 'the ones most likely to be filled by those who have been through higher education' (Department for Education and Skills 2003: 58). Clearly, the role of the state within processes of studentification should not be underestimated.

The existence of a growing pool of HE students also signifies a wider ideological and cultural transformation within society about the meaning and role of HE. One of the major manifestations of this change are individual and familial middle-class attitudes and perceptions that an important phase of the 'typical' lifecourse of middle-class individuals and households involves the movement away from the parental home to study at an HEI; hence, the overall rising expectations and aspirations of gaining access to HE. Crucial here, and in line with theorisations of the causes of gentrification (Ley 1980), are broader changes in gender relations and demographic patterns (e.g. Bondi 1991b), lifestyle preferences and repro-ductive orientations, such as the postponement or rejection of marriage, family formation and childrearing.

In England, the structural and ideological commitment to HE has enabled an increase of HE students from 1,720,094 to 1,990,625 between 1995/6 and 2000/1 (Higher Education Statistics Agency 2002), with 43 per cent of 18–30 year olds currently participating in higher education (Department for Education and Skills, 2003). It is not surprising, therefore, that the emergence of student ghettos has coincided with the marked expansion of HE in Britain during the 1990s. Particularly significant here is the subgroup of full-time undergraduate students, which increased from 1,107,841 to 1,210,165 between 1995/6 and 2000/1 (Higher Education Statistics Agency 2002), and who are most likely to reside in HMOs (Chatterton 2000). Indeed, it is this cohort of students which Chatterton (1999:

118–19) asserts are: 'analytically important because of the way in which they still largely determine the overall image of who a student is within British society, and their colonisation of certain areas of cities'.

At the same time, the laissez faire, and unregulated, approach of central government towards the supply of student accommodation is a key factor underpinning the current supply–demand of HMO for HE students. Despite the promotion and rising numbers of HE students, there is a serious lack of appropriate guidance and suitable resources for Higher Education Institutions (HEIs) to develop university-maintained accommodation. It is implicitly assumed that the private rented sector will 'mop up' the shortfall between the supply and demand for student accommodation.

Importantly, it is not being suggested here that residential concentrations of HE students did not exist prior to the 1990s. This discussion seeks to stress that in many English university towns the scale and magnitude of residential clusters of HE students has reached a threshold, whereby the supply–demand relationship of accommodation within HMO is imbalanced. As a result, the production of HMO has become a major institutional endeavour to discover new opportunities for profit. With this in mind, the discussion now turns to the production of studentified housing.

The production of studentified housing and economic reordering

The rigid definition of studentification, outlined earlier, points to the fundamental agency of 'landlord developers' (N. Smith 1979) within the process, yet it should be noted that HE students often move into many studentified areas, prior to institutional actors setting in motion intentional profit-maximisation strategies. This phase of pre-studentification (i.e. it does not usually involve the recommodification of single-family housing on a significant scale) is an important factor which illuminates the latent demand of HE students, and is key to the financial motivation of institutional actors. As Hamnett (1991: 181) states: 'most developers are risk averse and will not risk entering an area until demand is proven'. Moreover, this is a crucial point within the process of change when the existence of a rent gap between the actual value of single-family housing and the potential value of an HMO (N. Smith 1979) becomes evident. Subsequently, the production of an HMO and the realisation of long-term rental income from multiple students per annum can be viewed, therefore, as a closure of the rent gap. Of course, this is only a partial explanation of studentification, and in line with non-structuralist interpretations of gentrification, I would argue that studentification is not essentially a product of urban land and property markets in university towns (Hamnett 2000), but is inter-related with demand-related facets, such as residential preferences and consumption practices (see below).

Interestingly, the presence of a rent gap is not always tied to locations with devalued housing stock or areas – although it is widely acknowledged within discussions of gentrification that 'neighbourhoods and housing need not be deteriorated before being gentrified' (Beauregard 1986: 47). Indeed, many areas which have been influenced by processes of studentification, such as Clifton in Bristol, Headingley in Leeds, Hanover in Brighton, or Lenton in Nottingham, contain relatively exclusive high cost housing, and a middle-class residential composition. If studentification is subsumed under the rubric of gentrification, this therefore begs questions about the traditional assumption of gentrification involving 'the rehabilitation of working-class or derelict housing' (N. Smith and Williams 1986: 1).

Perhaps more importantly, the restructuring of the housing stock and the closing of the rent gap underpins a reordering and inflation of property prices, as the demand from HE students for accommodation within a student ghetto (which is increasingly promoted and marketed by institutional actors, e.g. letting agents) becomes more pronounced, in conjunction with the diminishing availability of suitable housing for conversion to HMO.

Moreover, in the British context the conditions of profitability are also tied to buy-to-rent mortgages with relatively low interest rates since the mid-1990s (which have also encouraged some parents of HE students to purchase housing, rather than absorb rental costs for student accommodation). Empirical evidence suggests that the availability of mortgage capital is a prerequisite of studentification (N. Smith 1979), although like gentrification: 'the centrality of mortgage finance, in itself does not create' studentification (Hamnett 1991: 1). Other influential factors include the absence of legislation requiring property owners to register HMO, and the lack of a national code of management practice for HMO landlords; thereby enabling some landlords to limit maintenance costs and longer-term capital investment. This latter point is important since studentification can be associated with a downgrading of the physical environment and housing stock, as property owners fail to upgrade or maintain HMO. Indeed, in Leeds and Brighton there is evidence of 'irresponsible' landlords intentionally 'running down' areas to encourage established households to 'sell up' and move out of the ensuing student ghetto. Clearly, this contrasts with many of the metaphorical associations of gentrification, and revitalised urban landscapes.

However, it is should be noted here that the scale of the downgrading is a relatively minor aspect of the urban change. When compared to the considerable physical upgrading and revitalisation of retail premises and culture-oriented services (i.e. pubs, café bars), links between processes of studentification and the physical downgrading of the urban landscape are generally limited. Of course, there may be specific enclaves within some university-towns where this supposition does not hold, given studentification unfolds in different ways and at different rates in particular places according to contingent conditions (e.g. housing stock).

It is important to stress here that processes of studentification do not explicitly encompass the new-build development of purpose-built HMOs for HE students, for example university halls of residence or flat units, or the large-scale redevelopment of former industrial or commercial premises. By contrast, this type of development has been integrated within recent conceptualisations of gentrification (Lees 2003a). Clearly, such developments do not fit within the rigid representation of studentification (i.e. recommodification of existing housing stock), outlined above. However, the supply and consumption of this type of accommodation is implicated in the studentification process, influencing the scale and pace of the recommodification, and the subsequent consumption by HE students of single-family or existing private rented housing. For instance, the presence of HE students residing in university-maintained accommodation heightens the visibility of students within a specific location and exacerbates the demand for 'student-centred' cultural and retail services. This is a key factor in the identity-making and reproduction of a student ghetto. Furthermore, empirical findings from Leeds reveal that HE students' spatial awareness and knowledgeability of potential residential options is often limited to the specific location of university-maintained accommodation, and this constrains their residential search when moving out of university-maintained accommodation and into the private rented sector, usually at the end of their first year of study (D. Smith 2002c).

Another key feature of studentification is the prominence of private rented tenure, and a reduction of owner-occupation. This is the inverse of gentrification (Hamnett 1991; Hamnett and Randolph 1986). Of course, the proliferation of private rented housing during studentification is bound up with the production of HMO for HE students, and the rate of this tenurial transformation is context-specific within and between different university towns. Findings from Leeds and Brighton reveal a combination of place-specific factors, for example the level of the resistance of established households to sell up and move out of the studentified location, and the capacity of institutional actors (i.e. estate and letting agents) to acquire or identify suitable property for investors or owners. Interestingly, in some locations which have been recently studentified and which had previously witnessed processes of gentrification, such as Headingley in Leeds, the subsequent unfolding of studentification may signify a profound tenurial reversal of the gentrification process. This issue raises important questions about the wider tenurial tenets of gentrification and urban change.

The spatiality of studentification

The production of HMO involves the conversion or sub-division of the internal space of properties to provide accommodation for multiple students. Hence, recommodification is usually restricted to properties with relatively large internal space, which are physically and economically conducive for conversion to an

HMO (see Redfern 1997a, 1997b, for discussion of domestic technological developments which enable gentrification). In line with theorisations of gentrification, the supply and availability of such housing stock does not necessarily lead to studentification (Hamnett 1991, 2000), yet this is one of the necessary prerequisites for studentification to take place. Importantly, the availability of such housing stock limits the breadth of locations which are potentially studentifiable, and ultimately underpins the spatial distribution of studentification.

In addition, the recommodification realms of studentification are not restricted to particular types of housing. Empirical findings from Leeds and Brighton show that a considerable variety of terraced, semi-detached and detached housing is recommodified during studentification; another comparable feature of gentrification, as Beauregard (1986: 41) notes, for instance: 'different types of housing stock might be rehabilitated'.

Nevertheless, processes of studentification often unfold within inner-city locations. In the English context, this is not surprising given the vast majority of established HEIs are located within inner-city areas, and a key factor within the residential decision-making processes of HE students is close proximity to the university campus. However, there is a geographical pattern to the distribution of studentified areas, with many tied to housing stocks and neighbourhoods often associated with the architectural aesthetics and styles of gentrification (see Jager 1986; Bridge 2001b), or as Ley (1981: 125) states: 'the desiderata of the culture of consumption'. Indeed, in many university towns studentification unfolds within areas that have been previously gentrified, or in areas which are adjacent to gentrified neighbourhoods. This finding is particularly important since it points to the formation of student ghettos within both working-class and middle-class enclaves. In the wider context of discussions of gentrification, this socio-spatial distinction raises questions about the class-related dynamics of the processes of change, and in particular wider issues of the long-term temporal effects of gentrification. For example, does studentification signify an emerging spatial expression of degentrification? At the same time, does studentification express a prelude to gentrification, or a form of 'marginal gentrification' (Rose 1984), in non-gentrified areas that bear the necessary prerequisites of gentrification (see Hamnett 1991)? These issues provide useful entrées for future research, and are particularly intriguing given HE students are often themselves associated with the pre- or early phases of gentrification (Ley 1996).

It should also be acknowledged that processes of studentification are not restricted to inner-city locations. In some university towns, such as Leeds and Bristol, studentification has spread outwards, penetrating into suburban areas as the processes of change have matured and gathered momentum. Empirical findings suggest that this spatial extension is predominantly linked to the agency of institutional actors, as they encounter additional 'single-family' or existing private rented housing stocks which are suitable for recommodification to HMO – rather than the explicit residential preferences of some HE students for suburban locations. It should be noted, however that such suburban areas are often relatively well-connected to university campuses by efficient public transport services and within close proximity to a student ghetto.

The migration specifics and population changes of studentification

A common effect of studentification are dramatic sociodemographic and population changes which are linked to distinct outward and inward migration flows (D. Smith, 2002b). In a similar vein to gentrification, studentification therefore 'necessarily prompts questions about migration' (Bondi 1999b: 204). However, there are major demographic and class-based migratory differences between the households that move in, move out or remain in the studentified location. Put simply, the assumption of a class-based transformation, or social upgrading (see for example, McDowell 1997), does not hold for studentification. Studentification involves the in-migration of a transient group of individuals, who are generally at an earlier phase of their lifecourse than conventional gentrifiers. The demographic profile of such in-migrants is dominated by single and childless young adults, with limited economic capital and non-participation in the labour market, seeking temporary rental accommodation, and with limited residential attachment to the studentified location (although some HE students may remain after graduation). There are also important class-related signifiers, with many 'traditional' HE students from predominantly middle-class backgrounds. As the Department of Education and Skills (2003: 17) note: 'Those from the top three social classes are almost three times as likely to enter higher education as those from the bottom three'.

An a priori starting point of many discussions of gentrification is that the process induces the 'displacement of one group of residents with another of higher status; entailing new patterns of social segregation' (Warde 1991: 227). This assumption of a spontaneous socio-economic upgrading, and the reconfiguration of the local class structure (see Bridge 1994; Badcock 2001 for fuller discussion), underlies dominant understandings of the non-gentrified population; this is despite a lack of empirically grounded accounts of gentrified households, a social grouping which are difficult to identify and track (Atkinson 2000a). However, a common profile of the stereotypical 'gentrified' individual is often reproduced within academic discourses of gentrification: working-class, marginal to the labour market, unemployed or under-employed, and with limited economic capital and earning potential. Perhaps more importantly, the displaced households are often perceived as being 'politically powerless', or as Beauregard (1986: 50) states: 'they are unable, because of their low economic status, to resist gentrification'. As a result, Beauregard asserts that the gentrified households are 'easily exploited by landlords if they are renting, unable to resist 'buyouts' by more affluent households if they are owning their housing, and unlikely to mobilise to resist' (ibid.). However, some recent empirical studies of gentrification have transcended the simplistic interpretations of the socio-economic upgrading of gentrification (Ley 1996), and have pointed to the replacement or displacement of middle-class social groups that have higher levels of economic and political power. As Bridge (1994: 32) asserts: 'not all those displaced are working class and not all the working class are displaced'.

This latter point is particularly pertinent to this discussion, given that student-ification often leads to the displacement or replacement of 'established' middle-class or working-class households, depending on the local context. Indeed, in some instances studentification results in the out-migration of gentrifiers. It is ironic, therefore, that in some gentrified locations which are now witnessing processes of studentification, the new middle classes that initially replaced or displaced industrial working classes from desirable inner city areas, may themselves be replaced or displaced by the children of the expanded new middle classes.

In line with empirical accounts of gentrification, established households often move out of studentified locations due to a combination of economic and socio-cultural factors (Atkinson 2000a, 2000b). On the one hand, the out-migration of some established households may express 'voluntary departure' (Bridge 2001b), as households sell their property, and move on, to take advantage of inflated property prices. On the other hand, some established households with relatively limited economic capital, such as first-time buyers or marginalised households in private rented accommodation, may be excluded from (buoyant) studentified housing markets. More significantly, it would appear that the (re)production of the different cultural ambiences and ideologies of student ghettos, and inter-connected changes in the local retail and services infrastructure, may underpin the out-migration of established households. For example, in many university towns the behaviour, recreational practices and attitudes of some HE students are perceived by established households as being 'anti-social', and detrimental to the social and cultural cohesion of the 'local' community. Such induced population movements thus bear many of the 'contagious' displacement tenets associated with gentrification (see Marcuse 1986 for fuller discussion).

In a wider social context, the migratory specifics of studentification mark a major social difference between gentrification and studentification, and expose different levels of class-based power. This factor underlies the recent widespread growth of local political action and movements to resist and contest processes of studentification in many university towns. By contrast to gentrified households, it would appear that studentified households have the economic and political prowess to contest and resist the processes of change. For example, the Leeds HMO Lobby has been established to co-ordinate the actions of local resident groups in Leeds, and to articulate the wider concerns of the established community. This group has illuminated some of the detrimental outcomes of studentification within the local context of Leeds, albeit influenced by their vested interest, and have now encouraged HEIs to develop accommodation strategies, and local planning and housing departments to acknowledge and monitor the rise of HMO, and develop a HMO landlord registration list.

Evidence from Brighton also shows widespread implicit resistance from some working-class households, with HE students remarking that some 'locals' are 'unwelcoming', 'intimidating', and 'anti-student'. As a result, HE students in Brighton tend to congregate in more familiar middle-class enclaves of the urban landscape; thereby perpetuating processes of studentification.

The cultural facets of studentification

Empirical findings from Leeds and Brighton reveal that it is necessary to focus upon the cultural choices and consumption practices of HE students to, in part, pin down why HE students concentrate within student ghettos and reside in HMO. To paraphrase Redfern (1997a), this suggests that 'students studentify because they can', rather than 'students studentify because they have to'. This is not to say that HE students have unbounded choice in the housing market when seeking short-term rental accommodation, or are not influenced by the intentional strategies of institutional actors and urban gatekeepers. Clearly, there are many economic and practical (e.g. lack of experience in searching for residence) limitations on the demands of HE students in the urban housing markets of university towns.

Given many HE students are at non-earning phases of their lifecourse (although an increasing number of HE students work part-time, Canny 2002), amassing appropriate levels of economic capital for bonds and rental deposits is likely to be difficult for many HE students; particularly given rising tuition fees and living costs. Nevertheless, many HE students often dismiss cheaper rental accommodation within locations that are not perceived as student ghettos, and choose more expensive rental accommodation in order to realise a 'student lifestyle' and 'student identity' within the student ghetto. It should be noted here, that some HE students in Leeds and Brighton undertake important trade-offs, often selecting lower-quality, and cheaper, accommodation within HMO at the periphery of the student ghetto, yet which is accessible to cultural amenities and services (D. Smith 2002c).

This latter point emphasises, in a similar vein to the socio-spatial concentration of gentrifier households (Butler 1997; Butler and Robson 2001a), that the clustering of HE students expresses the predilection for the distinct cultural and entertainment facilities often located within student ghettos, and HE students move proximate to such cultural consumption items (Beauregard 1986). Therefore, in line with Hamnett's (2000: 335) interpretation of gentrification, studentification 'is not simply a class or income phenomenon – it is also crucially linked to the creation of cultural residential preferences'. On the whole, such cultural practices bear many similarities to the self-conscious consumption strategies, lifestyles and ideological values and beliefs of gentrifiers (Ley 1994, 1996).

In light of this overlap between gentrifiers and studentifiers, it is valuable to draw upon Bridge's (2001a) recent discussion of the rational time-space strategies of gentrifiers. According to Bridge, 'early gentrifiers are seen as having large amounts of cultural capital even if their stores of material capital are small' (p. 206). It is argued that such cultural capital 'is deployed in lieu of material capital to achieve distinction', or in other words 'the set of values that privileges pro-urban lifestyles' (ibid). I would contend here that HE students share many similarities with such groups of marginal gentrifiers, albeit via different strategies to achieve distinction and social and cultural identity and belonging. In line with early gentrifiers, most HE students possess limited levels of 'individual' economic capital (although parental contributions are influential here), and often utilise the values, beliefs and meanings (i.e. cultural capital) tied to student lifestyles and identities to achieve distinction. The reproduction of the student ghetto, via the consumption practices of HE students to reside in HMO within a specific location, can therefore be viewed as the spatial expression of the student habitus.

Indeed, the predispositions of the student habitus appear to provide HE students with a sense of 'ontological security', during a potentially insecure and uncertain phase of their lifecourse. For many HE students, moving away from the parental home to study at a university often involves their first significant period away from the parental home, and leads to social interactions and co-residence with strangers. Therefore, the tendency of HE students to reside in HMO is tied to the search for a sense of belonging and membership to the wider student grouping, and signifies collective self-conscious acts of reflexive consumption to buy into the student lifestyle and realise a student identity. In line with Bridge (2001a), this cultural practice expresses the conscious, rational decision-making of HE students – a perception of a 'sound judgement' in light of the actions which they think other HE students will choose:

> If games are repeated there will be a history of prior interaction on which agents can draw to help make their decisions. This shared history means that class agents can be fairly sure of the beliefs of others and so can make sound judgements about how others will be thinking and likely to act in the knowledge that the others are also trying to judge how the class agents with which they are interacting will act.

> (Ibid: 210)

Similarly, Chatterton (1999: 119) claims that the distinctiveness of student ghettos enables 'identifiable students' ways of life to be developed which are internalised and embodied'. It is noted that the sharing of student housing, for example, provides a framework which nurtures and perpetuates 'a common set of student dispositions, or something like a student habitus'– thereby setting 'students apart from the non-student world' (ibid.).

Of course, and in a similar vein to gentrification, these cultural underpinnings are mediated by intermediaries, such as letting agents and cultural-service providers (D. Smith 2002a). These actors operate at the interface between the production-consumption facets of studentification via their marketing and promotion of student ghettos and accommodation, and thereby influence the residential and locational demands of HE students. For instance, Bridge (2001b: 214) reveals that the cultural practices of gentrifiers: 'are open to manipulation by the cultural workers or the critical infrastructure who attempt to move this co-ordination of expectation in particular directions'. Clearly, the role of intermediaries within processes of studentification should not be understated.

Studentification: the gentrification factory?

The previous sections point to studentification as a generational or cohort specific phenomenon, in a similar vein to Ley's (1996) notion of the 'hippies' of the 1960s and 1970s becoming the new class consumers of gentrification. Likewise, it can be postulated that studentifiers represent a potential grouping of future gentrifiers. In this sense, the social and cultural spaces of studentified locations may provide a 'training ground' for future gentrifiers, or represent a 'factory of gentrifiers'. The socio-cultural practices and consumer preferences of HE students, noted above, may therefore influence new expressions of gentrification, and the types of residential location, housing and tenure which are viewed as desirable by future gentrifiers. Similarly, this may influence the cultural consumption practices of future gentrifiers, and the predilections for particular types of retail and cultural services associated with the lifestyles of gentrifiers. This link between a distinct group of 'gentrifiers in the making' and future forms of gentrification stresses the need for lifecourse analyses to explore the individual and collective biographies of gentrifiers; a theme which has generally been understated within studies of gentrification (D. Smith 2002c; Bridge 2003).

This raises important issues for the study of gentrification. For example, do studentifiers represent a new (future) generation of gentrifiers (i.e. when their economic capital increases following graduation and entry into the labour market). Studentified spaces may be understood as important 'learning spaces', whereby the embryonic new middle classes sophisticate their levels of cultural capital and competences, and formalise (or reproduce) the values and beliefs of the new middle classes. In short, while gentrification is linked to higher education as the gateway through which professional status (connected with economic capital) and cultural capital may be transmitted, the lifestyles within ghettoised studentified areas provide a certain kind of symbolic capital. This form of capital represents an attempt to find security in areas of 'people like us' and one which is likely to be repeated in future location decisions upon graduation (Butler 1997).

Chatterton's (1999) discussion of the formation of student lifestyles may offer some valuable insights here. It is shown that student spaces, such as shared student housing, are 'arenas' where the rituals and rules of student life are learnt and embodied. Perhaps more importantly, Chatterton postulates that HE students then 'unlearn the rules of the student game', as their university career matures and develops, and enter into a 'process [which] represents annual learning of student rites and a distancing from the student infrastructure as the student is acculturated into less 'typical' student activities within the city' (p. 122). This practice, according to Chatterton, gives rise to some HE students exploring and discovering 'other areas and venues in the city which are not associated with traditional student culture' (ibid.). Clearly, if studentifiers are viewed as potential gentrifiers, such experiences may have important effects on future forms of gentrification, and the types of locations which may be gentrified.

The experiences of HE students may also have broader ramifications upon the gender, sexuality and lifecourse dimensions of future gentrification, with 'less-traditional' relations often being integral to 'typical' student lifestyles and identities. This is likely to have an effect on the normative expectations and attitudes associated with partnering, parenting, marriage and family forming of future gentrifiers; factors which have been shown to be pivotal to the causes and end results of gentrification (e.g. Bondi 1991b; Butler and Hamnett 1994).

Given the emergence of this group of potential gentrifiers, there is clearly a need for more sophisticated analyses of the wider temporal contexts of gentrification. For example, are current dominant understandings of gentrification based upon out-dated, historical expressions of urban revitalisation associated with the latter decades of the twentieth century, and perhaps linked to different structural and ideological conditions? Recent accounts of emerging forms of gentrification illuminate the urgent need to acknowledge this point, with authors increasingly refining understandings of gentrification (Lees 2002b). In this respect, different expressions of gentrification may be viewed as conceptual and historical markers of time, space, and society, which encapsulate the fluid relations between structure-agency, production-consumption and supply–demand. Gentrification may therefore provide a 'window' through which broader economic, societal, cultural and spatial restructuring can be viewed.

Discussion and conclusion

This chapter asks questions about the contemporary meaning of gentrification. By transposing studentification within a framework of gentrification, the previous sections have been closely aligned to recent discussions which, as Eric Clark's closing chapter suggests, transcend ideas of gentrification as a fixed marker of the (re)colonisation of the inner city by middle-class households and the displacement of working-class residents (Glass 1964). Instead, the term gentrification is increasingly being utilised as an all-encompassing, descriptive label of urban revitalisation. Importantly, this perspective is based on the premise that: 'The process of gentrification seems to have mutated so much that traditional definitions no longer seem apt' (Lees 2003a: 572). In particular I have argued that gentrification may be seen as much as a learned response stemming from early housing careers as to some inherent motive to gentrify.

In this reworked guise, the use of the term gentrification allows researchers to bring some assemblage to the multiple trajectories of urban revitalisation, which are known by a plethora of other names – according to the economic, cultural or socio-spatial distinctiveness of a particular process. But what unites these processes of change other than revitalisation, and what does the label of gentrification signify at a deeper theoretical level? A major commonality between the processes of revitalisation is the (re)production of geographies of social segregation and concentration, and the widening socio-spatial polarisation of different groups (see Dorling and Rees 2003).

Furthermore, these processes often lead to tensions between different social class and cultural groupings, and induce territorial claims about rights of ownership to space, neighbourhood and housing, and public (e.g. schools, health care, public transport) and private services (e.g. pubs, types of retail provision). This social division is manifest in the rise of local political action and community movements, and socio-cultural resistance and contest in many transformed urban landscapes; a common feature which is exemplified by studentification. Studentification can therefore be subsumed under the wider label of gentrification, and future research should compare the social and spatial significance of studentification and other forms of revitalisation.

In the British context, it is imperative here to recognise localised and regional contingencies when undertaking detailed examinations of geographies of student-ification. In particular, changing structural conditions tied to HE funding regimes and a growing diversity between groups of HE students point to the formation of uneven patterns of studentification. For instance, recent plans by central government to allow HEIs to charge differential 'top-up' tuition fees may result in a multi-tier HE system (Curtis 2003). It is envisaged that HE students will be polarised (Cottell 2001), with attendance at prestigious HEIs dominated by relatively affluent students moving away from their parental home to study (i.e. 'traditional' students), and less-affluent students paying lower tuition fees at less-prestigious HEIs in their local area, and residing in parental or family homes (i.e. 'non-traditional' students). As a result, processes of studentification may be confined to university-towns with prestigious HEIs, such as Oxford, Cambridge, London, Durham, Bristol, Leeds, Manchester, Nottingham and Sheffield. Likewise, it can be argued that the socio-spatial polarisation of HE students is further compounded by other recent legislative changes, such as HEFCE (Higher Education Funding Council for England) advising the Secretary of State for Education and Skills that the restriction of the MaSN (maximum student numbers) should be removed, thereby allowing a higher intake of HE students to the more prestigious HEIs.

These links between the supply–demand of HE and studentification may be usefully explored in other European and global contexts. Intriguingly, preliminary investigations suggest that processes of studentification may be specific to Great Britain. It would appear that studentification is bound-up with the HE system of 'young' adults moving away from their parental home to study in another location, and is tied to the supply–demand nexus which results in HE students often entering the private rented housing market for accommodation in HMO. The system of HE and migration patterns of students in a global context suggest that this is not the case. For example, anecdotal evidence from Northern Italy and Ireland shows that 'typical' HE students often attend a university within their local area or region, and may often travel back to their place of origin at weekends. Similarly, in other international contexts where individuals move away from the parental home to study, it is unusual for students to seek accommodation in private rented housing (e.g. Singapore, Indonesia). Examinations of the geographic scale of studentification may warrant further attention.

In conclusion, the emergence of studentification raises some important issues for scholars of urban revitalisation. These beg questions about future forms of gentrification and the characteristics of potential groupings of gentrifiers – thereby reiterating the value of problematising the meaning of gentrification. I would argue that this orthodoxy forms part of an ongoing endeavour within gentrification discourses, which is intrinsically connected to the dynamic nature of processes of urban revitalisation. The chapter therefore reaffirms the need for reflexive and critical perspectives when using the term gentrification to investigate emerging, and established, expressions of urban revitalisation. Twenty years on, Rose's (1984: 62) call for a reconceptualisation of 'our ways of seeing some forms of gentrification, and some types of gentrifiers' clearly holds significant resonance for understanding the broader revitalisation of urban space in the twenty-first century.

Note

1 Unfortunately, there is currently no official definition of HMO in Britain. In the English context, the definition of HMO varies within housing and town and country planning legislation. In the former, the Housing Act (1995) defines HMO as a house which is occupied by persons who do not form a single household. However, this raises the question: what constitutes a single household? In the latter, the Use Classes Order (1987) suggests that HMO is a house with more than six persons, not forming a single household. In this chapter, a working definition of HMO is adopted in line with Scottish legislation: a house with more than two people from more than two families. This is the definition espoused in the Houses in Multiple Occupation (Registration Scheme) Bill (House of Commons 2001).

6 Gentrification in post-communist cities

Luděk Sýkora

Introduction

Our knowledge of the gentrification of cities outside the west has often been limited by ideological and linguistic barriers as well as the more general impression that gentrification in other global regions has been muted or absent. However, it is increasingly clear that the implementation of market reforms in Eastern European 'post-communist' countries has often led to pronounced urban restructuring and neighbourhood changes that are, to some extent, similar to transformations mapped out for cities in the west. This chapter presents a review of current understanding of gentrification in selected post-communist cities. The post-communist world is both large and diverse and this chapter cannot cover the whole geographical area and encompass all the variety. It focuses on Budapest (Hungary), Prague (Czech Republic) and Tallinn (Estonia), three cities where gentrification has been researched and discussed, and builds upon this experience. Existing studies of other post-communist cities, such as Bratislava, Ljubljana or Warsaw, have not generally identified gentrification among the more important processes of urban change.

This chapter starts with three distinct stories of gentrification from Budapest, Prague and Tallinn. Then it will seek their implications for what we understand as gentrification more generally. Three particular areas affecting gentrification and the interpretation and explanation of neighbourhood change are scrutinised. First, urban decline during communism, second, models of housing privatisation and, finally, the rise of gentrifiers as a newly significant fraction of the middle classes. In conclusion we point to the specificities of gentrification in post-communist cities that might have some relevance for the general discussion of the process and its trajectories under differing systemic conditions.

Neighbourhood transitions in Budapest: gentrification in question

Budapest is perhaps the most often discussed example of gentrification in a post-communist city. Research here dates back to Hegedüs and Tosics (1991), who used the term 'socialist gentrification' for the description of public urban rehabilitation projects affecting two blocks in run-down areas of inner Budapest. The rehabilitation involved the relocation of inhabitants to flats in other public housing (mostly in the inner city), physical refurbishment and consequent allocation of upgraded apartments to new public tenants. In aggregate, new tenants had higher social status than the original population as they accepted higher rents for refurbished flats.

Opportunities for a more fully developed gentrification of neighbourhoods opened with the establishment of capitalism in the country. In his influential book *The New Urban Frontier: Gentrification and the Revanchist City*, Neil Smith presents Budapest as a showpiece of gentrification in post-communist Europe (N. Smith 1996). He argues that 'gentrification emerges hand in hand with the capitalisation of the Budapest land and housing markets' (N. Smith 1996: 173). The gentrification itself Smith associated with a privatisation of housing. Privatisation

> has led to a quite evident class shift in the composition of several Budapest neighbourhoods which are attracting large numbers of the newly emerging middle class. This gentrification is focused in several central districts, but as with gentrification in most cities it is highly visible, involves disproportionate amounts of new capital investment, and already has the momentum to become a major determinant of the new urban landscape.
>
> (1996: 176)

The conclusions of Kovács and Wiessner's (1999) study of urban and housing transformation in Budapest stand, however, in sharp contrast with Smith's findings.

> While renovation of the old building stock can often be observed in the case of business investments, we can hardly speak about it in relation to the housing sector, even in the privatised housing stock. Moreover, processes of physical upgrading and gentrification so typical for the western cities are practically unknown in Budapest until now.
>
> (Kovács and Wiessner 1999: 76)

Their view is in line with the findings of Douglas (1997) according to whom 'there is not gentrification in Budapest in the western European or American sense of the word. ... it would be difficult to find one neighbourhood in Budapest that could be termed "gentrified"' (1997: 190).

While Smith builds his view on the conviction that inner Budapest is being changed by a 'dramatic, perhaps unprecedented, shift from minimal to maximal investment in a newly evolving land and housing market' (Smith 1996: 173), there are many other voices stressing urban decline in inner cities (Dingsdale 1999; Kok and Kovács 1999; Ladányi 1997). Ladányi and Szelényi (1998: 84) admit that 'inner urban areas in Budapest are eminently suitable for gentrification', however, the reality is different as 'the new upper-middle class is leaving the inner city and the vacated areas are being filled with lower status groups, especially with the Roma poor' (1998: 83).

Kovács' (1998) paper which considered 'Ghetoization or gentrification?' does not directly answer the posed question. He stresses that there are both upward and downward processes in inner Budapest. Without doubt there has been a huge inflow of investment into the CBD bringing the development of commercial spaces and outbidding housing from the area. Commercialisation (the increase in commercial properties as a proportion of built environment) dominates this landscape (Kovács 1994) and even if some single apartments become gentrified it often fails to influence the general character of the neighbourhood. The existence of 'the kind of expensive restaurants, clubs and nightspots that mark many gentrifying neighbourhoods' (N. Smith 1996: 174) cannot be interpreted as being direct markers of gentrification activity.

The socio-spatial structure of Budapest has been influenced by increasing social disparities among the population leading to growing differences between inner city areas (Kovács 1998). The upward moves are concentrated especially in villa neighbourhoods in the western part of the city (Buda) which have always been the highest status residential areas. Much of their upward trajectory is related not to the mobility and displacement of the resident population but is an outcome of the relative social mobility of the existing population. Even the mobility and change of inhabitants is difficult to associate with forced displacement and gentrification as these have always been areas dominated by owner-occupied housing.

The inner-city neighbourhoods that were most severely affected by disinvestments and decline during communism now continue on a downward spiral. Segregation of the poor in the eastern part of the inner city (Pest) dominates the neighbourhood change in Budapest. In particular, Erzsébetváros in district VII and Józsefváros in the VIIIth district are often seen as examples of slum and ghetto formation. In this area are two blocks rehabilitated under communism and termed 'socialist gentrification'. The rehabilitation process did not continue in the 1990s and renovated houses remained isolated pockets of higher social status in an otherwise depressed district.

Regeneration in Ferencváros (district IX) provides a stronger example of an upward trajectory. The renovation project in an area that was a slum since World War II started during communism and continued in the 1990s through a public-private partnership company with the local council as 51 per cent shareholder.

The whole project involved the construction of new buildings on vacant lots, demolition and replacement of abandoned buildings in dangerous conditions, rehabilitation of properties in sound conditions and regeneration of public spaces including pedestrianisation. As is usual with many such renovation projects, residents are relocated to alternative dwellings without the option of returning. Most of the new dwellings are for sale rather than for the public rental tenure (Douglas 1997). The whole project can be seen as the publicly administered cleansing of the area in favour of the wealthy. It is a rather special case, whose nature is quite distinct from the market-led gentrification processes in western cities. However, the rehabilitation can impact on the wider area and induce spontaneous market-led gentrification leading to the displacement of lower-income households though, at present, it is rather an island of renewal in a sea of decline.

New niches in Prague's property markets

In Prague, gentrification developed in a small portion of the inner city, where it brought radical physical and social changes. Its significance within the overall urban change is not in its absolute extent but in the sharp contrasts between new and old within affected neighbourhoods. As gentrification is not the most significant process that shapes contemporary Prague it has not been significant in discussions of urban change. The central city and some adjacent inner city neighbourhoods were revitalised mostly through commercial developments including the displacement of residential by non-residential functions. In the second half of the 1990s, central and inner city urban development has been overshadowed by growing suburbanisation which is now the major process transforming Prague's metropolitan area. Within the residential environment, new developments are associated with suburban single-family homes and inner city condominiums. Nevertheless, from a qualitative perspective, gentrification is an important element of post-communist urban restructuring.

Old rental apartment houses have been reconstructed and transformed into both office spaces and luxury apartments in some zones of the historical core and nineteenth-century inner city neighbourhoods adjacent to the city centre. Gentrifying areas are densely built-up with four to five storey buildings with only few gaps allowing for new construction. Physical revitalisation takes the form of rehabilitation and refurbishment. Numerous commercial projects (office, retail, hotels) include full or partial demolition and new property construction. In housing, there are a few examples of condominiums being squeezed into the existing historic fabric.

The major gentrifying area is in Vinohrady, a neighbourhood that was originally an independent town growing in the second half of the nineteenth century outside the historic Prague fortification and was amalgamated to the city in 1922. Despite decline during communism, the area has always been seen as a good residential

6.1 Gentrification of multi-apartment rental housing in Prague's Vinohrady

address. Vinohrady itself is a large neighbourhood with a population of around 60,000 and gentrification has affected only some areas within it. Despite several cases of housing converted to non-residential use, residential change plays a more significant role in this area.

Residential gentrification is also proceeding in some parts of the historic core, namely at Malá Strana (Little Side). However, residential change is, in these spaces, overshadowed by business and tourist related developments. The main process transforming the city centre is commercialisation i.e. a growth in the share of non-residential uses in the city. Commercialisation proceeds through new commercial buildings constructed on vacant lots, the replacement of less 'economic' uses and the displacement of residential by non-residential functions in originally residential properties. Despite the abundance of gentrified residential properties commercialisation prevails in Prague's central city areas.

Neighbourhood revitalisation through gentrification and commercialisation is reflected in population change. The number of inhabitants of two central districts of Prague 1 and 2 (historic core and Vinohrady) declined by nearly one-fifth between 1991 and 2001. While some of this decrease has been caused by natural change, over half of it results from out-migration, people especially being displaced by non-residential functions. Gentrification also contributes to population decline. During reconstruction, smaller and modest flats are often combined to form large luxurious apartments. Besides the reconstruction of existing properties, in a few instances new condominiums have been in-filled into the existing historic fabric bringing new population.

The social status of the population is also growing faster than in other parts of Prague. The share of university graduates rose particularly in the two central city districts Prague 1 and 2 and also in Prague 6, which is traditionally the major area of upper-class residences (mostly owner-occupied villas). This points to displacement in neighbourhoods with existing high social profiles. It does not change the pattern of spatial distribution of population according to social status; it is strengthening existing differences. Nevertheless, it must be admitted that the social composition of gentrifying areas was socially mixed since the beginning of the communist period, when the dwellings of the bourgeoisie were subdivided and allocated to working-class households.

Despite gentrification occuring in areas where the social status of the population is already high, gentrifiers still significantly differ from the existing inhabitants. People who buy or lease renovated apartments are often western foreigners working in Prague who came to the city with the expansion of corporations into newly emerging markets. Also, more Czech nationals are taking part in this segment of the housing market. Gentrifiers substantially differ from the existing population by their income level and purchasing power. They usually work in the advanced services sector dominated by foreign-owned firms and where salaries are considerably higher than for other jobs.

The developers engaged in housing rehabilitation are often foreign owned firms aware of the potentially high gains from property refurbishment and have better access to foreign customers. They acquire whole buildings from private individuals who received these properties through 'restitution' (the return of properties confiscated during communism to former owners or their heirs), come to agreements with tenants who are then moved to replacement flats, refurbish housing to a high standard and either lease apartments or sell them to gentrifiers. In this way a special segment of Prague's residential property market developed, dominated by foreign developers and customers. This market segment is rather a small niche that affects only a limited number of housing units in certain areas of the central and inner city.

Gentrification in Prague had no pioneer stage in the way that many other western cities have. It started as a property-development business organised by foreign firms and targeted to a specific group of customers – generally western migrants working and living in Prague (Sýkora 1996). Local transformations, namely the establishment of property markets facilitated the process. Restitution transferred large numbers of properties to private hands (in the central zone and some segments of the inner city it was up to three quarters of all buildings) and created favourable conditions for the establishment of property markets and property redevelopment. The new owners have not had enough experience and capital to engage in property development and tended to sell newly gained property. Real estate in attractive locations quickly changed owners as real estate developers became aware of the possibilities to achieve high returns on their investments.

Gentrification in Prague is spatially very selective affecting only a small portion of the inner city. It is closely associated with commercialisation: the same developers are engaged in the rehabilitation of old properties for both offices and housing and some projects involve a combination of these functions. It usually takes several years and decades to change a neighbourhood through gentrification. Therefore, we can speak about gentrifying areas but about gentrified neighbourhoods with greater difficulty. Gentrifying places are characterised by a mixture of original population and gentrifiers, old and new establishments, refurbished and not-yet-renovated properties.

Old and new Tallinn

While central city and several inner city locations show signs of revitalisation in Talinn, there is only one inner city area undergoing gentrification. Its name is Kadriorg. It has always been a desired residential location. Despite the lack of investment during Soviet times and physical decline it retained the image of a prestigious residential area. However, there were internal differences. Housing consists of two to four storey wooden and stone multi-family villas and apartment houses. There are also downgraded single-family wooden houses. The older wooden buildings deteriorated seriously, had few or no modern conveniences and were occupied by elderly and working-class people. Inter-war stone buildings were in better physical shape; they contained relatively large apartments and their tenants often came from the administrative elite and intellectuals.

In Kadriorg, 30–40 per cent of buildings were returned to private hands in restitution and of these an estimated 70 per cent were then sold to new owners (Feldman 2000a). Those real estate developers that purchase these properties tend to buy the existing tenants an apartment in Soviet-era housing estates or pre-Soviet wooden housing in a less central location. In many instances the displacement does not happen immediately as the new owners wait and speculate on future developments. The renovation of existing properties started in the mid-1990s and by 2000, 10–15 per cent of apartments were refurbished (Feldman 2000a). Virtually all of them are in stone housing while most wooden housing remained in poor condition. At present, multi-apartment wooden houses in better condition are undergoing upgrading. Furthermore, new condominium complexes were constructed in this area, often on land returned to private ownership in restitution, or replaced demolished wooden buildings (Feldman 2000a; Ruoppila and Kährik 2003). Residential upgrading is often accompanied by the location of fashionable restaurants, architecture firms and offices. Feldman (2000a) suggests that about 15–20 per cent of population in Kadriorg are gentrifiers residing in both renovated properties and new condominiums. In the neighbourhood, gentrifiers live side-by-side with elderly and other disadvantaged populations. Gentrification brings not only social upgrading but also lead to social polarisation within the area.

According to Ruoppila (2002) much of the new construction and reconstruction in Tallinn has concentrated on Kadriorg. As the new and renovated housing is

6.2 Gentrification of art nouveau style multi-family villas in Tallinn's Kadriorg

affordable only to the wealthy, the spatial concentration of construction and rehabilitation indicates the spatial concentration of better-off households. Kadriorg developed into the most clearly visible pockets of wealth in the inner city placed within otherwise socially mixed areas. The analysis of Ruoppila and Kährik (2003) found that despite the rapidly expanded income disparities and the liberalisation of the housing market there was still a generally low socio-economic differentiation between Tallinn's city districts. Nevertheless, Kährik's (2002: 52) analysis of trends between 1995–9 shows that in apartment housing the economically disadvantaged population tend to concentrate in cheaper apartments with a low level of facilities, while apartments with all facilities have become more often inhabited by the households belonging to higher income groups compared to lower income groups.

Despite most recent housing development in Tallinn being located in newly suburban locales (Kährik 2002; Ruoppila 2002) processes of inner city neighbourhood change will continue. Tenants living in restituted housing are vulnerable to displacement and this housing segment is most likely to be further gentrified provided it is located in an attractive area. According to Kährik *et al.* (2003), about 40 percent of the owners of restituted stock in Estonia intend terminating existing leases of their tenants to renovate the building and let it for several times higher rent or convert it to a non-residential space. The pressure in the capital city and its attractive neighbourhoods is likely to be much higher. At present, there are, however, strong obstacles to forced evictions. Rent contracts in restituted housing are protected to 2007 and local governments in some large cities including Tallinn regulate rent levels (Feldman 2000a; Kährik *et al.* 2003), if these regulations are removed displacement can proceed more quickly. Interestingly, in Tartu, another Estonian city, the local government supports displacement. If the owner of restituted housing is willing to support financially a new housing purchase by its tenant, local government will provide financial support at the same level to a maximum of about US$2300 and the rest of the apartment price must be paid by the tenant (Kährik 2003: 228).

The character of gentrification in former socialist cities

In this chapter, gentrification is seen as a process of inner-city neighbourhood change by a simultaneous physical upgrading of dilapidated residential buildings and the displacement of the original population by more wealthy newcomers. The direct relationship between capital investment and displacement at the level of individual properties forms the nexus of gentrification. Property rehabilitation associated with the arrival of more wealthy inhabitants is likely to have wide implications for neighbourhood change. Residential gentrification is accompanied by the changing nature of restaurants, shops and other services located in the neighbourhood. Nevertheless, the side effects and accompanying features of gentrification should not be mixed with the core issue of the process, which is residential refurbishment and population displacement. Some authors like Cooper and Morpeth (1999) speak about 'commercial gentrification' in Prague. They mean central city upgrading associated with commercial functions. This process is in this chapter termed commercialisation, while gentrification is restricted to the residential field.

In this chapter, gentrification will be associated with established residential neighbourhoods, where old property is being refurbished. There can be new development on single lots or individual buildings extensions. Construction of large condominium complexes significantly contributes to urban restructuring through physical and social change, however, it is not considered here as gentrification.

The other crucial aspect of gentrification is displacement of original low social status inhabitants by a more wealthy population, often through eviction. Despite a number of unlawful cases of forced evictions in post-communist cities, tenants enjoy formal protection. Eviction is not a common mechanism behind displacement and gentrification. In rental stock, landlords interested in property refurbishment with an aim to lease or sell it for higher returns usually have to offer tenants replacement flats within city limits and attempt to come to an agreement to speed along their removal. This can be realised for the whole building, which is usually the work of institutional investors and developers. Some people can be pushed out from a revitalising area by rising prices and they usually move to more affordable housing in different parts of the city. Rent regulations, however, up to now largely prohibited such impacts. The replacement is often going on through voluntary moves out from the neighbourhood by a variety of people, while the new population consists of those who can afford to live there. Such a mechanism can gradually lead to the substantial shift in the aggregate composition of population.

Gentrifying neighbourhoods are often transformed simultaneously by a number of processes that contribute to general revitalisation. In the post-communist urban context the functional transformation from residential to commercial uses often goes hand in hand with the conversion of dilapidated tenement housing to luxury renovated condominiums. Neighbourhoods are therefore often transformed by both commercialisation and gentrification at the same time.

The social geography of the socialist city

Gentrification started to attract attention because it brought a significant reversal in the trajectories of suburbanisation in western metropolitan areas. In Eastern Europe the urban structure and socio-spatial pattern of socialist cities was somewhat different. City centres and some parts of the inner cities were traditionally high social status areas, while low social status people were generally located at the city periphery. The initial redistribution of inner city housing from bourgeoisie to working-class families often included the subdivision of large dwellings, which also brought a mixing of population and heterogeneity in the socio-spatial pattern. However, major changes were caused by a massive construction of new prefabricated blocks of flats in housing estates located on the city outskirts and uniformly allocated to the socialist middle class. Investment in new housing construction was the single priority and old inner city housing suffered from under-maintenance and dilapidation.

The implications of these changes were worse for inner-city working-class areas than for original upper social status neighbourhoods. Some inner-city housing was declared as uninhabitable. Entire buildings and their whole blocks were abandoned or used as warehouses and sometimes demolished and replaced by new structures. Households were allocated higher quality dwellings in new estates. However, a certain social bias was implicit in the administrative allocation concentrating less educated people, and especially gypsy minorities, into flats in dilapidated inner-city houses. Despite the general physical deterioration, there were significant differences between individual neighbourhoods. The inherently uneven nature of socialist inner-city decline, with original upper social status neighbourhoods keeping their character as 'good addresses' as well as deteriorating bad address districts, is a critical feature for understanding post-communist urban change and the urban geography of gentrification in particular.

Smith has asserted the role of disinvestment and capital devalorisation in the inner city as a crucial precondition for gentrification and has extended his analysis to the post-communist context: 'the opportunity for gentrification in Budapest lies in a protracted history of disinvestments' (N. Smith 1996: 175). However, physical degradation is a necessary but not a sufficient precondition for reinvestment and regeneration that are essential elements of the gentrification process. Smith's rent gap theory (N. Smith 1979) points to the crucial aspect: gentrification is likely to happen where the rent gap is widest or in other words where there is the best possibility for profit making from property redevelopment. In the context of the post-communist city we may argue that the best possibilities for such profits are in areas that have declined, are well located, but which also have attractive features to their residential environment. In other words the rent gap is widest in areas where there are no slums and where the actual rent is not necessarily among the lowest in the metropolitan area.

The rent gap is large because these are locations and properties where the intentions of investors to redevelop and sell and customers to pay for refurbished housing meet at such a high level of potential rent that in contrast with the actual rent this produces a significant rent gap. The largest rent gap, therefore, can be in areas that do not belong to the most deprived, in both physical and social senses. The presented case studies show that gentrification is not a process that would transform the existing socio-spatial pattern through the revitalisation of most deprived neighbourhoods. Gentrification is happening in areas that had the best residential places before communism, declined during communism and are now being refurbished to their former glory while segments of the population housed in the areas during communism are now being displaced.

Pathways of privatisation and property refurbishment

The rapid establishment of basic conditions for the development of a market economy, through privatisation and price liberalisation, led to a quick formation of real estate markets in East Central Europe (Ghanbari-Parsa and Moatazed-Keivani 1999). Properties could be traded and their price and nature of use began to be re-shaped by demand. After years of centrally-planned allocation of functions in urban space, households and firms could choose where to live, offer services or locate production. Their individual activity started to contribute to changes in the built environment, land use patterns and residential segregation. Provided there is demand for certain types of properties in certain locations, private institutional investors are certainly not missing new opportunities to realise profits on real estate development.

With regard to gentrification, the most influential factors have been housing privatisation and rent deregulation. In particular, different pathways in housing privatisation were crucial for both capital investments to physical refurbishment and the displacement of population bringing changes to neighbourhood social composition. Two forms of housing privatisation deserve particular attention: restitution and flat privatisation, that have created substantially different conditions for the mechanisms of neighbourhood change. The implications of both these privatisation approaches for gentrification must be considered in the specific context of inner city environments with prevailing multi-dwelling housing stock.

The restitution process returned property rights to former pre-communist owners or their heirs. In the context of the inner city, apartment buildings were transferred from the public landlord (state or local government) to private individuals. Former public tenants suddenly became tenants of private landlords to whom the ownership was returned. Restitution has been applied in the Czech Republic, Estonia, Germany, Slovakia and Slovenia. Prague and Tallinn are two examples of cities, where urban change was shaped by the restitution process (Sýkora and Šimoníčková 1994; Eskinasi 1995; Ruoppila 1998; Ruoppila and Kährik 2003). In central Prague and some inner-city neighbourhoods as much as three-quarters of residential buildings were returned to private hands through restitution. In Tallinn, restitution affected a much smaller part of inner-city housing stock. However, this impacted significantly on some small areas.

In the inner-city context, restitution created a large pool of new private owners of rental housing. The important factor is that the building as a whole remains in single ownership and can be redeveloped as one integrated unit. During redevelopment, former rental houses can be converted to condominiums with individual dwellings offered for sale. However, the redevelopment process and displacement of former inhabitants can be organised by a single landlord for the whole building. This makes for a significant difference from flat privatisation.

Rent has been regulated in public and private rental housing in the case of lease contracts signed under communism. This meant that rents could not rocket in desired central and inner-city areas pushing tenants out of rental stock. However, once the flat becomes vacant it is not subject anymore to rent regulation. As market rents in attractive locations were many times higher than regulated rents, there has been a strong impetus for private owners to switch their property from the regulated to the deregulated sector. The removal of tenants opens such an opportunity. Once the formal rental house is empty, it can be converted not only to market rent luxury flats, but also to offices or other non-residential spaces for lease (provided land use regulations allow such change) or to apartments for sale.

Flat privatisation has occurred in most post-communist countries. In Hungary and Budapest it was the single strategy of housing privatisation and local councils listed most housing for privatisation. The Estonian government applied right-to-buy legislation (Kährik *et al.* 2003) and in Tallinn, nearly all former public housing that was not subject to restitution was privatised in this way. As the result of privatisation, public housing stock owned by the municipality of Tallinn diminished from 63 per cent in 1995 to 6 per cent in 1999 (Kährik 2002). Privatisation in the Czech Republic has been less intensive reducing the former public housing to one half by 2001. In inner Prague, local governments started to sell some of the inner city apartments that remained in their ownership after restitution and individual flats have been offered for sale in housing estates.

Budapest provides a good example of flat privatisation and its consequences for neighbourhood change. Between 1990 and 1994, about two-thirds of former state dwellings were privatised in Budapest and great majority of them for a negligible part of their market value (see Kovács 1998; Bodnár 2001). The results of privatisation had a distinctive spatial pattern. While nearly all dwellings were sold in attractive and prestigious locations, it reached only 10–20 per cent in poor inner-city areas (Kovács 1998). Despite the low price, low-income people concentrated in eastern to southern inner-city areas could not afford to buy and were not interested in the purchase of dilapidated properties in undesirable neighbourhoods.

Huge discounts on the price mean that those who privatised dwellings in attractive locations could realise immense capital gains through sales or renting-out acquired property. Many people calculated these gains when they made decisions whether to purchase or not. Later gains from lease or sale of privatised flats allowed them to purchase or build new suburban homes. Their voluntary displacement while leaving the inner city provided them with an opportunity to capitalise the rent gap for their own pockets. Interestingly, flat privatisation in inner Budapest has contributed to suburban development while leaving the inner city in an uneasy situation.

The different methods of privatisation produce distinct ownership patterns within inner-city neighbourhoods that influence the pathways of neighbourhood change. Inner Prague is dominated by private owners of whole buildings, accompanied by local authority ownership of selected houses and a smaller share of owners of individual apartments. While some neighbourhoods in inner Budapest have very fragmented ownership of individual flats due to intensive privatisation, others still have large shares of local authority owned rental housing. In Tallinn, nearly all inner-city housing is in private ownership, whether it is restituted private rental stock, owner-occupied apartments or privately owned single-family villas. With regard to gentrification, restitution provided conditions for concentrated institutional investment and property refurbishment leading to gentrification. Fragmented ownership after flat privatisation has provided an obstacle for developers wishing to refurbish whole properties but in desirable places it can lead to a gradual physical revitalisation including population change.

Expatriates and local yuppies

The question remains as to whether post-communist cities provide new containers for the class fractions which have provided the demand for gentrifiable properties in the west. The case studies of three post-communist cities in this chapter show that there is certainly a growing demand for inner-city housing. In Prague, this demand is often associated with expatriates — western foreigners that arrived to the city with their employers. There is a clear link between the establishment of producer services that are the key institutional infrastructure linking the Czech Republic to the wider global economy allowing western companies to exploit emerging markets, and the demand of their well-paid young employees, with their preference for urban living. The highest spatial concentration of expatriates is in upper status villa neighbourhoods in the north-western segment of Prague 6. However, large numbers also concentrate in city centre and some adjacent inner-city areas, such as Vinohrady. As well as the ex-pats there are a growing number of local 'yuppies' most of whom prefer new condominiums as well as some older city quarters contributing to their gentrification.

The gentrifiers in Tallin's Kadriorg are young, well-educated, successful professionals of Estonian (compared to Russian) origin living as singles or couples without children. The presence of foreigners is not strong, as they are more spatially dispersed with a stronger presence in the Old Town, where change is, however, dominated by commercial building developments. Despite the strong internationalisation of Tallinn, the number of foreigners is not comparable with Prague where they form a distinct cluster in urban space and visibly impact on urban change in a particular neighbourhood. Budapest is a more tricky case. The city centre is full of the new rich showing conspicuous consumption habits (Bodnár 2001). While their places of consumption are clearly identifiable, it is less the case with their homes. As there is no true gentrification in inner Budapest, the question is rather who might be potential gentrifiers and what their alternatives are to inner city housing.

The growth of these professional groups has come about with the move in the economy and polity over the last decade or so. Many people now have opportunities to choose where to live limited only by their purchasing power which is growing for some groups. This is a very different situation from that under communism, when income differences were small and most of the urban population had no other possibility than to accept flats allocated by the authorities. The post-communist transition is characterised by much more pronounced social and income differentials shaped by two distinct but related forces: the transformation of the local economy and wider connections with the global economy.

The progressive edge of local economic restructuring including labour market changes, is associated with globalisation. The rapid liberalisation of local markets and removal of restrictions on foreign trade opened post-communist countries to the forces of global capitalism. Foreign companies established themselves to explore and exploit emerging markets. Major cities became spatial nodes within transforming economies, gateways linking individual countries with the global economy (Drbohlav and Sýkora 1996; Feldman 2000b). The infrastructure for this linkage was provided through the operation of newly established firms in the producer services sector. Well-paid employees of these firms, consisting of both western managers and specialists and a local, usually young labour force with good language and computer skills, form the core of emerging new middle class that is gradually building its presence in post-communist cities. This new middle class is an important social link of local urban life to international corporate culture (Bodnár 2001).

The lifestyle of these people, their consumption habits and presence in public spaces, has already changed the look of certain inner city localities (Temelová and Hrychová 2003). Despite these changes the new middle class is still small and fragile, as Bodnár (2001) warns us in the case of Budapest, its ephemeral visual presence will take some years to materialise in the built environment of the city. Among the new middle classes there is a substantial proportion of younger middle-aged households with children preferring new single-family housing in the city hinterlands. The gentrification of the older inner-city neighbourhoods seems neither universal nor a major residential strategy of the new middle classes, but may become more pronounced in time.

Conclusions

Gentrification is not generally a major factor in the transformations of post-communist cities. Nevertheless, it is significantly changing both the physical and social face of selected areas in many inner city neighbourhoods. Despite being linked to the housing demand of emerging new global middle classes, its realisation depends very much on local property market circumstances. Provided that ownership structures modulated by privatisation are favourable for the involvement of large private capital in housing refurbishment, the character of existing built structures can be rearticulated by developers and investors to meet the demand and realise profits. The pathways of housing privatisation are decisive in this aspect with restitution providing much better conditions than sales of individual flats.

Neighbourhood change through gentrification can be found in major economic centres, where wealth is created due to their role in the global economy and spent on quality housing. Property refurbishment is also evident in medium-sized and small towns, but in these locations it is more often associated with development of commercial properties. There are rare cases of small blocks of old housing that were refurbished and experienced a change of population The scale of such change is so small that it does not constitute neighbourhood change. Certainly, gentrification has not descended the urban hierarchy down to, for example, to small market towns like Český Krumlov in the peripheral area of the Czech Republic, as N. Smith (2002) suggests.

The geography of gentrification is selective, not only at the level of settlement structure but also within cities. Gentrifying areas in post-communist cities are small islands in a wider sea of stagnation, decline as well as other forms of revital-isation. Urban change in post-communist cities has been primarily driven by commercial developments. Within the residential sector, suburbanisation dominates landscapes of post-communist metropolitan areas, whether in Budapest, Prague, Tallinn or other post-communist metropolises (Kok and Kovács 1999; Kährik 2002; Sýkora 1999). Gentrification is not an equal alternative to surbanisation, however, it complements it as an expression of a growing variety of possible lifestyles and housing carriers.

Gentrification in Eastern Europe and in post-communist cities more generally is a result of a global–local interplay of markets in which local policies are embracing changes which attract inward investment and the classes which service these changes. 'New' middle-class gentrifiers are growing from an international economy that is linked to post-communist economies via the infrastructure of advanced services residing in major cities. Their services to an international clientele provide them with good incomes that allow them wider choices within consumption-oriented lifestyles. Beside demand fuelled by internationalisation, the supply of gentrified properties is also highly associated with international investment circles. Major developers are foreign companies that are well aware of profits that can be made on locally small but globally significant housing markets for international executive and professional classes. International property developers and investors have been up to now rather neglected in the gentrification literature. The same applies to foreigners that are members of the international class. Their strong visibility in post-communist urban change is given by the highly unequal income disparity at the individual level and capital strength at the level of property investors.

Post-communist gentrification has had no pioneer phase with little sentiment or desire for inner-city living. The process is driven by utilitarian demand for housing in convenient and pleasant locations close to the places of work for professional elites. On the supply side, it is a property business in a specific niche of urban housing markets. Landscapes of new urban life are being articulated on the stage formed by refurbished buildings emptied of their former content. Local governments support this social upgrading. If gentrification does enter public debate, conservation issues dominate so that displacement and other social consequences have not been considered at all. Households and individuals increasingly live their lives around the market allocation of property in post-communist cities. In tandem with this process politicians suggest that these markets are moving post-communist cities back to what they see as their 'natural state'. It appears that gentrification is progressively seen as an integral part of this adjustment.

Acknowledgements

The author greatly appreciates the advice of Anneli Kährik and Sampo Ruoppila on gentrification in Tallinn.

7 Exploring the substance and style of gentrification

Berlin's 'Prenzlberg'

Matthias Bernt and Andrej Holm

Introduction

'Gentrification' has been a significant topic in urban research for more than forty years according to its chronicling in the west. In the context of Germany and its capital city, social division and economic transformation have also brought changes at the neighbourhood level. This chapter describes the changes in this capital city and considers the changes at the neighbourhood level in Prenzlauer Berg, an area of the old East Berlin and now symptomatic of the gentrification of much of the inner city.

Depending on the researchers' intellectual background, analysis of gentrification has been based either on economic or socio-structural and cultural factors. Though nowadays, such a one-dimensional view is generally regarded as obsolete and researchers have tended to try and incorporate approaches taken by other schools into their own research. However, this has arguably not led to conceptual clarification. In contrast recent attempts to paper over the fundamental cracks between Marxist and liberal, supply-side versus demand-side explanations, and structure versus agency, tended to move discussions even further away from the possibility of reconciliation of these views: a synthesis, that moved 'beyond the positions of economics or culture' (Lees 1994b) has thus far been hard to find.

Apart from these older debates about supply vs demand an important issue remains over the relative generalisablity of the process that has been described as gentrification. As Sýykora in this book shows, gentrification has unfolded in different ways and means in cities that have moved from differing economic systems. Here we pick up on this theme but also consider the differing regulatory and tenurial systems that have affected the rate and distribution of gentrification activity in Berlin and other of the larger German cities. Finally we try to consider the adequacy of explanatory frameworks of gentrification given their origins in cities and countries dominated by stronger sets of property market relations and differing welfare regimes.

International comparative research has generally restricted itself to Australia, the United Kingdom and the United States. In comparing the gentrification of London, New York and Paris, Carpenter and Lees, for example, found that the course of gentrification depended in large part on a range of public policies, planning schemes and subsidies (Carpenter and Lees 1995: 300). The argument that national and regional context are crucial is also supported by a number of other contributions which have highlighted the role of national context in shaping local forms of gentrification activity (Kennedy and Leonard 2001; Lees 1994a; Badcock 1989; Musterd and van Weesep 1991).

With this article we try to push the project to move beyond these established positions further. Our main focus is on an attempt to confront established gentrification theories with a case in East-Berlin, where the framework under which gentrification has occurred is largely different from that of the United States or Great Britain in which the dominant theoretical lines and case studies have been identified and developed. Our main conclusion from this work is a call to embed gentrification research into a more advanced political economy of land and housing markets and an analysis of state intervention which has often been lost sight of in the minutiae of regular and in-depth case studies at the local level.

German research on gentrification

The international debate on gentrification has been picked up by a number of German social scientists. Some have even gone so far as to suggest that gentrification represented 'probably the most thrilling debate of recent years' (Helbrecht 1996: 2). What makes discussion difficult is not only a lack of comparative research at the international level, but also the state of German research on gentrification more generally. Though gentrification has since the late 1980s been seen as a hot topic on the German academic agenda and numerous articles have been written, empirical research was generally characterised by a positivist application of structural and consumption-side theories (Blasius 1993; Falk 1994; Friedrich 2000) and, while production-side explanations were often cited, they were applied much less often.

The reason for this is less national arrogance in the face of important and relevant urban debates, but rather a reaction to the situation in West German cities that appeared to differ so greatly from the conditions described in the United States and United Kingdom in relation to rent and value gaps. This has been due to a range of national characteristics that suggest significant and differing preconditions which may strongly affect the value of considering gentrification as a live topic for German cities, even while interest remained high. A number of local contingencies impact on the probability and nature of gentrification activity in German cities.

In the first place state intervention is much greater than in the west while a much lower degree of income polarisation at a national level and lower ethnic segregation contrast sharply with the US model of neighbourhood dynamics and locales that have been shaped by gentrification processes. Like the United Kingdom race is much less of an issue in urban social relationships and neither has there been the same degree of suburbanisation. Perhaps most important is the differing tenurial structure of Germany's housing stock. With renting forming nearly two-thirds of the stock (36 per cent private, 26 per cent social) (Balchin 1996) many might suggest that opportunities for tenure transfer and gentrification are pronounced.

Germany also differs from the western city model in terms of its traditions of urban planning and an urban culture largely different from that of the United Kingdom and United States which is linked to different attitudes to housing tenure (a distinctive 'tolerance' of renting rather than owning) and the larger degree of state intervention (Häußermann 1983). Traditionally urban planning always aimed on balancing socio-spatial disparities and applied large amounts of public money to prevent segregation. Also, zoning regulations and rent laws did a great deal to level socio-spatial disparities. Social housing, as an example, was for a long time not predominantly directed on the urban poor, but on broad strata of society. As a result segregation in German cities is visibly smaller than in their American or British counterparts.

Due to these special conditions German sociologists and geographers have generally assumed that urban change in their country would be slower, less dramatic and less pronounced than in US cities. Consequentially studies on the upgrading of German inner-city neighbourhoods were nearly exclusively engaged in the socio-cultural aspects of neighbourhood change. Their main focus was on household-types, lifestyles and invasion–succession cycles (Alisch and zum Felde 1990; Blasius 1993; Dangschat 1990; Dangschat and Friedrichs 1988), and with an impressive conscientiousness, phase models were analysed and typologies of actors were improved. The outcome was, however, often disappointing, both for the prediction of these processes and theoretical clarification (Alisch and Dangschat 1996).

These peculiarly German conditions for gentrification changed fundamentally with the reunification of East and West Germany in 1990. As the result of the 'return' of real estate properties to their original owners, or their heirs in the former GDR, a massive turnover of properties was brought about and markets suddenly started to play a previously unheard of role in new urban changes. This 're-commodification' (or what Sýkora in this book has called commercialisation) in the context of post-communist cities, of urban development could, of course, not leave German gentrification research unaffected. Inner cities were visibly upgraded by private capital and the face of the urban landscape changed dramatically. Furthermore, due to massive social changes the pre-conditions emerged on which a wave of gentrification could be expected. What made the issue thorny though, was the fact, that the East German housing stock faced a huge need for investment, although all data (due to the low incomes and a different socio-cultural differentiation in East Germany) showed a clear lack of demand for 'gentrified' housing. Nevertheless, as we show, a combination of local state agency, private capital and an urban culture increasingly celebrating centrality and a new infrastructure of entertainment has managed to overcome these apparent barriers.

Such processes of rapid gentrification, in the early 1990s, were then prophesied for many towns and cities in eastern Germany (e.g. Krätke 1991; Herlyn and Hunger 1994). Yet just a few years later these hypotheses were toned down by empirical investigations which suggested that early waves in cities like Berlin were not matched in less 'central' locations (Harth, Herlyn and Scheller 1996; Rink 1997; Weiske 1996). Harth *et al.* (1996) even went so far as to suggest that gentrification in East Germany would be 'halved' from initial estimates of its proliferation. Following the mid-1990s the view that gentrification was no longer a relevant theme for East German cities became widespread. Recent analyses have now indicated the opposite with gentrification widening its base (Franz 2000; SAS 1999; Friedrich 2000).

The puzzle of Prenzlauer Berg

The most prominent example of this confusion in academic discourse relates to the gentrification of East Berlin's Prenzlauer Berg. This is an old district in the immediate vicinity of the city centre but whose centrality was circumvented by the Berlin Wall and was therefore neglected during the lifetime of East German state socialism. However, following re-unification the area was declared a redevelopment zone ('Sanierungsgebiet'). It is here that our story starts.

It is hard to find another urban district in Germany about which so much has been written in the past ten years as Prenzlauer Berg (Mieterberatung and TOPOS 1995 and Mieterberatung and Stadtforschung 1998; Argus 1997 and 2000; Bernt 1998; Häußermann and Kapphan 2000; Borst and Krätke 2000; Holm 1999 and 2000; Reimann 2000). Moreover, despite many research investigations the only thing German urban researchers appear to agree on is that Prenzlauer Berg has undergone fundamental socio-spatial transformations during the last decade. However, while some scholars have identified a 'gentrification process' taking place in Prenzlauer Berg (Borst and Krätke 2000), others reject this view as too 'one-dimensional' (Häußermann and Kappan 2000: 197) and instead see a 'juxtaposition of upgrading and decline' which will continue for a long time to come (ibid: 177), or even anticipate that gentrification (especially on Helmholtzplatz) will be replaced by devaluation tendencies with the risk of 'social hotspots' forming.

The difficulty of interpreting and explaining recent and future changes in old East Berlin's inner areas suggests that the area, in some sense, exceeds the conceptual and empirical language and indicators of neighbourhood change in the city. This is perplexing but, as the difficulty is due not so much to a lack of quantitative data and research work, but rather the *nature* of the topic, it is a good starting point to discuss what it is that makes gentrification in Prenzlauer Berg so difficult to analyse. An examination of the assumption that Prenzlauer Berg is gentrified can thus not only clarify to what extent the findings of international gentrification research are relevant for a German neighbourhood and clarify the peculiarities of urban change in Germany, but may also advance our understanding of gentrification as a process that is deeply embedded into varying social and economic environments (Van Criekingen and Decroly 2003).

Examining neighbourhood change in Prenzlauer Berg

Our approach in this chapter is perhaps a simple one, to put the confusingly complex situation in Prenzlauer Berg into analytical order. In order to achieve this we framed a series of research questions which drew on conventional definitions of gentrification from the literature to see in what ways gentrification in Prenzlauer Berg converged and differed on these points. We compare these hypotheses with the available data and finally we draw conclusions concerning similarities and peculiarities characterising the changes in Prenzlauer Berg compared to gentrification processes in other countries.

We were concerned with three key assumptions. First, that, if gentrification is understood as a reinvestment process (N. Smith 1996), a verifiable rise ought to occur in investments in the dilapidated housing stock. These investments would have to be spatially concentrated and lead to an increase in the local property market and/or in rental prices. Second, regarding population changes, new household types with a higher social status (particularly in terms of income and formal qualifications) compared to the previous inhabitants would be expected to invade (Ley 1996). As a result an 'enhancement' of the social structure might be expected to occur, this enhancement being a consequence of migration movements. In connection with our first question, these changes would be particularly visible in refurbished buildings. Finally, parallel to the changes observed in the composition of the population and investment, a general shift in cultural discourses about the affected neighbourhood ought to occur, which in the meantime would be likely to acquire a reputation as being 'chic', trendy or a new locus of cultural activity more generally (Zukin 1991). This change in values would be likely to result in a new infrastructure of lifestyle restaurants, boutiques and delicatessens.

The property market and investment behaviour

Starting with the analysis of investment activity in Prenzlauer Berg over the past decade, a number of peculiarities were observed. A central precondition for gentrification – and one which is often taken as a matter of course – is the existence of developed property markets, which have to be in place before properties can start rising in price in a certain area. However, such a market simply did not exist in East Berlin in 1990. The market was only just emerging in Prenzlauer Berg due to the 'return' of real estate to its 'original owners' (in a manner with a marked similarity to that which Sýkora describes in this volume). In the central areas of the old borough, this accounted for some 70–90 per cent of the entire housing stock, leading to its rapid sale (cf. Dieser 1996; Reimann 2000). Since there was no generally accepted land price structure based on rational expectations and experience, the agreed-upon selling prices were largely speculative. Following an unprecedented speculative property boom (cf. Borst and Krätke 2000: 145ff.), prices positively exploded in the early 1990s, sometimes well in excess of €500 per square metre in inner-city areas of old housing. The property market has since noticeably cooled down, with prices for unrefurbished tenement blocks near the city centre dropping to €300–400 per square metre.

The overheating of the property price structure in Berlin in the early 1990s owing to speculation thus led – in contrast to the assumptions in our first question – to prices falling rather than rising over the course of the decade. The development of land prices hence ran against the expectations expressed here. However, this state of affairs is a consequence of the exceptional circumstances of German reunification, which led to a speculative 'bubble' on Berlin's property market, and this point can be expected to become less influential.

Other German peculiarities result from local state intervention. This chiefly concerns direct subsidies for modernisation and repair of unrefurbished housing offered by the government of Berlin which are linked with various rent and occupation obligations for the owners. Links might be seen here between the grant programme for repairs available in cities like London in the 1970s and which were also linked to gentrifrication activity (Hamnett 1973). Before German reunification, urban renewal in West Berlin was financed almost exclusively by public subsidies. However, because of the obviously greater need for renovation in the older East Berlin housing areas and the deep budget crisis in Berlin, this is no longer considered financially possible. For this reason in the course of the 1990s successively fewer funds were made available and the financing of renewal was left for private capital to fill the gaps, a process which was taken on board with relish given the priming effect of the local state and the newly perceived value of the location itself.

Above all, as Table 7.1 indicates, in the early 1990s refurbishment was largely financed by public money; until 1996 the ratio between publicly subsidised and privately financed refurbishment was about 2:1. Since then, public funding has been continuously reduced, and by 1999 the ratio had been reversed with only about a third of (extensive) refurbishment measures being supported by public subsidies, the rest being privately financed. In 2001, following a deep budgetary crisis, subventions were completely cut.

Nevertheless, thanks to the large-scale public subsidies in the early 1990s, around a sixth of the entire housing stock was refurbished using direct public grants. As a result, the local housing market contains a considerable 'welfare segment' where rent development, occupancy and the economic profitability of investment are

Table 7.1 Refurbishment progress in redevelopment zones in Prenzlauer Berg

	No. of dwellings	Modernised	%	Of which subsidised*	%	Of which privately financed	%
1994	32,202	811	2.5	811	100	0	0
1996	32,202	6,718	21	4,215	63	2,503	37
1997	32,202	8,186	25	5,002	61	3,184	39
1999	32,202	12,851	40	6,927	54	5,924	46
2001	32,202	16,938	53	8,536	50.4	8,402	49.6

* Includes subsidised schemes under the programmes 'Soziale Stadterneuerung', 'Stadtweite Maßnahmen', 'LEBE' 'Wohnungspolitische Maßnahmen' (figures taken from S.T.E.R.N., the 20th Report: 36 and the 21st Report: 23, as well as own research)

largely disconnected from market activities – at least for the duration of the grant programmes.

Another, probably more important, peculiarity stems from German tax legislation. The special depreciation possibilities enshrined in the *Fördergebietsgesetz* (Development Zone Act) meant that a considerable share of refurbishment costs for building owners in the 1990s was tax deductible. Until 1996 this form of depreciation allowed up to 50 per cent of refurbishment costs in the first year of investment to be offset against tax, this proportion being reduced to 40 per cent until 1998/9. These high indirect subsidies made refurbishing old housing extremely lucrative for investors with a large taxable income, especially if costs were high and rents low, since the 'costs' of investment could be transformed into tax savings for the partners involved. The lion's share of the yield from letting housing thus mainly resulted from claiming tax benefits, with only a small amount stemming from rental income. As the balance of investment could be evened out by tax advantages, investors could afford to do without high rental income for a while, as well as building in areas where no affluent demand was apparent. Therefore, investment largely took place irrespective of the rents realistically expected after refurbishment, and often irrespective of location.

Encouraged by the possibility of saving tax and due to the uncertainty about good or poor locations, refurbishment was widespread in Prenzlauer Berg. Even the area around Kollwitzplatz, which was generally considered to be especially attractive, did not attract significantly more investment than other districts.

In consequence investment activities show in Prenzlauer Berg a different spatial pattern from that which is traditionally known from international gentrification studies. A 'frontier of profitability' of the type observed in American gentrification areas (N. Smith 1996) has so far not emerged. Instead of having a clear 'frontier', gentrification in Prenzlauer Berg has had a restricted scattering of investment across the neighbourhood.

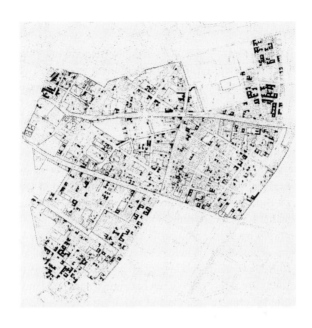

7.1 Refurbished dwellings in Prenzlauer Berg 1996 (data from STERN)

7.2 Refurbished dwellings in Prenzlauer Berg 1999 (data from STERN)

113

Housing market and rent development

Since only a dwindling fraction of dwellings in Prenzlauer Berg are inhabited by their owners, we now direct our attention to the development of rents – which, too, is an area that is strongly affected by federal, specifically east German, and local regulations. Generally speaking, rent inflation in Germany is subject to strict legal control, with the result that rents can only be increased gradually within a certain framework defined by the 'comparative rent system' (*Vergleichsmieten-system*). In addition, various transitional regulations were in force until 1998 in what used to be East Germany (GDR), which again provided narrow scope for rent increases. Furthermore, in 1995 local 'rent caps' were introduced in various city-centre districts in East Berlin which were designed to cap rents for a certain period at a socially acceptable level of around €3–5 per square metre.

What all these regulations have in common is that they provide far more protection for existing than new tenants. Whereas for example rent increases are limited to 20 per cent within three years (assuming no modernisation has taken place), rents for new contracts are freely negotiated between tenant and landlord. Moreover, the caps applying to certain boroughs and which are supposed to apply to all rent contracts are difficult to enforce when premises are rented to new tenants. A study of rent development in unsubsidised buildings hence found that new tenants paid a third more than existing tenants. In contrast to the rent-cap of €4, which generally worked for remaining tenants, new tenants pay an average rent of €5 (ASUM/ Mieterberatung 2003, own calculations), considerably higher than the general price level in both East (€4.5) and West Berlin (€4.4).

Since rent increases among the existing tenants can only be carried out gradually and within certain levels, market development is largely moulded by the development of the rents paid by new tenants. However, according to the *Market Monitor – Real Estate Market 2000* (BBU 2000) in which landlords were asked about the development of rents for new tenants, the areas of old city-centre housing in East Berlin are considered to be especially attractive for investors. Even though incomes in East Berlin are still below that of West Berlin, the level of rent agreed by new tenants is significantly higher than that paid in West Berlin. For example, whereas a maximum of €4.6 per square metre is demanded for refurbished housing in inner-city boroughs in West Berlin such as Charlottenburg, Schöneberg and Wedding, rents of up to €7.5 are paid in districts of old housing in East Berlin like Friedrichshain, Mitte and Prenzlauer Berg. Moreover, rents are tending to rise in these areas, whereas elsewhere in Berlin they are stagnating. Furthermore, East Berlin is characterised by extreme differences in the rent paid by new tenants in refurbished buildings (for example in Prenzlauer Berg they range from €2.6 to €5.9). This can be attributed to the effect of the rent caps in redevelopment and 'milieu protection' areas, which can hardly be enforced for new tenants, and which are far below the market level. Whereas the lower level of this range represents the effect of state rent caps, the upper level reflects the rent increase potential once these regulations expire. Rent in the district of Mitte are already very high, and aspiring market locations in the East Berlin boroughs of Prenzlauer Berg, Pankow and Friedrichshain are not far behind. In all other districts of Berlin, rents are stagnating.

It is important to stress that rising rents are mostly paid by new tenants, who have a weaker legal position than existing tenants. Rent increases – and as a result economic displacement – is here not only dependent on the market position of the locality, which could well be explained with the available knowledge on gentrification. Rather than that it is also to a certain degree determined by the different positions than legal frameworks offered for different types of tenants.

Population changes in the district

During the 1990s, the size of households in Prenzlauer Berg changed fundamentally. The proportion of single-person households rose by almost 20 per cent between 1991 and 2000, and now makes up about 60 per cent of all households, compared to the Berlin average of 48 per cent. The average number of persons per household has thus declined from 2.1 to 1.6, compared to the mean figure of 1.9 persons per household in Berlin in 2000 (2000 micro census). Prenzlauer Berg has developed into a neighbourhood dominated by young singles. In areas of older housing, a considerable decline has also occurred in the number of children and youngsters aged under 18. By contrast, the proportion of those aged 25–44 has risen from a third to over half.

A rising tendency towards higher educational qualifications has also been seen in Prenzlauer Berg. Despite the declining population size, the number of residents with the *Abitur* (higher education matriculation qualification) has increased. Whereas the number of people with solely lower school qualifications has fallen below the 1991 figures, the number of people with the *Abitur* has almost doubled. Prenzlauer Berg now occupies a premier position in this respect, since the average number of people with the *Abitur* in East and West Berlin has only increased by about a third.

A similar tendency is to be seen in the number of people with higher education qualifications. Whereas the number of vocational qualifications has stagnated or even fallen, the number of people with higher education qualifications has almost doubled in the area since 1991. The number of higher education graduates increased between 1991 and 2000 from about 15,500 to almost 35,000 – in other words more than one in four adults in Prenzlauer Berg has completed a degree course. This significant increase in the share of people with higher education sets Prenzlauer Berg apart from other Berlin boroughs.

This upward movement in educational degrees is not yet significantly reflected in income. Households' incomes, which were among the lowest in Berlin in 1991, are still below the East Berlin average – but, given the size of households (Prenzlauer

Table 7.2 Population in Prenzlauer Berg and Berlin by higher education certificate (Abitur)

| | Berlin | | Prenzlauer Berg | |
	No.	Index*	No.	Index*
April 1991	564,000	100	25,400	100
April 1993	654,700	116	31,000	122
April 1995	702,600	125	40,500	160
April 1997	752,400	133	49,500	195
April 1999	775,500	137	47,700	188
April 2000			48,100	189

Source: Berlin Department of Statistics, micro-census 1991–2000, * 1991 = 100

Berg 1.6/East Berlin 1.9), it is apparent that Prenzlauer Berg has reached an average level of prosperity. This apparent normalisation of income in Prenzlauer Berg masks significant differentiation, with a large gap between low and high incomes exceeding the average elsewhere in the city. Whereas nearly one in three households (31.5 per cent) has to make do with a monthly income of less than €700 (compared to the average in East Berlin of 26.97 per cent), 13.08 per cent of households have an income exceeding €1500 (compared to the average in East Berlin of 12.97 per cent; 1999 micro-census: E4), thus high and low earners live 'cheek by jowl'.

To summarise, we can see that the changes to the social structure in Prenzlauer Berg are congruent with the changes to be expected during a process of gentrification. In particular, educational degrees and the income distribution demonstrate a clear differentiation among the local population, indicating a pioneering phase of gentrification and the fact that 'invaders' are living next door to the usually 'displaced'. Moreover, these changes are not due to endogenous developments but are instead the result of enormous internal changes in the population structure of the neighbourhood. With a slightly varying total population of 130,000–140,000, between 1991 and 1999 over 225,000 people moved into and away from the Prenzlauer Berg (Berlin Department of Statistics). Mobility grew continuously; in the second half of the 1990s some 30,000 (about a quarter of the total population in Prenzlauer Berg) moved in or out of the area every year.

These population dynamics are highest where refurbishment has been carried out. Fluctuations are especially prompted by privately financed modernisation. A study of inhabitant structure in privately modernised buildings (Mieterberatung/ TOPOS 1998) revealed that 50 per cent of tenants only moved in following refurbishment. Another study put this figure higher at two-thirds (Häußermann, Holm and Zunzer 2002). The latest survey (ASUM 2003) estimates that more than 75 per cent of tenants have moved out suggesting a staggeringly high level of population displacement.

The rent, ages and household structure and income of new and old tenants differ greatly. Eighty-five per cent of new inhabitants are aged between 18 and 45. Older children as well as seniors are practically non-existent in this group. The majority of new tenants are single-person households. The employment rate is above the local average. Whereas only slight shifts are to be ascertained among existing tenants, the proportions of blue-collar workers, unemployed, pensioners and trainees are especially low among new tenants. By contrast, the relative numbers of self-employed and students are high.

The financial position of newcomers is correspondingly high. Extremely low household incomes of below €500, which in 1997 still accounted for 15 per cent of the population in the area (Argus 1997), have now almost completely disappeared. The occurrence of higher income groups is by contrast above average. As a result, the equivalent income of new tenants weighted by household size is significantly above that of not only remaining tenants but also those moving away and the local average. Because of their higher income, especially new tenants in privately refurbished dwellings can also afford higher rents and the average rent they pay is about €1.5 per square metre above that of existing tenants (Mieter-beratung/TOPOS 1998: 25).

Privately financed refurbishment, which in the 1990s accounted for two-thirds of the total refurbishment volume and which was continuously on the increase, hence clearly contributed to displacing poorer and larger households, which were replaced by smaller, higher-earning households. The changes already evident in the analysis of socio-structural change in the entire district are reflected here in an even more extreme manner. More generally the data shows a close connection between refurbishment, reinvestment decisions and population dynamics which has often been described in the wider gentrification literature (Berry 1985; Marcuse 1986; Dangschat 1988). Privately financed refurbishment can thus be seen as the segment of the local housing market in which gentrification has occurred in a way which strongly resembles that of accounts in the United States.

From Prenzlauer Berg to 'Prenzlberg'

As is well-known from studies of gentrified areas elsewhere, economic upgrading and changes of the social structure in Prenzlauer Berg have also been accompanied by an unmistakable cultural enthusiasm and an intensive media hype. This new

Table 7.3 Average equivalence income by household type (€)

Tenants in unrefurbished dwellings	838
Tenants in privately refurbished dwellings	1,257
Tenants in subsidised refurbished dwellings	1,048
Total population of redevelopment areas	1,051

discourse has celebrated the recent changes and challenges the older images of the neighbourhood. In the 1990s, Prenzlauer Berg was voted the 'funkiest part of town' by the lifestyle media and is currently regarded as the 'liveliest district of Berlin'. Almost all the major German newspapers have published reports on the area, and hardly any Berlin guidebooks can afford not to include a separate chapter on this now 'legendary' borough. Local events such as the opening of new bars by local heroes of the area's bohemian society or the annual Walpurgis Night celebrations receive national media attention and are reported in full detail in the press.

In the 1990s, this cultural boosterism increasingly became the basis for investments in a 'cultural' infrastructure. The blend of cafés, international cuisine, boutiques and delicatessens typical of other gentrified at the global scale can now be found especially around Kollwitzplatz, but recently also on Kastanienallee/ Oderberger Strasse and Lychener Strasse. 'Prenzlauer Berg' has effectively become a brand name which can be found in local names, an apparent aesthetic in the interior design of houses, shops and restaurants. Whereas in the past Berlin pubs were traditionally named after their location ('Dunckerquelle', 'Pappeleck'), the cuisine they served ('Hackepeter'/'Steak Tartare') or the principal ('Antons Bierstübchen'/'Anton's Beer Bar'), these days pub names feature intellectual puns and metaphors to appeal to their patrons' sense of place and consumption of these new spaces ('Frida Kahlo', 'Pasternak', 'Chagall Nr. 1–3', 'Bukowski'). One does not simply eat and drink on Kollwitzplatz; these days one enjoys the 'internation-ality of Alsatian cuisine' in a restaurant where the US President once dined, the lifestyle of the Russian aristocracy, or the feeling of drinking your beer amidst imagined poets and dissidents.

This infrastructure of 'conspicuous consumption' (Beauregard 1986) features a pronounced degree of spatial concentration. With the exception of the area around Hackesche Höfe in Berlin-Mitte and Simon-Dach-Strasse in Friedrichshain, no other place in Berlin contains so many pubs, cafés and restaurants as the area around Kollwitzplatz and its side streets. Figures from the area around Teutoburger Platz, where the pub trade is chiefly concentrated on Oderberger Strasse and Kastanienallee, show the seating already almost equals the total population of all ages in the surrounding blocks (BV Teutoburger Platz) – and is still rising. Yet just in a few streets little is to be seen of this culinary boom. In the blocks surrounding Teutoburger Platz there are just 0.46 pub and restaurant seats per resident, this situation being reflected to the north and south of Lottumstrasse and north of Eberswalder Strasse.

When considering the expansion of catering outlets over time, terms from the American lexicon such as the formation of 'waves', 'beachheads' and 'frontiers' are encountered (N. Smith 1992; Smith 1996; Abu-Lughod 1994b; Smith and Defilippis 1999). Whereas the area around Kollwitzplatz already had large numbers of pubs and restaurants by 1992/3, the roads to the north, east and west of the area (especially Danziger Strasse) were for a long time regarded as frontiers which could hardly be crossed, especially by more expensive restaurants; the few attempts which were made went bankrupt or were demolished. Only recently has this frontier begun to fade, and nowadays restaurants can be found on Helmholtzplatz and on Oderberger Straße/Kastanienallee which do not differ at all from their counterparts on Kollwitzplatz. Kollwitzplatz is now described in listings magazines as humdrum and boring, whereas the adjectives used for Kollwitzplatz five years ago are now being applied to Helmholtzplatz and Oderberger Strasse. The new 'urban frontier' is the railway embankment; everything beyond it is 'Indian territory' (N. Smith, 1996).

Conclusion: A familiar or peculiar brand of gentrification?

To sum up, the most important points regarding gentrification in Prenzlauer Berg are the following. The stock of old housing in the district experienced a considerable increase in investment in the 1990s. Instead of being concentrated on certain areas, this investment was broadly spread across a large area. As a result of state intervention the rental market split and the rents paid by both existing and new, privately refurbished and publicly subsidised households differ greatly. Nevertheless locations have emerged where high rents can be expected for a long time to come. The structure of inhabitants has fundamentally changed and is nowadays dominated by singles and DINKs (double income no kids) with higher educational qualifications. This trend is especially apparent in buildings refurbished with private capital, where new tenants have a much higher disposable income. Real investment in Prenzlauer Berg was accompanied by the district's symbolic upgrading. The myth of Prenzlauer Berg led relatively quickly (sometimes even before the buildings had been refurbished) to investment in a 'cultural infrastructure' with a pronounced spatial concentration belying its significance as an international destination and aspect of Berlin's wider cultural capital and cachet. All these major trends are absolutely congruent with what is generally considered as 'gentrification'.

Nevertheless, important peculiarities remain. Contrary to traditional reports from the United States direct and indirect subsidies resulted in investments being widespread rather than spatially concentrated and the rent increase (at least for existing tenants) is slowed down by a series of regulations. Urban change in Prenzlauer Berg is therefore puzzlingly split. On one hand, in the case of those dwellings where refurbishment is carried out with private money and where the rents for the new tenants are freely negotiated, gentrification and the displacement of poorer households shows classic features in its correspondence with the wider literature. On the other hand, a supply of substandard housing has remained throughout the district for a long period of time which is still being used by lower-income groups. As a result, poorer and wealthier sections of the population are living side by side, delaying the transition from a pioneer phase of gentrification.

119

A similar prolonging of this stage is linked to rent control legislation, which provides some protection for poorer households[1]. Spatial form, style and dynamic of gentrification are obviously different from the United States or the United Kingdom – and the reason for this can be found in the different patterns of home-ownership, in subsidies and rent laws. Prenzlauer Berg is thus certainly another case of gentrification; but one of a special kind.

But, if the aim of an analysis of urban change is not only to see whether the empirical reality fits with existing models, but to understand the actual patterns, dynamics and actors of a particular neighbourhood, the case also shows very clearly that an understanding of regulatory context is crucial. Trying to relate the case to more general scientific discussions, we thus mainly find implications for production-side arguments. In this respect the case of Prenzlauer Berg demonstrates very clearly that the particular features of a neighbourhood cannot be understood without at least some kind of analysis of the reinvestment process on one hand. On the other hand it also points at weaknesses in the current application of this kind of analysis, which often failed to go beyond general arguments and come to terms with the varying conditions under which real housing markets work. In this respect our analysis suggests that production-side arguments should be re-examined at least in two areas. First, the implied assumption that re-investments into the run-down housing stock are mainly conducted because of expectations of rising rents/ housing prices (and that there is therefore a clear link leading from investment to rising prices and displacement) has proved to be simplistic. The reasons why professional landlords took the decision to engage in the renovation of Prenzlauer Berg's dilapitaded dwellings was the availability of public subsidies, not because of rents. The theory that gentrification is caused by a rent-/price-/value gap has therefore to be reworked and embedded into a broader perspective.

Second, the rental income a particular landlord can extract does not only depend on supply and demand in the housing market, but also on legal frameworks that determine how, where and to what extent rents can be increased. As rising rents are seen as the main reason for the economic displacement of poorer households, which is the essence of gentrification, legal frameworks and the power relations between landlords and tenants, that they provide, should gain more attention.

Note

1 However, as these regulations expire after a certain period, the displacement of these residents is at best only postponed, not cancelled.

8 Outside the core

Gentrification in Istanbul

Tolga Islam

Introduction

After decades of gentrification debates, a vast body of literature has been accumulated on the gentrification process in the 'core cities', with an emphasis on London and New York, while little attention has so far been given to the cities outside the centres. One of the major reasons for this neglect is that these core cities went through gentrification much earlier than their counterparts in the periphery, where the middle classes clung to the core for longer (Butler 1995). However, the apparent biases of social geographers, which Ward defines as UK–US ethnocentrism, also played a role in the neglect in that 'too many Anglo-American geographers remain ignorant about processes operating outside of their own immediate cultural context' (1993: 1133). This chapter is one of relatively few studies attempting to fill this gap in the literature. It discusses the process of gentrification in a context outside the core. The chapter begins with a brief discussion on the nature of gentrification in Turkey as distinctive and related to the process described in the west before focusing upon the gentrification process in its major metropolis, Istanbul.

Gentrification in Turkey

In its classic sense, gentrification is a process of housing rehabilitation in which the middle classes move into and renovate old inner and central city housing hitherto occupied by working class and other lower income groups. This can, however, be regarded as too limiting a definition for research focusing on changes in social class in general and neighbourhood change in particular (Ley 1996: 34). In this regard, a broader definition of gentrification that places social change as a central variable in the process will need to incorporate redevelopment (Cybriwsky, Ley and Western 1986) as well as renovation of both commercial (Jones and Varley 1999; Kloosterman and Leun 1999) and residential units in both rural (Thrift 1987; Smith and Phillips 2001) and inner-city areas.

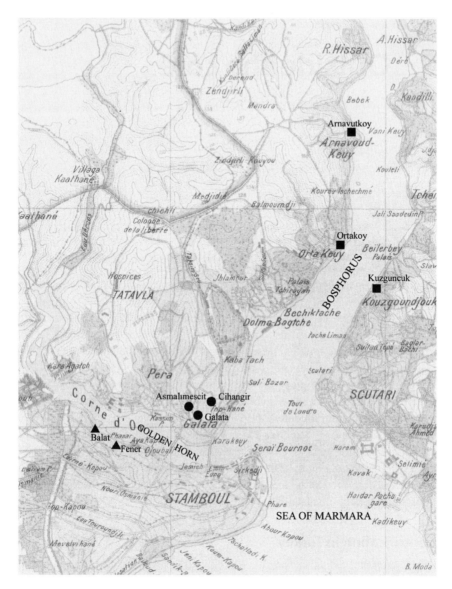

8.1 The gentrified neighbourhoods in Istanbul (Source: 1918 Engineer
Nedjib Map, Atatürk Library if Istanbul Metropolitan Municipality)
■ First wave gentrification
● Second-wave gentrification
▲ Third-wave gentrification

In fact we can often find these diverse aspects of gentrification in Turkey. For example, in Ankara, Turkey's administrative capital, gentrification has taken place through the redevelopment of a series of inner city squatter areas by renewal projects based on models of public and private financing. High-rise apartment blocks are constructed on the land once occupied by one- or two-storey squatter settlements, resulting in both the displacement and replacement of the squatter population by middle- and upper-middle income groups. These renewal projects involve the construction of luxury apartment blocks. The former blocks are donated to the squatter owners to encourage their consent to the project and the latter is sold to the upper-middle and upper classes by which the private construction firms compensate the costs of the former blocks and gain profit.

Two types of displacement are seen in these areas with between 50 per cent and 90 per cent of the original squatter population forced out depending on the areas' proximity to the city centre and prestigious areas (Dundar 2003). Squatter renters are not regarded as the participants of the project and are displaced involuntarily along with a fragment of the squatter owners who are unable to afford the new revenue maintenance costs of the new dwellings they are given. Voluntary displacement is also seen among this latter group, who sell their properties to gain profit.

Cases of rural gentrification can also be seen in Turkey, in a number of villages around the coasts of the Aegean and Mediterranean Sea such as the Behramkale, Adatepe and Yesilyurt villages of Çanakkale. Old houses in close proximity to the sea are bought and renovated by middle and upper-middle classes, coming from Istanbul and other major cities of Turkey, mostly for summer use. Replacement, rather than displacement, is more common in these villages as the local inhabitants mostly consist of home-owners. The main downside of this gentrification is to put these villages under the threat of becoming deserted and isolated areas, except for a small period in summer, since the great majority of gentrifiers leave their dwellings after their holidays end and move to their home towns.

It is in Istanbul, the economic and cultural capital of Turkey, that both commercial and the traditional 'ideal type' of gentrification has taken place. Here we find that much of the dilapidated late nineteenth- and early twentieth-century housing stock within the city bought and renovated by the members of the new middle class. In the remainder of this chapter, I discuss different aspects of these gentrification processes in Istanbul. I begin with a brief reference to the processes forming the background of gentrification in the city and continue with a description of the three waves of gentrification that have taken place citywide. I finally focus on the demographic and lifestyle characteristics of the gentrifiers and their reasons for moving to the case study area of Galata. In this section, I discuss the two necessary preconditions that have come about which have facilitated gentrification in Istanbul. I first explain the processes that have created the potential supply of gentrifiable inner-city housing and then describe the conditions that have produced the pool of potential Istanbulite gentrifiers and their cultural consumption requirements.

The creation of gentrifiable housing

As Beauregard suggests, two processes lead to the formation of potentially gentri-fiable areas: 'the creation of gentrifiable housing' and 'the creation of prior occupants who can easily be displaced or replaced' (1986: 47). The first process has its roots in Istanbul in the late nineteenth and early twentieth centuries. Most of the housing stock in the now gentrifying neighbourhoods belongs to that period. They were at that time inhabited by different ethnic and religious groups; Muslims and more predominantly non-Muslim minorities, notably the Greeks, Jews and Armenians, and – in some cases – European foreigners, both of whom constituted the middle- and upper-income segments of the society.

The second process began with the departure from these neighbourhoods of these dominant population groups. Until the 1940s, almost all the foreigners and significant numbers of minorities left their inner-city habitats due to the loss of economic opportunities that were present in the latter part of the nineteenth century. In the subsequent three decades following the 1940s, the remaining middle- and upper-income minorities left their neighbourhoods, this time disturbed by the political pressures 'to drive the non-Muslim population out' (Keyder 1999a).[1] In both migration waves, these minorities and foreigners left their neighbourhoods by moving out of the country.

This massive middle- and upper-income flight of the minorities coincided with the rapid industrialisation and urbanisation era of the post 1950s that had led to the massive influx into Istanbul of lower-income immigrants coming from the rural parts of Turkey. Although these migrants mostly settled in the squat that they themselves had constructed on the illegally occupied lands in the periphery, some of them also moved into these partly abandoned minority neighbourhoods, which led to the departure of the remaining minorities therein. In the 1960s and 1970s these inner-city areas were dominated by the rural migrants, who lacked the neces-sary resources to afford the maintenance and reinvestment costs of their properties. Hence, social decline was followed by physical decay, which led to further deterio-ration and devaluation. By the 1980s, these old minority neighbourhoods became apt places for gentrification, with the easily 'displaceable' occupants and inexpen-sive housing stock they possess.

The processes that have produced the potentially gentrifiable areas have set one of the conditions for the gentrification of the city. The next is the production of the potential gentry.

The formation of the new gentry: Economic, cultural, demographic and spatial restructuring processes of the post 1980s

The creation of the pool of potential gentrifiers is closely related to 'the production of a new professional and managerial labor force' and 'the cultural and consumption characteristics of part of that group' (Hamnett 1991: 184). The economic, cultural, demographic and spatial restructuring processes that have been taking place in Istanbul since the 1980s will then provide a basis for an understanding of the production of the potential gentry in Istanbul.

The year 1980 was the beginning of a new era for Turkey. The inward-oriented development policies of the former period were replaced with neo-liberal ones, which led to the greater opening of Turkey's economy to world capital flows. The clearest indicators of this aperture were perhaps the rapid increases in the volumes of foreign trade and foreign direct investments (FDIs). Between 1980 and 2001, the volume of imports and exports respectively increased five and ten fold – the former from 7.9 to 41.4 billion dollars and the latter from 2.9 to 31.3 billion dollars (SIS – State Institute of Statistics – 2001; 2002b), while the volume of authorised foreign direct investments expanded twenty-eight fold and reached 2.7 billion dollars in 2001, from 97 million dollars in 1980. The number of foreign capital companies operating in Turkey during the same period increased seventy-five fold, from 78 to 5841 and significant changes occurred in the composition of the FDIs, in that the share of industry fell from 91.5 per cent to 45.7 per cent, while that of services increased around six fold – from 8.5 per cent to 48.3 per cent (www.treasury.gov.tr).

Istanbul alone attracted most of this foreign activity. The city, by itself, accounted for 39.3 per cent of the imports and 46.6 per cent of the exports in the country as of 2001 (SIS 2002b), and hosted 41.8 per cent of the foreign capital and 58.1 per cent of the foreign capital companies as of 1997 (Berkoz 2001) and 95 per cent of the banking and other financial services as of 1999 (Ozdemir 2002). These changes were also reflected in the employment structure of the city. The share of industrial labour force declined slowly from 34.4 per cent in 1980 to 32.2 per cent in 2000 while new service industries increased their employment shares. FIRE (finance, insurance and real estate) services created 100,000 new jobs in each decade and increased their share in Istanbul's labour force from 5.3 per cent in 1980, to 7.1 per cent in 1990 and 8.2 per cent in 2000 (SIS 1983; 1993; 2002a). The media sector went into a boom, especially during the 1990s, and created new employment opportunities in media, advertisement and other related sectors.[2]

New core-like cultural consumption patterns were adapted by the Istanbulites in this liberal political economic climate of the 1980s, in which western values and consumables flowed freely. Indicators of these new lifestyles in the city were the arrival and proliferation of boutiques of world brands, new shopping centres, giant hypermarkets, fast-food chains, ethnic and world cuisine restaurants; bars, discotheques and night-clubs; and perhaps more importantly, the organisation of international festivals of film, theatre, music, jazz and art, hosting more than 2,500 artists and performers and capturing an annual audience of 300,000 (*The Washington Times* 5 December 2000). The latter also provides evidence of the growing numbers of artists in the city.

Demographic changes in the last twenty-five years toward smaller households have reinforced the effects of these new cultural consumption patterns. The average household size in Istanbul decreased from 4.9 in 1975, to 3.9 in 2000 and the number of children per woman at reproductive ages diminished to 41 per cent. One reason for this trend was the rapid increase in education and labour force participation levels among women. While only 2.2 per cent of the females in Istanbul were higher education graduates in 1975, this rate increased four fold, twice as much as the increase in males, and reached to 8.8 per cent by 2000. Similarly, the labour force participation rate of females increased nearly two fold, and reached to 27.3 per cent by 2000, from 14.9 per cent in 1980 (SIS 2002a).

These occupational and cultural restructuring processes are also accompanied by spatial transformations within the city. The city municipality implemented a series of urban renewal projects including the demolition of large areas of historic housing to open new boulevards in the central and inner city. The Istiklal Street in Beyoglu – the historic centre, was pedestrianised by transferring its traffic to these new constructed routes and became the focal point of cultural and leisure activities. By the same token, the flourishing service jobs are concentrated in the new central business districts that had emerged in the north of the historic centre along the Levent–Maslak axis (Enlil 2000). The implication for gentrification of this spatial concentration of jobs and – most notably – cultural facilities were to increase the desirability of the historic centre and create a demand for the housing therein.

The proliferation of new professional cohorts and the associated changes in the consumption and reproduction patterns since the 1980s have certainly contributed to the production of a pool of potential gentrifiers in Istanbul. This was, however, not sufficient to generate gentrification on the scale observed in the major core cities. In Istanbul, the pace of labour restructuring has been slow (Keyder 1999a). Naturally, the city has not witnessed the same dramatic rise in professional service jobs as the core. FIRE services, for instance, accounted for only 6.4 per cent of the labour force as of 1985 (SIS 1988), while this rate was 18.2 per cent in London and 17.3 per cent in New York in the same year (Sassen 1991: 199). This pool even diminished in the past few years due to the economic crisis in Turkey; which hit hardest the flourishing service jobs: some 23,000 bankers (*Cumhuriyet* 3 December 2001) and some 3,000 of 12,000 media workers (*The New York Times* 2 April 2001) lost their jobs following the severe economic crisis of February 2001. The accompanying demographic transitions have also been limited among these cohorts: the vast majority of professionals consist of families with children, and hence are more likely to prefer gated compounds (Keyder 1999b).[3]

Successive waves of gentrification in Istanbul

With the realisation of these two necessary conditions for gentrification – the production of the gentrifiable areas and the potential gentrifiers, Istanbul experienced the first signs of gentrification in the early 1980s, around three decades later than the core cities, notably London and New York.[4] This gentrification has taken place in three waves, each in a different region, each with a different motive.

First-wave gentrification

First signs of gentrification in Istanbul are seen in the inner-city neighbourhoods around the coasts of the Bosphorus, namely Kuzguncuk, Arnavutkoy and Ortakoy. It was the late nineteenth- and early twentieth-century two- and three-storey terrace houses – an alternative to the standard middle-class habitat of flats, and the invaluable coastlines nearby that had appealed to the first-wave gentrifiers in the early 1980s.

Gentrification began and proceeded as housing rehabilitation in these three neighbourhoods during the 1980s. However, it has been of a different nature in Ortakoy after 1992, following the reorganisation of Ortakoy Square by the local municipality. The area attracted bars, discotheques, cafés and other leisure activities in such an intense way that it disturbed the residential life and led to the departure of the gentrifiers who had settled there in the past few years (Ergun forthcoming).

In Kuzguncuk and Arnavutkoy, housing rehabilitation continued throughout the 1990s. Gentrification has been gentle in these two coastal neighbourhoods; displacement has been limited; diverse social groups still live side by side. In both neighbourhoods, the physical fabric – or at least the outside appearance – is mostly protected by the help of the Bosphorus Development Law of 1983, which outlawed

8.2 First wave – Kuzoquacuk

127

new construction along the Bosphorus that resulted in the renovation of the existing stock. Gentrification began in Kuzguncuk with the arrival of a well known architect into the neighbourhood in the late 1970s, who was followed by his architect and artist friends (Uzun 2001). 'It was not the artists', on the other hand, 'who blazed the trail and embarked on the gentrification of Arnavutkoy' (Keyder 1999c: 185); but the members of the 'information-intense sectors', probably because of the neighbourhood's easier access to the central business districts.

Second-wave gentrification

With the first-wave still proceeding, a second-wave of gentrification began in the late 1980s in Beyoglu – the historic centre – notably in Cihangir, Galata and Asmalimescit. Typical of these neighbourhoods are the late nineteenth- and early twentieth-century terraced apartment buildings with Bosphorus views and the intense cultural and leisure activities nearby that had emerged following the pedestrianisation of a major axis, Istiklal Street, in 1990. Given their more central location, it might well be expected for the first wave to have taken place in these neighbourhoods, rather than those in the inner city. In the absence of leisure facilities in the core throughout the 1980s, however, those coastal neighbourhoods of the first wave appealed to potential gentrifiers to a greater extent with the higher environmental amenities they had.

8.3 Second wave – Galata

Gentrification acquired a new momentum following the aforementioned revital-isation movements in the Istiklal Street and proceeded in each neighbourhood in a different way. In Asmalimescit, residential and commercial gentrification took place side by side; though the latter proceeded in a more intense way, probably for its greater proximity to Istiklal Street. The area is now under the threat of experiencing the same processes that had occurred in Ortakoy, losing the middle- and upper-middle class residents that it had gained in the last few years, who are largely disturbed by the too much intensification of commercial activities, especially the restaurants, just around their dwellings (Ak 2002 and interviews with gentrifiers in 2002).

Residential gentrification was more prevalent in Galata and Cihangir, albeit at different levels. Gentrification proceeded very slowly and affected only a small track in Galata after almost fifteen years since the first signs of gentrification had been seen. Galata has though a potential to experience gentrification on a more advanced level since it will gain a greater accessibility with the opening of a new metro exit during the following years. In Cihangir, on the other hand, gentrification diffused through at a rapid rate, especially after the mid-1990s; causing sharp increases in house prices and had transformed the neighbourhood into an upper-middle class district by the end of the decade. This divergence occurred between these two nearby neighbourhoods, most probably, due to the differences in their commercial bases. Unlike Cihangir, Galata hosts several industrial workshops operating on the ground floors of the apartment buildings, which greatly disturb the residential life with the pollution, unpleasant smell and potential risks caused by the use of industrial gas tubes they produce.[5]

Third-wave gentrification

In the late 1990s, gentrification spread to one of the poorest areas in the city, to Fener and Balat districts of the Golden Horn. As had happened in all the other gentrifying neighbourhoods, deterioration began in these areas with the replacement of middle-income minority groups by the lower status rural in-migrants after the 1950s. Many buildings initially built for single families were cut up into small units and became cheap rental stock for the poor. The already poor social and economic conditions worsened when trade activity was cut by the relocation of the industry on the Golden Horn during the 1980s.

The two neighbourhoods, with their inner-city location on the waterfront and late nineteenth- and early twentieth-century two or three storey terrace houses, have characteristics similar to the first-wave districts. There is, however, a gap of twenty years between the two waves due to a number of barriers against gentrifica-tion in Fener and Balat, including the existence of a very poor and religious population in and around the two neighbourhoods[6] and the presence of unpleasant smells caused by industrial pollution, which ended following the transfer of

8.4 Third wave – Balat

industrial uses and cleaning projects in the waters of the Golden Horn in the latter part of the 1990s.

These negative factors are mitigated in the late 1990s with the announcement of the rehabilitation of Fener and Balat districts programme, a 7 million euro investment project funded by the European Commission and implemented in partnership with Fatih Municipality that primarily involves the rehabilitation of around 200 selected houses (around one-seventh of the total housing stock in the two neighbourhoods) between 2004 and 2006. Although credits are only to be given to the existing home owners that have bought their properties before 1997, this promise of a multi-million euro institutional investment became an appropriate recipe for gentrification: it acted as a catalyst and helped gentrification occur earlier than it would without any outside interference. The dynamics of the third-wave are therefore different from the gentrification of earlier decades which has taken place in a more spontaneous way. Here, institutions, whether they intend to or not,[7] can well be seen as the main instigators of gentrification, given that 'institutional involvement' has been prior to gentrification[8] and gentrifiers were aware of the programme when they moved in (Islam forthcoming).

Gentrifiers

I earlier described the processes that have created the pool of potential Istanbulite gentrifiers on a city level analysis. Here, I draw the social profiles of a fragment from that pool on a neighbourhood level study. The data I use here is based on a survey carried out in the summer of 2002 in a case study area in Galata,[9] one of the second-wave neighbourhoods, with twenty-three homeowner gentrifiers – which I estimate constituted between a range of one-third or half of the total set of owner occupier gentrifiers in the region.[10] I used snowball sampling during the surveys since it was not possible to differentiate the dwellings of gentrifiers from those of non-gentrifiers with an 'eyeball survey': in Galata renovation had mostly taken place inside the dwellings of gentrifiers as their apartment buildings mostly contained many low-income residents, who lacked the necessary financial means to participate in the renovation of the whole façade. To minimise the shortcomings of snowball sampling, I began with different links and kept conducting surveys until it came to a point where respondents began to suggest the same links. In the following discussion, I will present answers to the questions of who the gentrifiers in Galata are, to what extent they conform with the ideal gentrifier profile and why they gentrify.

Gentrifiers have similar social backgrounds across the world , however, distinguishing they are within their cultural context (Carpenter and Lees 1995: 288). They are the highly educated professional cohorts who generally consist of singles and childless couples mostly in their youthful or early mature lifecycle stages (Ley 1996; Butler 1997; Munt 1987; Gale 1978; Hamnett and Williams 1980; Hamnett 2003b). The Galata gentrifiers conform with this general profile in many respects.

They are highly educated: all the respondents and their partners had at least an undergraduate university degree; six of the twenty-three respondents (26 per cent) also possessed masters or doctors degrees. Almost all the respondents knew at least one foreign language at an advanced level, one-third of whom knew two or more.

The members of a 'cultural middle class', which Ley defines as the 'professionals in the arts and applied arts, the media, teaching and social services' (1996: 15), were heavily represented among the gentrifiers: 77 per cent of the respondents belonged to this group. Architects and journalists within this cohort, who constituted 42 per cent of the total respondents, played a central role in the gentrification of Galata, probably because of their greater sensitivity to the historic value of the neighbourhood. This cultural middle class also had similar political affiliations with their counterparts found elsewhere: 83 per cent of the respondents supported leftist parties, while none showed tendencies to rightist parties (see Ley 1994 and Butler 1995 for a discussion about the politics of the cultural middle-class gentrifiers).

The managerial and financial cohorts, who are supposed to enter the gentrification cycle 'in its final stage' (Ley 1996: 193), were absent in the neighbourhood. This is one indicator that shows the premature level of gentrification in Galata. These groups are well represented in the other gentrified neighbourhoods in the city like Cihangir (Uzun 2001) and Arnavutkoy (Keyder 1999c), where the process proceeds on a more advanced level.

The respondents appear to be older than the gentrifier prototype of households who are 'in the youthful or early mature stages of lifecycle' (Hamnett and Williams 1980: 473): almost half of them were over fifty and 74 per cent over forty.

The more mature generations' greater representation among the gentrifiers is not only specific to Galata; similar results are also reported in other gentrified neighbourhoods in Istanbul.[11] This can be partly attributed to the lower levels of participation of younger cohorts to the Turkish housing market: younger Turks tend to continue living with their parents until they get married. Moreover, it is rather difficult for the younger generations to afford to buy a house since there are no mortgage institutions to give long-term credits and 'hence individual home-ownership is either directly financed by private savings or by short-term commercial and suppliers' credit' (Oncu 1997: 71).

The household structures of the gentrifiers also conform to the ideal gentrifier profile drawn from single households and childless couples: only four of the twenty-two households had children, each had one child living with them; which was either for the reason that younger cohorts postponed childbearing or the children of the mature gentrifiers had grown up and left their family homes. The average household size of the twenty-two gentrifiers was 1.86, less than half of the 2000 citywide average of 3.9 and the percentage of single and two-person households among gentrifiers was around four times as many as that of the citywide average. Changing gender composition of the labour force was also reflected in the occupational structure of the gentrifiers. Almost all the female respondents (and the partners of male respondents) in Galata were economically active; which is significant compared to the 2000 citywide women labour force participation rates of 27 per cent. There was also a strong association between partners working in the same sector.

Perhaps the clearest indicator that shows the distinction of gentrifiers in Galata from other social groups in the city was the high rates of cohabiting (18 per cent) or other non-family households (4.5 per cent), regarded as a radical attitude in a Muslim society. This high incidence of non-traditional household composition, which is also common in other gentrified districts across the world (see Butler 1997, for the case of Hackney, London) is one example of how significant the changing cultural and demographic values and lifestyles are in the formation of gentrifiers. It also suggests that gentrifiers conform to 'global' lifestyles and are less tied to religious ties or cultural common rules than other social groups, including the traditional middle classes, in the city.

The respondents were asked to rank the nine possible reasons for moving into Galata, first from unimportant to important and then from one to nine in order of importance. The desire to live in an old house or environment and being near to cultural and leisure activities were cited as the most important two factors for moving in. They received the largest number of 'important' (100 per cent) and 'very important' (65 per cent) responses. The respondents gave a greater emphasis on the former factor, which they ranked first in importance almost three times as many as the latter. This shows the aesthetic appeal of late nineteenth- and early twentieth-century housing and the historic Galata Tower to the gentrifiers.

The lifestyles of the respondents explain why being in close proximity to cultural amenities was of considerable importance to the gentrifiers: nineteen of the twenty-three respondents attended the cultural or leisure activities in Istiklal Street, the cultural axis nearby, for at least once a week, fourteen of them more than once. Moreover, 74 per cent of them ate dinner out at least once a week, 43 per cent more than once. This also demonstrates the low levels of household production among the gentrifiers. The respondents' cultural orientation is another indicator that illustrates their difference from the 'old middle classes' who live a more traditional life. It also shows how important the revitalisation movements taking place in Istiklal Street since the 1990s are on the gentrification process of Galata.

The factors ranked as third and fourth in importance were respectively the scenery and the reasonable house prices: both were considered as important by 87 per cent of the gentrifiers while the former was ranked first in importance more than two times as many as the latter, which is hardly surprising given the magnificent Bosphorus viewpoints that the neighbourhood has. The economic factor of reasonable house prices is preceded by three cultural factors in the ranking. This, together with the fact that the other economic factor of regarding house purchase as an investment for future is identified among the least important reasons, suggests that cultural preferences played a more central role than economic reasons in the respondents' decision to gentrify.

Ranked as fifth in importance, a relatively low importance was given to proximity to work. However, this is not revealed in the employment patterns of the gentrifiers: 83 per cent of the respondents who worked had jobs within walking distance of their homes; around one-third of this group use their homes as offices. Social mix, ranked as sixth in importance, was not identified as a significant factor by the respondents. The interviewees were indeed mostly neutral to the idea of living side by side with lower status groups; they neither sought it nor felt discomfort. The respondents cited 'the presence of friends and relatives in the neighbourhood' among the least important factors in their decision to gentrify, albeit over half of them (52 per cent) had friends in Galata before they moved in.[12]

Conclusion

Istanbul has been experiencing three waves of gentrification in the past twenty-five years. First signs of gentrification are seen in the Bosphorus in the early 1980s, which is followed a decade later by a second-wave in Beyoglu, and a recently sparked third-wave in the Golden Horn. Despite their geographical diversity, the gentrified localities are similar in that they all are the former minority neighbourhoods that contain a specific housing stock, namely late nineteenth- and early twentieth-century row houses or apartment buildings with distinct environmental amenities like nearby shorelines or views of the sea.

The analysis of the gentrification of all three waves has identified the importance of local factors on the gentrification process. Each wave started with a different dynamic: it was the high environmental amenities in the first wave, intense cultural and leisure activities in the second and an institutional investment project in the third that are the driving forces. It is again because of the local differences that the rapidity and extent of gentrification varies between and within (i.e. in the second wave between Galata and Cihangir) the three waves.

Institutions, local authorities or other non-profit organisations, have played a major role in the constitution of these local contextualities. Their influence is particularly felt in the third wave, where the announcement of a multi-million euro rehabilitation programme into Fener and Balat proved an appropriate recipe for gentrification. Albeit to a lesser extent, institutional intervention is also seen in the second wave, where pedestrianisation of a major axis by the city municipality gave start to the revitalisation movements in the historic core, and also in the first wave, where legislation helped to preserve the old houses and in Ortakoy a renewal project by the local municipality caused a shift in the structure of gentrification.

It is in the analysis of the gentrifiers that we move beyond these local factors and see the global forces behind. The Istanbulite gentrifiers are the products of the same occupational, cultural and demographic restructuring processes that have taken place across the globalising cities of the 1980s. This is highlighted in the case study in Galata. The Galata gentrifiers, except for being a little older, are in great conformity with the gentrifiers across the world: they are highly educated singles and childless couples that largely belong to the cultural middle class. In some respects, the characteristics that unite the gentrifiers in Galata with their global counterparts also distinguishes them from the traditional middle classes and other social groups in the city (i.e. high rates of cohabiting couples). It is also revealed from this study that, the Galata gentrifiers are largely affected by cultural factors, namely the historic environment, proximity to cultural facilities and the scenery, rather than economic reasons, in their decision to gentrify.

I have sought, in this chapter, to demonstrate how gentrification, a process widely known as a core city phenomenon, has taken place in Istanbul. Gentrification started here around three decades later than its counterparts, notably London and New York, and has mostly been modest and on a lower scale. Little divergence is, however, observed between Istanbul and the core with respect to the nature of gentrification: in both contexts gentrification has largely taken place as the rehabilitation of old inner-city housing by similar social groups. The differences are therefore not a matter of kind, as Ward (1993) states, as in the case between the core world and Latin America, rather they are a matter of degree, time, rapidity and scale.

Notes

1 Among the ideological factors that had driven the middle and upper-middle class minorities out were the imposition of an enormous wealth levy on non-Muslim businessmen of the city in 1942, the riot which destroyed Greek property in 1955 – related to the Cyprus conflict between Turkey and Greece, and the legislation requiring the departure of those with Greek citizenship

in 1964. This political environment mostly affected Greek citizens. Jews, on the other hand, had generally left their habitats following the the establishment of the state of Israel in 1948 and its offering citizenship to Jews across the world.

2 From one state-run black and white TV channel in 1982, there are now more than twenty national TV channels, almost all of which broadcast from Istanbul. In the 1998 OECD report on communications, the Turkish radio-TV sector took the lead between 1995 and 1997 in the development of this sector, showing an increase of 24.3 per cent, more than seven times as much as the average increase of 3.4 per cent in OECD during that period (cited in http://www.mfa.gov.tr/grupc/cj/cje/07.htm). The printed media also showed an expansion; one indicator is the increase in the number of magazines published, which reached to 110 in 1999, from twenty in 1990.

3 Among the pool of potential gentrifiers, the shortage in the supply of professional service workers has a greater importance than that of the cultural middle class cohorts in the explanation of the relatively lower levels of gentrification in Istanbul compared to the core. Since the latter group usually plays a pioneering role on the eve of the gentrification process, they do not affect the scale of the process as much as the former group.

The shortage in the supply of potential gentrifiers, I argue, is the primary reason for the relatively low levels of gentrification in the city but other factors – albeit subsidiary – also exist, including the absence of mortgage institutions to finance housing, large scale developers' distance to the gentrification market, the Turkish middle classes' heavy reliance on private cars, heavy bureaucratic procedures required to renovate historic buildings and absence of any government policies to encourage gentrification.

4 Gentrification in London and New York began in the 1950s and 1960s, proceeded rapidly during the 1970s and was almost complete in many parts of the two cities by the 1980s (Carpenter and Lees 1995; Smith 1996).

5 Cihangir has further advantages compared to Galata such as the better viewpoints, closer proximity to both Istiklal Street and Taksim Square – the hub of transport links and the wider roads that are more accessible by cars – which is an important factor given the heavy reliance of middle and especially upper-middle classes on private transport.

6 See Ley (1996: 107) for discussion of the relation between gentrification and being near to poor and religious neighbourhoods.

7 The aim of the rehabilitation programme, on the other hand, is as in the title of S. Williams (2000), 'rehabilitation not gentrification', that is 'to improve the economic and social life of the inhabitants of Fener and Balat, as final beneficiaries' Press release of representation of the European Commission to Turkey (2003, March 5), online. Available HTTP: http://www.deltur.cec.eu.int/english/fener-balat-en.rtf (01 September 2003). Indeed, there are some measures in the programme to prevent displacement and replacement, such as rent controls and prohibition of sales for around five years in those 200 buildings to be renovated by the programme. Although they may help to delay – rather than prevent – displacement and replacement in these selected 200 houses for a certain period, these measures say nothing about hundreds of others that are not included to the programme. Given the presence of 60 per cent rates of renters in the area (*Étude sur la réhabilitation des quartiers de Balat et Fener à Istanbul* 1998), the scale of displacement is likely to be high once gentrification moves from the current initial levels to more mature stages – which has a potential to occur especially after the completion of the rehabilitation of 200 houses by 2006 (Islam forthcoming).

8 This also contradicts to the argument put forward by Munt that 'gentrification starts prior to institutional involvement' (1987: 1178).

9 Galata is used here to refer to the area located just around the historic Galata Tower and along its eastern axis, where residential units are more prevalent, notably the Serdar'i Ekrem Street and the axes parallel to it. Dogan Apartment – the three blocks containing around fifty dwellings, which experiences gentrification on a much more advanced level than the whole neighbourhood, is excluded from the study to have a clear picture of the gentrification taking place neighbourhoodwide.

10 The full results of this survey can be found in Islam (2003a) and another version of it is also available in Islam (2003b).

11 Uzun reports that the mean ages of the household gentrifiers and their spouses are respectively 47.5 and 44.9 in Cihangir and 50.9 and 44 in Kuzguncuk (2001: 130).

12 The desire to live in a house was the factor identified as the least important by the respondents: only two of them were living in houses; both of whom however stated it as the most important second factor for moving in. Indeed, this preference was mostly irrelevant for the gentrifiers in Galata since the vast majority of the building stock consisted of apartment buildings. It is, however, likely to have a far greater importance on the first and third wave gentrification that has taken place in houses.

9 Gentrification and neighbourhood dynamics in Japan

The case of Kyoto

Yoshihiro Fujitsuka

Introduction

Gentrification is a well-known phenomenon in western countries but less has been said about the cities of Southeast Asia where urban and neighbourhood processes offer significant variations. However, the inner-city areas of East Asian countries, especially Japan, have also experienced similar processes and upward neighbourhood trajectories. World cities, like Tokyo, have been identified as primary sites of gentrification activity given their location within a 'space of flows' and as locations wherein a growth of service functions to administer their status in the global economic context. Some writers have already commented that the gentrification in Tokyo (Cybriwsky 1998; Sassen 1991) is characterised by a movement of young professionals to traditional housing in the *shitamachi*, or inner city and relatively poor areas.

In fact gathering information on gentrification in Japan is very difficult. In terms of English-language research there have been very few studies and the issue has not received much coverage by Japanese academics. This chapter therefore examines the characteristics of Japanese gentrification using the case of Kyoto, Japan's ancient capital. The case study is used as an example of the gentrification found across other Japanese cities. The chapter asks, what characterises the gentrification process in these cities and how may it be distinguished from a broadly western conception of the process.

There are several broad characteristics of urban environments that have led to gentrification in East Asian countries. First, most traditional urban houses, for example, the traditional Korean urban house, Hanoak or shophouse, in Southeast Asian cities, are often small and low-rise. The Hanoak are only one storey because of the unique Korean floor heating system known as ondol. These units do not have enough rooms for multiple families to live in one house. In areas where market pressure has increased these units have only become available for better-paid dwellers. In contrast, most shophouses in Singapore were overcrowded and the small size of traditional townhouses meant that they had to be demolished and superseded by new larger residential buildings where real-estate markets have escalated.

A second feature of the region is the construction of large new residential buildings, controlled not by unified design, but by those heights and ratios of total floor space to site area, which are maximised in areas of acute land costs. Because of these pressures the historical landscapes of many of the inner cities have been lost or totally changed. In the case of 'moon village' in Seoul, high-rise condomin-iums have been constructed where many traditional but deteriorated houses were once concentrated. Like the slum clearance and redevelopment of many western cities former residents found themselves displaced and were moved into temporary accommodation during the redevelopment; however, they could not afford to live in new condominiums after their construction (Gelezeau 1997). This illustrates the role redevelopment plays in transforming areas, with former poorer inhabitants being displaced to make way for the present affluent inhabitants. However, some East-Asian countries, such as China, have attempted to put ameliorative policies in place where municipal governments have sometimes been requested to pay attention to the negative effects of gentrification by promoting urban renewal which is more socially equitable (Qiu 2002).

A further feature of East-Asian cities is the traditional houses of urban areas which have increasingly been preserved since the 1980s. In the case of Chinatown in Singapore many shophouses were demolished to build large condominiums. Since 1986, however, the government decided to start preserving these traditional urban houses in four communities, and most of them are occupied by fashionable shops and restaurants. Unfortunately, this policy caused many former inhabitants to lose their houses resulting in the break-up of local communities (Yuan *et al.* 1998). In Seoul the municipal government created a policy to preserve traditional urban housing for foreign sightseers during the Seoul Olympics in 1988. Kahoedong, a feudal upper-class community, was preserved, but the regulations were strict and affluent households abandoned the district to maintain their own houses, resulting in the deterioration of the district. With the deregulation of height restrictions from ten to sixteen metres in 1994, the construction of higher buildings became possible, and new residents came to live there (Kim 1997). In all these stories of redevelopment, new high-rise buildings have generally supplanted older architectural styles and indigenous communities, in common with many western cities. As a preservationist movement has grown, often linked to tourism and local economic development, this has also promoted the preservation of historical houses which has attracted affluent households.

The characteristics of Japanese inner cities

The conditions of Japanese inner cities differ from those found in British and American inner cities. The concentration of political, economic and cultural functions in the Tokyo metropolitan area limits inner-city problems, but inner-city problems appear in six other major cities including Osaka and Kobe (Narita 1995). The physical decay of the residential area built after the war, the downsizing and depression of economic activities, decreasing population and aging society are some examples of problems found there. These problems are not remarkable in other major cities such as Sapporo, Sendai, Hiroshima and Fukuoka. In Tokyo, inner-city problems, such as physical deterioration and aging exist in the Eastern and Southern wards of Taito, Sumida, Arakawa, Oota and Shinagawa (Takahashi 1992); however, they are not considered serious because of the relative social and economical equality of the inhabitants in the communities. If this restraint factor becomes weak, for example, by increasing the number of new immigrants from Asian countries, the inner-city problems of Tokyo are likely to become actualised (Narita 1999).

Intense competition for land and dwellings has pushed prices in Tokyo up to some of the highest in the world in the 1980s (Sassen 1991). However, property prices have been decreasing during the continuing economic slump that has led to high rates of mortgage arrears and indebtedness. Japan has around 60 per cent home-ownership, but this rate has been decreasing slightly since the late 1990s because of uncertainties regarding land values (Forrest *et al.* 2003).

The decline of the traditional townhouse and the construction of condominiums

Most Japanese houses are made of wood and are generally one or two storeys. In fact, most houses in the inner cities are relatively small, with a capacity for only one or two families. In most Japanese cities, rows of houses in the inner-city areas were burnt down during World War II. However, Kyoto was not as severely damaged as other cities during the war. Rows of historic houses, made of traditional materials, remained intact in the inner-city area. This paved the way for their demolition for redevelopment (Table 9.1) as small-scale houses were replaced by modern apartment buildings or condominiums.

The booming economic expansion of the 1980s enabled real estate companies to make large investments of capital in the inner-city area. Speculators bought inner-city properties and demolished houses for redevelopment resulting in the loss of a significant number of historic houses. In 1978 pre-war wooden houses made up more than 50 per cent of Kyoto's inner city housing (Table 9.1), but the lack of laws protecting such sites, combined with the redevelopment caused this number to drop drastically in favour of large buildings.

Table 9.1 The percentage of wooden houses in inner-city areas of four large cities in Japan

Year	1978	1983	1988	1993	1998
Tokyo wooden houses	24.0	18.0	14.7	12.0	10.3
prior to 1945	4.8	3.2	1.9	1.2	0.8
Osaka wooden houses	50.2	47.2	35.1	29.1	27.4
prior to 1945	19.6	15.5	10.6	7.2	5.3
Nagoya wooden houses	50.3	37.1	33.4	25.6	20.0
prior to 1945	28.7	27.7	20.9	19.3	16.2
Kyoto wooden houses	73.8	67.5	55.7	45.7	40.3
prior to 1945	54.2	44.0	31.9	23.2	17.0

Note:
The wards of inner city of Tokyo, Osaka, Nagoya categorised by Narita (1987) are used.

The 1980s witnessed skyrocketing land prices and the resulting property speculation led to the construction of a large amount of condominiums. A lot of historic houses were demolished to clear the land for the construction of condominiums, thus displacing many tenants with little in the way of public policy to intervene in this wholesale loss of housing and communities. In Kobe, the construction of condominiums attracted white-collar workers employed in the city centre who preferred good accessibility to the train station (Hayashi 1995). In Osaka, changes of inhabitants through the demolition of pre-war inner-city housing for condominium construction involved gentrifiers who preferred to live in rented apartments near the city centre before child rearing (Nanba 2000).

Large-scale redevelopment attracted affluent dwellers to a waterfront district in Tokyo (Takagi 1994, 1996). Skyscraper condominiums, which have emerged in inner-city areas in recent years, are very popular with the affluent as they provide good accessibility to the city centre, good views from higher floors, high quality spaces and good amenities. The phenomena of the recent population recovery of inner Tokyo differs slightly from the gentrification of western cities because they were induced partly by the supply of public housing (Yabe 2003) and without the eviction of former inhabitants (Sonobe 2001). However, this massive construction of condominiums has led to the almost total turnover of local communities.

Gentrification in Kyoto

The only large city with a large amount of traditional houses remaining in Japan is Kyoto. Since most of the buildings were constructed before the war, they have deteriorated and have not been rehabilitated. In terms of comparison with western cities which generally have a large stock of traditional houses, Kyoto is an appropriate city for the purpose of comparison. The preservation of traditional houses, however, has been less important locally. During the 1980s contemporary policies were not adequate to prevent the demolition for construction of condominiums and apartment buildings which induced gentrification. This section presents the case of Kyoto, and discusses the characteristics of gentrification in Japan.

Early gentrification in Nishijin district

Kyoto is the centre for producing and trading kimonos, traditional formal wear in Japan. Kimono industries are typically traditional manufacturers. Most factories are small and run by families because special techniques are needed to weave and draw unique designs on the kimonos. As kimonos are very expensive, younger people rarely wear them so that the kimono is losing popularity and the industry is in decline.

In the inner city of Kyoto factories are concentrated in two districts, Nishijin district, a historical weaving centre, and the western part of the central area, where Yuzen process dyeing and related factories are located. Both districts are integrated industrial-residential areas, where small factories have accumulated. A lot of factories of the Yuzen dyeing process and the Nishijin weaving moved to an outside area or were closed, and the sites became unoccupied. The reuse of these sites has become an important local urban policy.

The population decreased severely in the inner-city area in the 1980s, causing a change in its social structure. The population, especially the younger generation, was rapidly decreasing in the district because it was difficult for them to inherit properties due to the expensive inheritance tax. As a result the percentage of the elderly and the poor rose. However, there were several districts that had population growth in the central and inner-city areas during the same period. Most of the population growth was caused by the construction of new condominiums and apartment buildings in the Nishijin district (Fujitsuka 1992).

During the early and mid-1980s a number of residential buildings were constructed mainly in the place where the textile industry once stood. They were popular because of the unique neighbouring historical townscape whose streets were lined with neat rows of houses, close distance to the city centre, and the relatively low cost of living. These factors encouraged new types of people to come and live in the district. Most notable was the increase of white-collar workers in the tertiary industries located in the central area. This phenomenon was recognised as a burgeoning of gentrification in the district (Fujitsuka 1992).

Late 1990s gentrification in the central area

In the late 1990s there was a massive population increase in Kyoto's central area. Population grew in most central census tracts and the rate was even higher than

10 per cent in census tracts located in and around the CBD (Figure 9.1). In these areas, a lot of Machiya, Kyoto's traditional townhouse, remain. During the 1980s, however, demand for offices was very high in the CBD; a number of houses had already been demolished and replaced by office buildings (Fujitsuka 1990). In terms of the social structure of population, professional and technical workers increased in several census tracts in the central areas of Kyoto. The four districts of Jouson, Tatsuike, Honnou and Meirin, were selected for a survey (Figure 9.2) to research the characteristics of gentrification, as the change in the amount of professional and technical workers from 1995 to 2000 in small areas was seen as a useful indicator. Five small areas in which the amount of workers increased by more than twenty persons were selected as study areas (Figure 9.3). The background of gentrification is examined and compared to the case of Nishijin during the 1980s in the following sections.

Depreciation of land prices

Many modern condominiums, constructed in the 1980s, were very expensive. Condominiums were often used as the objects of short-term speculation because land values skyrocketed during the bubble period, and then peaked in the beginning of the 1990s. After that, they fell rapidly year-by-year. Japan's economic collapse was the turning point for gentrification: real estate transactions stagnated during the first half of the 1990s. Since land values fell severely, most land was left unoccupied in the 1990s. After the bubble economy burst, disinvestment again became prominent in the inner-city areas of Japanese cities.

over 10%

5 ~ 10%

0 ~ 5%

-5 ~ 0%

-10 ~ -5%

under -10%

9.1 Change of population in Kyoto (1995–2000)

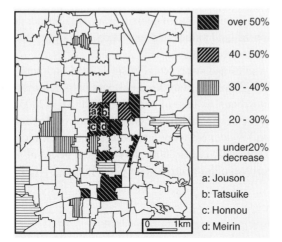

9.2 Increase rate of professional, technical workers in Kyoto (1995–2000)

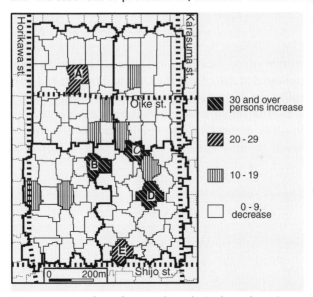

9.3 Increase of professional, technical workers in central Kyoto (1995–2000). (Black bold lines show boundaries of census tracts)

Urban revitalisation became an important policy for stimulating the Japanese economy after the recession. In recent years, the construction of residential buildings was encouraged and newcomers to the inner-city areas increased. The primary factor contributing to the increasing number of new residential buildings in the central area was the substantial depreciation of land prices after the economic collapse. Like many cities in the west, however, gentrification re-emerged after the mid-1990s in Japanese cities, almost at the same time as Smith (1996) relates the process in New York City. A second wave of gentrification was further driven by the preceding depreciation of land values and existence of unoccupied sites which drove the process in inner-city areas.

In the study areas street values had risen severely since 1986 and peaked in 1991 (Figure 9.4). From 1991, however, they became extremely depressed. In 2000 those prices became almost equal to those of 1985. Most of them in 2000 were about one tenth of 1991. As the price of land became cheaper, some of the condominiums were bought as second residences. New gentrifiers were wealthier than pioneer gentrifiers in New York's case (Lees 2000), however the prices of newly gentrified property was lower than older gentrified property in Kyoto's case.

Displacement

In the 1980s the main purpose of developers was to collect small sites and merge them into larger sites (Ueno *et al.* 1991) because such transactions made a large profit. A number of household displacements were evident at this time. There are many Yuzen dyeing factories in the Jouson and Honnou tracts, however, some of them closed in the 1990s (Table 9.2). Since they had a close relationship with wholesalers in Muromachi streets located in the Tatsuike and Meirin tracts the closure of the latter followed in the 1990s. They had to downsize and sell their land, which often resulted in a decline in property values; at worst, some of them became bankrupt, and even the employee dormitory became the object of property sales (Kawabata 1996). The demand for office buildings also decreased in the

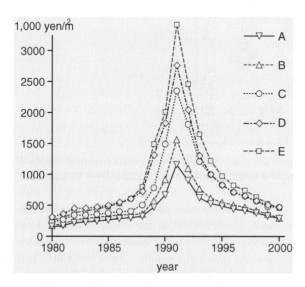

9.4 Changes of street value in research streets in central Kyoto

1990s because of the recession. Many condominiums and apartment buildings constructed on the sites were re-leased or sold by the kimono companies in financial difficulties.

In the study areas there were seven new condominiums. Prior to being condominiums the land had been occupied by eleven houses, two shophouses, four wholesalers, one factory, seven tracts of unoccupied land and three parking lots in 1994. Therefore the construction of condominiums was made possible by the existence of merging these sites. Since the demand for residential buildings increased in the late 1980s, they were built on sites where houses had previously been demolished, therefore, displacement of households increased in the period. The sites from which inhabitants had been displaced were then used as parking lots or remained vacant before the construction of condominiums.

On the other hand, construction of a high rise building creates other problems. Construction of large-scale condominiums caused many problems for the neighbouring inhabitants such as the lack of sunshine, poor ventilation, and electrical interference (Figure 9.5). If a new building has satisfied all legal conditions the client's obligation is only explaining the building's plan to the neighbouring inhabitants before construction can begin. The Kyoto municipal government decided not to negotiate actively in building struggles after the privatisation of agents confirmed the plans. There may be no better way to protect the neighbouring inhabitants' rights.

Characteristics of gentrifiers in Kyoto

The population of the study districts saw an increase in professional and technical, clerical, and retail workers and, despite the decrease in production, process workers and labourers. Table 9.3 serves to illustrate that gentrification is associated with wider population recovery. This section examines the attributes of population in the study small areas (Table 9.4) compared to the case of the 1980s.

In the 1980s most of the people moving into the Nishijin district were from within the city. However, in the latter half of the 1990s, people came mostly from other wards in Kyoto city. The number of people moving from the suburbs was relatively few, judging from the fact that small numbers came from the Kyoto prefecture; the greater part of the newcomers were from inside the city. Thus, the pattern of movement appeared to represent not a back-to-the-city movement but, rather, a stay-in-the-city pattern, similar to the result found by Gale (1980).

Compared with the supply of detached houses or tenement houses, the supply of condominiums and apartment buildings largely resulted in a massive increase in the population of those small areas. Most newcomers tended to live in the new modern condominiums. In terms of dwelling tenure, some were owner-occupied condominiums and others were leased apartment buildings.

Table 9.2 Change of number of textile industry and wholesaler

Textile industry	Kyoto city		Nakagyo ward		Jouson		Tatsuike		Honnou		Meirin	
	factory	worker	factory	worker	factory	worker	factory	worker	factory	worker	factory	worker
1995	4764	23011	844	3924	89	405	22	76	88	357	18	54
2000	3393	14747	646	2606	77	319	18	44	69	242	13	29
1995–2000	-1371	-8264	-198	-1318	-12	-86	-4	-32	-19	-115	-5	-25
Wholesaler	shop	worker	shop	worker	shop	worker	shop	worker	shop	worker	shop	worker
1994	8088	88916	1736	20328	109	657	155	2504	103	807	245	4923
1997	7274	79689	1511	17285	91	569	148	2216	96	750	208	3955
1994–7	-814	-9227	-225	-3043	-18	-88	-7	-288	-7	-57	-37	-968

Table 9.3 Change of workers' occupation (1995–2000)

	Nakagyo ward	Jouson	Tatsuike	Honnou	Meirin	A	B	C	D	E
Professional, technical workers	959	103	66	120	116	23	36	41	20	48
Managers and officials	-664	-39	-7	-18	-15	-1	2	15	-3	0
Clerical and related workers	36	61	27	95	67	36	25	41	12	34
Sales workers	-519	106	32	15	31	23	29	23	-2	29
Service workers	185	56	-5	32	19	4	7	5	6	1
Production process workers and labourers	-1584	-55	-2	-29	-2	-2	9	12	1	6
Others	436	62	10	-9	-3	13	0	0	0	0
Total	-1151	294	121	206	213	96	108	137	34	118

9.5 The sacrifice of neighbouring inhabitants in the Honnou district

In the case of the 1980s, condominium residents were singles and young couples in their late twenties or thirties, and most of the couples had one or two children. It is a feature of Japanese gentrification that the predominant types of residents are families with children (Fujitsuka 1992). In the case of the 1990s the young are also the predominant type of resident, but also the number of relatively older residents increased. Some of the residents are over forty years old, including singles and families with children.

The other types of buildings are leased apartment buildings which consist of single rooms with a private kitchen and bath whose residents are single and mainly students. Since they preferred to live in upgraded comfortable dwellings, landlords have constructed such apartment buildings for them. The phenomenon was thought of as gentrification by landlords, and the residents were marginal gentrifiers (Fujitsuka 1992). In the second half of the 1990s, judging from a large amount of private rented houses, the small area E is an appropriate case, but it also includes condominiums where two or more people live. The size of rooms in apartment buildings is relatively small. Most of the inhabitants were single in their late teens to early thirties.

There has also been a population growth stimulated by this supply of new houses. There are some detached houses in the areas researched, however, their share of population growth is not so large. Most of them are owner-occupied, however in recent years the Machiya Club (2002) has begun to introduce empty traditional houses on the Internet to people who want to live in such dwellings. The number of individual gentrifiers was not so large but has recently begun to increase.

Table 9.4 Characteristics of gentrifiers (1995–2000)

	A	B	C	D	E
Change of household members					
1 person	45	56	30	40	33
2 persons	27	51	24	40	7
3 persons	12	10	17	25	−1
4 persons	2	5	7	12	4
5 and more persons	−1	−1	6	0	1
Address of newcomers in 1995					
Nakagyo ward	29	61	26	27	25
Kyoto city	87	95	74	126	33
Kyoto prefecture	9	19	12	23	4
other prefecture	40	62	36	55	24
Tenure of dwelling (households)					
Owned houses	79	122	76	100	28
detached houses	−2	3	4	2	3
apartment houses, flats	80	118	72	98	25
Private rented houses	1	2	9	18	15
detached houses	−1	1	0	0	−1
apartment houses, flats	2	7	9	18	17
Issued houses	1	−2	0	1	0
Area of floor space in apartment buildings and flats					
floor space per household	68.4	71.3	67.5	69.8	49.1
15 years of age and over					
Employed persons	96	118	108	137	34
Persons attending school	5	7	9	9	3
Change of five year groups					
0–4 years old	15	16	20	26	9
0–4 → 5–9	0	−2	7	10	1
5–9 → 10–14	−1	2	7	5	4
10–14 → 15–19	6	6	7	7	3
15–19 → 20–24	7	9	9	18	11
20–24 → 25–29	22	47	17	23	6
25–29 → 30–34	28	23	26	30	14
30–34 → 35–39	16	29	21	33	8
35–39 → 40–44	12	19	17	22	6
40–44 → 45–49	15	8	13	16	4
45–49 → 50–54	13	25	19	19	1
50–54 → 55–59	9	14	10	15	4
55–59 → 60–64	3	6	6	8	−1
60–64 → 65–69	−1	−1	5	4	2
65–69 → 70–74	2	2	4	9	−1
70–74 → 75–79	−2	2	0	4	1
75– → 80–	−6	−2	1	2	−7

Note:
Area of floor space in apartment buildings and flats is a value which divide difference of total area of floor space by difference of households number.

Concluding remarks

In the introduction to this book it was observed that particular areas of the globe have been little-explored in relation to the gentrification agenda. In many countries the absence of evidence on gentrification should not be viewed as the absence of the process. Gentrification in Japan appears to have started later but bears many of the hallmarks of the process in western cities even while the neighbourhood and city contexts differ in many respects. The absence of many building controls has led to gentrification peculiar in its physical modernity with many of the traditional areas of housing that would often have been attractive to the middle classes in the west, replaced with high rise blocks. This suggests a different gentrification aesthetic which remains to be explored in more detail. In the context of Southeast Asia we may make other observations; there appear to be similarities of the large-scale demolition of inner-city houses and differences of skyrocketing Japanese land values. This chapter ends with three concluding remarks.

Effects of gentrification

Gentrification is limited to some districts where closed factories and wholesalers' shops exist and whose locations are relatively good. Population growth was not prominent in the districts far from the city centre because large residential buildings had not been constructed. Being close to the city centre, gentrification occurs at the place where the sites are available. Inhabitants of residential buildings changed after the 1980s. A wider range of ages and households moved to the central area. There is a possibility of redressing the lopsided situation of the population in terms of macro urban policy.

A key policy issue remains the continuing redevelopment of many cities. While gentrification was seen to bring social life and diversity to already mixed areas in cities like Tokyo (Cybriwsky 1998) the longer-term result has been a social 'rinsing' of neighbourhoods with the displacement of poorer households as well as significant developer interest in the more varied older neighbourhoods. It is not clear, at this stage, what a policy for the amelioration of gentrification in Japanese cities might look like. However, a distinctive challenge resides in the notion that clean lines, modern style and technologically driven design represent clear moves forward all of which pose a distinct challenge to a discourse seeking to celebrate diversity and traditional lifestyles.

Physical shape of gentrification

Gentrification is visible by the construction of high-rise residential buildings such as condominiums and apartments. If this trend continues the local inhabitants and the attractive townscape of historical houses will be lost. There is a danger that the uniqueness of these districts will not be maintained. In recent years, however, reuse or rehabilitation of old historical houses has increased in Kyoto. Some

Gentrification in Spain: an overview

Over the past two decades, Spain's major cities have undergone important economic, geographic, social and political restructuring processes (Fernández Durán 1999; Benach 2000; Monclús 2000; Rodríguez *et al.* 2001). While these efforts reflect the specific features of the situation in Spain, they are also comparable to processes taking place in other urban contexts (Marcuse and Van Kempen 2000; Soja 2000).

In Spain, the gentrification phenomenon began to be identified in the 1990s as a process which, though still incipient (in many cases circumstantial, sporadic and relatively small in scale), quickly gained importance wherever restructuring was going on in the central core of the country's larger cities (Vázquez 1996; Martínez Rigol 2001; Sargatal 2001; V. Rodríguez *et al.* 2002; Vicario and Martínez Monje 2003).

To give an adequate view of gentrification in Spain, two key factors must be borne in mind. The first, which helps to understand how the Spanish context differs from other situations, concerns the historical 'residential model' in Spain (Díaz 1989). Here, as elsewhere in most southern European countries, urban central districts – often nineteenth-century 'new towns' built for the bourgeoisie – still are prime residential areas of the middle and upper-middle classes. Accordingly, the potentially gentrifiable space in major Spanish cities basically concerns only two types of area: (1) the historical centre or 'old quarter', often subject to decades of decline and decay, where the contradictory processes of gentrification and foreign immigration can both be found; and (2) certain working-class and industrial areas which in recent years have come to be seen as 'opportunity' areas as a result of their strategic location and/or of urban planning requirements. Indeed, these are the two areas most focused on in studies of gentrification in Spain – e.g. in Barcelona, the Raval neighbourhood of the city's old quarter (Martínez Rigol 2001; Sargatal 2001) and the industrial working-class district of Poblenou (Gdaniec 2000; Marrero 2003); in Madrid, the old quarter (Vázquez 1996; V. Rodríguez *et al.* 2002); in Bilbao, the old district known as Bilbao La Vieja (Vicario and Martínez Monje 2003).

The second factor, which is crucial for understanding the broad range of situations existing within the urban context of Spain, concerns the role of local government and the nature of urban politics. Here, gentrification, whether ongoing or potential, appears to have made its greatest strides in cities governed by aggressively entrepreneurial councils that have endeavoured to boost their city's competitive position in the new global economy by launching large-scale, flagship urban development projects aimed at restructuring and reimaging the inner city. The clearest example of this is Barcelona (Benach 2000; Monclús 2000), and therefore it is no surprise that most of the literature on gentrification in Spain concerns this city.

In this regard, perhaps a comparison of Madrid and Barcelona will be of help in understanding the diversity of gentrification experiences in Spain. In the case of Madrid (Ayuntamiento de Madrid 2001), the local government's major urban projects, and the interests of the private sector, are concerned with city expansion through new urban developments on the immediate outskirts (e.g. Operation Chamartín and the Prolongation of La Castellana). Therefore, we cannot speak of a 'back to the centre' phenomenon in the capital, either public or private. Consequently, in Madrid gentrification seems to be a highly sporadic process limited to specific areas in the old quarter and driven for the most part by the private sector (V. Rodríguez *et al.* 2002). In the case of Barcelona, however, the situation is quite different. Here, since the mid-1980s, urban regeneration strategies have focused on transforming the urban centre in preparation for the hosting of major international events (the 1992 Olympics and the Universal Forum of Cultures in 2004). Due to territorial limitations, most of the large emblematic projects have taken place in established parts of the central city – namely the old quarter or Ciutat Vella and Poblenou. As a result, gentrification in Barcelona is a more generalised and significant phenomenon than in Madrid. Moreover, it seems to be closely linked to 'new urban policies' for urban regeneration and, therefore, is led and promoted by the local government (Gdaniec 2000; Marrero 2003).

Likewise in Bilbao, gentrification is also closely linked to the development of central city projects, as we shall see in the rest of this chapter.

Bilbao: urban regeneration strategies and their socio-spatial effects

Today, after two decades of swift and devastating de-industrialisation that eventually made of Bilbao a prime example of an 'old industrial city in decline' (Martínez Monje and Vicario 1995), the city has enjoyed a spectacular turnaround and is now in the midst of an extraordinary urban 'renaissance' based on a number of initiatives undertaken in the 1990s to restructure and reimage the city (Rodríguez and Martínez 2001). As a result of such strategies, Bilbao – with the Guggenheim Museum as its hallmark – appears to have become a standard reference for urban studies, or even as *the* model of urban regeneration for other cities affected by decline (Crawford 2001; Sudjic 2002).

However, although the urban regeneration strategies deployed in Bilbao are touted as unique, innovative and exemplary, in fact they are a rather recent continuation of a model first devised years ago by cities such as Pittsburgh, Birmingham and Glasgow (Gómez 1998; Rodríguez and Martínez 2001). Bilbao is, therefore, a significant example of the well-known approach dating from the 1980s where flagship property-led redevelopment projects are central ingredients of urban regeneration (Moulaert *et al.* 2003).

Urban regeneration strategies

In the late 1980s, the Bilbao and Bizkaia councils became convinced of the need to devise and implement planning strategies designed to combat the steady decline begun at the end of the 1970s. This thinking gave rise to the Strategic Plan for the Revitalisation of Metropolitan Bilbao (initiated in 1989 by the Basque government and the provincial council of Bizkaia) and the Master Plan for Bilbao (initiated by the Bilbao city council in 1985).

Generally speaking, the revitalisation strategies adopted in these plans were based on six key elements. First, planners embraced a new vision for the city, a 'post-industrial vision' (Esteban 2000), whose prime objective was 'to secure our place among the "world-class" metropolitan centres' (Diputación Foral de Bizkaia, 2001).

Second, if economic revitalisation was to take place, it would first be necessary to alter the city's image (Gómez 1998). That is, the negative picture associated with de-industrialisation and decline would have to be done away with, and a new image associated with art, culture and advanced services created in its stead – an image of Bilbao as a better-looking, creative, attractive city.

Third, this change in image would be achieved through transformation of the city's physical environment and the use of aggressive place-marketing campaigns (Rodríguez and Martínez 2001). This opened the door to large emblematic projects and riverfront redevelopment undertakings (Abandoibarra, the Isozaki 'Gateway' project), the creation of new cultural facilities (the Guggenheim Museum, Euskalduna Conference and Concert Hall), the construction of new trade fair and conference infrastructures (Bilbao International Exhibition Centre), etc. To ensure that these additions would stand out as symbols of 'renaissance', and that they could be featured in place-marketing campaigns, the authorities resorted to big-name architects for their design: Frank Ghery, Sir Norman Foster, Cesar Pelli, Arata Isozaki, etc.

Fourth, there was a downtown bias to the urban regeneration strategies adopted. The existence of abandoned industrial sites and derelict waterfront areas near the central business district and in the heart of the affluent residential area provided the city council with its first 'opportunity areas': non-residential sites with high potential for commercial property development where flagship schemes could be undertaken (A. Rodríguez et al. 2001). Thus, from the very beginning, the transformation of the downtown area was considered crucial to the attempt to restructure the image and the economy of the city as a whole.

A fifth feature of urban regeneration is the increasing importance of urban leisure economies. Judging by the results obtained to date, the so-called 'Guggenheim effect' seems to have been more successful in attracting visitors and possibly developing a cultural tourist industry than in attracting international capital investment and strategic functions (Gómez and González 2001). Thus, the local authorities have had to rely increasingly on urban revitalisation strategies based on arts, culture and entertainment.

A final feature is the emergence of a new urban governance system (A. Rodríguez *et al.* 2001) in which an increasingly important role is being played by novel agencies such as Bilbao Ría 2000 – an urban development corporation engaged in revitalising degraded areas or industrial zones in decline for new property investment – and Bilbao Metrópoli-30 – a public-private partnership set up to implement the Strategic Plan and operating in fact as a lobbying institution.

Flagship projects and the remaking of the central urban landscape

Once in place, the regeneration strategies devised for Bilbao received a great deal of criticism (Gómez 1998; Esteban 2000; A. Rodríguez *et al.* 2001). Two main issues are of special interest due to the socio-spatial consequences they entail – the predominance of market logic applied to redevelopment projects, and the downtown bias inherent in this regeneration model.

Regarding the first issue, it is clear that the strategists who devised the redevelopment projects see the city basically as a commodity with exchange value; where 'opportunity sites' are said to exist wherever there is room for profitable reinvestment; where the principle of self-financing adhered to by Bilbao Ría 2000 and 'the overwhelming emphasis on efficiency and financial feasibility [have] left the project[s] captive of a short-term return maximization logic that subordinates the strategic component to the requirements of speculative redevelopment' (A. Rodríguez *et al.* 2001: 176).

The second issue, the downtown bias, is easy to understand in light of the above. From the very first, urban regeneration strategies concentrated on the 'opportunity sites' located in the city's central district (Abando). This, then, gave rise to a new central urban landscape and waterfront, featuring high-priced, high-rise housing and office blocks, luxury hotels, new shopping and entertainment facilities, museums, convention centres, riverside promenades, etc. Although the powerful presence of the Guggenheim Museum Bilbao seems to give the downtown a touch of 'originality', it is actually the same urban landscape that can be found in cities such as Baltimore, Glasgow and Barcelona (N. Smith 1996; McNeill and While 2001).

In Bilbao city centre (see Figure 10.1), two large-scale redevelopment projects illustrate both issues well: Abandoibarra and the Isozaki 'Gateway' project.

Abandoibarra, a 35-hectare site previously devoted to port facilities and a shipyard, is considered the most emblematic project of those undertaken by Bilbao Ría 2000. The area skirts the river between the Guggenheim Museum Bilbao and the Euskalduna Conference and Concert Hall. The development, which was begun

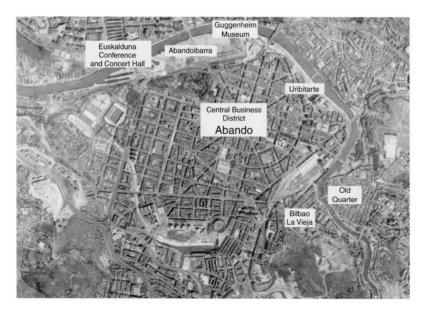

10.1 Bilbao city centre (Source: Diputacion Foral de Bizkaia)

in 2000, is a project designed by Cesar Pelli. Its main elements include new luxury flats, a Sheraton hotel, a commercial/recreation centre, office space, and the Maritime Museum of Bilbao.

The Isozaki Gateway, begun in late 2002, is a project designed to transform Uribitarte, a 4.2-hectare quayside area just up river from the Guggenheim Museum. The architect's striking design calls for the construction of a small citadel containing luxury flats, cinemas and restaurants. Unlike Abandoibarra, the Isozaki Gateway is a project undertaken by private initiative on privately owned land. Nevertheless, the local authorities have not only paved the way for its development, but have also included the Isozaki venture in their place-marketing campaigns as if it were one more emblematic project produced by public initiative.

The 'perverse effects' of this regeneration model – i.e. the socio-spatial consequences of these projects – seem obvious. First, it has contributed to the rise in housing prices in the city as a whole. Within the wider context of steeply climbing dwelling prices all over the country, the high expectations of economic revitalisation generated by the new projects (the so-called 'Guggenheim effect'), have sent prices soaring in adjacent neighbourhoods as well, eventually affecting the entire city.[1] Between the years 1997 and 2002, the average cost of housing rose nominally by 104 per cent in metropolitan Bilbao (Ministerio de Fomento, 2003). Consequently, by early 2003, Bilbao had become one of the most expensive cities in Spain, with prices similar to those of Madrid and Barcelona.

Table 10.1 Socio-economic characteristics of the population, Abando and Bilbao, 1986–96

	Abando			Bilbao		
	1986 %	1996 %	% change	1986 %	1996 %	% change
Upper SEGs (employers, managers, professionals)[a]	35.4	45.4	42.2	15.7	22.9	60.0
Young professionals (upper SEGs 25–39 years old)[a]	13.4	17.7	46.3	7.1	10.4	62.0
Manual workers (skilled and unskilled)[a]	17.1	11.5	–25.2	38.2	30.7	–11.7
Employed[b]	43.7	51.5	8.3	41.4	44.7	3.9
Professional, technical and managerial[c]	41.8	53.9	39.0	20.7	30.3	52.0
Banking, finance, insurance and business services[c]	15.9	21.7	47.1	9.5	13.1	43.5
Young adults (pop. 25–39 years old)[d]	19.0	23.3	14.7	20.6	24.4	11.1
Higher education qualifications (University)[b]	33.6	41.7	19.7	16.0	21.3	36.5

Source: EUSTAT (1999)

Notes

[a] Percentage of economically active population.
[b] Percentage of working age population.
[c] Percentage of employed population.
[d] Percentage of total population.

Second, it has exacerbated social and territorial disparities in the city. The downtown residential areas, always inhabited by the city's more affluent citizens, have had their socially exclusive nature reinforced to the detriment of other neighbourhoods which, though deteriorated and in need of investment, did not offer the same 'opportunities'. Clearly then, the new emblematic projects are all enabling the city's central district to become ever more exclusive and 'privatised'. Table 10.1 enables us to visualise part of this process of consolidating Abando as 'a consumption based renovated space catering to the demands of the urban elite' (A. Rodríguez et al. 2001: 176).[2]

Thus, as has happened in other European cities, Bilbao is becoming another example of how large-scale urban development projects can actually accentuate social exclusion and polarisation in the city (Moulaert et al. 2003).

The new opportunity areas and the process of gentrification

As we have seen, the regeneration strategies pursued to date in Bilbao have focused mainly on the redevelopment of derelict inner city areas with potential for commercial development. The fact that these are non-residential sites located in a district always associated with middle- and upper-middle class residences would not seem to imply the existence of gentrification in the strict sense, if we understand by that 'the rehabilitation of working-class and derelict housing and the consequent transformation of an area into a middle-class neighbourhood' (Smith and Williams 1986: 1). However, the recent identification by the City Council of new 'opportunity areas' in the city makes us believe there is a real possibility that the regeneration process under way in Bilbao might ultimately lead to gentrification of some of its deprived inner-city neighbourhoods.

In April 2002, the Mayor of Bilbao presented the main conclusions reached by Andersen Consulting in a study entitled 'Opportunity Spaces for the City of Bilbao' commissioned by the council. According to the document, the city needed to 'continue exploiting more opportunity areas and projects to enhance its competitiveness' (Ayuntamiento de Bilbao 2002: 3). To this end, the Andersen report recommended that over a hundred strategic and business projects should be undertaken during the next twenty years in six areas of the city.

As can be seen from the above, once the best located sites with greatest potential for commercial development (i.e. sites such as Abandoibarra and Uribitarte) have been exploited and recapitalised, it is essential to identify new areas with sufficient appeal to merit new investments, attract new activities and transact new business. The projects proposed for these new 'opportunity sites' would transform them physically, economically and socially to enable them to occupy the place and fulfil the role assigned them by 'experts' in drawing up their 'desired vision' for Bilbao. If, as is the case, one or another of these 'recently discovered opportunity areas' is in fact a deprived housing neighbourhood, its new status will almost certainly make of it a candidate for gentrification. In the next sections, we analyse the case of one such area, Bilbao La Vieja.

Bilbao La Vieja: from 'exclusion' to gentrifiable neighbourhood

Bilbao La Vieja as an 'excluded place'

The area usually referred to as Bilbao La Vieja (BLV) actually consists of three neighbourhoods located in the Old Quarter of Bilbao: San Francisco, Zabala and Bilbao La Vieja *per se*. With a surface area of 38 hectares, BLV has a population numbering close to 14,000, or 4 per cent of the city's total. Today, BLV occupies a space of undeniable centrality (see Figures 10.1 and 10.2). In spite of this factor, however, it remains isolated and cut off from the rest of the city. Physically speaking, its isolation can be accounted for by the existence of three barriers keeping it effectively separate from the surrounding neighbourhoods: railway tracks on one side, the abandoned mines of Miribilla in the hill behind, and the Nervión river below. Socially speaking, the visible signs of physical and social decay, together with the bad reputation created by drugs, violence, crime and prostitution, have finally ostracised BLV, rendering it the status of an 'excluded place' (Sibley 1995).

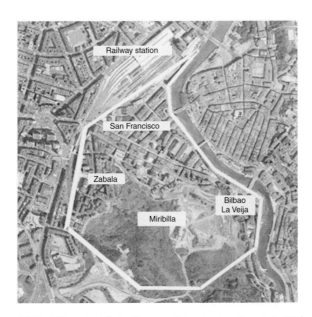

10.2 Bilbao La Vieja (Source: Diputacion Foral de Bizkaia)

The deterioration of BLV is made particularly apparent in the council's Integrated Rehabilitation Plan for Bilbao La Vieja, with its mentions of high unemployment, school truancy and dropout rates; high percentages of contagious disease and infant malnutrition; lack of social and cultural facilities; high rate of derelict housing; dwindling business activity; rising street crime, and so on (Ayuntamiento de Bilbao 2000: 40–55). It is no surprise, therefore, that BLV should be considered by the public authorities as 'the most degraded area in the Basque Country' (*El Mundo*, 7 June 2000).

Bilbao La Vieja as a gentrifiable neighbourhood

BLV appears to be immersed in a self-perpetuating process that makes it increasingly stigmatised and unattractive. However, this is really only one side of the coin. On the other there are a number of characteristics that make the area potentially attractive to the better-off – i.e. gentrifiable.

First is its strategic location. BLV is located right next to the central business district and to the exclusive neighbourhood of Abando. It is within easy reach of Bilbao's star redevelopment projects, plus it lies on the same bank and just up river from Bilbao's new waterfront. Moreover, its centrality is being reinforced by different projects designed to eliminate the physical barriers cutting BLV off from the rest of the city. The upper portion of the Miribilla area rising behind BLV

10.3 Bilbao La Vieja: a 'cabaret' in a tenement building

Table 10.2 Socio-economic characteristics of the population, Bilbao La Vieja and Bilbao, 1986–96

	Bilbao La Vieja			Bilbao		
	1986 %	1996 %	% change	1986 %	1996 %	% change
Upper SEGs (employers, managers, professionals)[a]	6.6	15.2	135.0	15.7	22.9	60.0
Young professionals (upper SEGs 25–39 years old)[a]	3.3	8.4	161.1	7.1	10.4	62.0
Manual workers (skilled and unskilled)[a]	47.5	35.8	−22.8	38.2	30.7	−11.7
Unemployed[b]	33.7	36.1	20.6	25.8	26.8	9.5
Retired and pensioners[c]	22.4	24.5	14.2	14.3	20.3	44.8
Elderly (60 years and over)[d]	24.2	26.8	11.1	17.2	24.5	33.3
Registered foreigners[d]	1.4	2.4	73.3	1.1	1.3	5.1
Lone parent[e]	8.8	10.2	19.0	9.2	10.7	22.2
Low education levels (primary and less)[f]	72.7	61.7	−11.4	58.6	48.3	−15.5

Source: EUSTAT (1999)

Notes
[a] Percentage of economically active population.
[b] Percentage of workforce.
[c] Percentage of population aged 16 or over.
[d] Percentage of total population.
[e] Percentage of the total number of households.
[f] Percentage of working age population.

is being transformed into a new residential area. Bilbao Ría 2000 is currently renovating the quays and building a riverside promenade that will connect BLV to Uribitarte, the Guggenheim Museum and Abandoibarra.

Second, BLV offers architecturally interesting housing at low prices. Although some buildings are in a state of ruin, many could be salvaged and renovated. Moreover, this could be done at comparatively low cost. Property prices have declined steadily in BLV since the 1980s, and the council has launched a BLV home purchase and renovation aid programme to help underwrite such efforts.

In the third place, a large portion of the population inhabiting BLV is particularly vulnerable and could easily be displaced from the area. Table 10.2 shows the significant presence, both in 1986 and in 1996, of vulnerable population sectors: manual workers, unemployed, elderly pensioners, and so on. To these must be added the large numbers of foreign immigrants and national ethnic minorities (Spanish gypsies) who, for different reasons, were not included in the official figures.[3]

In the fourth place, the existence of a nucleus of gentrifiers is another factor which highlights the potential of BLV for future large-scale gentrification. Often referred to as 'urban pioneers' to underscore their role as 'early-stage gentrifiers', the term seems useful to us here despite the objections raised against it (Lees 1996). During the 1990s BLV began to attract increasing numbers of a heterogeneous sector of the city's population – artists, designers, professionals – which could be loosely described as its 'bohemia' (Florida 2001). The existence of architecturally interesting housing and commercial premises at low prices; the 'atmosphere' of the neighbourhood and its cultural diversity are some of the factors helping to explain their interest in the area. In BLV, the arrival of the

10.4 Bilbao La Vieja's riverfront: buildings undergoing remodelling along the new promenade

'pioneers' is today easily visible. They have occupied and renovated housing, opened art galleries and studios, shops, tapas bars and cafés, and new night life is now available. However, the scope of this incipient gentrification is still quite limited. Within the area as a whole, the weight of these groups, while growing, is still small in comparison with the vulnerable population (see Table 10.2).[4] In spatial terms moreover, the process is mostly a case of 'spot rehabilitation' clustered along the lower fringe of BLV – the area least degraded and best connected to the rest of the city.

Obviously, the existence of a gentrification trend initiated by 'urban pioneers' and taken up later by other agents is certainly nothing new (Beauregard 1986). What makes them worth highlighting in the case of BLV, however, is something different. Their presence may mark the starting point of a future spontaneous, large-scale, market-led gentrification process, but so far it is slow in coming, due mainly to the area's deadly image and the existence of other areas with greater appeal and safer for investment. But what should be noted is that the presence in the neighbourhood of this relatively consolidated nucleus of bohemians was one of the major arguments used in targeting BLV as one of the new 'opportunity areas'. We shall return to this point later.

Bilbao La Vieja and local government: the generation of a potentially gentrifiable neighbourhood

BLV has long been one of the neighbourhoods most neglected by the local authorities. Until the end of the 1990s, local government intervention in BLV was restricted to a few scattered initiatives, most of which were simply physical measures with little effectiveness. Meanwhile, the neighbourhood continued to decay at an alarming rate, with more and more voices clamouring for decisive action. As a result, the local government drew up an integrated action plan for the area.

The integrated plan for the rehabilitation of Bilbao La Vieja

The first measure came in 1995, when a Rehabilitation Board was set up with members drawn from the neighbourhood associations and the council. Next, at the insistent urging of the Rehabilitation Board for greater co-ordination among the agencies at work in the area, a new body – the Interinstitutional Council of BLV – was set up at the end of 1999. With funds made available by Bilbao Ría 2000, the Interinstitutional Council drew up the Integrated Rehabilitation Plan for Bilbao La Vieja, San Francisco and Zabala (IRP) (Ayuntamiento de Bilbao 2000).

The changes called for in this five-year plan (2000–4) cover social and community issues through programmes designed to improve the quality of life of citizens;

local development through aid to existing businesses and job insertion programmes; urbanistic development through the rehabilitation of the urban
environment; and citizen safety to ensure peaceful community relations.

Although this plan places emphasis on solving the internal problems of the
neighbourhood, its approach is mainly physical. Public intervention under the
IRP from 2000 to 2004 calls for far greater investment in urbanism than in social
intervention and community development (€105.1 million vs €65.3 million).

Hence, taking into account the excessive emphasis on physical rehabilitation,
the lack of a truly integrated approach, the short-term initiative focus, plus the
absence of any real citizen participation, it is doubtful that the IRP will resolve
the social problems affecting the resident population of BLV. Indeed, neighbourhood protests have become more strident and community associations are
demanding that the authorities revise the plan or face a boycott (*El País*, 8 May
2003).

Bilbao La Vieja as a new 'opportunity area'

As noted earlier, the Andersen report has identified BLV as one of the city's
'opportunity areas'. This designation would seem to indicate a significant change
in official thinking about the role of BLV in the 'new' Bilbao and how the area
should be regenerated.

The 'Guggenheim effect' and the 'new' Bilbao

Before we examine the outlook for BLV, it would be helpful to review the main
characteristics of the 'new' Bilbao. The 'Guggenheim effect' does not appear to
have worked when called upon to attract international capital and advanced
services, although it did prove effective in creating a new city image associated
with art and culture, thereby making it possible to pursue an economic revitalisation strategy based on the 'new leisure economies' (Plaza 2000).

However, there are doubts about the museum's capacity to adequately spearhead
the rise of a dynamic, flourishing culture and tourist industry. Some claim that it
is simply a transnational corporation's 'franchise': a museum that in any case is a
mere cultural showcase that contributes nothing to cultural production *per se*
(McNeill 2000; Gómez and González 2001). Hence the 'flip side' to this 'first
Guggenheim effect'.

Our findings are similar when we consider the 'second Guggenheim effect':
the revaluation and enhanced residential appeal of the downtown area. As noted
earlier, the great expectations generated by the city's flagship projects have had
a huge impact both on the city's image and on its real estate market. Bilbao is now
perceived by its citizens as a more appealing place to live. For the local authorities,
this means the possibility of stemming the significant population loss – particularly

among the middle class – that Bilbao has been suffering since the early 1980s (Martínez Monje and Vicario 1995). Today there are signs that would seem to indicate a relative change in this situation. Since the end of the 1990s, the housing market has gained momentum in Bilbao with stepped up demand, purchase-sale transactions, rehabilitation operations, etc.

However, as was to be expected, this lively real estate activity has resulted in the rapid disappearance of building lots and a sharp increase in land and housing prices. Hence, if the local authorities wish to retain or attract middle-class residents, they will have to identify adequate spaces for new housing developments. They will need to 'create' neighbourhoods with sufficient appeal for the type of population – young, qualified, creative – that they want to help make up the 'new' Bilbao (Bilbao Metrópoli-30 1999).

A 'new' Bilbao La Vieja for a 'new' Bilbao

In view of the above, it is not difficult to discover the 'opportunities' offered by BLV to the 'new' Bilbao. For one thing, the regeneration of BLV would make it possible to sharpen and complete the image of Bilbao as a city of art, culture and tourism, and would contribute as well to the economic revitalisation of the city along the lines of the 'new leisure economies'. In the report on the Opportunity Spaces in Bilbao, the existence of 'a functioning art colony' – i.e. the 'pioneers' or bohemia referred to earlier – was identified as one of the neighbourhood's prime 'competitive advantages'. On this premise, BLV has been identified as an area 'with a clear bent towards the artistic and cultural which, if adequately managed and enhanced, will help to drive the economy of the local community and the city as a whole' (Ayuntamiento de Bilbao 2002: 18). A number of measures have been proposed to augment and take maximum advantage of this asset, including the boosting of existing arts-based cultural facilities (the young artists' centre *Bilbo Arte*, and a theatre known as *Bilbo Rock*) and the creation of performing arts and music centres, a multimedia school, galleries, restaurants, etc. In addition, the grants and subsidies already available for the purchase and rental of housing and commercial premises, as well as the probable location in BLV of the new university building for advanced courses in fine arts plus a new students' hall of residence will make it possible to attract students and young artists to the area. Finally, the development of a marketing plan will help to transform the image of the neigh-bourhood (Ayuntamiento de Bilbao 2002: 18–19).

Clearly then, this is a 'typical' example of a strategy aimed at creating an arts and cultural quarter (Law 1992). But besides helping to intensify the bright side of the 'Guggenheim effect', BLV as an arts quarter could also help to attenuate its dark side. BLV is now perceived as an ideal 'complement' for the Guggenheim Museum: a space destined not only for consumption, but also for cultural produc-tion, a space that will be open to new trends and young artists – 'the 'Montmartre' of Bilbao' (*Deia*, 6 June 2002).

165

Furthermore, a regenerated BLV will mean new residential opportunities to attract or retain the 'new' population desired for the 'new' Bilbao. The authorities therefore appear to be striving to make of BLV the 'bohemian enclave' of Bilbao. No doubt they are thinking of the key role attributed in the recent literature to such enclaves, and their ability 'to attract people, harness their creative energy, spawn new innovations, and generate economic growth' (Florida 2001: 2).

The new vision desired for BLV would transform it into a novel, dynamic neighbourhood able to help in forging the 'new' Bilbao. To meet this objective, the local government is using culture as a tool for urban regeneration. But similar experiences in cities like Barcelona (Gdaniec 2000; Marrero 2003) show that these initiatives can have negative effects as well. As Gdaniec has argued:

> These regeneration schemes are based on culture as their motor, but through their policy approach … this culture is not inclusive and the rehabilitation favours an elite over local residents. In other words, these programmes tend to lead to processes of gentrification and segregation.
>
> (2000: 382)

Therefore, it does not seem unjustified to claim that the regeneration of BLV runs a real risk of becoming a gentrification process promoted and sponsored by the local authorities.

Conclusion

The case of Bilbao, an old industrial city, examined in this chapter shows how ubiquitous the phenomenon of gentrification is. It is not exclusive to large, or global, cities, but appears as well in regional capitals which, like Bilbao, are trying to reposition themselves in a wider global economy.

In the case of Bilbao, we have endeavoured to show the relation between gentrification and the spatial, economic and political restructuring being under-taken in the city, pointing to how one of the effects of the urban regeneration policies designed to restructure urban cores may be the gentrification of deprived inner city areas. In this regard, the experience of Bilbao has enabled us to highlight the important role played by local government in creating potentially gentrifiable neighbourhoods.

BLV is the most deprived neighbourhood in the city, and yet it has a number of characteristics that make it potentially so attractive (i.e gentrifiable), that it has been targeted as an 'opportunity area'. It was selected because it offers good opportunities for 'completing' the restructuring and reimaging of the city, for developing the city's economy along the lines of arts, culture and tourism, and for enhancing and broadening the 'Guggenheim effects'. The designation of BLV would appear to indicate that any projects put forward for the neighbourhood's revitalisation will be linked and subordinated to the wider strategies for regenerating the entire urban core. That is, the regeneration measures for BLV seem designed to enhance the city's image more than to solve the internal neighbourhood's problems; to create cultural and residential facilities for an elite more than to meet the social needs of the local population; to produce exchange value (both symbolic and economic) rather than use value.

At first sight, these regeneration schemes may be welcomed by the area's 'normal' or mainstream residents and neighbourhood associations, since they apparently will contribute to solving BLV's most pressing problems. On the other hand, however, these programmes tend to lead to processes of gentrification, and there is abundant evidence pointing to the negative neighbourhood impacts of this phenomenon (Atkinson 2002).

Therefore, if the projects devised for BLV are finally approved and implemented, there is a real possibility that the neighbourhood's regeneration will lead to a process of gentrification promoted, organised and sponsored by the local authorities. Hence, the gentrification of BLV – should it finally become a reality – can be seen as yet another 'Guggenheim effect'.

We can ask, therefore, whether gentrification is the inevitable destiny of all deprived inner-city neighbourhoods offering 'opportunities' for this model of urban regeneration. Whether, as claimed by Smith and Williams (1986: 221–2), 'what remains is the Catch-22 character of the problem' for vulnerable residents of Bilbao La Vieja and other similar neighbourhoods is an important question that remains unanswered.[5]

Notes

1 Following closely on the economic expansive phase of the years 1997–2001, the real estate market also began a spectacular expansion of its own, characterised by sharp increases in housing prices. This development, while international in scope, has been especially pronounced in Spain (Banco de España 2002; Ministerio de Fomento 2003).

2 Unfortunately, statistics from the 2001 census are not yet available, making it necessary to compare 1986 data with figures from 1996, when the Guggenheim Museum was still under construction. Given the evolution in housing prices, however, it seems safe to assume that the upward trend shown in Table 10.1 simply rose at a sharper rate thereafter.

3 For one thing, the census does not include ethnicity among its definitions. For another, the use of a person's place of birth as a proxy is not entirely satisfactory, since many 'irregulars' foreigners do not figure in the census.

4 The formula employed by EUSTAT to define and classify socio-economic groups does not make it possible to take an adequate measure of 'bohemia'. We have had to content ourselves, therefore, with using the 'upper socio-economic groups' as a proxy.

5 In view of the latest projects formulated for Bilbao, the answer appears to be 'yes'. This would seem to be the destiny awaiting Olabeaga. Located strategically on the waterfront next to Abandoibarra, Olabeaga is a small working-class neighbourhood associated historically with the river port and the shipyards. The draft plan for its 'regeneration' calls for the expropriation and demolition of almost all housing to make way for a new residential area.

11 Local limits to gentrification

Implications for a new urban policy

Kate Shaw

It is forty years since the phenomenon of gentrification was first observed in the United Kingdom, and debate has swung from what causes it to what its effects are, to what to do with it. There is a huge literature offering causal explanations on the essentially market-driven process, divided broadly along the lines of production versus consumption and economics versus culture, but with an emerging 'consensus' that both sides have a part to play (Lees 2000, 1994; Shaw 2002). The effects of gentrification continue to be disputed, with some views accentuating the positives: new investment, building improvements, and others the negatives: displacement of low-income households and social homogenisation. Perspectives on appropriate policy responses are shaped, not surprisingly, by perspectives on the effects.

What is not in question is that gentrification plays out differently in different places, and that the process is deeply affected by local context (Ley 1996; Lees 2000; N. Smith 2002). This differentiation has interesting implications. It suggests that certain conditions favour gentrification or limit it, increase the pace or slow it. Indeed, government interventions in the most recent, third wave of gentrification (Hackworth and Smith 2001) are openly encouraging the process by employing strategies that have been seen to 'work' elsewhere, from street improvement programmes to large public-private redevelopment projects to arts-led brownfield regeneration proposals. Factors that limit the passage of gentrification, however, receive less attention in policy and academic communities.

A review of research in Europe, the United States and Australia during the second wave of gentrification reveals that particular characteristics do slow the process, with the result that the negative effects are not as marked. Insofar as these local specificities are reproducible, they hold strategic implications for a different kind of policy response. That governments have not shown much interest in such a response is in part a failure of urban researchers to communicate their conclusions that gentrification carries real social inequities (Lees 2003a) but indication also that policymakers prefer where possible not to see the negatives. Over the last two decades this has been due in part to the reluctance of neo-liberal governments to intervene in market processes. In 1994 van Weesep observed that 'in the present mood of deregulation, privatisation and decentral-isation of governmental responsibilities, the public sector has little room to manoeuvre' (p. 77). This third wave of gentrification is somewhat different: the problem is no longer whether to intervene, but in whose interests? Now is the time, perhaps more than any in the last twenty years, for the gentrification research community to ensure strong links with, and a good flow of information to, urban policymakers.

This chapter combines new research with a review of the relatively small component of the literature that observes factors that limit gentrification, and draws out common characteristics that, whilst they do not halt the process (nothing will, says van Weesep 1994: 81), might inform this new kind of urban policy. Before engaging fully with the question of what to do with gentrification, however, there needs to be some agreement on its effects. Only after consensus on the complexity but, I will argue, coherence of the variations observed will researchers and policy-makers be able to develop nuanced policy responses that allow cities to experience the benefits of gentrification while limiting its inequities.

First, can we agree on the problem?

There can be no doubt as to the benefits of gentrification: many old cities, in Europe in particular, need re-investment in their residential buildings and infra-structure. While the longer-term solution is to remove incentives for the withdrawal of investment in the built environment in the first place – or at least circumscribe the opportunities for sustained disinvestment (N. Smith 2002) – this will not resolve existing problems. Gentrification repairs buildings and increases the property tax base so that local governments can fund improvements to streets and services. The 'urban regeneration' programmes operating throughout Europe are designed to stimulate private investment through public-private partnerships that govern-ments hope will improve infrastructure and reverse the depopulation of struggling regions.

Not all these strategies 'succeed' by any means, but it is of concern to researchers of gentrification that those that do create as many problems as they answer (Lees 2003a; Zukin 1995). As Zukin points out, successful arts and tourism-based regeneration initiatives inevitably create tensions between the economies of scale required for a successful tourist industry and local quality of life:

At best, residents would have to endure environmental and social irritations such as traffic congestion. At worst, property values would rise so high residents would no longer be able to afford to live there.

(Zukin 1995: 107)

Lees observes simply that 'much of this urban redevelopment caters exclusively for the well to do' (2003a: 571). The irony of course is that gentrification proceeds most confidently in the places that need new investment least: gentrification-induced displacement is so far from the reality of the heavily de-industrialised cities of Europe and rust-belts of America, where governments are trying to promote 'gentrification' through urban regeneration projects in order to alleviate problems of crumbling infrastructure and miserable poverty, that it is simply not an issue. Not yet. But urban regeneration programmes must carry the caution that, if they are successful – that is, if urban regeneration becomes gentrification – then their logical extension is expensive housing, an increase in the white middle-class population and exacerbated social inequalities (N. Smith 2002).

The dilemma in Australian cities is not dissimilar. Renovation of dilapidated housing in Melbourne, Sydney, Adelaide and Brisbane has improved the condition and increased the longevity of buildings. It has preserved some of Australia's heritage, not only through the restoration work but because subdivision of apartment blocks into multiple ownership, a characteristic of gentrification in Australia, significantly reduces the likelihood of future demolition. Associated street and infrastructure improvements are generally perceived to be a good thing. State (regional) governments are embracing major redevelopment projects that bring private investment into former industrial areas such as docks, riverbanks and rail-yards, while the inner cities continue to gentrify with little need for government assistance. And the experience of researchers, housing workers and tenants' unions is that low-income tenants in the city and around former brownfield sites are suffering major rent increases, forcing them to move or driving them further into poverty.

International research repeatedly shows that gentrification-related displacement is significant (Atkinson 2002). One of the obstacles to consensus on this point is that displacement is notoriously difficult to document on a statistically significant scale. First, there is a problem in the distinction between 'involuntary' and 'voluntary' moves, and in assessing what this actually means. Second is the difficulty of tracking large numbers of displaced households, and third, of establishing the impacts of the move. As most people who move out of a gentrifying neighbourhood go to a less-gentrified neighbourhood with better housing for the same rent or equivalent housing for less, 'respondent satisfaction' with their new home is an ambiguous measure.

Nevertheless, there are many small studies using quantitative, qualitative and combined methods that provide evidence of displacement due to gentrification, predominantly of 'poor white and non-white households ... the elderly, female-headed households and blue-collar/working-class occupational groupings' (Atkinson 2002: 9). There are no serious studies demonstrating that displacement does not occur, but a small number of quantitative studies suggest that displacement is not in itself a negative, for example Vigdor (2002) and various US Department of Housing and Urban Development reports. These studies tend not to seek qualitative information such as how far the displacees have moved from their friends and networks, what the effect is of the disruption to their daily life patterns, how they feel about the move or whether they are using community services – where these exist – in their new neighbourhood more heavily as a result. Nor do they attempt to assess the effects in the gentrified city of increasing social homogeneity or polarisation. These studies of course provide the justification for government decisions to not respond to gentrification and let it proceed unimpeded (Vigdor 2002).

As gentrification advances, however, low-cost housing does become harder to find. We know that in Melbourne, the number of rooming houses (providing single-room occupancy for most vulnerable tenants) decreased by 60 per cent in the last decade (Department of Human Services 2003). The 2001 census shows that the percentage of households with incomes in the lowest quartile declined dramatically in gentrifying Melbourne localities, and increased in outlying and regional areas (Department of Sustainability and Environment 2003). Data such as this, which verifies the experience of workers in the housing field, corroborates the 'over-whelming academic evidence that gentrification tends to harm rather than help neighbourhoods' (Lees 2003a: 573).

While some policy perspectives on gentrification are shaped by ideological assessments of its effects and the 'perceived logic' of positive outcomes rather than systematic research (Atkinson 2002: 15), it is clear from the literature that many differences in perspective derive from different experiences of the process. These range from improvements to the built environment with little residential displacement, to significant social upheaval with unseemly increases in conspicuous consumption. In its early stages, gentrification's positive effects seem to outweigh the negatives; in its advanced stages this relationship is reversed.

There is an argument that the processes of urban change in cities at different levels in national and international urban hierarchies are entirely different (Van Criekingen and Decroly 2003). Rather than disaggregating the concept of gentrification into fragments with little theoretical unity, I think it is more helpful to locate gentrifying cities on a continuum where their position is determined in part by their position in the urban hierarchy – that is, by the relative strength of their economy and nature of their labour markets. Small-scale variations in gentrification – between municipalities within a city, neighbourhoods within the municipality – can be similarly viewed in the context of municipal and city hierarchies.

The classic stage model of gentrification has come in for a bit of a beating lately (Van Criekingen and Decroly 2003; Lees 2003b). While its boundaries need to be blurred, the model adequately accounts for the experience of cities in a perpetual state of 'marginal' gentrification (Van Criekingen and Decroly 2003): if a city's economy is not strong enough there is no reason why gentrification would proceed past that point. The insight that the stage model gives us of gentrification's progression should not be abandoned along with its evidently flawed prediction that all gentrifying areas will ultimately have reached the same end-state (Lees 2003b). The stage model – or gentrification continuum – need not imply that gentrification always does progress, nor that all cities will move through all stages, nor, indeed, that there is any 'end' to the process. Is this conception chaotic? No: it simply reminds us that gentrifying cities have common causal elements (disinvestment in the city, cheap housing close to the inner-city scene and the prospect of significant revalorisation), similar effects (displacement and reduction in social diversity, if conditions for reinvestment are right) and, critically, the same policy alternatives.

The conditions that determine a city's position on the continuum can change: a sustained strengthening of the local economy and increase in highly paid jobs in the advanced tertiary sector will see a city quickly gentrify beyond the marginal stage. Researchers in these places, rather than amusing themselves by dismantling the concept, would be better to focus on policy initiatives to protect their relative social egalitarianism in the event that their ongoing marginality does begin to change. The factors that determine change in the urban hierarchy are usually beyond the influence of any single government, but there are other elements, that facilitate or limit gentrification, that are within the reach of local policy.

Community workers and housing activists in Europe understand this: many are in favour of the current programme of national and European Union funding for cities and regions experiencing greatest poverty, but work with low-income communities to increase bottom-up control of spending decisions and ensure they are not displaced or otherwise disadvantaged (Robinson and Shaw 2003). Others are carefully watching the social housing sales (an urban regeneration strategy in itself) and trying to reach agreements with city governments on minimum social housing levels. When these levels are approached, the city can expect resistance from activists and squatters (Draaisma 2003). Overall, the suggestion is that urban regeneration is a reasonable policy to kick-start under-used, declining or deprived cities or regions, as long as another kind of intervention occurs to maintain a low-income housing stock if and when the place actually begins to gentrify. So, what are these interventions, and how realistic are they?

Local limits to gentrification

An approach that advocates intervention to protect low-income residents from gentrification must be based on a sound analysis of the factors that appear to have an impact. In the great mass of gentrification literature, there are a few contributions that elaborate on local differences in the way gentrification proceeded in its second wave in the 1980s. Many North American, European and Australian cities demonstrated unevenness in the pace and extent of gentrification. Where the pace was slow and the extent limited, at least two of four common characteristics appeared to be in play. First and foremost was a housing stock not particularly conducive to gentrification. Second was some security in housing tenure. Third was the relative 'embeddedness' of local communities and presence of political activism. Fourth was a local government willing to intervene in the interests of low-income housing. These factors are connected and cyclical.

What follows is a summary of the effect of these characteristics, drawn from literature on gentrifying localities in Philadelphia and New York, United States; Montreal, Vancouver and Toronto, Canada; London and Paris, Europe; and Sydney and Adelaide, Australia, with additional research from the locality of St Kilda, Melbourne.

Local housing characteristics

In his research on gentrification in US cities in the 1980s, Beauregard (1990) identified four inner-city neighbourhoods in Philadelphia at various stages in the process. Society Hill was fully gentrified, Spring Garden partially gentrified, Northern Liberties slowly gentrifying and Fishtown not at all. He found the type and quality of housing stock to be important. Buildings in Society Hill are typically large colonial and Georgian houses and eighteenth-century row houses (terraces). They are brick and spacious and well-suited to rehabilitation, and were occupied until the 1960s mainly by low-income white households. Substantial disinvestment prior to the 1950s resulted in dilapidation and large areas were designated for urban renewal and demolished. New construction took the form of low-rise townhouses and high-rise luxury apartment towers. By 1970, housing built in the previous ten years constituted 53 per cent of the total stock. The local redevelopment authority acquired many of the existing old houses for resale on the basis that their new owners rehabilitate them to conform with guidelines for historic preservation, and by 1980 the area was regarded as gentrified.

Approximately 40 per cent of Spring Garden's housing units were demolished in the 1960s and 1970s. Certain areas were designated for renewal, and the city built a college in one of these areas which helped stabilise the surrounding commercial precinct. The remaining houses were mainly brick rows that were readily converted to large, luxury condominiums (individually-owned units). Gentrification in the late 1970s and 1980s was rapid, and displacement of the local community was widespread. But levels of new construction were low and in 1990 the neighbourhood still contained empty lots and abandoned buildings, and many low-income residents continued to live on the fringes. Spring Garden was polarised and its gentrification incomplete.

The third neighbourhood, Northern Liberties, is a former industrial area with mainly working-class Victorian rows. These were of poorer quality and lacked the decorative elements of Spring Garden and Society Hill. Early disinvestment, abandonment and demolition were widespread, and small factories and larger row houses were purchased cheaply, especially by artists seeking combined studio and living space. Beauregard says it took more than two decades of slow but continuous gentrification before new construction began to occur, and that only then did the process escalate.

Of the four neighbourhoods, that which gentrified least was Fishtown, furthest from the central city and with a solid working-class Catholic community. It has the greatest number of small houses, no slum clearance and virtually no new construction. It experienced very little disinvestment, in fact, with little change in the housing stock over the years and very slow turnover. Importantly, it also had by far the highest proportion of home-ownership of all the neighbourhoods studied.

In a collection of stories about the Lower East Side in New York, Abu-Lughod (1994a) attributes the area's persistently 'multicultural proletarian' character to a number of highly specific attributes relating to its location in New York City, one of which is the nature of the housing stock. The Lower East Side is made up mainly of tenements (blocks of flats built closely side-by-side) 'thrown up to accommodate the streams of poor immigrant workers' in the nineteenth century (1994: 6). Their small size and lack of ornate features ensured that they remained a source of low-cost housing. Their proposed clearance was intercepted by the Depression, and in the late 1930s the city concentrated on construction of new public housing projects that served to further discourage potential gentrifiers decades later.

A more complex story emerges in Canada. Rose (1996) observes that Montreal's most gentrifiable housing consists largely of sizeable greystone triplexes (rows of three) built in the late nineteenth and early twentieth centuries for the middle classes. Working-class areas were razed in urban renewal programmes in the 1970s and replaced with condominiums and townhouses. In the 1980s deteriorated inner-city housing was targeted for 'civic beautification' by the city, which offered renovation subsidies to non-profit groups and private developers for rehabilitation. But for reasons linked to 'the particular history of city-building in Montreal's older neighbourhoods' (1996: 147) the triplexes were interspersed with smaller and lower-quality units and newer in-fill apartments which continue to sell or rent at lower prices, providing a still important source of relatively low-cost private housing. Pockets of in-fill public housing and housing co-operatives funded under federal and provincial programmes help sustain the presence of low-income households in what Van Criekingen and Decroly (2003) identify as a continuing state of marginal gentrification.

In a comparison of gentrification in Montreal, Vancouver and Toronto, Ley (1994) suggests that contingencies of housing sub-markets such as age and construction materials attract 'divergent housing classes harbouring different political sympathies' (pp. 68–9). He argues that housing forms that lend themselves least to cost-effective renovation – timber construction rather than brick or stone, for example – attract 'risk oblivious' early gentrifers who are more likely to welcome social mix and social stability for low-income earners. He speculates, with support from local ethnographic studies, that later arrivals are more likely to oppose social housing and be attracted to newly-built condominiums, being 'risk averse, preferring the new face of the neighbourhood over the old' (Ley 1994: 69). The central thesis here is that the lower the level of new construction in localities with housing stock that does not renovate well, the greater the likelihood of social diversity.

In Melbourne, Australia, the nature of the housing stock is similarly significant. The first areas to gentrify in the 1970s, East Melbourne, Carlton and Fitzroy (Logan 1985) were mainly made up of elegant two-storey terraces and single-storey but quite detailed Victorian workers' cottages. St Kilda, on the other hand – a seaside locality a little further out from the central city – was something of a holiday destination in the late nineteenth and early twentieth centuries, resulting in an unusually high proportion (for Australia) of holiday flats and guesthouses. Because of the critical role these played in the postwar housing crisis, St Kilda's high density housing was not demolished in the slum clearance programmes of the 1950s. A second wave of construction in the 1960s increased densities further with mainly cheap, small flats in 'six-pack' blocks. A quirk of history meant that St Kilda's construction standards were amongst the lowest in Melbourne at the time, and by the mid-1970s three-quarters of the locality's housing stock was made up of apartments, making it the most densely populated municipality in the nation. These were nowhere near as well-disposed to gentrification as terrace houses and workers' cottages, and their size kept rents and purchase prices down for far longer than other parts of Melbourne. Even now, St Kilda's 'studio apartments' (i.e. bedsits, converted 'six-pack' flats and motel rooms) still provide relatively affordable housing for low- to middle-income groups (Department of Sustainability and Environment 2003).

The particular nature of the housing stock has a real impact on gentrification. Large dwelling spaces, detached houses or terrace and row-houses, decorative construction and slum clearance programmes followed by up-market construction contribute greatly to an area's gentrification potential. Small houses and apartments, inexpensive construction, avoidance of clearance and modest in-fill developments limit both the pace and extent of gentrification.

Housing tenures

There is a clear inverse relationship in Beauregard's work between gentrification and the rate of owner-occupation at the commencement of the process. It is widely accepted that as gentrification proceeds home-ownership increases, but less noted is the observation that the higher the owner-occupation levels to start with, the lower the likelihood of gentrification gaining a strong hold. This is due in part to the restriction on the number of properties entering the market, and in part to the consequently 'embedded' communities discussed in the next section.

Beauregard attributes Fishtown's highly limited gentrification in the main to the security of home-ownership, the stability of the community and the refusal of many of the residents to sell up and move. While high and equitable levels of home ownership are almost beyond the influence of any single government, other forms of secure tenure are easier to provide, and it is instructive to examine the impact of such security on gentrification.

Carpenter and Lees (1995) compare the processes of gentrification in the suburbs of Park Slope in Brooklyn, New York; Barnsbury in Islington, London and the Marais in central Paris. All three had eminently gentrifiable building stock and are now substantially gentrified. What is worth noting here is the role of rent controls. These produced different results in each city, with widespread abandonment of buildings by their owners in Park Slope to avoid paying property taxes, occasional 'winkling' (where tenants were bribed or harassed into leaving so the landlords could relet at higher rents) in Barnsbury and a 'high incidence of sitting tenants' in relative security in the Marais (1995: 294). The effect of housing security in the timing of gentrification in Paris is marked. In 1986 the change in government from Socialist to Gaullist brought an end to rent controls, and the Marais, once the most densely populated district in Paris, gentrified immediately. But the large proportion of rent-controlled housing that continued into the early 1980s 'was a crucial factor in postponing gentrification in the Marais' to twenty years later than in London and ten years later than in New York (Carpenter and Lees 1995: 294).

In his study of Glebe, an inner-locality of Sydney, Engels (1999) notes that a large number of local small-scale individual landlords (with one or two investment properties) and the traditionally high home-ownership levels in Australia hinder gentrification. In particular, Engels argues that 'the continued persistence of private renting and working-class owner-occupancy sectors in Glebe acted as a brake on the supply of gentrifiable housing re-entering the market for middle-class purchase and occupation' (1999: 1479). An exception to this pattern was the first area to gentrify in inner-Melbourne (Logan 1985) where the predominantly working-class and new immigrant home-owners of Carlton and Fitzroy willingly sold up in the late 1970s to capitalise on the land price increases and buy into the 'Great Australian Dream' of the quarter-acre block in the suburbs. Carlton and Fitzroy were the first in the first wave of gentrification, when inner-city living was still pointedly unfashionable in mainstream Australia. The extent of 'voluntary replacement' (where it can be quantified) is influenced by the relative embeddedness of local culture.

An important characteristic of Melbourne is that prior to 1967, individual flats were not available for purchase. This made St Kilda unusual for another reason: not only did it have more than one-third of all the flats in inner-Melbourne, but it reversed the national proportion of 70:30 owner-occupiers to renters. This attracted and aided a subculture of renters (already defined in Australia as people who were 'different' to the home-owning norm) in dwellings the antithesis of the Australian Dream. It drew people with little other choice, Eastern European immigrants, and marginal gentrifiers – that 'economically struggling avant-garde of artists, graduate students and assorted bohemian and counter-cultural types' (Rose 1996: 132). In the 1970s St Kilda's population was dominated by low-income young adults and elderly people; the rents were cheap and vacancy rates high, resulting in relatively secure rentals. As we will see in the next section, this had a profound effect on the pace of local gentrification.

Longevity of tenure, through home ownership, secure private rental, public or community housing, plays a vital role in limiting gentrification. It limits the number of units on the market, reduces attractiveness to higher-income purchasers, minimises displacement and allows the development of embedded local communities. These communities have their own role to play.

Embedded local communities

According to Beauregard there was little community resistance to gentrification, despite massive displacement, in the first neighbourhoods in Philadelphia to undergo gentrification. When the process picked up in Spring Garden however, and low-income, mainly Hispanic residents began to be forced out, the strong social network that centred on the local church became a base for active opposition. Community initiatives included attempts to establish renter households as home owners, picketing the openings of converted blocks, obtaining city assistance to purchase and adapt an old school for low- and moderate-rent apartments and supporting plans to convert a local building into a shelter for the homeless. The low amount of upmarket construction in Spring Garden is not explained by Beauregard, but it seems likely that local resistance acted as a disincentive to wavering developers. The level of home ownership in Spring Garden was so low, however, at 12 per cent in 1980, and the financial inability of most members of the Hispanic community to become home-owners so entrenched, that their resistance was eventually undermined. They were pushed to the fringes of the city, but in 1990 remained an important part of the neighbourhood's culture and imagery.

The least gentrified of Beauregard's case studies, Fishtown Philadelphia, also organised against gentrification. Local neighbourhood associations and elderly people's organisations joined a city-wide coalition to gain property tax relief for long-term home owners in gentrifying neighbourhoods. Fishtown's insularity – 'newcomers' are often regarded as such for the first ten to fifteen years (Beauregard

1990: 869–70) – its slow turnover in properties and deliberate policy of transacting sales through local agents helped limit the area's gentrification potential.

Community politics on the Lower East Side of New York city were fierce – a complicated combination of housing project tenants, squatters, low-income Latino communities and counter-cultural and middle-class private renters. The neighbourhood partly succeeded in repelling the 'attack' of gentrification by its ability to mobilise in its own defence (Abu-Lughod 1994; N. Smith 1992) and a cross-subsidy plan was agreed upon that provided affordable housing units through the rehabilitation of city-owned tenements. Abu-Lughod notes that the outcome was assisted by 'larger economic forces' – that is, the recession of the early 1990s – but concludes that the East Village 'succeeded, by this combination of positive effort and negative climate, in protecting itself from total transformation' (1994: 340).

In the late 1990s Montreal's inner-city population continued to be diverse. Gentrifying neighbourhoods are made up of increasing numbers of 'economically marginal professionals', many of whom live in different kinds of households in terms of family structure, gender, sexual orientation and ethnic identification. According to Rose these early gentrifiers move to the inner city because of the 'difficulties, not only of affording housing, but also of carrying on their particular living arrangements in conventional suburbs' (1984: 63). She proposes that the strength of existing social groups is a critical factor in the endurance of social diversity in some inner-city neighbourhoods. Working-class European immigrants and other well-established cultural groups not only remain in Montreal's inner city, but make common practice of renting out units at below market rents to other members of their community (1996: 156). Low-income and low-skilled households are represented in approximately similar proportions to the entire Montreal metropolitan area. In 1996, economically marginal professionals continued to constitute a significant proportion of the populations of neighbourhoods that had gentrified through renovation. Van Criekingen and Decroly (2003) suggest that it remains so.

Caulfield (1994), Ley (1994, 1996) and Ley and Mills (1993) offer similar accounts of the power of community. Caulfield argues that early gentrification in Toronto was itself the result of a left-populist movement which drew support from a range of socio-economic strata. Early gentrifiers have their own definition in the literature: often on higher-incomes than marginal gentrifiers, they include a 'cultural new class' drawn from 'tertiary-educated professionals in the arts, media, teaching and academic positions as well as public sector managers in regulatory and welfare activities' (Ley 1994: 56). They have links with 'avant-garde arts circles and leftist political organisations', are the most urbanised of the 'new class fractions', and the most predisposed toward a home in the central city (Ley 1994: 57). According to Caulfield, early gentrifiers were characterised by a concern with the 'practices of property capital and of growth-booster civic officials that were systematically destroying the social and physical fabric of inner-city neighbourhoods, especially low and moderate-income neighbourhoods' (Caulfield 1994: 222). He says their decisions to locate in the inner-city were implicitly political, centred on a range of social, economic and environmental dilemmas confronting the city:

> in other words, they generally understood that settling in an older inner-city neighbourhood was not just a personal housing choice but was linked to a wider socio-political context; in this respect, [the] respondents clearly sensed the social nature of their residential activities – their 'collective' and 'conscious' character, terms central to Castells's model of urban movements.
>
> (Caulfield 1994: 223)

The 'social nature' inspired early gentrifiers to unite to protect the local building stock from luxury condominium developments. The most forceful argument in defence of their community was 'that the local state should not be sanctioning the wrecking of a substantial number of affordable units at a time when Toronto's housing costs were quickly moving beyond the means of most moderate-income households' (1994: 37).

An important aspect of St Kilda's development was the timing of entry of its flats into the home-ownership market. The changes to subdivision laws in the late 1960s came at a time when the municipality was still regarded as undesirable by the gentrification industry (developers, both domestic and professional, real estate agents, financiers, place-marketeers and the media). The locality's reputation as a place to live according to alternative values (or a place of debauchery, depending on where you stood) preceded its entry into the affordable home-ownership market with clear repercussions. Early gentrifiers were attracted to the newly available, secure and affordable housing in a place that, in the 1970s, still repelled more conservative people.

Cultures of alternative values tend to contain a politics of resistance. In St Kilda, a culture of resistance evolved over decades to become part of local tradition. Later gentrifiers who did not consider themselves in any way politically active found themselves in a social milieu where resistance is part of everyday discussion and practice, etched into the locality's physical fabric and collective consciousness. It is largely because of the longer-term communities that the local council has maintained the political will to provide for its most disadvantaged residents, through the largest local government housing program in Australia and a continuing commitment to state-owned housing in the municipality, amongst other things. It is on the strength of this, indeed, that the city has a base for its now conspicuous celebration of social and cultural diversity.

Relatively high levels of owner-occupation or security in rental housing tenure appear to limit gentrification not only by constraining displacement but through the direct contributions of the consequently embedded local communities. The nature and strength of the local communities in the cases considered here determined the resolve of residents – many of whom were low-income – to increase the housing security of those without access to home-ownership, or keep property rates low, or simply resist the invasion of higher socio-economic groups.

Local government

Vital among the strategies of local communities is their influence on, and ability to work with, local governments. Whereas the role of national and regional governments in the second wave of gentrification was generally confined to passive support for private investment, local governments have more flexibility. Local governments represent 'our most accessible democratic institutions' (Rayner 1997: 160). Because they are small and democratically accountable in very direct and local ways, they have the potential 'to be highly effective in shaping the local built environment and associated matters to do with the quality of life in their communities' (McLoughlin 1992: 121). Rayner stresses their genuinely participatory potential: 'people can participate in local government, not only by voting councils in and out of office, but also by influencing their decisions between elections' (1997: 161). Local governments have land-use and social planning powers. They can require developers to adhere to locally-determined practices. They can lobby regional and/or central government for funding and legislation to protect low-income tenants and housing stock. They may be ignored or overridden, but they have strong mobilising and electoral power.

Ley (1996) suggests that traditional left policies in local government in Vancouver in the 1980s limited its gentrification well into the 1990s, both in area and depth. In the early 1980s a socialist party with a strong anti-poverty agenda controlled the city council (Ley and Mills 1993) and provided some CAN$4 million a year to non-profit housing groups (Ley 1996). Alexander (1998) observes that resistance from tenants to redevelopment in the late 1980s led to the formation of a powerful residents group, the Downtown Eastside Residents Association, which worked with the city to protect low-income housing and which has since become a leading social housing developer in its own right.

Ley and Mills suggest that the social protests throughout Canada in the late 1960s, oriented mainly at freeways and urban redevelopment megaprojects, transcended immediate land use conflicts with 'a new politics of inclusion' (1993: 272) leading in the 1980s to the formation of new civic political parties in all cities. These parties supported replacing high-rise public housing estates with housing co-operatives – 'socially mixed with an income range' (p. 274). By 1988 over 52,000 co-operative housing units were built throughout Canada, mainly in metropolitan areas, providing the security of tenure necessary for maintenance of social diversity.

Badcock (1989, 1993) provides an interesting analysis of the roles of regional and local government in the gentrification of Adelaide. The city of Adelaide was run-down and experiencing substantial disinvestment in the 1970s, but the two levels of government managed to reverse that situation while protecting their low-income residents. Badcock suggests that gentrification, in the narrow sense of residential rehabilitation, was the third best reinvestment response after high-rise office and high-rise residential construction. He argues that government intervention played a crucial role in shaping Adelaide's gentrification. First, via local policy in the 1970s that was largely responsible for abandonment of the first two redevelopment options, partly in response to the community opposition they generated. Second, the state housing authority, the South Australian Housing Trust, under a social democratic Labor government in the late 1970s, acted to offset the loss of low-cost accommodation by substantially increasing low-rise public housing in the inner-city. The program purchased, restored and built in-fill housing in areas previously avoided by private developers, thus achieving dual objectives:

> ... by providing a lead in the rehabilitation and redevelopment submarkets with some very innovative projects, the government was able to advance its social policy objectives ... and 'prime' the inner city property market at the same time.
>
> (Badcock 1989: 137)

By holding before it 'the promise of stimulatory funding' (1989: 142) the state administration was able to secure local government support for the inner-city housing program. The housing authority 'played a vital role as a catalyst in the early years of revitalisation, and ... has indirectly induced further gentrification in neighbourhoods that otherwise would have remained investment "backwaters"' (1989: 137). Increased public and private investment ensured the improvement of the local building stock, and the increase in public housing ensured minimal displacement.

It was state rather than local government here that made the critical progressive intervention, but it was the combination of the two levels of government with community politics that achieved the joyful outcome of improved housing quality and assured social equity (Stretton 1989). Resident opposition to high-rise development, whether public or private, turned to support for the housing authority to produce public in-fill developments, rehabilitations and spot purchases. These attracted people 'with modest demands for space and few cars: children, students, nurses, and hard-up tenants of public housing' (Stretton 1989: LII) – an exemplary mix of marginal and early gentrifiers, sufficiently stablised prevent advanced gentrification.

Local government in St Kilda was shaped by community politics in the 1980s, also in a period of Labor state government. Independent left candidates gained control of the council in the late 1980s and extracted substantial state support for the fledgling community housing program – an act that was instrumental in perpetuating a culture of egalitarianism. The Housing Association has since become self-sustaining and council commitments to social diversity and environmental sustainability are now permanent features of local community and corporate plans. Residents of St Kilda continue to express their support for these commitments through local elections and participation in decision making between elections.

What are the implications of this for progressive politics? To become involved in local government. For progressive local government? To nurture strong, participatory communities? Combined, they can do much.

Developing equitable urban policy

In all of the places where the pace of gentrification was slowed and its extent limited, at least two of four common characteristics were in play. First and most important was a housing stock not particularly conducive to gentrification. Small unit sizes, simple forms and inexpensive construction have a real impact. The particular character of the housing stock in these cases is of course the result of the particular history of those localities, but the implication for future planning practice is clear. Local planning systems that encourage and support the construction of small, simple and consequently affordable medium to high-density apartments will go quite a way to modifying the most negative effects of gentrification.

Security in housing tenure can also be determined to a degree by local policy, through community or social housing and support for housing co-operative arrangements. The task of ensuring secure private rental and high levels of home-ownership is more often a regional or national government responsibility, and then hard to effect, but the significance of secure housing on the passage of gentrification should not go unmarked.

Embedded local communities, while they cannot be manufactured or guaranteed, are a likely and direct result of long-term secure housing. Participation in local politics is a culture in itself, and needs time to develop. Responsive local government is a direct result of politically active communities, although of course this does not ensure a progressive regime in itself. The particular political character is determined by a slightly more subtle process: gentrification carries its own dynamic. Residents of full-floor apartments or townhouses with private parking and elaborate security systems can be expected to support continuing gentrification. Occupants of high-density, car-free bedsit developments, on the other hand, are likely to support policy interventions designed to maintain social diversity only if it is in their own interests in terms of lower-cost retail and recreational facilities.

Progressive local governments can protect existing affordable housing, produce more social housing and encourage the production of affordable private housing. They can use the planning system to judiciously apply maximum standards in dwelling size and help to ensure a stock of relatively low-cost apartments. The absence of a car-parking space, for example, reduces a purchase price in inner Melbourne by AUS$40,000. Local governments can capitalise on their social and cultural diversity by engaging their lower-income residents in genuine consultative processes. They can provide leadership in values as well as practice, supporting a culture of openness to social housing, for example, and actively discouraging intolerance and prejudice.

The timing of these interventions is critical. The appearance of marginal and early gentrifiers in a locality may be the thin edge of the wedge, but as they rarely if ever displace existing residents (van Weesep 1994) their presence may limit advanced gentrification if they can purchase cheaply or rent with some security. The time for progressive interventions is in these early stages, as it is at this point that they are most effective and realistic. Secure and affordable housing for low to middle-income groups creates conditions for a community politics that can resist the inequitable distributive effects of urban social restructuring. This is an iterative relationship: policy interventions work in the interests of groups that themselves help shape local circumstances, reinforcing the legitimacy of the interventions and the government making them. It is then possible for other, complementary social policy initiatives to follow.

The third wave of gentrification is characterised by interventionist governments working with the private sector to facilitate gentrification: quite a shift from the typical second-wave position of passive support. The distinction may be important; at the very least it heralds a transition from the early neo-liberal resistance to any intervention in the market. If they can intervene, governments have to make choices. For any government of a gentrifying locality, it must be clear that displacement of low-income tenant households becomes more severe as gentrification advances, and that to prevent displacement a range of housing types is required. This does not mean equal policy emphasis on all types of housing: gentrification supplies the upper-end of the market and will continue to make structural improvements. It is up to the local and regional government to look after the rest. This might mean a dual role, stimulating urban regeneration and intervening if and when the area begins to gentrify, to ensure the benefits of gentrification without its inequities.

For governments presiding over areas not completely gentrified, and for those whose electorates are nowhere near that point but someday may be, there is a clear message: particular demographics generate their own momentum, and can be steered. A gentrifying demographic will always bring local politics to a critical point. Should councils encourage a range of housing types to retain the area's diversity, or cater for the aesthetic and amenity demands of more wealthy in-movers? The response to this choice sets the pattern for subsequent decisions. As more and more cities gentrify, more local governments have to make these choices. They can be strengthened by engaged communities, and supported by urban planning associations, peak government bodies and social justice bodies. They can be assisted by research that demonstrates the reality of displacement and provides the basis for equitable policy interventions.

This research needs to get out of the academic journals, into the newspapers and onto the streets. Politicians, policymakers, planners and communities have to examine their commitments to multicultural, diverse, socially equitable and environmentally safe cities, because these elements do not persist or expand of their own accord. Strategies to ensure their continuity exist, and they are relatively simple. The problem is not lack of alternatives or policy initiatives, but their political meanings and the consequences of their implementation. The answer to the question of whether such interventions are realistic of course relates to the electoral viability of local governments taking such a stand. What we need now from the gentrification research community is not more discussion of gentrification's causes and effects, nor the production of dissociated explanations for variations that rob the concept of its political currency. We need effective communication of what we already know and principled public discussion about the nature of the cities we want to inhabit in the twenty-first century.

Acknowledgements

Thanks to Ruth Fincher and Tom Slater for their comments on an early draft of this chapter.

12 Poland and Polonia

Migration, and the re-incorporation of ethnic aesthetic practice in the taste of luxury

Jerome Krase

Gentrification is generally described as the process by which higher status residents displace those of lower status in neighbourhoods which, by definition, are contested. Originally considered as a uniquely English and then a related urban American phenomenon of the middle class moving into poor and working-class urban areas, today gentrification is recognised in virtually every corner of the globe. This chapter considers the interesting cases of gentrification in the Polish American neighbourhood of Greenpoint, Brooklyn and in Krakow, Poland. I have attempted to observe transnational ethnic connections and photographed indications of the process of gentrification in the two different venues and at two different times. It is argued that although the direct causes of gentrification in these locations are historically different, there is something about gentrification as a symbolic semiotic activity or aesthetic practice that can be grasped via the use of image-based research and consideration of contrasted streetscapes as spatial semiotic examples of Pierre Bourdieu's *Distinction* (1984). These ideas are illuminated by a selection of photographs taken by the author in both locations which build on earlier aesthetic treatments of the gentrification process (notably Jager 1986).

Visual methods and the aesthetic of gentrification

In both Greenpoint and Krakow, my research method was relatively simple. After I designated the area to be visually surveyed and/or documented I proceeded to photograph street by street, the public 'faces' of the neighbourhood, especially its residences and shops. I tried to get the widest shots of the face-block and then focus attention on particularly interesting aspects of the scene. I also took field notes to remind myself of things that might not be apparent from the photograph alone. My routes were recorded on city (Krakow) and neighbourhood (Greenpoint) maps, which made it possible to re-shoot, for comparison, the same scenes at later dates.

In terms of visual sociology Prosser and Schwatrz (1998) argues that 'Taken cumulatively images are signifiers of a culture; taken individually they are artefacts that provide us with very particular information about our existence'. Photography is an especially valuable tool for qualitative researchers as they result in the creation of a 'different order of data, and, more importantly, an alternative to the way we have perceived data in the past'. Visual, photographic, research can enhance quantitative research as well. Grady (1996:14) describes it is an organised attempt to investigate 'how sight and vision helps construct social organization and meaning and how images and imagery can both inform and be used to manage social relations'.

Finally, Rieger (1996: 6) noted that among its many other advantages 'photography is well-suited to the study of social change because of its capacity to record a scene with far greater speed and completeness than could ever be accomplished by a human observer taking notes'. This was especially important for me in my second trip to Krakow during which I had much more limited time to re-shoot the cityscapes that I had documented in the late 1990s. Most valuable for us in studying gentrification in urban landscapes is 'how the techniques of producing and decoding images can be used to empirically investigate social organization, cultural meaning and psychological processes' (Grady 1996: 14). It is obvious that this ties in neatly with our introduction to Bourdieu and visible expressions of class and ethnic cultures or 'taste' which has been attempted in a pioneering effort using photography to explore the 'Icons and Images of Gentrification' in Lincoln Park, Illinois by Suchar (1992).

Visual aesthetics and class taste

Most research and writing about gentrification is as a problem of social and commercial displacement, and the injury to less affluent residents and proprietors who are priced out in the process. My scholar-activism in the 1970s focused on urban blight and its symbolic relationship to white flight. I worked on preventing or reversing the stigmatisation of inner-city neighbourhoods because of the in-migration of non-whites. This was done, in part, by promoting a positive image of the areas through the visible expression of middle-class American values seen in architectural styles and local history (Krase 1982).

Although concerned with the concrete objective consequences of the phenomenon, my own special interest in gentrification is as a visible style or perhaps as 'taste'. There is a great deal of discussion in the professional and lay literature about what exactly constitutes gentrification, but it appears to me that gentrification is like the proverbial duck: if it looks like it, it is it. I may be on shaky ground here but the role of intuition in formulating theory on the occurrence and 'look' of gentrification seems important. Even before census figures might show changes in tenancy, a patient and embedded observer may sense that something qualitative is happening on the scene such as the up-scaling of storefronts and homes. More importantly processes like displacement require on the spot monitoring and observation in order to capture a process all too often long gone from accounts provided by survey data. At the very least a spectrum of methodological and epistemological approaches are required to capture the breadth of dimensions that gentrification presents to the social researcher.

Pierre Bourdieu's *Distinction* between the taste of 'necessity' and the taste of 'luxury' might help us to understand how spaces become more attractive to gentry and therefore more attractive to more advantaged consumers of housing, goods, and services:

> Taste is the practical operator of the transmutation of things into distinct and distinctive signs, of continuous distributions into discontinuous oppositions; it raises the differences inscribed in the physical order of bodies to the symbolic order of significant distinctions … Taste is thus the source of the system of distinctive features which cannot fail to be perceived as a systematic expression of a particular class of conditions of existence, i.e. as a distinctive life-style, by anyone who possesses practical knowledge of the relationships between distinctive signs and positions in the distributions – between the universe of objective properties, which is brought to light by scientific construction, and the no less objective universe of life-styles, which exists as such for and through ordinary experience.
>
> (1984: 174–5)

Taste, then, is a mechanism by which subtle distinctions between things take on much more resonance in terms of social class divisions. The middle class has the power to define 'good taste' and this is a source of social power: to make their aesthetic distinctions into social divisions. We can think of gentrification then as a shift in semiotics or the meaning of space/place changes as opposed to merely the social alteration in the space/place. The same objects may mean different things to people who are members of different classes and as result have different tastes for the same things. It is a movement from a space dominated by expressions of the taste of necessity to those of a taste of luxury.

I frequently refer my students to the difference of opinion regarding food tastes. When I was a child we were served coffee in the morning with hot milk. For my mother it was a rather cheap breakfast, especially when combined with stale bread. Therefore, I am amazed by the price the gentry and others pay for *caffè latte* or even more expensive *café au lait*. Other food tastes which have undergone similar transformations are sun-dried tomatoes and polenta both staples of once under-nourished Italian peasants. It should be noted that in some cases the vernacular of ethnic or working-class neighbourhoods, the patina, or ambiance if you will, is commodified but at the same time tamed or domesticated, namely 'themed'. This is frequently expressed in stories in the real estate sections of newspapers in global cities touting the most recent frontier neighbourhood which describe working-class people and working-class places as giving the area a pleasantly rough character. In order for the upscaling of the neighbourhood to be successful, however, such roughness and related apparent danger must be tamed.

Bourdieu goes on to say:

> As can be seen whenever a change in social position puts the habitus into new conditions, so that its specific efficacy can be isolated, it is taste – the taste of necessity or the taste of luxury – and not high or low income which commands the practices objectively adjusted to these resources. Through taste, an agent has what he likes because he likes what he has, that is, the properties actually given to him in the distributions and legitimately assigned to him in the classifications. (175)

In this way the working-class individual who can only afford his lowly estate expresses a preference for it and looks down upon the yuppies invading his neighbourhood as paying too much for local products.

Perhaps we need here another example of how taste is either explicitly or implicitly part of the discourse of gentrification in both the scholarly and popular media. I first came across the idea of a specific type of commercial establishment, the coffee shop, as a semiotic of gentrification when reading Atkinson's 'Domestication by cappuccino or a revenge on urban space?' which owes part of its title to Sharon Zukin's sarcastic description of the design-led strategy of revitalisation for Bryant Park, New York City as 'domestication by cappuccino' (2001: 4). A recent *New York Times* article by John Leland (2003) 'A new Harlem gentry in search of its latte', adds support to the notion of 'exotic' coffee as gentrification cachet. He writes: 'What is the relationship between home and a good cup of coffee? On first reckoning, coffee (or tea) organises space and movement; in the brewing of a serviceable cup, a house becomes a home'.

Yet there is also a public way that coffee shapes the sense of home, even from down the block. If you sketched the foot traffic around a cup of expresso, for example, you might see the pattern of intersecting lines that Jane Jacobs described in her 1961 book, *The Death And Life Of Great American Cities*. To Jacobs, the number of opportunities people have to cross paths with their neighbours correspond with the quality of life in the neighbourhood. According to Leland, attracted to iced cappuccino on a hot summer day at the corner of Malcom X Boulevard and 125th Street were a Harlem architectural historian, an editor of a new neighbourhood newspaper and a marketing rep for a new local brewery called

Sugar Hill. The appearance of amenities here in Harlem, similarly, both reflects and facilitates the real estate boom in an erstwhile stigmatised ghetto.

Atkinson, continues, writing about commodification and theming of public spaces which tames them and erodes the sense that they are open to all (2001: 4). The contribution of this present chapter is to think of another dimension of public space visibly open to all. Just as a shop window scene or a sign invites one inside, it also may repel or make other observers feel unwelcome. In short, residents inhabiting the same space may feel repulsed or attracted by changes in the symbolic and aesthetic qualities of both 'their' neighbourhoods. The simplest analogy for this might be reading the menu posted outside the restaurant before deciding to enter. In deference to ' Domestication by cappuccino' we will see how coffee and other tasteful and tasty commodities are displayed in both gentrifying Polish Greenpoint, Brooklyn and gentrifying Krakow, Poland.

Greenpoint

Greenpoint is one of the many Brooklyn neighbourhoods that my students and I have been studying for decades. It is a residential, commercial, and industrial waterfront neighbourhood in the northwesternmost section of Brooklyn. It has a long history of industrial development, the legacy of which still exists today in the form of abandoned and deteriorating buildings and many environmental problems. The Community District (Brooklyn #1) is home as well to power plants, a sewage treatment plant, an incinerator, numerous waste transfer stations, a radioactive storage facility, and polluted waterways. It also has great potential. It is virtually surrounded by waterfront properties, and has easy access to Manhattan by public transportation. Even its local rust belt has provided temptation for artists seeking affordable space, and inspiration.

Some local anti-displacement groups see the increased number of loft conversions threatening the neighbourhood with gentrification. Because of its historical undesirability as a residential neighbourhood it has maintained a few die-hard ethnic enclaves and attracted immigrants seeking co-nationals, and low rents. The population of the Community District has increased every decade since 1980 and in 2000 was 160,338 and almost evenly divided between white non-Hispanics and Hispanics. About 10 per cent of the population is neither Hispanic nor white. Ironically, residential mixing of groups is the exception and not the rule in the area and the most visibly diverse areas are also those which show signs of gentrification or other transition. As reported on the the Metropolitan Waterfront Alliance website:

'Despite challenges, Greenpoint is a diverse and lively neighbourhood'. According to Laura Hoffman, a Greenpoint resident and member of the Friends of Newtown Barge Terminal Playground, 'You could be at one end of the neighbourhood and think you're in Poland and walk to the other and think you're in Asia'. According to Rob Peters of the North Brooklyn Development Corporation, 'In the next five or ten years we are going to see a lot of change along the waterfront … It will be interesting to see how this all plays out'. From recent activity it appears that change is already taking place.

(Focus on Greenpoint)

There are also many excellent publications on Greenpoint from which to draw upon for the related issues of ethnicity, immigration, and gentrification. Perhaps the best overall assessment is that provided here (paraphrased) by DeSena as in her research she had focused most specifically on the issue of housing and ethnicity. One should note the special irony in the context of this chapter that immigrant Poles were seen as a social resource to prevent the influx of black and Latino renters, only to find themselves later being invaded by gentrifiers in various forms because of the neighbourhood's proximity to Manhattan. Even more ominous today, after a decade of further de-industrialisation for the working class, is the proposed re-zoning of industrial spaces and the waterfront. In 1990, DeSena wrote that she thought the future of Greenpoint would be difficult to predict:

> Until now, white residents have been able to maintain a predominately white neighborhood. There has been a pool of white individuals who want to rent and buy in Greenpoint, However, as minority populations in new York City and Greenpoint increase, and as old time residents die, the possibility of maintaining a white neighborhood seems unlikely … The influx of Polish immigrants in Greenpoint must also be considered. It is possible for them to displace Hispanics in northern Greenpoint and continue using defensive strategies in the northern and southern sections, especially since they seem to be the neighborhood's major investors. These refugees, some of whom are here illegally, work a number of different jobs and live under substandard conditions in order to save money. Some buy houses with cash and others obtain mortgages from the Polish Slavic Federal Credit Union. One resident remarked that these Poles are presently Greenpoint's power brokers because they have the capital for investment … Another possibility for Greenpoint's future is gentrification.

> There are a few streets in Greenpoint, which arc made up of brownstones and brick townhouses. Gentrification has taken place on many of these streets, and is illustrated by an asking price of $400,000 for one of the brownstones, considered an outrageous price for Greenpoint by local people. Residents who grew up in the neighborhood cannot afford to buy homes there. Moreover, the availability of these houses is advertised in *The New York Times*. Waterfront loft space is occupied by artists. An annual house tour in Greenpoint is also held, another hint of gentrification. There rents for commercial property on

Manhattan Avenue have tripled in some cases and some chain stores have moved in, such as Genovese Drugs and Fayva shoes, Greenpoint residents are not defending against gentrification. They don't need to because the housing market is so fierce that most 'Yuppies' interested in Greenpoint are white. Like homeowners in Long Island City, Greenpoint homeowners would like the neighborhood to be gentrified. From the point of view of residents, their housing investments would pay off, the neighborhood would be upgraded, and Hispanics would be displaced. Most do not recognize that many other residents such as their tenants, neighbors, the elderly and possibly they themselves could also be displaced. Some residents expressed concern about Greenpoint receiving publicity in *The New York Times* and *Village Voice*: 'I'd rather people don't know about us (the neighborhood) because I like it the way it is' ... Some realize that people who are attracted to Greenpoint would change the neighborhood's present character.

Gentrification by renters is also possible, especially since Greenpoint has been described as an area with 'affordable rentals'. And the impact that the redevelopment of Long Island City, which is just across the Creek, will have on Greenpoint remains to be seen. The Port Authority of New York and New Jersey has proposed an investment of $100 million for infrastructure work, an additional $400 million from private investors to construct 'offices', apartment buildings, stores, performing art spaces, and scientific research facilities.

(DeSena 1990: 118–20)

DeSena did not yet see the trend of up-scaled stores and the artists on Bedford Avenue and north Greenpoint where Polish immigrants were displacing and 'pre-displacing' Latinos. Now Poles are losing territory to the gentry as reflected by the store windows and signs of the upscale clothing stores, new bars, dance clubs, restaurants, and, of course, coffee shops. Higher income, established professionals are also buying up the stock of historically and architecturally significant residential structures. Even some of the traditional, working-class Polish restaurants and food stores are trying to appeal to yuppies by becoming more 'international' or 'continental' in appearance and offerings. Notice in the photos that follow how the meaning of the dingy working-class scene outside of a Greenpoint bar/dance club is appropriated and transformed by the scene inside.

My own interest in Greenpoint was academic and essentially semiotic, and it was here in 1994 that my first step on the visual comparison between Polonia and Poland was taken. Gentrification was not the focus of my research but rather ethnic vernacular landscapes. Although I have written extensively on ethnic vernacular architecture these two photographs of city neighbourhood homes in Greenpoint and in Krakow are more effective in demonstrating the aesthetic practices of ethnic groups. It must be noted that the vernacular of the ordinary Pole is one designed

12.1 Greenpoint. Bar/dance club exterior

12.2 Greenpoint. Bar/dance club interior

for rural and small town environments. In both these cases that aesthetic has been used to transform an urban space as migrating rural Poles countrified their city homes. One should especially note the visual decorative outlines of both places which gives them a rustic look despite their urban location. This is a general form which I observed and photographed throughout Poland.

As I wrote:

> In Greenpoint, commercial signs in the Polish language had almost disappeared by the 1960s. Only a few enterprises, semiotically adorned with red and white signs, crowned Polish eagles, or Polish place names survived the transitions. In the 1990s, young immigrant Poles fill the spaces left by their assimilated co-nationals and share the neighborhood with remnants of the older Polonia. Interestingly, many of the newer Polish businesses are not marked by the

12.3 Countrified urban dwelling in Greenpoint

12.4 Countrified urban dwelling in Krakow

stereotypical red and white, or eagle motifs of previous generations. Greenpoint is now dotted with signs in Polish announcing everything from food to professional services, multipurpose *Agencja*, and other work-related signs.

(Krase 1997: 26)

One obvious expression of newer Polish commercial vernacular can be found in the form of a Polish meat store only about one short block away from the bar/ dance club scene in Figures 12.1 and 12.2. It can be compared in its rather crude and obvious commercial expression to one in Krakow in the images which follow.

In 2000, a few months before I left for my second visit to Krakow, the westward expansion of the Polish immigrant community had clearly been checked by the intensified gentrification in the north side of Greenpoint. On the streets the clash could be seen as a battle of signs on local commercial streets where Asian-fusion

12.5 Greenpoint. Meat store

12.6 Krakow. Meat store

and other up-scale, chic restaurants shared visual space with working-class Polish ones. The contest was reported in New York City newspapers. Writing a few years ago in the *Sunday Daily News*, Lorraine Diehl stated: 'While the north side is prime – particularly along Driggs and the busier Bedford Avenue, where cafés, a sushi restaurant and a juice bar stand alongside longtime ethnic establishments – the grittier south side is starting to come into its own'. According to Bourdieu, intellectuals have the – 'power to elevate vulgar artifacts to distinctive works of culture' (1984: 282).

Perhaps artists do as well as indicated by the irony, perhaps even subliminal 'Polish Joke', of gentrification in the form of 'the Galleries Pierogi'. As reported in Diehl's article the gallery is located in a former cork factory. Artists have been going to Williamsburgh/Greenpoint in search of the space they no longer can afford in Manhattan's once gritty now chic SoHo. Gentrification and displacement is an issue which is often found in the Polish-language newspaper *Nowy Dziennik* ('Polish News') as a major problem for immigrant Poles. There are increasingly stories in *Nowy Dziennik* about the impact of gentrification and the general housing problems for Poles in both the United States and Poland expressing a transnational urban plight connected by ethnic identity and migration.

It is appropriate at this point in this visual essay to provide images of how commodities are displayed in gentrifying Brooklyn, which can be compared to similar ones in Krakow. The first is the 'Bean', a coffee shop in Greenpoint (Figure 12.7). It has all of the elements of the understated upscale storefront versions of which we shall see in later images. It is interesting to contemplate the point at which such more or less independent perhaps even indigenous commercial development will be overwhelmed by the likes of Starbucks. The second photo (Figure 12.8) is an example of clothing and/or other boutique-like storefronts that are increasingly apparent in the area. It must be remembered that these enterprises are as likely to be Polish as not in Greenpoint as the area is the destination for some the hippest young Polish immigrants. One should also note how cryptic the signage and displays are as compared to the previous meat stores. It is by this process of subtlety and understatement that the neighbourhood begins to lose its ethnic, and working-class, character.

Krakow

In Krakow my primary interest was in making visual connections between the Polish American neighbourhoods I had already photographed such as Greenpoint, and the places in Poland from which residents had emigrated. In the spring of 1997 I received a Fellowship Award from the Kosciuszko Foundation and Polish Ministry of to 'explore Polish vernacular architecture' and lecture on 'multiculturalism in American urban life' at the American Studies Center of the Jagiellonian University, in Krakow. Once in Poland, I was drawn to the issue of displacement and gentrification through my conversations with Krakowians about issues such as the developing housing shortage and related rising rents. Most connected the problem to the increasing number of foreign businesses locating in the city, and the post-socialist return of properties to pre-socialist owners. This transfer included individual property owners and larger institutions such as the Roman Catholic Church.

Indicators of the growing affluence in the city help to explain the changing appearance and related gentrification of neighbourhoods in the city. According to Noworol and Serafin:

12.7 Greenpoint. 'Bean' coffee shop

12.8 Greenpoint. Upscale clothing shops on Bedford Avenue

Krakow is Poland's historic capital and is one of the country's most important economic centres. As a cultural and academic centre, Krakow is second only to Warsaw. Over 1.2 million live within the urban area of which 740,000 (1996) live in the City of Krakow (including temporary habitants). The city is one of a kind – the only large population centre not destroyed in World War II. Visitors are struck with how history and tradition intermingle with the move to a market economy and local democracy that have been under way following the collapse of communism. The city with its long traditions of education, commerce and culture is known as the capital of southern Poland (1997).

In the photos (Figures 12.9 and 12.10) of a Krakow branch of Citibank and Pizza Hut we can see how the mere visual presence of global financial institutions and fast food chains can overwhelm the traditional architecture of the medieval city.

Noworol and Serafin continue by noting that there is a growing private sector coupled with growing disposable income as well as a trend towards privatisation of the state or public sector. Other, more positive economic signs for the city were that unemployment in the years 1992–5 was much lower than the national average. In Krakow, consumer spending has increased with a related increasing availability, affordability of goods and sophistication of consumer products. By 1996, there were 14,582 retail outlets in Krakow and almost all were in private ownership. This represented a sixfold increase in the number of shops since 1987. As a semiotic of the triumph of capitalism they noted 'For instance computers and cellular telephones have become not just tools but also symbols of a fast-approaching consumption-oriented high-tech world. Moreover, growing affordability is accelerating consumer spending'. Not unrelatedly it was also reported that 'Krakow City's housing needs are enormous: approximately 30,000 families have no self-contained dwelling and several thousand families live in sub-standard housing' (Noworol and Serafin 1997).

I interviewed a young couple from the United States who owned an American-style café. They explained that Poland offered greater opportunities for people like themselves, but interestingly had complained to me that they might be forced in the near future to close their business. In Krakow, there is a long tradition of the Polish Kawiarnia (modelled on the Austrian Kaffeehaus) and outdoor cafes; somewhat subdued however during the socialist period. As a post-socialist city after 1989, the renaissance of cafés have virtually erased the typical Bar Mleczne which abounded during the socialist period and by 2000 was an occasional, privatised, relic. These rather mechanical and cheap eating places could be best described as offering adequate food and poor service at reasonable prices. The influx of foreign businesses into the most desirable areas of Krakow, especially the beautifully preserved historic centre, *Stare Miasto*, had driven rents skyward

12.9 Citibank

12.10 Pizza Hut

both in the centre, and the neighbourhoods close by where their café was located. A traditional pre-socialist version of Krakow coffee as well as an equally upscale outdoor café on the Central Square (Rynek) are shown in photos below (Figures 12.11 and 12.12). The re-emergence of such elegant and relatively expensive eateries in Krakow's centre is the most often evidence given of the success of the local economy. It would be hard to imagine scenes such as these in its socialist incarnation as a city dominated by tastes of necessity as opposed to those of luxury.

A further complication of Krakow's renaissance was property of Jews that had been 'transferred' by various, but always questionable, means to non-Jews during the Nazi occupation and subsequently redistributed during the socialist period. Also, by the 1990s the cities of Poland still lacked a large enough cadre of indigenous entrepreneurs. Most of those who might have filled such economic roles in the past were a missing population cohort, who had been either murdered

12.11 Upscale tea and coffee shop

12.12 Outdoor café on the Rynek Square

or fled from Poland after 1939. Those who survived World War II were effectively removed from business by the socialisation of the economy.

At the time of my first visit to Krakow the Polish government had not yet settled the claims of the Catholic Church for the return of the extensive properties it had owned throughout the country. I visited the apartment of a priest I had come to know who lived in a complex of buildings in the Stare Miasto originally owned by the Church and used exclusively for clergy. The socialist government had forced the church to share the residence with non-clergy renters. My friend was unabashedly looking forward to the time when it would revert to its previous status. Two of my colleagues at the Jagiellonian University had a similar problem, and shared similar anticipation, but at a smaller scale, as their family home was also shared by non-family members at the insistence of the state. My Polish informants also spoke of how Poles, primarily a rural and small-town people, first moved into the city, and the socialist-planned new city of Nowa Huta especially, where they brought their animals with them, and did not know how to use the 'modern' spaces and facilities.

Ethically, legally, and morally the most challenging problem is the properties of Jews forced to abandon or quickly sell their homes and businesses and flee the Nazis. Even more tragic, of course, was the property confiscated after the imprisonment and eventual extermination of Jews in nearby Oswieciem (Auschwitz). Krakow's oldest Jewish neighbourhood, *Kazimierz*, was used as the ghetto staging area for the transportation. During my 1997 visit it had just begun a slow process of 'recovery' fuelled initially by (partly post-Holocaust) tourism, and then by renovations and restorations of properties, non-profit religious and cultural organisations. Several of the students in my American Studies class told me that *Kazimierz* was a kind of 'in' place for the student, artist, and intellectual crowds. This attraction to the neighbourhood of bullet-pocked walls, rubble cluttered lots, and crumbling buildings, was described primarily in terms of low rents and cheap food, as well as proximity to the university. The photos below indicate the past and present of Kazimierz in an interesting way. The first (Figure 12.13) is a faded sign for a hatter painted on what was at the time a semi-abandoned building. The business sign is an indication of the past industrial and working-class history of *Kazimierz*. The second scene (Figure 12.14), in 2000, of a new restaurant, which also has a wonderful coffee shop, is an example, perhaps, of the re-appropriation of part of the ghetto by contemporary Jewish businesses and organisations. The restaurant is adjacent to the historic R'emuh synagogue and cemetery.

My goal was to survey the streetscapes of the widest possible variety of Krakow's neighbourhoods. As a result I photographed about a quarter of the residentially developed zones of the city and related convenience and shopping streets. On my first visit I noticed a great deal of construction, demolition, and renovation activities in what obviously had been physically neglected areas. According to long-time Krakow residents, Krakow was experiencing an explosion of commercial and business activity. Shops and restaurants had sprung up all over the city but especially towards the most desirable centre.

My second visit to Krakow took place in conjunction with the Annual Meeting of the Polish Institute of Arts and Sciences in America at the Jagiellonian University in June, 2000. At this time I carefully retraced my steps, and looking for changes in the appearance of spaces and places I had photographed in 1997. For signs of gentrification, I focused most attention on the *Stare Miasto*, and continuous residential zones of Nowy Swiat, Piasek, Nowy Wies, and Kazimierz. Nowy Swiat,

12.13 Faded sign, Kazimierz, 1997

12.14 Szeroka restaurant, Kazimierz, 2000

Piasek are adjacent to the Stare Miasto along its western edge and has a dense mixture of housing, offices, and shops. Nowy Wies is almost exclusively residential and lies just outside the second ring of the city to the northwest. Kazimierz was at one time a dense mixed residential-commercial district that lies south east of the city's historic centre. Gentrification in Krakow had also been inadvertently stimulated by the upcoming return visit home of the 'Polish Pope'. In anticipation of the huge crowds the public faces of the municipality had been scrubbed clean and public streets and transportation systems had been greatly improved. As a result of an agreement with the European commission, Poland had also begun a process of reducing the use of soft coal for heating and industry. Gasification of residential heating was a major sign of improvement.

Below are photos of what I call naïve, elegant (pre-socialist), and upscale shop windows in various Krakow neighbourhoods. At one level they can easily be compared with those found in Greenpoint, Brooklyn. For me, the naïve display is the most interesting. When stores began opening in Krakow owners with little or no experience in retailing also had little sense of commercial display. In Figure 12.15 we see poison displayed with food. Note also religious symbols for Easter and Palm Sunday. Elegant Shop windows such as the one shown below (Figure 12.16) are part of the long pre-socialist urban history of Krakow and are increasingly in evidence as Krakow re-emerges as a sophisticated international business and cultural centre. These displays are easily associated with this region of Poland's historic association with the Austro-Hungarian Empire. In Figure 12.17 of Claps, as we saw in Greenpoint, the sign and window display offer at most hints of what is sold inside.

As to official explanations for Krakow's housing shortage, Ken Kopstein (2000) reports that under the communist regime, housing became a social right, not a market-based economic enterprise. The state, through state-owned industry and large co-operatives, became the provider of much of the housing. By 1989, the state controlled about 60 per cent of the housing stock. Individuals continued to construct homes, but from their own resources. By the end of the communist era, about 40 per cent of the housing stock was privately owned, much of which was in the rural areas. The state produced 7 million apartment units in the postwar period up to 1989. Much of the housing built by the state was in urban areas and was characterised by poor construction quality and suffered from lack of maintenance while central heating plants were often inefficient. These utilities were controlled by the state and operated on a non-economic basis. Housing received considerable subsidies and residents became accustomed to paying much less than cost recovery for housing, far less than market value. The communist regime produced more housing units than were built after the transition because of the substantial subsidies provided to the sector. However, even the state production of housing was not sufficient to supply what was later to be perceived during the transition as adequate numbers of units for a growing population, which contributed to the perception that there was a substantial housing deficit or 'gap' in the nation (Kopstein 2000).

The United States Agency for International Development provides the following scenario for Poland's housing problems:

> Poland entered the 1990s with a stock of housing well below the European standards to which the country aspired, and with a declining rate of housing production. In the early 1990s, there were 296 housing units for every 1,000

12.15 Naïve shop window, Krakow

12.16 Elegant window, Krakow

people, compared with 334 per 1,000 in Slovakia, 397 in the Czech Republic, 383 in Hungary, and 481 in Western Europe. The housing stock was in an abysmal state of repair: a widely accepted estimate was that 11.4 per cent of the stock needed immediate replacement and that 8 per cent needed major repairs. Housing production had fallen from 150,000 units in 1989 to a reported 62,000 in 1996 (1997 and 1998 witnessed a small recovery – although we suspect that actual completions are significantly higher than the numbers officially reported). These conditions were the consequence of a deep recession, a lack of affordable mortgages, lack of confidence in the financial sector, and a poor legal, institutional and regulatory framework.

(USAID 2002)

Although people in the rural areas were somehow building their own housing, the new Poland inherited no institutional infrastructure for urban housing delivery.

12.17 Upscale clothing window, Krakow

There was no such profession as 'developer'. The only available form of home financing was subsidised but severely restricted credit from the State Savings Bank, PKO BP. There was little ability on the part of local governments to facilitate any form of private housing construction. The public sector had no resources to maintain or renew its housing stock for low-income households, but were maintaining rents of 'social housing' at an unsustainably low level. All of these problems were a legacy of central planning. At the same time, popular perception was that housing was a right, a social good to be provided by government (USAID 2002).

From the perspective of tenant organisations in Krakow the 'invisible hand' has been more ruthless. For example, Zygmunt R. Kich (2000) reports that:

The 'Tenants in Defence of the Law' association was founded in Kraków in the late 1999 by the residents of the 'no-one' tenement houses that were unexpectedly repossessed by someone who claimed to be the successor or plenipotentiary of the former owner. As a rule such houses were immediately sold for a fraction of their market value. Such a sale is a disaster for the residents. It must be noted here that people in Poland have been rather bound to their houses, mainly because of the mentioned 'specific renting mode'. Therefore it is quite common that a tenant stays for decades in one flat. During such a long stay he puts much labour and money in the maintenance, refurbishing and major investments. The sale usually unleashes hell: the landlord tries by any measures to get rid of the tenants, he cuts off the water and gas supplies, breaks the electricity, or does other similar nice things. Apart from losing their input to the flat sooner or later the tenants face the eviction.

I was able to see the accelerating loss of affordable housing on the streets of Krakow when I revisited in 2000. Then, many of the central neighbourhoods I canvassed showed signs of renovation and restoration. Below are two examples. These two photographs are literally before and after shots at the same location. In the first (Figure 12.18) we see a beauty parlor (*Fryzer*) which was on the ground level of *Wila Jadwiga,* an urban mansion of a type which dominated the once elegant neighbourhood of Nowy Wies. In the second (Figure 12.19) we see that the beauty parlour is now gone as the handsome homes facing the village green are in the process of being reoccupied by the new and returning urban elite. During the socialist period many of the most substantial homes in this area were taken over by the government for public or governmental uses. While on my first visit, in 1997, one such building was being used as a nursery school and others as government offices. Upon my next visit those structures were privatised and undergoing extensive reconstruction.

Conclusion: tracing gentrification trajectories in ethnically linked neighbourhoods

If we were to suspend our ideological beliefs for a moment we might find some gross historical similarities between Greenpoint, Brooklyn, United States and post-socialist Krakow, Poland. For one they are both places that have suffered extensive physical deterioration in the 1970s and 1980s only to find themselves desirable destinations for higher status migrants by the turn of the century. At the largest scale are plans for the development of the NYC waterfront and the growth of Krakow as an international business and tourism centre gateway to southern Poland, or *Malapolska*.

Another shared cause for these metamorphoses is that they offer aesthetic enticements to potential gentrifiers, most of which are beyond the scope of this chapter. Visual enticements, however, are well within our purview, such as what I have termed the 'shabbily chic' (Krase 1993) or the patina of poor and working-class areas. In such neighbourhoods structures exhibit their history visually as in the evidence of an industrial or 'seedy' past. Areas like this seem to act as magnets to the young and especially the creative classes and this seems to be about more than the simple economics of this situation.

I have attempted in this chapter to bring into focus examples of the process in before and after photographs. I also sought to bring to the attention of those interested in gentrification that this visual and visible aesthetic practice appears almost ubiquitous. By looking at the process taking place in spaces created by a single ethnic group in their new host and old countries we can see the invasion

12.18 Fryzer, Krakow, 1997

12.19 Krakow. Wila Jadwiga, Krakow, 2000

and succession of class and lifestyles as a global phenomenon. Ethnic groups as well as neighbourhoods have their own 'look'. This makes it possible to tease out of the landscape visual indicators of gentrification; some of which are simultaneously causes and effects of the process.

Holding somewhat constant the ethnic aesthetic dimension also helps us to see what is local and/or ethnic and what is apparently international if not a universal aesthetic of gentrification. What we have done in this chapter is to see via processes of migration and immigration how Polish ethnicity is expressed in the urban vernacular landscapes in both the home country and abroad. In a parallel discussion we were able to observe how these, at first 'ethnicised', spaces were subsequently transformed via an apparently global process of secondary colonisation in the form of gentrification. In many ways then gentrification is a threat in these similar spaces. The ethnically Polish enclaves, at home and abroad, are threatened both socially and visually as they are incorporated and re-styled through the 'taste of luxury' that gentrification has directed at these spaces. Ironically, global processes of population migration in earlier waves may have both precluded and facilitated subsequent recolonisation through processes like gentrification.

The international cognitive geography of many travellers often relates to newly 'respectable' central city neighbourhoods wherein the surprise of civilised spaces can now be experienced. These once scarified, tamed areas can be found in Warsaw, Glasgow, Barcelona or Prague and such places appear as successful replicated models of economic development based on clean, predictable and socially respectable spaces. In short, gentrification is an international process that is also connected by ethnic ties and aesthetic practices. Not only are local residents and businesses displaced but the symbolic representations of people and their activities are as well. I have observed and photographed the process of gentrification in once poor and working-class urban areas in many countries and on several continents. As a visual researcher what has struck me is the similarity in the way that gentrified spaces and place look. What do these visual images tell us about gentrification? It seems to me that the common image/aesthetics provide evidence for a kind of networked process; when one sees it repeated in places as diverse as Turkish Kreuzberg in Berlin, and Malay Bo Kaap in Cape Town one feels that there must be a common origin or substance to the process that is in many ways more tangible than its delineation through theory or empirical measures.

Allow me to speculate about the significance of this work for gentrification in a global context. One might argue, as has been suggested to me, that the similarity of these refashioned landscapes implies that the same forces may be directing gentrification. In some cases poor and working-class ethnic images and practices of place are also appropriated. Like Wendy Shaw's chapter in this volume and her impressions of the heritage industry in Sydney, cultural remnants are salvaged as urbane souvenirs expressing the way it used to be, especially in 'local' restaurants or specialty shops. In this sense some working-class ethnicity serves as a catalyst for some forms of gentrification. For example, one- and two-family homes, which reflect pride in accomplishment of Italians and African-Americans in Brooklyn, New York's Carroll Gardens and Fort Green respectively, have been especially attractive.

Residential architecture in working-class areas survive as opposed to the same structures in more extreme poverty zones where buildings have been razed or burnt to the ground leaving little to 'reclaim'. As I wrote about neighbourhood preservation and related issues in the 1970s; in many other cases the process of removal is much more brutal and akin to slash and burn. This results in the obliteration of poor and working-class communities once decisions are made to 'renew' the urban landscape (Krase 1982). In a related vein, there has also been an obvious need to create safe but 'appealing' zones in central cities and the expropriation ethnic and other interesting spaces can facilitate this redevelopment. Such spaces can become what I have called elsewhere 'ethnic theme parks' which, at their extreme, are dioramas of sorts.

Despite displacement of most of the 'natives' the most famous of American Little Italies are preserved as spectacles for the appreciation of tourists, and the streetscapes which are used by film crews shooting 'locations' for Mafia movies. Manhattan's Mulberry Street, and the world famous feast of San Gennaro takes place in an Asian neighbourhood decorated with 'Italian' store fronts, street furniture, and outdoor cafés where restaurateurs recruit 'swarthy' waiters from Latino communities. A few ethnically sympathetic vendors might attempt to recreate Italian markets, but many are more likely unashamedly hawk 'Kiss Me I'm Italian' buttons, ethnically offensive bumper stickers, miniature Italian flags, and almost anything else in red, white and green' (Krase 1999).

The allure of the slightly dangerous, perhaps exotic, ethnic working-class districts often attract the first wave of gentrifiers who in many instances are young professionals seeking the affordably 'in' or artists seeking authenticity. This is demonstrated as much in the transformation of Caroline Ware's Greenwich Village (1994) into Jane Jacobs' later version (1992b) as in Trastevere, Rome where merchants, workers, and artisans have melded with Italian Yuppies. At least in the initial phases of gentrification in all these working-class neighbourhoods the taste of necessity was visually transformed into the taste of luxury. Finally, I must admit that I am not naïve enough to suggest that individual aesthetic decisions are the most powerful force in the production of gentrified urban spaces. However, in Greenpoint and Krakow the move from Polish luncheonettes and *Bar* Mleczne, to Bean and the American Café, may well precede their future displacement by Starbucks and Subway. In these stories of local change ethnicity and the appropriation of aesthetic practice appear important and neglected aspects of transformations in a wider international and urban context.

13 Outside the metropole

Gentrification in provincial cities or provincial gentrification?

Paul Dutton

Introduction

The first half of this chapter uses empirical evidence to demonstrate that gentrification is a significant socio-spatial process in relation to its magnitude: affecting a variety of disinvested residential and commercial stock of inner-city areas and involving tenure transformation and the creation of high-status social spaces in inner-city areas. Gentrification presents policy challenges in light of the transformation it engenders in local housing markets, including the removal of 'affordable' rental units and the displacement of lower income residents. However, such findings rely heavily upon empirical research clustered around inner-city neighbourhoods of high order and global cities.

Examination of empirical evidence highlights the importance of context (i.e. the extent to which gentrification is dependent on temporal and historically inherited characteristics) at the metropolitan level in producing an uneven geography of gentrification.

Drawing upon the work undertaken in the United States by Wyly and Hammel (1998), a set of conditions, which mediate the magnitude of gentrification, are located. Owing to a dearth of empirical research activity undertaken outside London in the United Kingdom, and indeed in cities located further down national and regional urban hierarchies across Europe and the United States, it is argued that future empirical research activity should focus on the nature of the process in the context of provincial cities. Such activity would provide a clearer picture of the importance of context in mediating the gentrification process.

The first section concludes with a proposition that the significance of context, in relation to specific and particular conditions found at the metropolitan and neighbourhood level, presents a theoretical problem: if the characteristics of particular actors, identified as central to the gentrification process, and whose actions and sets of inter-relationships result in gentrification of neighbourhoods, vary depending on the metropolitan and neighbourhood context in which they are found, it questions the ability of producing a unified theory of gentrification centred upon the characteristics of 'gentrifiers'.

Flowing from these concerns, three research questions are identified, and direct empirical research activity in the context of the regional city in the United Kingdom chosen as a case study. First, we consider how the specific context of the chosen city mediates the significance of gentrification in relation to its magnitude. Second, we identify manifestations of gentrification in the chosen regional city and their characteristics, and finally, we test empirically whether gentrification inscribes a set of similar socio-spatial patterns and characteristics regardless of where it is found.

The second half of the chapter outlines findings of research undertaken of the process in the regional city of Leeds.

The incidence and significance of gentrification

The occurrence of gentrification has been located in cities caught on the 'upside' of economic restructuring, involving the expansion of service-sector industries and the concomitant return of private capital investment flows to inner-city housing and land markets. Empirical research has found gentrification to be an active process across a number of continents, and shown the phenomenon as 'quintessentially international' (N. Smith 1986: 18). A considerable body of research has identified the historic development of gentrification in high order international and global cities including New York (Zukin 1986; Fainstein and Harloe 1992; Smith and DeFilippis 1999; Lees 1995, 2003b) and London (Munt 1987; Lyons 1996; Butler 1997; Atkinson 2000c; Hamnett 2003b) and demonstrate the increasing intensity and magnitude of the process.

However, some urban geographers have voiced scepticism of its empirical significance (Berry 1985; Bourne 1993) and offer a prognosis of the demise of gentrification. Although theoretical frameworks used by critics to question the significance of gentrification have been disproved empirically in particular cities as the process has developed over the past two decades, their concerns do suggest a need to consider further the influence local conditions have on the magnitude, intensity and consequences of gentrification in particular urban contexts. Indeed, the evidence identified highlights an association between the spatial unevenness of the process and the nature and extent of post-industrial economic restructuring in particular urban contexts.

The geography of empirical evidence of gentrification

Despite the considerable body of case study material gathered of gentrified neighbourhoods over the past three decades, in the context of the United States, Wyly and Hammel found, with only limited exceptions, empirical evidence to be in a 'handful of now-familiar cities and neighbourhoods', making 'comparable estimates of the magnitude and intensity of gentrification ... elusive' (Wyly and Hammel 1998: 305).

In the United Kingdom gentrification has been observed in a number of cities outside London (Williams 1984). However, with the exception of a small number of contemporary published research in Bristol (Bridge 2003), Edinburgh (Bondi 1999a), Manchester (Wynne and O'Connor 1998) and Leeds (Dutton 2003), most published empirical research, which could assist in understanding the geography of gentrification and the importance of local conditions in various cities in the United Kingdom, uses empirical data gathered across London.

The preceding debate directs research activity to concentrate on the importance of context in future analysis of gentrification. Other researchers of gentrification have already identified such a concern, most notably Lees (2000, 1994), Hammel (1999a) and with co-author Elvin Wyly (Wyly and Hammel 1998).

The work by Lees (1994) attempted to understand both generalisations and the importance of the specifics of context in the gentrification process, by looking firstly at the comparisons between the two cities of London and New York, and also New York, London and Paris (Carpenter and Lees 1995). Additional research in London considers empirically the diversity of gentrification at the intra-urban level (Butler and Robson 2001a).

However, much urban research that focuses upon the role of particular 'global' cities within an increasingly global economy, informs us that similar socio-economic dynamics are occurring in these cities (Sassen 2000a and 2000b).

The research agenda: the significance of context

Lees (1994) identifies the 'specifics of context' at three spatial levels of locality, city and country. Similarly, Hammel argues

> (t)o understand certain aspects of the gentrification process, any analysis must consider at least ... the metropolitan area and the neighbourhood.
>
> (Hammel 1999a: 1292)

Wyly and Hammel's (1998) investigation into the context and contingency of gentrification in the United States, identified a set of conditions at the metropolitan level that were important in mediating the process of gentrification. First, they believed a city's employment structure influences the demand for gentrified residential settings by high-wage service workers, and the production of the potentially gentrified often marginalised or excluded from local labour markets. Second, the varied roles of private and public sector agencies influence the supply of residential developments and run down, devalorised 'gentrifiable neighbourhoods'. Also, conditions in urban housing markets mediate the interaction of supply-and-demand-side processes of gentrification. For instance, 'tight' housing markets, commuting distances and planning controls are important factors. Finally, they identify processes of segregation and separation on class and racial lines in particular cities that mediate the process of gentrification. These factors provide a schema by which to assess the importance of historical and contemporary factors mediating gentrification in particular urban contexts.[1]

Undertaking analysis at the neighbourhood level raises a deeper theoretical problematic and provides another spatial level upon which to develop an appreciation of the importance of context in understanding the geography of gentrification.

The pulse of high-status occupational growth has increasingly become linked to the socio-spatial rhythms of the expansion of gentrification across global cities of London (Lyons 1996; Butler 2003) and New York (Lees 2000). However, research findings in Edinburgh (Bondi 1999b) and Manchester (Wynne and O'Connor 1998) indicated characteristics of gentrifiers differed from those in London and other high order cities. This evidence questions the extent to which the actions of gentrifiers in these cities should be seen as a distinction strategy of a particular fraction of the middle class, and raises a theoretical problematic. Considerable dexterity is required to construct a generalisable theoretical frame-work from such diverse strategies of inner-city residents – found in lower order provincial cities – to explain the universal occurrence of gentrification regardless of context.

Recent evidence from a comparative case study of two second order cities, Brussels and Montreal undertaken by Criekingen and Decroly (2003) led the authors to propose a delimitation of the concept of gentrification. They argued that differing explanations are required to suit particular forms of gentrification. Separate and distinctive causal processes bring about 'Yuppification' – the classic stage model of gentrification found most often in high order and global cities such as London and New York and 'marginal gentrification' (Rose 1986) found in cities whose,

> position in the international urban hierarchies are relatively modest and where labour markets offer relatively few highly paid professional jobs in the advanced tertiary sector.
>
> (Criekingen and Decroly 2003: 2453)

Bridge (2003) suggests differentiation between the role global city gentrification plays in class formation and a more restricted and ambivalent class process-taking place in gentrified areas in provincial cities such as Bristol in the United Kingdom.

These discussions resonate with a general theoretical concern raised by Wyly and Hammel (1998) in the context of the United States. Do conditions and processes specific to particular localities 'represent causal elements' of gentrification? If they do, it questions the ability to offer a universal description of the process of gentrification and implies greater complexity in producing a general explanation for gentrification.

With few recent and notable exceptions, owing to the lack of supporting empirical research literature or asking the wrong research questions in studies outside high order cities, it has not been possible, so far at least, to consider and develop our understanding of the importance of context at the metropolitan level and to question the sensitivity and suitability of contemporary explanations to account for the development of gentrification in provincial cities.

To consider the importance of context, analysis will therefore be at two differing geographical scales: at the metropolitan and neighbourhood level. The research investigates the importance of conditions at the metropolitan level in mediating gentrification processes, and at the neighbourhood level to identify the characteristics of gentrifiers in the chosen regional city.

Gentrification in context: gentrification in the regional city of Leeds

Historically, the urbanisation of Leeds was a product of the agglomeration of industrial production sited close to and within the inner core. Such growth allowed Leeds to become a major centre of industrial production in the United Kingdom (Burt and Grady 1994). Since the early 1970s, employment in manufacturing in Leeds has recorded absolute declines, and as a consequence the loss of working-class blue-collar occupations close to the inner core (Burt and Grady 1994). Evidence from the 2001 census suggest that the processes of counter-urbanisation and the haemorrhaging of population encountered in industrial cities of the United Kingdom such as Leeds, is still the trend albeit at a less dramatic rate than previous decades (refer to Figure 13.1).

However, Leeds has been a recent beneficiary of spatial and sectoral restructuring of the British economy. The development of Leeds as a regional financial service centre (Tickell 1993, 1996), with an established infrastructure across the range of financial services has led to the growth of highly skilled occupational groups. Reflecting its relative economic prosperity, Leeds enjoys higher (average) house prices than the West Yorkshire region as a whole (Cole *et al.* 2003).

Economic restructuring and the Leeds economy

Returning to the work of Wyly and Hammel (1998), and their identification of particular factors at the metropolitan level that mediate gentrification: their first set of conditions translates into a consideration of how the employment structure

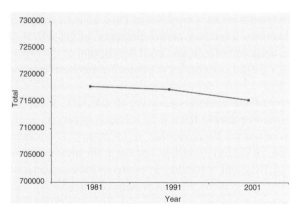

13.1 Leeds metropolitan district population

of Leeds influences the demand for gentrified residential settings by high-wage white-collar workers, and the production of the potentially gentrified.

Since the 1980s, Leeds has experienced an influx and intrinsic growth of specialist firms in the financial and business service sectors (Figure 13.2), and by the later part of the 1980s became a major employer of professionals in the region. Over the period 1981 to 1991 service sector employment in Leeds increased by over 20 per cent and by 1991 employed some 73 per cent (225,000) of total employment. Net growth was focused upon the sectors of banking, financial, insurance and business services (+18,300). The inner core of Leeds witnessed an expansion of service-sector industries, and secondly an influx of a large cohort of professional and managerial occupations (*Leeds Economy Handbook*, 2002). In the ten-year period between 1992 and 2002 employment growth continued to be dominated by these occupations. Professional and managerial occupations totalled 107,900 employees working in Leeds Metropolitan District (MD) in 2002, and represented an increase of 31 per cent since 1992, with projections for growth to be higher over the next decade (*Leeds Economy Handbook*, 2003). The growths in these occupations were against a backdrop of overall employment growth in Leeds MD (Dutton 2003). Such occurrences suggest the existence in Leeds of a potential demand for inner-city housing.

The historical legacy of the built environment of Leeds

In Leeds the actions of private and public sector actors have influenced the supply of residential developments and run down (devalorised) gentrifiable neighbourhoods close to the inner core. Historical socio-spatial processes, associated with private sector suburban house building and local state interventions in housing and land markets, have heavily influenced contemporary conditions allowing 'piecemeal' gentrification to take place in Leeds.

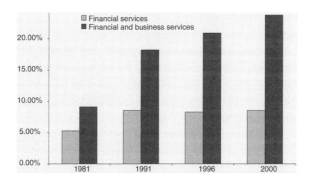

13.2 Percentage of employees in financial and business service sectors in Leeds metropolitan district

The process of suburbanisation involving spatial differentiation of social classes and decentralisation of the upper and middle classes from central Leeds had begun in the early part of the nineteenth century. However, the hope for middle-class residential exclusivity within the centre and north of the inner city throughout the nineteenth century was rarely realised (Treen 1976). The character of industrial production quickly led to a degraded environmental quality of the inner core of Leeds. Competition for other land uses and the better returns in providing smaller housing for the large and expanding working-class populace of Leeds squeezed out any remaining high status residential uses close to the inner core. Local economic expansion during the nineteenth century was accompanied by the construction of vast quantities of back-to-back houses; a total of 78,000 were built between 1787 up to 1937.[2] By 1920 the urban industrial structure of Leeds was established, and back-to-back totalled 70 per cent of the city's total housing stock (Gibson and Langstaff 1982).

Local housing and planning policy interventions in Leeds from the mid-1930s to the early 1970s, during periods of national government policy drives for comprehensive housing redevelopment and renewal, led to the demolition of 35,000 back-to-backs and restricted the supply of available and potentially gentrifiable devalorised neighbourhoods close to the inner core. Inner-city working-class communities were displaced to council built 'garden suburbs' in Leeds such as Gipton or rehoused in mostly high density, high-rise public housing developments surrounding the urban core, particularly to the east and south of the city (Gibson and Langstaff 1982).

By the later part of the 1970s the impact of the process of de-industrialisation together with slum clearance and redevelopment policies by the local housing authority resulted in a blighted inner-city urban landscape. Over 500 acres of cleared land remained unused, with over two-thirds allocated for non-residential land use. The scale of obsolescence in Leeds was immense, 'creating the impression of a scorched earth policy' (Gibson and Langstaff 1982: 256).

The industrial heritage of Leeds has left a deep socio-spatial footprint and has influenced subsequent interventions in local housing and land markets. Leeds has inherited large tracts of inner-city spaces suitable for the redevelopment and renewal of industrial/manufacturing areas into residential spaces for higher income groups to take place. Conversely, the housing and urban policy legacy of the city has limited the magnitude of piecemeal gentrification close to the inner core. The process of gentrification spreading out and away from established inner-city high status neighbourhoods, identified in middle-class cities such as London was not a possibility in such an industrial urban structure. No such elite neighbourhoods remained in the inner core of the city of Leeds.

Contemporary housing market conditions in Leeds

Cole *et al.* (2003) identify the emergence of a two speed housing market, of rapid house price inflation together with areas of low demand. Analyses of Land Registry figures by Cole *et al.* (2003) show that the average house price in Leeds for the period October to December 2002 was £105,590, with price inflation between 1999 and 2002 of 60.1 per cent. However, the fractured nature of the housing market in Leeds is also suggested: 41 per cent of the city of Leeds postcode sectors experienced a reduction in relative house prices between 1999 and 2002.

Although neighbourhoods in North Leeds do supply a concentrated number of professionals and managers working in the central core of Leeds (Harland 2001), the expansion of these occupations has been partially absorbed through an increase in levels of commuting. Leeds City Council calculated over 2 million people are within 30 minutes' driving distance from Leeds. Large towns such as Harrogate, a spa town with historic 'exclusive' middle-class settlements and possessing a substantial stock of Victorian and Edwardian housing within easy commuting distance from Leeds, export a high percentage of its commuting professionals and managers to the centre of Leeds (Harland 2001).

The rapid increase in private rental accommodation in the north of Leeds provides another temporal factor in mediating the gentrification process in the city. The following section draws on the research undertaken by Smith (D. P. Smith 2002a, 2002b). Leeds witnessed a dramatic increase in the student population from 18,705 in 1989/90 to 34,772 by 1999/2000 (D. P. Smith 2002b). The increase in demand for term-time residential accommodation was not supported by a concomitant expansion of university provided campus accommodation; rather it was met through the local private rental housing market.

> The expansion of student population has been associated with the increase for demand for private rental accommodation on short-term leases, and thus

the bourgeoning supply of rental accommodation by private landlords and property-letting agents.

(D. P. Smith 2002b: 15)

Neighbourhoods located to the North West of the centre of Leeds, and within close proximity to Leeds University and Leeds Metropolitan University, have witnessed an expansion of student lets. Smith (D. P. 2002a) identifies retail services in the Headingley area of Leeds have become increasingly geared towards student lifestyles (fast-food outlets and themed bars), and allows him to conceptualise these socio-cultural changes as 'studentification'.

The gentrified areas of Leeds

The Calls

An inner-city location was selected for the research. This area consisted of developments along either side of the River Aire, close to the central business district of Leeds, and to the commercial and retailing centres. The area consists of brownfield developments and renovated warehousing converted into residential apartments between 1984 to 1991, with some additional developments built at the end of the twentieth century. This form of gentrification relates to Warde's (1991) developer-led form of gentrification.

The Claremonts

A second area 'the Claremonts' centred on a cluster of streets around Claremont View and Claremont Road situated within an area described as Far Headingley which is to the north west of the city and approximately two miles from the city centre. It is close to the University of Leeds and Leeds Metropolitan University, a local shopping centre and schools. The Claremonts includes sizeable Victorian terracing built for the middle classes of Leeds. However, the later part of the nineteenth century saw the character of the area 'compromised' with the infill of two-storey plain fronted terraces similar to the working-class terraces and cottage style terracing found in more central areas of Leeds. In addition the area includes early twentieth-century 'Edwardian' four-storey semi-detached in-fill properties. These later properties include purpose-built basement flats and maisonettes, as well as family houses. In the late 1960s the city council established a General Improvement Area covering a number of streets within the area, consisting of late Victorian artisan terraced houses.

Chapel Allerton

Another early suburb of Leeds, again within two miles of the inner core but further east of 'The Claremonts area was also chosen. The houses in this area were constructed during the later parts of the nineteenth century, consisting of two- and three-storey Victorian terracing around a small park, with some later semi-detached housing and Type III back-to-backs. Such an area had included a local authority designated General Improvement Area and a Housing Action Area. There are areas of local authority housing of traditional construction, built in the later part of the 1970s.

Research design

Analysis of the 1981 and 1991 census, using data sets collated from the enumeration district level identified these three neighbourhoods undergoing a process of gentrification. Social upgrading was identified: all three areas witnessed rapid increases in the proportions of SEG Class I (Professional and Managerial SEGs: 1, 2, 3, 4, and 13) and Class II (Intermediate non-manual SEGs: 5 and 6) relative to both ward and city level. Figure 13.3 demonstrates the increases amongst Class I and II between 1981 and 1991 in all three gentrified areas.

A set of physical variables, relating to the lack of amenities, were identified to signify the process of economic upgrading and investment taking place in the identified gentrified areas (GAs). Using such data as a reflection of disinvestment in each unit of analysis suggests that disinvestment in the built environment in 1981 was higher in the Claremonts and Chapel Allerton neighbourhoods than their respective wards (Figure 13.4). By 1991 the gap had closed between the percentage of dwellings in the GAs lacking amenities and other units. Such data provide a strong indication that, in the 1980s, all three neighbourhoods underwent both disinvestment compared to its local environment, and subsequent re-investment.

The value of offering additional comparative units of analysis 'in order to explore the nature of gentrification relative to other forms of urban change' (Bondi 1999a: 266) is an often-missed opportunity in gentrification research. Therefore, in addition to the three gentrified areas a fourth suburban neighbourhood was selected. This area consisted of 1950s semi-detached houses located on the edge of the built up area of the City of Leeds.

Analysis of data from the Land Registry were used to identify the percentage change for average house prices (yearly) between 1995 and 2003, and suggests rapid house price increases for the postcode sectors of the three GAs, relative to Leeds as a whole. While house price inflation for Leeds, for all types of property was 105 per cent (£51,830–£106,164), the postcode sectors of the three gentrified areas by comparison, witnessed far higher price inflation. The Claremonts had 133 per cent inflation (£45,379 to £105,772). The Calls increased by 177 per cent (£52,575 to £145,527), and Chapel Allerton by 171 per cent (£51,892 to

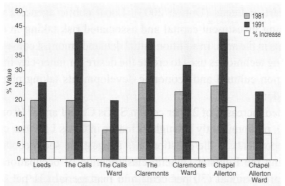

13.3 Increases in economically active residents in SEG I and II in Leeds MD, gentrified areas and their wards

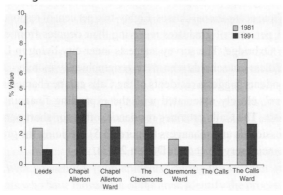

13.4 Percentage of properties lacking one or more basic amenity

£140,586). House price inflation in the suburban area of the Moseleys was lower than the three GAs at 123 per cent (£68,631 to £153,028).

Additional data were collated during spring 2001 by questionnaire (262 households in the three gentrified areas and a further 55 households from the suburban neighbourhood. In addition, in-depth interviews of residents in the three gentrified areas were undertaken (30 householders) together with estate agents, property developers, domestic and corporate lending managers, and local officials.

The nature of gentrification in Leeds

The Calls

The development of up market residential housing in and around the Calls marked the beginning of a nascent inner city private housing market in the city. I identify the role of public–private partnerships in preparing and creating the potential of

new road to more 'human' cities, where memory, identity and community might be better preserved. However, as the pattern of such redevelopment started to gain the attention of the press who saw the prospect of new seaports inspired by Barcelona or Boston and forecast the development of neighbourhoods like New York's SoHo, other critics of this 'urban interference' were soon evident. Social scientists and planners, informed by the critical literatures of geography and sociology and by authors like David Harvey, started to point out the danger of an emerging gentrification and of using revitalisation to carry out a social cleansing in areas that were to be classified as historical or relevant to the memory of the wider nation.

A rising concern at this time was whether this gentrification in Brazilian cities represented a similarly anti-social force in the way that it has for other advanced countries and global cities (Atkinson 2002). In this chapter I use both the terms gentrification and commodification as metaphors of social/spatial change, in a circumscribed manner, meaning that not all shifts in the social and physical character of space, not every piece of evidence relating to this 'creative destruction' might be seen as gentrification.

In fact we can observe a process of what we might term 'proto-gentrification' in Brazilian cities in the redevelopment and urban embellishments that were inspired by European programmes, such as Haussmann in Paris, in cities across Brazil from São Paulo to Rio de Janeiro and Recife at the beginning of the twentieth century (a theme Eric Clark picks up on at the end of this book). However gentrification has become a more important theme in the last forty years and one which has intensified during the last two decades. In this period, in Brazil, as in other countries, one can observe a shifting of the notion of planning in cities, often termed creative destruction, which included the preservation and revitalisation of old non-heritage areas of towns. Areas demarcated as historical centres are now being preserved and restored to attract the attention of new people, the media and capital, rather than some wider attempt to construct a perennial symbol of nationhood as in the past.

Latin American gentrification?

In considering what gentrification is we might revisit the Chicago School's perspectives on the neighbourhood as a kind of zone. Space as an analytical category has not always been present in sociological debates, commonly interpreted as an epiphenomenona of social relations. However, for writers like the anthropologist Antonio Arantes, space is important as a landscape of human action and creation (Arantes 2000a: 84). For that reason, gentrified processes may be seen as a distinct process of urban renewal which, in a sense, acts to *replace* places. I propose to use gentrification in this narrower sense, as a subset of wider issues covered by terms like urban preservation, rehabilitation, urban renewal and revitalisation.

In the 1982 postscript of the classic work of the 1960s *Urban Villagers*, Herbert Gans defines gentrification as basically a private version of urban renewal:

> The term comes from England, but it is apt because affluent people are taking over the homes and neighborhoods of less affluent ones. The American term is 'revitalization', which presumably refers to healthier property values and tax receipts, not to the replacement of the lifeless poor by the lively rich.
>
> (Gans 1982: 390)

Although both Neil Smith and Saskia Sassen argue in favour of including new urban development as gentrification, of expanding the concept, I assert that the concept may be strictly used in the Brazilian context when shifts at the neighbourhood scale may be better perceived in terms of social structure or occupation rather than in spatial terms. The notion of commodification of areas, wider than gentrification and including it, is a very well known theme in Brazilian urban history – a trajectory of speculation and eviction in most cities. Gentrification becomes, in a narrow sense, a powerful concept, able to expose the social changes that lie behind some initiatives of cultural preservation that, in *appearance*, are the opposite of urban speculation. In Brazilian urban history, renewal has been linked to the processes of creative destruction, to tear down entire areas in order to rebuild them. Gentrification shows that savage speculation and soft revitalisation might cause similar impacts: the removal of popular groups, but under an epic public rhetoric of preservation.

Thus, the key questions of this chapter can be identified as the following. Can we find gentrification where there is no displacement of the poor by the 'gentry', but where a curious blend of slums, tenement houses and working-class houses next to upscale stores, coffee houses and restaurants now exist which are geared up to both local and global tourism? Is the use of these neighbourhoods by the middle classes as places to visit and tour an appropriation of the social uses to which these spaces are put on a daily basis even when the gentry return to their vertical and horizontal new condominiums and gated communities? Gentrification processes in central and/or historical areas are not simply a matter of who lives in the housing, but also of tourism, leisure and cultural activities – all of which are transitory processes but nevertheless inflect on the daily processes of the neighbourhood.

In Brazil we can compare this metaphor to another, older one, written by the French anthropologist Claude Lévi-Strauss after living in São Paulo in 1935:

> Some mischievous spirit has defined America as a country which has moved from barbarism to decadence without enjoying any intermediary phase of civilization. The formula could be more correctly applied to the towns of the New World, which pass from freshness to decay without ever being old. Once,

a Brazilian girl student, after her first visit to France, came to see me with tears in her eyes: Paris, with its blackened buildings had struck her as being dirty. Whiteness and cleanliness were the only criteria by which she could judge a town. But those excursions outside time prompted by the contemplation of monumental architecture and that ageless life characteristic of the most beautiful cities, which have become objects of contemplation and reflection rather than mere instruments of urban functioning: these are things beyond the scope of the American towns. In the cities of the New World, whether it is New York, Chicago or São Paulo (and the last two have often been compared), it is not the absence of traces of the past that strikes me; this lack is an essential part of their significance. Unlike those European tourists who sulk when they cannot find another thirteenth-century cathedral to add to their 'bag', I am happy to adapt myself to a system with no temporal dimension, in order to interpret a different form of civilization. But then I fall into the opposite error: since these towns are new and derive their being and their justification from their newness, I find it difficult to forgive them for not remaining new. In the case of the European towns, the passing of the centuries provides an enhancement; in the case of American towns, the passing of years bring degeneration. It is not simply that they have been newly built; they were built so as to be renewable as quickly as they were put up, that is, badly. When new districts are being created, they are hardly integral elements of the urban scene; they are too gaudy, too new, too gay (sic) for that. They are more likely stands in fairground or the pavilion of some international exhibition, built to last only a few months.

(Lévi-Strauss 1973: 95, 96)

Socio-spatial shifts have been accompanied by the annihilation of older cities, but not always destruction of the whole urban fabric, as in the well-known fire that ruined Chicago in 1871. Small pieces of older eras remain side-by-side with newer ones. If Lévi-Strauss is right, such rapid shifting is typically American, both North and South. If the former Chicago was made of wood and the latter of stone and iron, São Paulo in 1870 was made of mud and we cannot write about a later one. However, other new cities, in the space of a century, like Rio de Janeiro and others, have made such leaps and transformations of their built environments.

Now I move on to examine some emblematic cases of revitalisation, commodification and gentrification in Brazil by looking more generally at changes in Rio de Janeiro, Salvador, Recife and São Paulo. Of course this is a non-exhaustive overview of revitalisation and gentrification in Brazil but these examples provide their own historical and geographical particularities. Salvador and Rio were capitals of the country; these two and Recife are coastal and have ports; Salvador and Recife are in the northeast of Brazil, in contrast to Rio and São Paulo, southeast, what is often seen as an axis of economic and political power. But they have in common an emphasis on trade in culture and leisure services that has also fuelled a wider revitalisation and gentrification in many neighbourhoods in these cities. And all them are subject to the same outward discourse which has tried to challenge the imagery of decayed downtowns, beggars, hustlers, whores and empty buildings that are now clean, vital, and full of people that now come to newly renewed restaurants, museums and local/global stores.

The decline of the central state in neighbourhood revitalization

Most cases of private sector-led preservation start spontaneously, with groups of workers accumulating in single buildings or through campaigns conducted by well-known artists and intellectuals or by the press. Common to all these changes is a shift of the use of a building or an area, enhanced by a cultural 'aura' which suggests a kind of civilising of such native places. The decline of modernist/state-centred perspectives in the practice of preservation in Brazil meant that imperial and early republican buildings were increasingly valued for preservation and revitalisation. This was the case with buildings in Rio, such as *Casa da Alfândega* (Customs), now *Casa França-Brasil* (France-Brazil House) and the offices of Bank of Brazil, now a cultural space sponsored by this financial institution.

In São Paulo, the emblematic case has been *Estação Julio Prestes* (Julio Prestes Station) which was built between the 1920s and the 1930s and which is now a concert hall and *Sala São Paulo*, where the São Paulo Symphonic Orchestra has concerts. In Rio de Janeiro, a municipal law created in 1984, the *Corredor Cultural*, and a technical group to evaluate it has created a team of prestigious intellectuals, writers, artists and journalists. The narratives of downtown tours that these key actors were involved in creating showed that the town was much more than simply a coastal resort. This was the first time that an area of a town, an urban site, was preserved by the city government rather than through wider state or federal initiatives.

The revitalisation which can be seen in progress in Brazil follows a set of international urban models of revitalisation such as that of Baltimore's South Sea Port, Puerto Madero in Buenos Aires and Lisbon, for the Expo 98, or Barcelona for its Olympic Games. This model, of strategic urban flagship programmes takes advantage of international events to attract capital and visibility. Such models have widely been seen as successful examples of the articulation of planning, marketing and management and in the creation of mixed uses and partnerships between government, communities and entrepreneurs.[1] I now turn to consider some key examples of gentrification and the different ways in which these cases have developed in recent years.

Pelourinho, Bahia

The former Brazilian capital, Salvador, now more than 2 million inhabitants, has recently revitalised its downtown, an area known as Pelourinho. Often seen as a 'pearl' of the Brazilian baroque style from the 1950s, the centre of Salvador, Bahia remained an abandoned locality largely deserted by the middle and upper classes that started to occupy newer neighbourhoods by the sea. Pelourinho means a column of stone or wood, situated in a square or other collective space, where criminals or slaves used to be both exhibited and punished. In the example of Bahia, the surrounding area kept this name linked to an instrument of torture.

After 1910 wealthy families that lived in the area started moving to new neigh-bourhoods by the sea and to new houses with gardens. The neighbourhood remained a place occupied by poorer people, jobless, prostitutes and hustlers – images fixed by the novels of the well-known *baiano* writer Jorge Amado:

> Beggars by the doors at night. Near the stairs, couples embracing in the presence of the cynical gaze of neighbors. Who cares? This is the end of the world in the center of the city, in the heart of Bahia. The uncleanness is complete. (…) In former days the nobles lived here. (…) The pelourinho was in front of the two-story houses. … This is the ascendance of Pelourinho.
> (Amado 1964: 104, author's translation)

When Amado published his city guide, the state of Bahia was waking up from a period of absence of economic projects between 1930 and 1950, a period of significant urbanisation for São Paulo, Rio and Belo Horizonte. By the time of postwar redemocratisation the old centre of Salvador was then registered as a national monument by IPHAN (Instituto do Patrimônio Histórico e Artístico Nacional (Historical and Artistic National Heritage Institute)), the state institution that has defined and sought to preserve the cultural heritage of the country.

IPHAN had been created in 1937 by a group of Brazilian intellectuals and self-proclaimed modernists as a key policy of the government of Getulio Vargas. In a few decades it had defined the contours of a state policy based on the construction of national symbols, preserving especially Portuguese heritage from the colonial period (1500–1822). The strong motivation of the institute formed a strongly state-centred preservation movement which went on until the 1980s and 1990s when processes of globalisation and neo-liberal urban policies influenced many policies in Brazil.

In 1967, Michel Parent, representing UNESCO visited Salvador and compared it to Toledo, Spain, for its churches, sights and traditions. In the same year, it created a covenant between SPHAN, the company for metropolitan development of Salvador, and created an Institute for Artistic and Cultural Heritage of Bahia (IPAC), with the goal of promoting a solution for the historical centre's perceived problems (Pinho 1996: 74). According to Pinho, the keynote of IPAC was welfare work and the revitalisation of the area was linked to social promotion for its population. During this time, if the preservation and revitalisation was not merely a matter of cultural affairs but also the planning of the metropolitan area, it remained a state-centred policy. This programme created museums, professional schools, health offices, restored a church, a colonial manor house and the medical school – the first in the country. In 1980, among the almost 1,000 old buildings, there were three antique shops, twenty-five artisans stores, ten artists studios, three museums (of sacred arts, afro-Brazilian heritage and of medicine) and the announced plan was to include the residents of the area in the plans.[2] In 1985 the area was declared a World Heritage site by UNESCO, subsidised by an inventory conducted by IPAC, and this designation, in turn, became crucial to new campaigns for the restoration of local buildings.

IPAC's proposals were to obtain permission for both residential and mixed uses in the area; the consolidation of tenements for the lower classes; informal economic activities; artisans and non-formal activities; the maintenance of the municipal and state government buildings; and finally the interests of local residents. In 1987, the mayor decreed Pelourinho a *Parque Histórico* (Historical Park) and in the plan it was taken for granted that issues like the safety of visitors, special methods of administration, protection against fires, public cleaning, and a wider cultural agenda would remain paramount. However, this was largely achieved through disciplining itinerant commerce in the form of pedlars, tourist guides and traffic.

Between the 1970s and the 1990s, this project had the side-effect of shifting public opinion to create a demand for intervention into the informal and 'dirty' uses of the area (Pinho 1996: 76). The ministry of the state governor Antonio Carlos Magalhães obtained a massive and aggressive restoration involving the eviction of local families with no dialogue with Brazilian or *Baiana* society. The revitalisation of the 1990s focused almost solely on tourists and indicated a shifting in the methods of intervention as well. The Pelourinho, now known as a historic centre, became a special designated part of the town with a concern to create new opportunities that might build on the widespread monuments and more than 5,000 buildings under governmental trust. The IPAC proposal of mixed uses never emerged. With houses rented by the state government, Pelourinho became a commercial, tourist and private sector quarter rather than the mixed-use neighbourhood envisaged initially by UNESCO. As Marinho de Azevedo proclaimed, 'No one thinks of Pelourinho as a Salvador neighbourhood, but as a tourist attraction' (p. 134).

Bairro do Recife, Pernambuco

In the neighbourhood of Pernambuco, the situation was the opposite from Pelourinho. Olinda, the Portuguese colonial town four miles distant from the capital of Recife was given architectural urban status in 1979. In Recife itself, particular houses, churches, chapels and fortress were protected by SPHAN. The place where the town was founded, called Bairro do Recife was not included in this, perhaps because it represents the site of the city's foundation through the earlier Dutch invasions rather than the later Portuguese colonisation. Since it was not in the colonial baroque style, but inspired instead by Dutch architecture and later 'Haussmannised' the area was left out of wider plans for revitalisation, suggesting the need for an identification of statehood to be registered in local revitalisation actions.

In 1993, soon after the start of revitalisation in Pelourinho, rumours began that Recife would be the next frontier for development. In the city of Recife, the capital of the state of Pernambuco in northeast Brazil, the area targeted for revitalisation was one of the oldest areas of the town. In fact while the elites of Pelourinho were leaving, in Pernambuco the area was being reconstructed in line with changes made by Haussmann in Paris with a widening of streets and the displacement of many residents. In 1993, the area was decorated with wall inks to paint the façades of Old Recife while the city hall and the Fundação Roberto Marinho (a cultural and educational foundation sponsored by a major broadcasting and press corporation) offered tax advantages for investment in the area. During this period the Minister of Culture announced that heritage was now an important aspect of economic development with the private sector 'discovering' the Bairro do Recife and initiating new cultural and tourist projects for the area. At this time the IPHAN decided to designate the area as a national heritage site and asked UNESCO to classify the area as a World Heritage Site, a designation which so far has not been given.

According to Proença Leite, there was no way in which the poor image of Recife could be salvaged. The Bairro do Recife, or Old Recife, was a small port island close to Olinda, the headquarters of the *capitania*[3] of Pernambuco. The Arrecifes grew as a commercial port and this continued until the Dutch colonial arrival which introduced a new urban landscape with plans based on the Maurits-Stadt. The new city of Mauricio de Nassau, that of the conqueror, had narrow houses, like those of the Netherlands. However, today the landscape is neither Portuguese nor Dutch, but *belle époque*, with wide avenues that connect the river and the sea lined with eclectic buildings. The reform was conducted by the *Societé de Construction du port de Pernambouc* and reflected the modernising, social cleansing elements of planning ideals of the early twentieth century in Brazil.

The preserved Olinda was considered a jewel of Portuguese colonisation which was classified a national monument in 1968 and protected by the state. The plan for revitalisation of Bairro do Recife had three main aims. The first was to turn the neighbourhood into a 'regional-metropolitan center', a groundwork for the service sector (leisure and culture). The second was to make the place one which promoted spatial physical concentration in order to create an urban spectacle and finally, to maintain the site as a centre for tourists, both Brazilian and international. We may agree with the conclusions of Leite who saw the notion of a space of urban spectacle as a strong indicator of the presence of gentrification as much as the economic development of the area. As in Pelourinho, like Salvador, Bahia, the gentrification of Bairro do Recife meant that the affluent had constructed new and temporary bonds with the place. They go there, as night or 'weekend gentrifiers' which conflicts with other local users and counter-users of these spaces.

Rio de Janeiro

In Rio de Janeiro, the *Corredor Cultural* (Cultural Corridor) project stands somewhere in-between the state-centred and local models of economic development and the gentrification that I have been describing. Initiated by the municipal government, with private partners, it was followed and completed by the Monumenta program. Gentrification is a relatively new theme among these urban changes but one that has become a new desired agenda, both politically and intellectually. On the one hand, this can be seen in the move from state cultural policies to local private ones while, on the other, with a move from modernist planning ideals to those celebrating 'diversity' and difference under the mantle of gentrification. The *Corredor Cultural* project, as a program of the Rio de Janeiro city hall, started in 1979, in order to protect a downtown assemblage of buildings which were not exceptional (by the IPHAN criteria), from demolition. In these years of political redemocratization, the dismantling of the remaining dictatorship, the centre of the arguments of preservation shifted from a notion of the intrinsic exceptionality of monuments to their contribution to a wider quality of urban life.

The pioneers in this case are institutional, either public or private, ones. Moreover, the hidden agenda appears to be that private individuals, 'young, well-to-do, and free-spending' would move to occupy old houses emptied by the successive shifting of urban centres in such towns. In Brazil, as in many countries, people were keen to listen to discourses in which 'declining', 'decayed' zones were seen as sites of revitalisation. It perhaps does not need to be stated that these terms are, rather than value-neutral descriptors, evaluations which create images of lifeless areas which needed to be energised and changed socially.[4] In many cases those people living and working in these areas, often in the informal economy, were almost independent of the wider dynamics of the wider city and region. The *Corredor Cultural* programme preserved and or rehabilitated 4,000 buildings through tax subsidies and an emphasis on the implanting of cultural spaces. According to Lia Motta, these actions indicated a wish to isolate the area like a shopping mall and to build a scenery for consumption. A sign of gentrification was felt in 1991 when activity at the fishery entrepot virtually ceased. Although there are still some remains of fishing activity there, the movement is pale if compared to what it used to be. It is an area of few dwellers but a significant amount of users – 200,000 pedestrians every day – where one can see a blend of white collar workers, state servants, street vendors, cultural spaces, popular restaurants and *botequins* (taverns) (Motta 2000: 281–2).

I now turn to examine the emblematic case of the failed project of a Guggenheim museum in Brazil.

Brazil's Guggenheim affair

Having a 'Gehry' or, who knows, a 'Koolhas', in order to take part of the new cultural global paradigm, would contribute to the re-constructions of the image of the city [Rio de Janeiro] at a international level.

(Vicente del Rio)

In 2000, Thomas Krens, the president of the Guggenheim Foundation, visited Brazil to choose a city for a new museum. In Rio, he visited the area of Copacabana beach, but declared to the press that the foundation wished to build the museum using a Frank Gehry design in a *favela*, or slum area, in order to create significant social benefits and promote the revitalisation of a problematic area. The press widely welcomed the possibility of having a Guggenheim museum in Rio de Janeiro inspired by Bilbao's example (as described by Vicario and Monje in this volume). It was seen as a significant lure for tourism and wider investment as well as a new international landmark for Brazil more widely. It was proposed that the new museum might even have more than one building, with the most important in Rio, and other smaller units located in Salvador and Recife.

In Salvador, the proposal was to have a Frank Gehry building, in partnership between the museum and the city hall in order to revitalise the lower-town area while in Recife the museum would be in a site between Olinda and Bairro do Recife which I discussed earlier. According to the Secretary of Culture, the museum was to be sited close to the port in order to function as an anchor for further investment. In Rio, the museum was seen as the possibility to create new partnerships which would help clean the Guanabara Bay and revitalise the docks area. Precedents for this action were seen not only in Bilbao's case, but also Sydney and, as so often, Barcelona.

In the beginning of 2003, the new Ministry of Culture and musician Gilberto Gil, argued that pursuing a Guggenheim in Brazil should not be a priority when compared with interests like preserving Brazilian cultural heritage while pointing out that the foundation would ask for US$20 million to allow the use of the label. At this time, a group of around 1,200 people, including a range of intellectuals and artists, asked the ministry to denounce the project, arguing that a museum in Brazil should not be designed by an European architect. This ultimately led to a furious quarrel between the federal government, Gil and the mayor of Rio, the latter foreseeing around 300,000 visitors each year which could justify the US$130 million investment for royalties to the architect (Nouvel), payment for the label and the construction of the building.

By this time, the nickname of the museum had become Mac-Guggenheim, suggesting both a franchise and a colonial commercial force that might move to Brazil. Initiatives of the Guggenheim in New York, such as exhibiting *couture* as art, were also severely criticised. The comparison between the costs of the museum in Rio, compared to others abroad, twice the cost of the museum designed by Santiago Calatrava for Milwaukee, and three times the expense of the design of Tadao Ando in Fort Worth, both wealthy towns in a rich country, led many politicians to ask for a restraining order to obstruct the new project. Furthermore the IPHAN argued that the docks were located near a preserved church, so that the architect would have to get permission to build the museum.

The drama summarised here is interesting in relation to wider debates about cities and symbols in a global context. Catherine David, the curator of Kassel Documenta, pointed out the cultural colonisation and alienation imposed by potentially accepting this museum instead of financing existing museums in the country, specially those in Rio. Other sectors demonstrated a new pride in Brazilian architecture, arguing that the presence of Oscar Niemeyer and Paulo Mendes da Rocha did not need to be supplemented by Koolhas, Gehry or Nouvel. The museums themselves in Rio complained about their existing budgets and other museums argued that with the kind of money that was being proposed many local urban problems could be addressed in order to attract resources and tourists to the city.

Out of this debacle there was perhaps curiously little said about the possibilities for social dislocation and displacement that an obvious new wave of gentrification might bring to the city. In the argument as a whole we can identify a range of contradictory themes with culture embraced as a strategy for revitalisation where this did not damage Brazilian pride in city heritage and identity. The transformation of many neighbourhoods which was already leading to gentrification and commercial displacement was embraced where this resulted from local partnerships and new cultural programmes but rejected where a global franchise was involved. In short, a new urban colonialism was seen as legitimate where this was driven from within the state but problematic if pushed from outside.

São Paulo

In the 1930s, two researchers form North America carried out some of the first urban-sociological studies in Brazilian towns. Samuel H. Lowrie and Donald Pierson – two North American researchers in the tradition of Chicago School – wrote, respectively, about the patterns of living and housing of the *paulista* working class, and a comparison between the different zones of the town. Their affiliation with the methods of the Chicago School of sociology were clearly in evidence. Reading them several decades later we can see that, in the first case, the working-class neighbourhoods they studied remain those neighbourhoods where the descendants of pioneers in the urban industrial workforce reside. Most of these were Italian and Spanish, who had moved both in social and economic terms. The

Mooca and Bras are now oddities, industrial neighbourhoods in a period of relative de-industrialisation for Brazil, neither poor but not as affluent as other areas. No matter how much some initiatives tried to recreate an aura of old São Paulo the vision of a New York SoHo style loft area was never realised.

São Paulo, the 'South American Chicago', as it was described on tram adverts, has changed in many aspects and is now the largest metropolis of the southern hemisphere. Pierson compared the poorest and wealthiest neighbourhoods in 1940. We can now see that his poor side of the town is now not so poor since the new peripheral housing of the urban poor took place in the 1950s. However, the three wealthiest zones remain so.

The geography of this segregation started to be designed around the time of the Abolition of Slavery in 1888 and the proclamation of the Republic in 1889. As Rolnik points out, the slave town was lightly segregated and the houses of owners, commerce, workshops, and popular housing were all located between the two rivers that first delimited the town. The borders between social groups were clearly defined and in the main relationship of the city at that moment, both the *senhor* (landlord) and slave lived within the *senhor's* properties (Rolnik 1997: 30–1).

During the First Republic (1889–1930) popular neighbourhoods were produced and crossed the railway route to Santos, a port 60km from São Paulo. Between 1911 and 1914, a major urban redevelopment demolished whole quarters in the centre to build wider avenues and streets, squares, offices, stores and a theatre inspired by the Parisian Opéra. By this time, as in European towns, the themes of urban debates were on hygiene and sanitation. Since then, as Rolnik emphasises, a legal/extralegal ambiguity has allowed the creation and preservation of an elite territory protected from uses seen to debase these areas.

Unlike Salvador e Recife, São Paulo city was not landmarked by IPHAN. It was considered too eclectic, immigrant and industrial to be identified as a national symbol. When the state of São Paulo founded its landmark institutions the centre had already changed to become a historical place. However, in the 1950s the centre was the locus of cultural activities: two new museums were located there, together with many cinemas and art galleries.

By the 1960s, after the military *coup d'état*, a large number of migrants from the northeastern states of the country moved to São Paulo and started to use the central area for economic activities such as street vending, shoe shining, selling herbs, itinerant preachers, prostitutes and hustlers among others. These various activities had in common only their non-legal character and their poor social origins in the eyes of the local state but they shared the urban space with white-collar and other middle-class workers of the centre's firms. In 1995 the downtown area offered 38.5 per cent of the job opportunities in the city (Frúgoli 2000: 60). Between 1975 and 1979, a Plan of Revitalization re-classified some streets as pedestrian ones, restored major buildings and inventoried those others to be preserved. Afterwards, the mayor regretted these actions, especially the pedestrianised streets, because, in his terms, they became a permanent 'Persian market' of the informal economy.

When a leftist female mayor won the election by the end of 1988, one of the initiatives to revitalise the centre was the transfer of the city hall from a park in the south of the city, built by Oscar Niemeyer for the 400th anniversary of the city in 1954, to an old mansion in Parque Dom Pedro in the old downtown area in order to induce revitalisation to the east side of São Paulo, to Brás, a traditional working-class neighbourhood.

In 1991, a group of entrepreneurs created the Associação Viva o Centro (Save the Centre Association), which aimed, in their words, to put an end to years of decay, abandonment and challenges to the urban core where the members of the association were located (Frúgoli 2000: 69). Among these institutions was the Bank of Boston whose CEO declared on many occasions that the association should have in mind as positive examples the Marais, in Paris and Covent Garden in London. Also mentioned as urban role models were the reoccupation of areas in Boston and Seattle, Fisherman's Wharf in San Francisco and, again, Barcelona.

Since 1991, the *Viva o Centro* had to deal with different municipal powers: a left-wing mayor, two right-wing mayors with evident liaisons with real estate investors and, recently, another (female) left-winger mayor who is also an important leader of the same political party of the new elected president of the country. This mayor now promotes the Monumenta project in São Paulo, but at the same time the staff of the municipality have an anti-gentrification discourse and have projects to bring back people to live downtown which include both the low-waged as well as the middle classes. Recently a decayed hotel was converted into social housing, with loans from a federal state bank, an example of the PAR project as we will see.

It is difficult to compare Brazilian towns to European ones, along any frame of reference and especially with regard to gentrification. São Paulo now has around 10 million inhabitants and every day 3 million people occupy its downtown area. Since the early twentieth century it has been a commercial and business centre. However, the shifting of the city's sense of centrality to Paulista Avenue and then to the southwest of the city has changed the character of the site. It is now an area with hotels, finance institutions and, nevertheless, a considerable number of empty buildings. The ongoing revitalisation is centred on converting the area to new cultural uses. Train stations are turned into museums or concert halls. Bank headquarters have become cultural spaces, while the issue of removing the street vendors and sheltering the homeless are permanently under tense negotiation. The unevenness of uses and users of these urban spaces is now more evident and still poses considerable challenges for investigation.

While in São Paulo and Rio de Janeiro, 20 per cent live in *favelas*, this amount reaches 46 per cent in Recife. In this picture of poverty, some recent initiatives, should be mentioned. There is very little social housing in elected central areas of cities such as São Paulo, Salvador, São Luis and Campinas but there is now a program of retrofitting older buildings to accommodate the low-wage population called Programa de Arrendamento Residencial (PAR). This was initiated in 1999 by a federal public bank, one of the few not recently privatised in Brazil, with the aim, when applied to historical and central areas of providing dwelling places for the lower classes with houses leased for fifteen years upon which time the dweller can opt to become an owner. The maximum value of each house is about US$10,000 to close the rent gap created by abandoned buildings in central areas and to provide social housing no longer located in the periphery of the larger cities. Although PAR was not conceived in order to rehabilitate houses, but to construct new ones, it has often been used to perform this function.

In some cities, such as São Paulo and Campinas, revitalisation processes have gentrified areas for cultural and leisure purposes while also de-gentrifying other areas to provide social housing. In Campinas PAR resources have been applied to revitalise a group of working-class houses near the disused railway. The train station is becoming a cultural and events space, and the same municipal policy aims to restore historical housing for social purposes. Both practices and discourses are now happening at the same time and mostly in the same areas. The revitalisation issues, including whether to encourage gentrification or not, have re-vitalised urban debates and action in a country where the oldest areas of the cities are often less than 500 years old and where the majority have been destroyed and rebuilt many times in a short time. We might hope that the possibility remains that other uses for revitalisation like the PAR programme may be found rather than always simply leading to more gentrification.

Conclusion

Although Brazilian cities have clearly participated in global processes of economic and cultural exchange they have more often appeared as the recipients rather than the protagonists of these global flows. Brazil's moves from a heritage-based and state-centred urban policy has been demonstrated by new moves towards local partnership and cultural designation as key strategies for economic development which have also brought about displacement and gentrification in many neighbour-hoods in the larger cities. This has also brought challenges to what have been seen as intrusive forces of colonial capital in the form of the failed Guggenheim develop-ment in Rio even while culture is promoted as an internal strategy of re-colonisation and even revanchism in some city contexts.

What I have attempted to develop in this chapter is a brief glimpse of some of the key changes in the emblematic spaces of some of Brazil's cities that allow us to understand something of the specificity of changes in these cities and some of their neighbourhoods. Certainly gentrification in Brazil appears to reflect existing competition between cities within Brazil as well as between other cities at a global scale. In a historical context, as Eric Clark notes in this volume, these processes of colonisation stem back to much earlier periods.

While some Brazilian cities can be located within a wider second tier of cities in global context there is also often fierce competition between them. In any case these flows of global capital and state policies directed at economic revitalisation have demonstrably not been directed at solving some of the more intractable issues related to the Brazilian urban system. Like much of Latin America Brazil contains large towns and cities in which it is estimated that about 50 per cent of the population dwell in 'informal' residential spaces. This profound urban poverty which has featured in prize-winning films like *City of God* highlight places where hopelessness and violence lives side by side with gated communities, international centres of tourism and pleasure as well as spectacle. As with gentrification in other cities across the globe, gentrification has not provided a resolution to these contradictions and social injustices.

Notes

1 Del Rio, Vicente, *Em busca do tempo perdido. O Renascimento dos centros urbanos*. http://www.vitruvius.com.br/arquitextos/arq000/esp028.asp, 10/10/2003.
2 *Guia dos bens tombados na Bahia*, pp. 152–3.
3 *Capitania hereditária*: an administrative division of Brazil during the colonial period whose possession was inherited by the descendants.
4 In Portuguese, the etymological roots of the term *revitalization* (revitalização) are more evident than in English, for *vita*, in Latin, is *vida* (life).

15 Out of squalor and towards another urban renaissance?

Gentrification and neighbourhood transformations in southern Europe

Petros Petsimeris

Introduction

This chapter examines the forms of gentrification processes in the core cities of southern Europe. Special emphasis is given to the relationships between gentrification and temporality, its historic context and to the particular types of gentrification found in this region. While there is an important bibliography on the structure and the evolution of the southern European city (Gambi 1973; Aymonino 1977, 2000; Zevi 1997; Martinotti 1993; Leontidou 1990; Tsoulouvis 1998; Capel 1977), a limited number of studies focused on gentrification have been undertaken. These have mainly been PhD theses or studies in progress. However, this does not mean that the phenomenon has not been analysed. A number of monographs have studied the process of embourgeoisement, the social segmentation of housing and of inter and intra-urban mobility closely related to the gentrification processes.

A number of analyses of intra-urban or intra-metropolitan spaces and neighbourhood transformations have been made to date which include Gambi (1973) and Zevi (1997) for the main Italian cities, Dalmasso (1971) for Milan, Cederna (1956, 1965) and Seronde-Babonaux (1980) for Rome, Dematteis (1973), Petsimeris (1998, 1991) for the cities of the Italian industrial triangle (Turin, Milan and Genoa); Castells (1981) for Madrid, Ferras (1976) for Barcelona and, finally, Leontidou (1990a, 1990b) for Athens and Tsoulouvis (1998) for the main Greek cities. Other authors have studied the question of historic centres (Cialdini and Faldini 1978; Comoli et al. 1980) and privatisation and speculation in these centres (Crosta, 1975; Potenza 1975). Such studies have had an important influence in Spain and in Greece but also in other European countries but much less so in the English-language geographies of these cities. The purpose of this chapter is to build on these studies in the context of renewed questions about the gentrification of various cities in southern Europe which have generally been under-examined.

An ignored process?

For the south European cities there have been few studies concerning the gentrification process according to the definition given by Ruth Glass. The term gentrification was initially neglected and scholars have used other terms such as 'affinage du centre' or 'imborghesimento'. In the mid-1980s some scholars used the term but changed the spelling (gentryfication) and nowadays the term has been broadly adopted with adaptation of the pronunciation 'gentrificazione', 'jentrification', 'geantrification'. It thus became fashionable in usage by the media and was frequently confused with wider processes of imborghesimento (embourge-oisement). Regardless the term remains unpopular for left-wing politicians for many 'non ha senso' and for some continental former radical geographers gentrifi-cation is a fixation of the Anglo-Saxons who perhaps see it everywhere. We should admit that it is an uneasy term to use and in southern Europe after a period of neglect it became a fashionable term used both as abuse or in uncritical ways. To some extent every painting of a façade, every bar selling Illy coffee or increases in the number of white-collar workers was often seen as gentrification without any debate about what these changes really constituted.

The places most affected by gentrification, the historic centre, had not had a better chance of change than was now emerging and what had been a neglected area had often become a place of perceived physical, social and cultural renewal. The term 'centro storico' was ignored in a similar way as the term of gentrification. Gambi has pointed out the use and abuse of the term 'centro storico' and the complexity of its delimitation. In the *Dizionario Encyclopaedico Italiano*, one of the most prestigious and comprehensive repertoires of Italian language, in its 1956 and 1960 editions does not mention the term. However, in the edition of 1970 the term appeared with a new definition of 'centro direzionale' or CBD. According to Gambi this is also 'because the difficulty of a generally accepted definition of the term and also to the fact that the question of the historic centre is not an abstract exercise but is linked everywhere with the policies of intervention for its conservation or transformation'. In other words the city centre had little linguistic sense in the context of these cities and that the rise of a central city terminology profoundly affected new possibilities for state sponsored revitalisation in these areas.

Gentrification as fashion

Here I adopt ideas relating to fashion found in the writings of Simmel to to describe gentrification processes in southern Europe. According to Simmel:

> fashion is a form of imitation … in changing incessantly it differentiates one time from another and one social stratum from another. It unites those of a social class and segregates them from the others. The elite initiates a fashion and when the mass imitates it in an effort to obliterate the external distinctions of class abandons it for a newer mode a process that quickens with the increase of wealth.
>
> (Simmel 1957: 541)

We can argue that fashion certainly affects the ways of life and housing choices for the wealthy. In southern European cities it would appear that there were different 'fashions' expressed in terms of the location, ways of life and type of housing sought by elite groups. What differentiates the southern European cities from their American and British counterparts is that the elites have always had a residential location in the centre. Indeed, we can also argue that gentrification is not a recent phenomenon in the region but one which affected its cities during the Renaissance and the eighteenth and nineteenth centuries.

Southern European cities are highly heterogeneous and complex, and the processes of gentrification are for this reason very different in terms of its temporality and spatiality. Although we might trace early processes of gentrification here during the renaissance, contemporary gentrification arrived at the end of the twentieth century as a result of a search for distinction by the elites in a wider context of the homogenisation of the urban landscape due to the urbanisation of the 1950s and 1960s. The following suburbanisation, selective reurbanisation and de-proletarianisation fuelled the processes of gentrification. The main difference with the global cities of Britain and the United States is that while they had a stronger architectural heritage they also had a much smaller number of economic elites. They also had a dual urban core in terms of social and functional structure with the rich often living side-by-side with poorer groups. Through a number of examples we now examine patterns of action and propose a provisional typology of the gentrification phenomenon in southern Europe. In particular we will try to answer the following questions. Is gentrification a new phenomenon? What are the processes of gentrification affecting the main metropolitan areas in the region? Finally, what might we see as the key differences between these processes and those of other advanced capitalist cities?

Earlier forms of gentrification

Contrary to those generalisations which consider the southern European cities as pre-industrial entities in terms of their urban processes and urbanity, the analysis presented in this chapter shows a greater complexity of the social division of these spaces and appropriation through gentrification. Despite the identification of gentrification by Glass in the London of the mid-1950s, in the southern European cities and not only there, this process was in action at least by the eighteenth and the nineteenth centuries. As Walter Benjamin pointed out, Haussmann's physical restructuring of central Paris had many facets but the main result of this was the complete functional and social appropriation of the central areas of Paris.

Other similar phenomena were enacted across Europe where the destruction of city walls took place or where there were demolitions in order to create a modernised city. One of the most extraordinary of these events was the demolition of part of central Florence for the realisation of its *Piazza della Repubblica*. Here we can see the arch on which, in Latin, one can read the hostile attitude of the new urban pioneers of the time after the eviction and destruction of the former neighbourhood. The demolished neighbourhood is defined as 'secolare squalore' amongst which were, in fact, many important buildings of architectural heritage, including those by some of the masters of the medieval and Renaissance periods. The inscription reads 'il centro della città da secolare squalore a vita nuova restituito 1895' (the centre of the city after centuries of squalor brought back to life).

The thousands of tourists enjoying their capuccinos and aperitivos in the piazza are probably not aware that it was in this very area that 'cardo' and the 'decumanus maximus' (the heart of Roman Florence) were conjoined and that the inscription relates in fact to the revanchism of the city's elite of that time. Amongst the so-called 'squalor' had been demolished the Jewish ghetto, the *Mercato Vecchio*, and an important part of the economic structure of central Florence. This case is not isolated; similar processes affected other southern European cities before and after this year.

In Turin the beautification of via Dora Grossa (now via Garibaldi), one of the main axes of the pre-industrial city and one of the most beautiful cities of Europe in terms of its urban design, suffered the consequence of important functional and social changes (Comoli *et al.* 1980; Magnaghi and Tosoni 1980). For Sabater (1990) the development of the Cerdà Plan in Barcelona at the end of the nineteenth century also had similar important consequences in terms of the city's gentrification and displacement of both its elites and lower income groups.

All of this suggests that processes of gentrification are as old as the 'modern' city, if not older, and have occurred in a much wider range of urban contexts that the existing literature would often have us believe. Equally old is the revenge of the winners, or appropriators, the big and small Haussmanns of these various cities. Similar operations took place during Mussolini's era with the 'help' of important masters of rationalist architecture. The various 'via Romas' show us the formal result in terms of the aesthetic character of many central neighbourhoods. Here again the pre-existent communities, or 'squalori', were transformed and broken and a new urban space created that was rectilinear, ordered, with granite columns and regular façades were born in a context of eviction and succession (Cederna 1979).

Fashion, mirrors, imitation and diffusion

A number of scholars describing the processes of urban change in US and British cities in the 1950s pointed out rapid changes in the use, succession and incompatibility between older forms and new uses. For example, Rossi described the changes in the American city in the following way:

> The city changes without cease. Homes give way to factories, stores and highways. New neighbourhoods arise out of farms and wasteland. Old residential districts change their character as their residents give way to different classes and cultures. Business districts slowly migrate uptown. Mansions of yesterday sport 'rooms to let' signs today. Tenements once rented to immigrant European peasants, now house migrants from our own rural areas. How do these dramatic changes come about? In the past industry and commerce in their expansion encroach upon land used for residences. But, in larger part, the changes are mass movements of families – the end results of countless thousands of resident shifts made by urban Americans every year. Compounded in the mass, the residence shifts of urban households produce most of the change and the flux of urban population structures.
>
> (Rossi 195: 1)

Nine years later Ruth Glass (1964) was describing the dramatic changes in Inner London and the transformation of modest buildings into 'elegant, expensive residences' with significant increases in their value and with important consequences in terms of social succession. Are similar processes to be found in Southern Europe?

In southern European cities we have seen former hospitals and asylums transformed into hotels, institutions for the poor and elderly turned into research institutions and business schools, while houses are transformed into university departments and flats to fashion design studios or small 'studio' firms. In addition, former mills and pasta factories have become luxurious apartments, stables transformed into ateliers for young architects and young artists. Meanwhile, inexpensive popular tavernas and trattorie are transformed into exclusive restaurants. Entire high-streets with a range of commercial functions are invaded by more luxurious fashion functions. At the same time there is an important augmentation of the price of property and a dramatic decline of the population of the core areas.

These various changes have resulted in a decrease of residence in core areas, evictions and massive succession within the functional structure of the city. Price increases have affected all types of property and there has been a demand for buildings and flats that were often considered residual and neglected during the 1970s. At the same time the transformation of Italy, Greece and Spain, from nations of emigration to nations of immigration, had the consequence of the arrival of massive flows of international migrants, mainly from the less developed areas of the world. This led to the rapid change of certain areas that became specialised in ethnic businesses or a mix of traditional handcraft and new ethnic activities. Some parts of the historic centre, areas in proximity to the railway stations and some central places, also assumed the function of ethnic sociability.

The form of the intra-urban space

The southern European city is a mosaic of social zones which are socially, ethnically, culturally and economically differentiated. In the historic centres the types of distribution of the different income groups reflect the interaction of labour and housing markets which act as filter for the selection of activities and social groups. The increasing importance of home ownership has resulted in a decline of mobility and the consolidation of existing social forms (Padovani 1996; Leontidou 1990a, 1990b).

A number of positive or negative externalities have been conditioned by the social, economic, ethnic and cultural structure of these intra-urban spaces. Of the historic centre in particular this has not depended on local characteristics and local forces but more and more from a mix of local and international events. Even if we use the term gentrification to designate these various changes it is still not clear whether this is the same thing. The rigidity and complexity of social divisions associated with the contradictory characteristics of the residential stock (hetero-geneity in economic, social, artistic, architectural and historic terms), give rise to processes of appropriation and/or reappropriation of some segments of the housing market.

In certain neighbourhoods (particularly those which are either central or pericentral) one can witness processes of expulsion and the substitution of lower income groups by higher income groups. In the historical centre or central core, originally with town houses for the wealthy, and later occupied by the first arrivals of immigrants (filtering down between 1950–70) have often become higher-class areas (reverse filtering). It is this part of the city that is affected by processes of gentrification. But it is important to underline the heterogeneity of this area in terms of architectural typologies, form, type, degree of decay, flexibility for refurbishment or adaptation, location. In terms of heritage this area has an important architectural variety. Not all of these types appear to be gentrifiable due to quality of the materials and costs of transformation. Certainly what is nowadays the centre was the whole of the city and as such was heterogeneous in terms of its social groups, functions and buildings.

In the pericentral belt of the central city there were more varied styles. Since the beginning of the twentieth century city authorities have often located public housing on the edge of the area. Some of them are of good quality and have been gentrified (from lower-income groups to medium-income groups after the 'right buy' of the 1980s). Many of these pericentral neighbourhoods experienced gentrification processes due to their good accessibility, low congestion and important functional structure at the local level.

In the longer term upper-class areas that are environmentally the most attractive, such as areas of low-density housing, have always been occupied by the wealthier sections of the population. These areas have had a tendency to attract more and more high-income groups. When saturated younger generations have often chosen to occupy niches in the historic centre and pericentral areas this increases the tendency of gentrification in these areas.

Finally, in the outer city, or 'le periferie', high-rise housing of lower quality has dominated with lower-middle and working-class groups occupying them. In these areas there has not generally been what we might call gentrification but due to wider changes in the economic base of the city there have been processes of social succession where working-class households have been substituted by white-collar or students over time. However, in some areas of urban renewal and transformation from brown field areas to tertiary areas, such as universities, residential areas have shown gentrified islands in a sea of uniformity.

Urbanisation and homogenisation of the urban landscape as drivers of gentrification

After the 1950s the main urban areas of Spain, Italy and Greece experienced huge concentrations mainly during the period between 1950–70 followed by a period of suburbanisation mainly after the 1980s and a decline of the city core (Tsoulouvis, Petsimeris, Nello, Dematteis). This had important consequences in terms of the production of space, land uses and urban and architectural forms. Areas characterised by urbanity and complex typological articulation in terms of architecture design and urban design were transformed into a much more homogeneous landscape. The processes described by a number of scholars Pikionis (1985), Psomopoulos for Athens (1977) and Insolera (1980) could be generalised if we change the toponyms and suggest a *general model* of development of the south European city:

From 1950, and particularly after 1960, a rapid outward movement of population took place. This resulted in the linear expansion of urban development along the major circulation axes and a closing up of existing built-up areas. The north of Athens, along the foothills of Mt Penteli, and Mt Parnes, and in the regions between Peania and Koropi to the northeast of Mt Hymettos, new primarily residential areas sprang up. At the same time, almost all the coastal sections in the study area witnessed extensive construction of second homes and tourist facilities. Astronomic land prices and the absence of effective housing programmes caused large sections of the population to move to cheaper land in areas not covered by any town planning regulations. This uncontrolled development has led to severe abuses of the land. Uses have been irrationally distributed and areas have been created with many incompatible uses, also residential settlements have expanded into areas that should have been reserved for other purposes. These practices were greatly facilitated by legislation which permitted the parcelling of large tracts of land into small plots, plus the lack of any zoning or other effective controls over land speculation and building designs.

(Psomopoulos 1977: 121)

Insolera, describing the urban sprawl in Rome on the basis of aerial photos, suggests that at the beginning of the period 1960–80, Rome took form of a 'discontinuous megalopolis' during which *abusivismo* (illegal urban development) became widespread and Roman rural environs, originally characterised by an undulating landscape, were completely changed through the construction of houses and intensive built-up sprawl. Apparent here were changes of the built environment into two clear types, one where the street predominated and the other where no design was particularly distinguishable (Insolera 1980).

For Lila Leontidou (1990) this formalised duality was due to a market duality where, in Greece:

popular suburbia was combined with independence from the capitalist market. The expansion of capitalism took the form, not of rationalization and concentration of capital, but that of the domination of a rather competitive and speculative market over the previous widespread informal housing sector. The Greek housing and land market were traditionally dual, composed of a dominant capitalist/speculative and a subordinate owner-built/informal sector; landownership was fragmented; and the role of planning was minimal. Capitalism then expanded and came to control housing production, and the dual market was increasingly unified through the suppression of the informal sector.

(Leontidou 1990: 269)

In fact the urban landscape suggested that building in the city had created dense built volumes and extreme population concentration (up to 1,000 persons per hectare). Historical landmarks, such as neoclassical public buildings, were surrounded by bland architecture of white cubic forms (Papageorgiou-Venetas 2002). During the 1950s and 1960s thousands of migrants from rural areas and remote regions located in the older parts of the historic centre where they remained economically and socio-culturally divorced from the high-level service structure that was to emerge at that time. In the 1990s third-world immigrants were also concentrated into the same spaces. This colossal and rapid influx of new population occurred in the absence of any substantial policy of 'controlled growth' on the part of the national and local authorities. Post-1970 immigrants mainly settled in residential areas in or close to the city centre. In the early 1970s they took up residence in the mid- and upper-income areas and in some predominant working-class areas.

Following a period of deurbanisation and deindustrialisation the city centre was now affected by abandonment and gentrification, reflecting long-term changes in the economy of the city centre with a shift from manufacturing to service industries, and a corresponding shift in employment in the tertiary sector. At this time large parts of the workforce were made redundant forcing a corresponding reduction in their ability to pay rent. Increasing professionalisation and concentration of management and technical functions obversely created demand for higher-income housing.

These processes have had important spatial consequences, not least of which is the expulsion of blue-collar workers from the central and peri-central housing markets described earlier and where professionals and managers are exerting increasing levels of demand. New housing adjacent to the Central Business District (CBD) reflected these changes and the increasing co-presence of renewal policies. The pull exerted by one group on the changing economy of the CBD fitted with the push against by another. For the higher-income, young households, all roads now led to the historical centre while, for the working class, all roads led to a social and geographical periphery. Thus, the increasing polarisation of the economy was reflected in the increasing polarisation of neighbourhoods: at the one end, deurbanisation, deindustrialisation and abandonment, while, at the other, selective re-urbanisation and gentrification.

In this context a period of gentrification can be interpreted as a search for alternative locations by the elites in the context of an increasingly homogenised and poverty-stricken periphery. However, not all the cities have the same level of gentrifiable buildings and not all cities have attracted international, national or regional elites as potential gentrifiers. In addition, in a hierarchy of desirability Thessaloniki's and Athens' heritage housing stock is far behind that of Rome's, Madrid's, Barcelona's or Milan's.

The cores of the metropolitan areas have been characterised by strong social polarisation that is at its most extreme in the case of owner-occupied housing for lower income groups. The levels of segregation and dissimilarity indices here have increased in a context of deurbanisation and deindustrialisation. In historic centres there has been a marked social polarisation between higher-income groups located in renewed housing, and minority ethnic groups concentrated in areas of deprivation. Due to filtering lower-income groups are able to move into more central locations, especially when the central area begins to decay. However, due to either cultural reasons and/or low incomes, these groups have benefited less from the central location and upscale services (shops, theatres, etc.) than the higher social groups.

After the period of quantitative urbanisation there was a phase of huge selection of the social groups in the centre of the main Italian cities. During the period 1981–91 there was a decrease in the active population but this trend is the result of two parallel but contrasting phenomena. On the one hand the process of professionalisation, and on the other, the process of deproletarianisation of the urban social structure. This was evidenced by a substantial increase (around 50 per cent) in the number of people in the social groups at the top of the social hierarchy, and a dramatic decrease in the numbers of persons in the working-class group (around 30 per cent).

From the comparative analysis of the core cities of the Italian industrial triangle (Turin, Milan and Genoa) it can be demonstrated that the decline of population in the core areas has not affected all social groups. During the period 1981–91, Turin, Milan and Genoa saw a decline of the population (–12.7 per cent, –11.12 per cent and –3.31 per cent respectively). Similar tendencies have been observed in Florence. This evolution has affected different social groups in different ways. By disaggregating the different components of the active population one can see that the upper socio-professional groups (professional, managerial and business owners) are increasing substantially. White-collar and self-employed groups have remained stable or in slight decline while the working-class group (lavoratori dipendenti) have recorded dramatic declines. This is not the only effect of the deindustrialisation but also the effect of a selective filtration through the housing market.

The decline of the working class has been greater in the cities where the restructuring processes were more substantial (Petsimeris 1998). In the case of Milan between 1971 and 1991 saw its active population pass from 684,000 in 1971 to 584,000 in 1991 and at the historic centre from 54,000 to 39,000 respectively. However, the upper social groups increased from 55,000 to 144,000 and in the historic centre from 10,000 to 20,000. The working class meanwhile decreased from 263,000 to 137,000 and from 20,000 to 5,600 in the historic centre. In short the decrease of the working class was –48 per cent in Milan city and –71 per cent in the historic centre while the number of managers increased by 92 per cent.

Similar changes have been observed in Rome, Florence and Bologna. However, this is not an Italian tendency. It is demonstrated in changes for the other metropolises of northern Europe and for Spanish and Greek cities (Tsoulouvi and Leontidou, *London and Paris*). From an empirical analysis of southern European cities it is clear that the centres of the bigger cities had the role of filter for select social groups. The selective urbanisation of the elites and this cultural change had as a consequence the search for diversity and heterogeneity in an urban landscape of increasing homogeneity. The following areas serve as further examples that can help us to understand the changes taking place in southern European cities today.

Athens

Plaka is a condensation of Greek history with traditional ways of life and its many small tavernas. It was mainly developed during the nineteenth century and in particular after 1832, the date of the proclamation of Athens as the capital of Greece. The residential area is mixed with monuments of the Byzantine and Turkish periods and the architectural style is a mix of the popular architecture of Greece and elements of neo-classical architecture imported by the Bavarian first king of Greece. The population of the area was traditionally a mix of popular workers' quarters with some villas for the wealthy and middle classes of the nineteenth century. After this period there was a decline of the population and an out-migration of the elites that moved towards neighbourhoods in central Athens or to the suburbs of the north. After this apparent decline started, a period of re-appropriation by newer elite fractions became apparent. These groups were now looking for a new, more exclusive style of life and for buildings with more architectural character and investment value. Again, it is possible to argue that this was linked to the processes of homogenisation taking place in the urban landscape of that time.

The neighbourhood is located in the contiguous area in the northern and eastern part and is contiguous to the commercial and administrative centre of Athens to the north and the limits of the ancient agora in the west. It is one of the most ancient quarters of Athens and one of the most visited areas by tourists. It is associated as an important attraction in terms of its heritage, cultural symbolism and centrality. The area has never really had the same kind of social diversity and heterogeneity of other historic centres like that of Rome, Madrid, Barcelona, Milan and Turin which were more diverse in their composition. The area, after a period of filtering and abandonment, experienced a massive tourist influx, thirsty for Greek folklore (with its bouzouki and folk music areas, traditional Greek fiestas), and a parallel development of handicrafts and craftsmen. Since 1980 there have been important public policies which have looked to upgrade the area and have, as a consequence, served to gentrify the area through a process of social and functional succession. All things now are 'proper', the traffic is not as chaotic, the neo-classical architecture and two-to-three-storey buildings have been restored and the traditional popular characters, most of which were immortalised by the popular neo-realist cinema of the 1950s and 1960s, have now been transformed. However, the degree of gentrification in Plaka has never been as significant as that which we may find in cities like central London and New York.

Venice

Analysing Venice is complex. In one sense the whole area can be considered as a historic centre given its relatively small size and heritage. We will limit ourselves here to present the many hotel developments and luxurious apartments in the relatively poor island of Giudecca. Giudecca will be well-known to urban scholars from Wirth's research on the origins of the Jewish ghetto. The island was also named 'Spinalunga'. This area, after a period of upgrading as a summer resort for the wealthy, became a poor area through processes of investment in industrial uses for the island. One of the most impressive buildings on this area is the Mulino Stucky Mill. This building was designed by Ernst Wullekoph and commissioned by an English entrepreneur at the end of the nineteenth century, but was abandoned in the mid-1950s.

According to *piano regolatore* policy documents:

> the Giudecca Project includes a series of steps which make use of unused industrial areas or old abandoned buildings in order to bring jobs to the island. The project includes the Mulino Stucky congress centre, parks and partially public residential areas that will be offered at reduced prices (p. 84).

In terms of housing on the island there is the explicit admission that the structural plan can do little for the level of prices and the decline of population. However, much of this decline has been due to the inability of lower-income groups to access the prohibitively priced housing. However, there have been measures introduced for the hundred and more evicted families and a provision to build new houses for these people or negotiate the rent between the municipality and the landlord. In 1993 there were seventy-two such contracts. We should also emphasise that the municipality of Venice was very sensitive in terms of social housing because they refused to sell the 4,132 they owned. In fact this case was taken to the constitutional court. Venice shows processes of both privatisation as well as a resistance to gentrification through the attempt to preserve low-income groups in the city.

Rome

Like Venice, Rome may be considered a vast historic centre, particularly the area within the Aurelian walls. In this city there are similar processes of gentrification affecting other historic centres and a significant demand for housing. Here I look at those areas that have been gentrified due to the recycling of brown field land. The former pasta factory of Pantanella has been transformed by a development agency into luxurious housing explicitly referring to the tastes of those urbane clients they wish to attract. Shortly after a Mercedes dealership arrived as well as a 'bingo' hall (rather oddly given its working-class associations in the United Kingdom) and numerous luxury bars. The area of development filtered down after the cessation of the local industry and appropriated by immigrants as with other urban centres. The development had at least two objectives: to liberate the area from this marginal population and to integrate the abandoned brown field area into the rest of the city. The development sought to attract yuppies and young affluent groups who might come to spend the weekend in Rome. In practice there are also processes of studentification (the students of wealthy parents), in the sense that Darren Smith uses the term in this volume; investment purchases and couples with children.

A similar development has also been initiated in the industrial area of Rome close to the Ponte delle sette industrie. In this area another developer has transformed the Vatican Mills by converting them into luxury apartments. In terms of form it is quite similar to the architecture one sees on the waterfronts of Liverpool or London. It is also close to a very popular area of Rome in the form of the main industrial area of the capital, though less important when compared with the industrial areas of Milan, Turin, Athens and Barcelona. After the conversions were completed 'yuppy cars' (Swatch and Minis) could be seen in abundance as well as promotions for festivals of dance and music. Residents appear to consider themselves as part of a big community while an upmarket baby shop is opening in front of the building, an irony given the lack of children in the development itself. Even more ironic is the constutition of the households themselves who, in their younger years, would have been opposed to the renewal of the historic centre and its gentrification.

San Salvario-Valentino, Turin

Our final case study is that of San Salvario-Valentino which formed one of the early extensions of the city of Turin. Città quadrata is the main historic centre of the western expansion of the boroughs contiguous to the medieval city. The eastern side (Corso Massimo d'Azeglio parallel to the river and next to the park of Valentino) is now occupied by the faculty of Architecture of Turin University. On the west side it is delimited by the railway station of Porta Nuova. On the north it is contiguous with the historic centre, the administrative and commercial area of Corso Vittorio Emanuele, and to the south the quarter of Lingotto where there the Lingotto industry of Turin and now directional headquarters of Fiat is located.

This area is one of the most complex in terms of a typology of gentrification activity in the region. It is characterised by the presence of eighteenth- and nineteenth-century buildings, though not as prestigious as other areas in the city. In the past the area was a concentration of ethnic and religious minorities (Jews, Valdesians, Protestant and Catholic communities). One of the most important aspects of this area is the presence of the universities which led effectively to a 'student invasion' of the housing stock and a net gain in functions taking place in these areas. In the segment of the neighbourhood delimited by Via Madama Christina and Corso Massimo d'Azeglio the presence of students is significant and a number of university faculties are are also located there.

In the neighbourhood there is a significant diversity of architecture, mainly luxurious buildings dating from the gentrification and renewal of the area in the 1960s and 1970s. On the western edge and centre of the neighbourhood was an important concentration of low-income groups during the late nineteenth century and later during the 1970s. Many of the changes in the area relate to the presence of the university, to a process of studentification and the influence felt due to the proximity of the faculty. In this process students were more able to compete for accommodation than medium- to low-income groups of one or two earners living in the area. The area thus became occupied by academics, professionals and dual income families, but also working-class families (some who had arrived from the south that arrived in Turin in the early 1960s and 1970s).

The historic residential part constitutes around half of the total area. The area as a whole is now ranked as one of the four wealthiest areas in Turin. However, though the process of gentrification has been extensive it has never fully dominated because of the range of architectural forms in the area as well as the range of vertical and horizontal dwelling types and the mix of housing conditions and decay.

The area started to become the centre of the media attention after the *Stampa* newspaper started referring to an immigration problem. Some residents of the neighbourhood began to act as vigilantes against Africans and Albanians who had moved to the area. The involvement of right-wing parties began with requests to have a greater police presence in the area while left-wing parties started to request more immigration controls. The neighbourhood became a centre of attention for the media, both nationally and internationally. The result was the decrease of property prices in the area along with panic selling and one of the most well-known and respectable areas of the city became a national landmark now known as a ghetto. Even respectable newspapers (*Il Manifesto* and *Le Monde diplomatique*) carried articles titled 'Turin; city with a ghetto at its heart' with a photo of an immigrant black man on his balcony behind a line of drying clothes.

The end of the story is that the situation in San Salvario has changed. The results of the 2001 census will, no doubt, reveal important changes while field trips already show important works of rehabilitation in the area. While some people bought their flats because they were unable to move or because they wanted to stay, things are now becoming less problematic though policing remains strong during the night and there is a significant drug market at the junction between Via Santanselmo and Via Principe Tomaso. A certain number of big developers have bought entire buildings now being rehabilitated into housing for middle-class households with a large increase in their value.

In terms of retailing there are now more ethnic bars, cheap telephone and internet centres, kebab shops which were non-existent in Turin in the 1970s and 1980s, as well as food shops for African and Asians. There remain areas that may be gentrified in the future even while other areas within the neighbourhood may be likely to continue filtering down income groups in the area. The new complex situation suggests a kind of urban poker in which entire buildings are being speculated upon with the outcome being a new set of winners and losers in a neighbourhood that has seen a tumultuous history. Like the other case studies featured here San Salvario shows a complex pattern of appropriation in the form of gentrification with an attendant process of displacement while, at the same time, the areas often retain an impression of strong social diversity in ways which perhaps differ from the gentrified neighbourhoods of the United Kingdom or United States.

Conclusions

Gentrification in a range of southern European cities has taken place alongside their counterparts in the urban north and west. The chronology and location of gentrification activity here appear outside the frames within which the debate has traditionally been focused. While it is difficult to suggest a south European 'type' it is also clear that the gentrification has some particular features while carrying a set of underlying and shared features with that seen elsewhere. Nevertheless, a reading of the architectural and physical form of these cities appears essential in understanding the relatively significant and socially selective move to the central city. In addition I have argued that notions of urban revitalisation, captured by the inscriptions of past city fathers, suggest much earlier waves of gentrification, displacement and an anticipated urban renaissance predicated on rising above the squalor that lower class uses of the central city appeared to represent.

We may conclude that gentrification processes have often not had the same root causes and intensity as those of North America and Britain mainly due to the form of the historic centres and their social and functional complexity. The main similarity between these two contexts concerns the core city in terms of its economic, social and symbolic centrality. In Athens, Barcelona, Madrid, Rome, Milan and Turin the inner areas have experienced increasing concentrations of population with higher incomes. Another similarity concerns the rapidity of urbanisation and concentration of population (mainly internal migration) to the core areas from the 1950s to the 1970s and, after the 1980s, the attraction of economic migrants from Africa, Asia, Latin America and Eastern Europe towards the city and in particular in the core areas. Thus we can identify a bifurcation in the trajectories of many neighbourhoods in these cities with simultaneous downward and upward social changes.

The main differences in the patterns of urban change I have looked at here concern the degree of urbanisation and the physical structure of the historic centres. In Greece the historic city centres are not as large in terms of residential capacity and architectural complexity as those of the main Italian and Spanish cities and the conservation is far behind that of the Italian historic centres. Today these urban agglomerations are undergoing a process of profound socio-economic change, and like practically all metropolitan areas and large cities which grew very rapidly during the postwar boom, are now having to face the consequences of stable or declining populations. In addition the industrial sector is declining in importance in terms of employment and no longer has such a strong influence as a locational attractor.

The generally muted existence of a new or expanded middle class is not particularly sustainable in the Italian, Spanish and Greek context. Nevertheless, socially selective settlement in the inner-city areas appears all the more pronounced when set against the population loss of many of the urban centres. Cities like Rome and Barcelona do appear to have become more connected to an international set of flows but this is as much linked to immigration of desperate groups of refugees as to a weightless trans-urban elite. This is also true of many of the neighbourhoods I have spent many years exploring. Gentrification appears as a partial but increasingly important phenomena but one which has rarely been a total force. However, we should be wary of the goals of urban planners and policy-makers all looking to emulate the success of cities like Barcelona and perhaps increasingly seeing the saviour of the city increasingly as the middle classes. Is it possible that a new urban renaissance is intended but which will repeat history? The possibility remains that a programme is being unwound which will again strive to rise above the perceived 'squalor' imposed on the lives of the affluent by the poor, the migrant and working classes.

16 The order and simplicity of gentrification – a political challenge

Eric Clark

We came with visions, but not with sight. We did not see or understand where we were or what was there, but destroyed what was there for the sake of what we desired. ... And this habit of assigning a higher value to what might be than to what is has stayed with us, so that we have continued to sacrifice the health of our land and of our communities to the abstract values of money making and industrialism.

(Wendell Berry, *The Gift of Good Land*, 1982: 82)

As the concept of gentrification celebrates an even forty years, some of the most basic questions about the process itself remain contentious. What is gentrification? What are its root causes? There are surely no lack of answers, though these are largely stamped by disciplined convention. The purpose of this chapter is to revisit these basic questions and formulate answers that facilitate 'having gentrification clearly in view' so it can 'be scrutinized effectively' (Beauregard 1986: 54).

I will argue for a broader definition of gentrification than is commonly found in the literature. Our overly narrow definitions render the concept genuinely chaotic by conflating contingent and necessary relations. This effectively interferes with probing underlying causes and slants our view towards particularities. I will also argue for a more inclusive perspective on the geography and history of gentrification.

I will argue that the root causes of gentrification are: commodification of space, polarised power relations, and a dominance of vision over sight associated with what Wendell Berry calls 'the vagrant sovereign' (1977: 53). We are so busy pursuing superficial particular truths we lose touch with and fail to maintain these deeper more universal truths about gentrification. I will argue that we need to break with the present norm insisting upon emphasising and focusing on the chaos and complexity of gentrification. We wrongly assume that seeking to identify order and simplicity in gentrification is tantamount to reductionism and simple-mindedness, and that critical thinking requires us to stick to the lodestars of chaos and complexity. This overriding tendency in gentrification research is not unrelated to more general trends in social science where there has been 'a remarkable turn-around in radical political sensibilities' which has seen the social construction of objects of study dominate over other discourses of understanding (Sayer 2001: 687).

A question less frequently posed is: why does gentrification lead to violent conflict in some places and not in others? Another purpose of this chapter is to suggest what the key factors are behind this difference and argue for more engagement in developing policies and practices effectively removing the bases for severe conflict. I will argue that two key factors are degree of social polarisation and practices surrounding property rights. In places characterised by a high degree of social polarisation, short on the rights of users of place and long on the rights of owners of space (i.e. where there is an abundance of vagrant sovereigns given free reins), the conflict inherent in gentrification becomes inflammatory. That is not so in places characterized by relative equality and judicially practised recognition of the rights of users of place.

I doubt any reader of this volume will have failed to notice the connection between the title of this chapter and the title of Robert Beauregard's influential chapter in *Gentrification in the City* (Smith and Williams 1986). It may appear that I aim to show just how wrong Beauregard was. Not at all. I agree with Beauregard's basic arguments and regard his seminal work among the best on gentrification.[1] My complaint is not with Beauregard but rather with how his thoughtful statement has been received and used in ways I see as misdirected. Generally interpreted as a call to recognise and focus on the chaos and complexity of gentrification, Beauregard's genuine concern for the 'essence of gentrification', its 'essential meanings and underlying causes', its 'essential form', and the 'structural forces necessary for its general form' (1986: 35, 36, 40) has been glossed over. Indeed it would not surprise me if Beauregard would find in the literature since 1986 a need to recognise the order and simplicity of gentrification, every bit as much as its chaos and complexity.

Beauregard's 'theoretical goal was to penetrate the layers of ideology and positivist social research which clothe gentrification, yet not probe so deep as to pass by its concrete manifestations' (1986: 54). An alternative title of the present chapter indicating its purpose and direction might be 'Gentrification: probing deep'. I suggest we need more deep probing, and that this does not preclude sensitivity to the particulars and contingencies of gentrification processes in specific contexts. On the contrary, it can help us to grasp better these manifestations as opposed to resigning before their complexity.

In the end, the arguments forwarded provide a base for presenting a challenge to gentrification research. The challenge is to engage in comparative analyses with a focus on policy issues in order to foster a politics of place in which the playing field is evened, the voices of all actors involved and influenced more fully recognised and the conflicts inherent to gentrification openly negotiated.

Gentrification: an elastic yet targeted definition

Gentrification is a process involving a change in the population of land-users such that the new users are of a higher socio-economic status than the previous users, together with an associated change in the built environment through a reinvestment in fixed capital. The greater the difference in socio-economic status, the more noticeable the process, not least because the more powerful the new users are, the more marked will be concomitant change in the built environment. It does not matter where, and it does not matter when. Any process of change fitting this description is, to my understanding, gentrification.

There are more often than not a variety of qualifiers attached to definitions of gentrification which narrow it down to more specific contexts. 'Gentrification is an inner city process'. Why? The process occurs in other places as well, which social change in many Scandinavian fishing villages attests to. This means that any explanation for it taking place predominantly in inner cities must be based on scrutiny of contingent relations of historically specific contexts. 'Gentrification takes place in residential areas'. Why? Are not daytime and workplace populations as relevant as night time and residential populations? What about the gentrification of waterfront warehouses and shipyards, for instance Aker Brygge in Oslo? 'Gentrification involves the rehabilitation of architecturally attractive but unmaintained buildings'. Why? In many instances, yes, but these are hardly necessary or definitive. For years I have waited for the convincing argument why renovated buildings can be sites of gentrification, but not new buildings replacing demolished buildings. With as much anticipation, I have awaited the succinct delineation between rehabilitation and clearance/new construction, wondering in which category the cleared lot with braced and girded façade will fall.

It is easy to confuse narrowness with precision, but when qualifiers are not based on relations necessary to the phenomenon, they detract from precision, the narrowness being arbitrary rather than meaningful. For some phenomena, racism for instance, a broad definition is more accurate and therefore more interesting than a narrow one, the additional qualifying abstractions of which may work in social contexts to reproduce the broader phenomenon they supposedly narrow in on. This is easy to see in the case of racism, where narrow definitions cluttered with qualifiers protect racist perspectives from scrutiny. Perhaps we should be asking ourselves, and empirically investigating, to what extent our narrow chaotic conceptions of gentrification play a role in reproducing the phenomenon we claim to zero in on.

Abstractions based on non-necessary relations lead to chaotic conceptions, and

'No amount of sophistication in research methods can compensate for such sloppy abstractions' (Sayer 2000: 19–20). There is a simple reason for these abstractions slipping into our conceptions. Causal forces are commonly found in contingent relations, analysis of which is therefore necessary for adequate explanation of a concrete process – for instance the location of a gentrifying neighbourhood. But being necessary for explaining a particular case is different from being a necessary relation basic to the wider process. Central location may be one important cause of the process in some cases, but abstracting this relation to define the process leads to a chaotic conception of the process, arbitrarily lumping together centrality with gentrification. What becomes of gentrification in rural areas? Calling it something else would involve just another form of chaotic conception based on another form of bad abstraction that arbitrarily divides gentrification, 'thereby "carving up" the object of study with little or no regard for its structure and form' (Sayer 1992: 138).

There is nothing chaotic about gentrification in inner cities and in rural areas, in neighbourhoods and in non-residential areas, through rehabilitation and through demolition/new construction. There is, however, something chaotic about conceptualising gentrification according to these aspects, since none of them stands in a necessary relation to its occurrence.

This may seem like hair-splitting, but it has consequences. The qualifiers 'inner city', 'rehabilitation' and 'residential' have been repeated enough times to become entrenched. Time and time again when inquiring about gentrification in cities I have visited the answer has been, 'No, we don't have gentrification processes here', only to find out later, after follow-up questions occasionally spurred by visual evidence, that there was gentrification going on, but not in the inner city, not through rehabilitation of buildings, and not in old residential neighbourhoods. The collective efforts of gentrification researchers have given the world a chaotic conception of a process we are supposed to know much about. How can we expect others to have more rational conceptions than the ones we generate as researchers?

This kind of chaos, not the mundane chaos associated with complexity, needs to be addressed. I agree with Atkinson (2003b: 2347) that 'the problem of gentrification is less its conceptualisation and more about the need for a project which will begin to address the systematic inequalities of urban society upon which gentrification thrives', and will address this below. I believe, however, that our infatuation with a shifting and complex understanding of gentrification and our predominantly chaotic conceptualisations of the process hinder recognition of that need and render ourselves poorly equipped to fulfil it. There is nothing quite so useful as good theory.

Another conventional truth I want to dispute concerns the time-space delineation of gentrification. There is a story about the historical origin of gentrification that reads like a mantra: once upon a time (the early 1960s to be more precise), Ruth Glass discovered the very first instance of gentrification in a London neighbourhood. She is accredited in so many words as having found and identified a *new* process whereby a *new* urban gentry transformed working-class quarters. The story conflates the origin of the concept with the origin of the phenomenon. Ruth Glass did indeed coin the term in 1964, but it is careless to turn this into an assumption that we have here the origin of the phenomenon.[2] This is untenable even with the narrowest of definitions, yet is repeated with sufficient frequency to become believed.

With the definition forwarded above it would be a tall task to show that gentrification started in London in the early 1960s. This 'process of conquest' (N. Smith 1996: xv) goes at least as far back as the mid-1800s when Friedrich Engels observed spatially concentrated displacements of workers to make space for new 'spatial fixes' of capital in search of potential profits and land rents. And did not Haussmann's remodelling of Paris entail in some places the two kinds of change associated with gentrification? Urban history holds many examples of gentrification far earlier and far away from 1960s Islington. Holding on to the story about gentrification's origins in postwar London is grounded in convention, not critical thought.

There is a similar story about the global spread of gentrification. Confident proclamations ring out: Gentrification is now global! The problem with this is not if gentrification can be observed in places around the world, but is again the issue of time: it is *now* global. The broader, more 'rational' (less chaotic) conception of gentrification argued for here extends not only the history but also the spatial scope of the phenomenon beyond the received limitation to large postwar western cities. This is again a matter of conflating concept with phenomenon. It is more accurate to say that the concept of gentrification is now global, diffusing as the geographic foci of gentrification research has expanded. The extent of occurrence of the phenomenon from a global historical perspective remains however largely uncharted.

If the global reach of gentrification is not new, it is certainly widened and accentuated by what Neil Smith calls 'the generalization of gentrification as a global urban strategy', based on 'the mobilization of urban real-estate markets as vehicles of capital accumulation' (2002: 437, 446). The language of this strategy is sugar coated with images of revitalisation, regeneration, renewal, reinvestment and redevelopment, while its legitimacy is anchored in the 'necessity' to become a 'global city', a 'creative city', an attractive city, in competition with other cities. The social costs of the strategy are, if at all recognised, deemed necessary and unavoidable (Asheim and Clark 2001; Lund Hansen, Andersen and Clark 2001).

Theorising order in contingency

A rational, non-chaotic conception of gentrification must be delineated by under-lying necessary relations and causal forces as distinguished from contingent causes and relations. The root causes of gentrification are: commodification of space, polarised power relations, and a dominance of vision oversight characteristic of 'the vagrant sovereign'. Much energy has been spent in the gentrification literature distinguishing between and arguing for and against production/supply-side theory and consumption/demand-side theory. But neither side is comprehensible without the other, and all present theories of gentrification touch bottom in these basic conditions for the existence of the phenomenon.

The commodification of space opens up space for conquest, facilitating 'highest and best' land uses to supplant present uses (Blomley 2002), or as David Harvey puts it, 'forcing the *proper* allocation of capital to land' (1982: 360). Note the normative naturalising tendency – who would care to argue for lower and worse uses or improper allocations? It works in tandem with the seeking of vagrant sovereigns to realise visions through the economic exploitation of potentials, destroying the actual in the process. Polarised power relations – economic, political and judicial – are a necessary condition for the tandem dynamic to work: the more polarised, the more forceful and active the dynamic.

As a process of conquest, gentrification is related to colonialism, a relation laid bare in Neil Smith's analysis of *The New Urban Frontier* (1996). Colonialism suggests another geopolitical scale, but the underlying forces of commodified space, polarised power relations and the impulsive roamings of vagrant sovereigns connect the two processes (cf. Cindi Katz 2001 on 'vagabond capitalism'). Gentrification is colonialism at the neighbourhood scale, though the structures and mechanisms involved are by no means limited by neighbourhood boundaries, as ties to foreign direct investment and 'global city' politics makes abundantly clear.

The following passage from Wendell Berry's *The Unsettling of America* is not about gentrification, but provides nonetheless a concise formulation:

> Generation after generation, those who intended to remain and prosper where they were have been dispossessed and driven out ... by those who were carrying out some version of the search for El Dorado. Time after time, in place after place, these conquerors have fragmented and demolished traditional communities, the beginnings of domestic cultures. They have always said that what they destroyed was out-dated, provincial, and contemptible. And with alarming frequency they have been believed and trusted by their victims, especially when their victims were other white people.
>
> (Berry 1977: 4)

This is as relevant in the 'new' urban post-industrial frontier as it is in the 'old' rural agricultural frontier.

The dreams and visions of vagrant sovereigns disembed and displace those of present users, a process powerfully facilitated by the operation of land markets in capitalist space economies. Potential land rents are boosted by how much vagrant sovereigns are willing to pay to realise their dreams. Actual land rents are limited by how little present users can afford in order to hang on to their dreams. Though the political economics of the rent gap mechanism and its underlying structures are vastly more complex (Clark 1987, 1995, 2004; Harvey 1982; Sheppard and Barnes 1990), this simple relation of conquest is essential to its workings.

> As long as ideas of a feasible and desirable alternative to capitalism are in short supply, the possibility of capitalism within a moral society becomes the next best thing to which to turn.
>
> (Sayer 2001: 705)

Gentrification leads to violent conflict in many cities (N. Smith 1996). In other places we can observe a 'more benign unwinding of the process' (Atkinson 2003b: 2343). I believe a comparative analysis aimed at understanding why this process turns into tumult in some places and not in others would find two key factors to be degree of social polarisation and practices surrounding property rights. In places characterised by a high degree of social polarisation, short on legally practised recognition of the rights of users of place and long on legally practised recognition of the rights of owners of space, the conflict inherent in gentrification becomes inflammatory. Not so in places characterised by relative equality and legally pract-ised recognition of the rights of users of place. If so, this indicates a direction for political engagement aimed to curb the occurrence of gentrification and to change societal relations such that when it does occur (and it will), conditions are established for more benign ends.

This kind of comparative analysis is strikingly absent in the gentrification literature. Academia, it seems, does not encourage interest in policy issues and political engagement, rewarding instead awareness of the 'chaos and complexity' of the phenomenon. While there is no lack of critique of gentrification as a strategic policy, there is a dearth of effort to outline alternatives or to the variability of grounded impacts in a wider variety of settings. This poses a considerable challenge to gentrification research.

Conflicts arise between interests associated with linear rhythms of 'consecutive-ness and reproduction of the same phenomena' (users of place seeking continuity in place) and interests associated with cyclical 'rhythms of new beginnings' (owners of space, vagrant sovereigns seeking new 'rewards'), as rents flow through the circuit of built environments (Lefebvre 1996: 231). The 'essential and determinant factor is money' argued Lefebvre (1996: 225), and concluded:

> When relations of power take over relations of alliance, when the rhythms of 'the other' make impossible the rhythms of 'the self', then a total crisis explodes, with the deregulation of all compromises, arhythmy, implosion-explosion of the city…
>
> (1996: 239)

While conflict is the necessary outcome of the forces at play, it is possible to reduce conflict and foster 'more benign unwindings'. Compromise can be regulated. Gentrification cannot be eradicated in capitalist societies, but it can be curtailed and the playing field can be changed such that when gentrification does take place it involves replacement rather than displacement, however difficult it is to draw an unambiguous line between them (Atkinson 2000b).

Gentrification underscores the importance of developing radical alternative politics of place and provides a field in which negotiations can be pursued and alternative politics honed. Where 'recognition is distorted by distribution' (Sayer 2001: 704), this needs to be addressed, partly through mechanisms of redistribution, partly through insistence on recognition in spite of warped distribution. We need a politics of place whereby political priorities are 'established out of the open but fair power-play between agonistic actors and their competing and often conflicting claims' (Amin 2004: 39). And we need to acknowledge that it is not a simple issue of defence and conservation: 'Challenges to the current construction and role of a place may sometimes be a more appropriate strategy than defence' (Massey 2004: 17).

To move successfully in this direction, we need to avoid the pitfall of simple division into conquerors and victims:

> We can understand a great deal of our history … by thinking of ourselves as divided into conquerors and victims. In order to understand our own time and predicament and the work that is to be done, we would do well to shift the terms and say that we are divided between exploitation and nurture. The first set of terms is too simple for the purpose because, in any given situation, it proposes to divide people into two mutually exclusive groups … The terms exploitation and nurture, on the other hand, describe a division not only between persons, but also within persons. We are all to some extent the products of an exploitative society, and it would be foolish and self-defeating to pretend that we do not bear its stamp.
>
> (Berry 1977: 7)

Visiting Malmö, Neil Smith asked me to show him the battlefields of gentrification. At the time, I was at a loss to explain that there were processes of gentrification in Malmö, but no battlefields. Conflicting interests, displacement, personal tragedies, yes, but not the desperation behind battlefields. The cumulative outcome of political and legal battles in Sweden during the twentieth century set the stage for less violent ways of dealing with inherently conflictual processes of change. I believe it is fair and accurate to say this is changing, with increasing polarisation and decreasing concern for the rights of users of place. Perhaps there will in the foreseeable future be gentrification battlefields also in Sweden. That depends on our willingness to face up to the 'faces of oppression' (Young 1990; cf. Harvey

1993), to develop relations of alliance between the interests of linear and cyclical rhythms. It depends on our capacity to see the order and simplicity of gentrification, and our willingness to participate far more courageously in the political challenge it presents.

Notes

1 It is unfortunate, however, that the understanding of chaotic conceptions Beauregard conveys is inaccurate. Given the authority the chapter continues to enjoy, this has not been helpful in edifying appreciation of the problems underlying chaotic conceptions of gentrification and how a more rational conception may be tailored.

2 David Harvey, *The Economist* and others have noted that globalisation is a new and fashionable term for imperialism. Similarly, gentrification is a middle-aged term for a process for which the victims may have had words long in use. This is pure conjecture, but I would wager a pretty penny that a good urban social historian could find some of those words with a modicum of concentrated effort. Little did Ruth Glass and whoever coined globalisation know just how successful their memes would be!

References

Abu-Lughod, J. (1994a) *From Urban Village to East Village: The Battle for New York's Lower East Side*, Oxford: Basil Blackwell.

Abu-Lughod, Janet L. (1994b) 'The battle for Tompkins Square park', in J. L. Abu-Lughod (ed.) *From Urban Village to East Village*, Cambridge: Blackwell, pp. 233–66.

Aitkenhead, M. *et al.* (1975) 'Rehabilitation, renovation and social change: the Gerrard-Logan Area', unpublished paper, Division of Social Science, York University (Toronto).

Ak, B. (2002) 'Strateji yokluğu, Narmalı Han ve diğerleri', *Istanbul*, 41: 136–8.

Alberdi, B. and Levenfeld, G. (1996) 'Spain', in P. Balcin (ed.) *Housing Policy in Europe*, London, Routledge, pp. 170–87.

Aleksander Noworol and Rafal Serafin, 'Krakow towards a sustainable urban life'. Economic Commission for Europe (ECE)Workshop on Encouraging Local Initiatives Towards Sustainable Consumption Patterns (2–4 February 1998, Vienna, Austria).

Alexander, I. (1998) 'Community action and urban sustainability: hope for the millennium?', *Urban Policy and Research*, 16(2): 107–16.

Alisch, M. und Dangschat, J. S. (1996) 'Die Akteure der Gentrification und ihre Karrieren', in J. Friedrich und R. Kecskes (eds) *Gentrification; Theorie und Forschungsergebnisse*, Opladen: Leske und Budrich, pp. 95–129.

Alisch, M. und zum Felde, W. (1990) 'Das gute Wohngefühl ist weg – Wahrnehmungen, Bewertungen und Reaktionen von Bewohnern im Vorfeld der Verdrängung', in J. Blasius und J. S. Dangschat (eds) *Gentrification – die Aufwertung innenstadtnaher Wohnviertel*, Frankfurt/M. und New York: Campus, pp. 277–300.

Amado, J. (1964) *Shepherds of the Night*, London: The Harvill Press.

Amin, Ash (2004) 'Regions unbound: towards a new politics of place', *Geografiska Annaler B*, 86, 33–44.

Anderson K. (1993a) 'Constructing geographies: "race", place and the making of Sydney's Aboriginal Redfern', in P. Jackson and J. Penrose (eds) *Constructions of Race, Place and Nation*, London: UCL Press.

Anderson K. (1993b) 'Place narratives and the origins of the Aboriginal settlement in inner Sydney, 1972–73', *Journal of Historical Geography*, 19(3): 314–35.

Anderson K. (2000) '"The beast within": race, humanity, and animality', *Environment and Planning D: Society and Space*, 18: 301–20.

Anglen, R. and Curnutte, M. (2000) 'Housing group made deals with insiders', *The Cincinnati Enquirer*, 11 February.

265

References

Arantes, A. (2000a) *O espaço da diferença*, Campinas: Editora Papirus.

Arantes, A. (2000b) *Paisagens paulistanas*, Campinas: Editora da Unicamp.

Argus (1997) 'Ermittlung gebietstypischer Mietobergrenzen in den Sanierungsgebieten Helmholtzplatz, Kollwitzplatz, Teutoburger Platz, Winsstraße, Bötzowstraße in Berlin-Prenzlauer Berg', Berlin: Unpublished.

Argus (1999) 'Längsschnitt-Untersuchung über die Wirkung von Mietobergrenzen auf die Mietentwicklung im freifinanziert modernisierten Wohnungsbestand in den Sanierungsgebieten von Prenzlauer Berg', Berlin: Unpublished.

Argus (2000) 'Wohnmobilität in Sanierungsgebieten. Wegzugsmotive von Haushalten aus den Sanierungsgebieten in Berlin-Prenzlauer Berg 1994 bis 1999', Berlin: Unpublished.

Armstrong, H. (1994) 'Cultural continuity in multicultural sub/urban places', in K. Gibson and S. Watson (eds) *Metropolis Now*, Australia: Pluto Press.

Asheim, Bjørn and Clark, Eric (2001) 'Creativity and cost in urban and regional development in the "new" economy', *European Planning Studies*, 9: 805–11 (guest editorial in special issue on creative cities and social costs).

Ashworth, G. and Turbridge, J. (1990), *The Tourist Historic City*, London: Belhaven Press.

ASUM und Mieterberatung (2003) 'Sozialstudie zur Fortschreibung der Sozialen Sanierungsziele und der Mietobergrenzen für die Sanierungsgebiete von Prenzlauer Berg', Berlin: Unpublished.

Atkinson, R. (2000a) 'The hidden costs of gentrification: displacement in central London', *Journal of Housing and the Built Environment*, 15(4): 307–26.

Atkinson, R. (2000b) 'Professionalisation and displacement in Greater London', *Area*, 32: 287–96.

Atkinson, R. (2000c) 'Measuring gentrification and displacement in London', *Urban Studies*, 37: 149–65.

Atkinson, R. (2001) 'Domestication by cappuccino or a revenge on urban space'. Paper presented at Institute of British Geographers, University of Plymouth. 5 January, 2001.

Atkinson, R. (2002) 'Does gentrification help or harm urban neighbourhoods? An assessment of the evidence-base in the context of the new urban agenda'. ESRC Centre for Neighbourhood Research, University of Glasgow, Paper 5, http://www.neighbourhoodcentre.org.uk

Atkinson, R. (2003a) 'Domestication by cappuccino or a revenge on urban space? Control and empowerment in the management of public spaces', *Urban Studies*, 40(9): 1211–45.

Atkinson, R. (ed.) (2003b) 'Gentrification in a new century: misunderstood saviour or vengeful wrecker? What really is the problem with gentrification?' *Urban Studies*, (special issue), 40(12): 2343–50.

Aymonino, C. (1977) *Lo studio dei fenomeni urbani*, Rome: Officina Edizioni.

Aymonino, C. (2000) *Il significato delle città*, Venice: Marsilio.

Ayuntamiento de Bilbao (2000) 'Plan integral de rehabilitación de Bilbao La Vieja, San Francisco y Zabala', Bilbao.

Ayuntamiento de Bilbao (2002) 'Bilbao, ciudad de oportunidades', Bilbao.

Ayuntamiento de Madrid (2001) 'El proyecto de Madrid'. Online. Available: http://www.plandesevilla.org/eventos/declaracion/doc/ponencia_madrid.pdf (29 May 2003).

Badcock, B. (1989) 'An Australian view of the rent gap hypothesis', *Annals of the Association of American Geographers*, 79: 125–45.

Badcock, B.A. (1991) 'Neighbourhood change in inner Adelaide: an update', *Urban Studies*, 28: 553–8.

Badcock, B. (1993) 'Notwithstanding the exaggerated claims, residential revitalization really is changing the form of some Western cities: a response to Bourne', *Urban Studies*, 30(1): 191–5.

Badcock, B. (1995) 'Building on the foundations of gentrification: inner city housing development in Australia in the 1990s', *Urban Geography*, 16: 70–90.

Badcock, B. (2001) 'Thirty years on: gentrification and class changeover in Adelaide's inner suburbs, 1966–96', *Urban Studies*, 38: 1559–72.

Balchin, P. (ed.) (1996) *Housing Policy in Europe*, London: Routledge.

Banco de España (2002) 'El mercado de la vivienda en España', *Boletín Económico*, September: 51–61.

Barnes, Julian E. (2000) 'The trendy frontier? Eastward Ho! in Brooklyn', *New York Times*, 30 July: A29.

Barnes, T. and Duncan, J. (1992), *Writing Worlds: Discourse, Text and Metaphor in the Representation of Landscape*, London and New York: Routledge.

Baum S. (1997) 'Sydney, Australia: a global city? Testing the social polarisation thesis', *Urban Studies*, 34(11): 1881–901.

BBC (2002) 'E-cyclopedia's glossary of 2002', Online. Available at http://bbc.co.uk/1/hi/uk/2614839.stm.

BBU – Verband Berlin-Brandenburgischer Wohnungsunternehmer (2000) 'BBU-Marktmonitor. Der Immobilienmarkt Berlin-Brandenburg 2000 – Wohnimmobilien', Berlin: Unpublished.

Beauregard, R. (1986) 'The chaos and complexity of gentrification', in N. Smith and P. Williams (eds) *Gentrification of the City*, London: Unwin Hyman.

Beauregard, R. (1990) 'Trajectories of neighborhood change: the case of gentrification', *Environment and Planning A*, 22: 855–74.

Benach, N. (2000) 'Nuevos espacios de consumo y construcción de imagen de la ciudad de Barcelona', *Estudios Geográficos*, 61(238): 189–205.

Benevolo, L. (1996) *Venezia il nuovo piano urbanistico*, Bari: Editori Laterza.

Bennett, T. (1993) 'History on the rocks', in J. Frow and M. Morris (eds) *Australian Cultural Studies: A Reader*, Sydney: Allen and Unwin.

Bennett, L. (1998) 'Do we really wish to live in a communitarian city? Communitarian thinking and the redevelopment of Chicago's Cabrini-Green Public Housing Complex', *Journal of Urban Affairs*, 20(2): 99–116.

Berichte zur Stadterneuerung in Berlin, Berlin fortlfd. = Senatsverwaltung für Stadt-entwicklung (continued): Reports on the progress of urban renewal activities in Berlin, Berlin.

Berkoz, L. (2001) 'The interregional location of foreign investers in Turkey', *European Planning Studies*, 9(8): 979–94.

Bernt, M. (1998) *Stadterneuerung unter Aufwertungsdruck*, Bad Sinzheim: Pro Universitate Verlag.

Berry, B. J. L. (1964) 'Cities as systems within systems of cities' *Proceedings of the Regional Science Association*, 13: 147–63.

Berry, B. J. L. (1972) *City Classification Handbook*, New York: Wiley.

Berry, B. (1985) 'Islands of renewal in seas of decay', in P. Peterson (ed.) *The New Urban Reality*, Washington, DC: Brookings Institution.

Berry, W. (1977) *The Unsettling of America: Culture and Agriculture*, New York: Avon.

Berry, W. (1982) *The Gift of Good Land*, New York: North Point Press.

Bhabha, H. K. (ed.) (1990), *Narration and Nation*, London and New York: Routledge.

References

Bhabha, H. K. (1994) *The Location of Culture*, London: Routledge.

Bilbao Metrópoli-30 (1999) *Informe de Progreso 1998*, Bilbao: Asociación Bilbao Metrópoli-30.

Blasius, J. (1993) *Gentrification und Lebensstile: eine empirische Untersuchung*, Wiesbaden: Deutscher Universitätsverlag.

Blomley, Nicholas (2002) 'Mud for the land', *Public Culture*, 14: 557–82.

Boddy, M. (1980) *The Building Societies*, London: The Macmillan Press.

Bodnár, J. (2001) *Fin de Millénaire Budapest: Metamorphoses of Urban Life*, Minneapolis and London: University of Minnesota Press.

Bondi, L. (1991a) 'Progress in geography and gender: feminism and difference', *Progress in Human Geography*, 14: 438–45.

Bondi, L. (1991b) 'Gender divisions and gentrification: a critique', *Transactions, Institute of British Geographers*, 16: 290–8.

Bondi, L. (1992) 'Gender symbols and urban landscapes', *Progress in Human Geography* 16(2): 157–70.

Bondi, L. (1999a) 'Gender, class and gentrification: enriching the debate', *Environment and Planning D*, 17: 261–82.

Bondi, L. (1999b) 'On the journeys of the gentrifiers: exploring gender, gentrification and migration', in P. J. Boyle and K. H. Halfacree (eds) *Migration and Gender in the Developed World*, London: Routledge, pp. 204–23.

Bondi, L. (1999c) 'Between the woof and the weft: a response to Loretta Lees', *Society and Space*, 17: 253–5.

Bonomi, A. (1995) *Privatizzare Venezia: Il progettista imprenditore*, Padua: Marsilio.

Bonyhady, T. (1995) 'The battle for Balmain', in P. Troy (ed.) *Australian Cities: Issues, Strategies and Policies for Urban Australia in the 1990s*, Cambridge: Cambridge University Press.

Borst, R. und Krätke, S. (2000) *Berlin – Metropole zwischen Boom und Krise*, Opladen: Leske und Budrich.

Bourdieu, P. (1984) *Distinction: A Social Critique of the Judgement of Taste*, London: Routledge.

Bourne, L. (1993a) 'The demise of gentrification? A commentary and prospective view', *Urban Geography*, 14(1): 95–107.

Bourne, L. (1993b) 'The myth and reality of gentrification: a commentary on emerging urban forms', *Urban Studies*, 30(1): 183–9.

Bowler, A. and McBurney, B. (1991) 'Gentrification and the avant-garde in New York's East Village: the good, the bad and the ugly', *Theory, Culture and Society*, 8: 49–77.

Boyer, M. C. (1998) *The City of Collective Memory: Its Historical Imagery and Architectural Entertainments*, Cambridge, MA: MIT Press.

Brenner, N. (1998) 'Global cities, global states: global city formation and state territorial restructuring in contemporary Europe', *Review of International Political Economy*, 5(1): 1–37.

Bridge, G. (1994) 'Gentrification, class and residence: a re-appraisal', *Environment and Planning D*, 12: 31–51.

Bridge, G. (2001a) 'Bourdieu, rational action and the time-space strategy of gentrification' *Transactions of the Institute of British Geographers*, 26(2): 205–16.

Bridge, G. (2001b) 'Estate agents as intermediaries between economic and cultural capital: the "gentrification premium" in the Sydney housing market', *International Journal of Urban and Regional Research*, 25(1) March: 87–101.

Bridge, G. (2003) 'Time–Space trajectories in provincial gentrification', *Urban Studies*, 40: 2545–56.

Burt, S. and Grady, K. (1994) *The Illustrated History of Leeds*, Derby: Breedon Books.

• Butler, T. (1995) 'Gentrification and the urban middle classes', in T. Butler and M. Savage (eds) *Social Change and the Middle Classes*, London: UCL Press, pp. 188–204.

• Butler, T. (1997) *Gentrification and the Middle Classes*, Aldershot: Ashgate.

. Butler, T. and Hamnett, C. (1994) 'Gentrification, class and gender: some comments on Warde's gentrification as consumption', *Environment and Planning D*, 12: 477–93.

• Butler, T. and Robson, G. (2001a) 'Social capital, gentrification and neighbourhood change in London: a comparison of three South London neighbourhoods', *Urban Studies*, 38: 2145–62.

• Butler, T. and Robson, T. (2001b) 'Coming to terms with London: middle-class communities in a global city', *International Journal of Urban and Regional Research*, 25: 70–86.

Butler, T. with Robson, G. (2003) *London Calling: the Middle Classes and the Remaking of Inner London*, London: Berg.

BV Teutoburger Platz o.J. (2001) 'Gaststätten- und Restaurantgewerbe im Sanierungsgebiet Teutoburger Platz und den angrenzenden Milieuschutzgebieten'. Unpublished manuscript, Berlin.

Cable, V. (1999) *Globalization and Global Governance*, London: Royal Institute of International Affairs.

Cameron, L. and Craig, M. (1985) 'A decade of change in inner Sydney', *Urban Policy and Research*, 3(4): 22–30.

Campos Venuti, G., Costa, P., Piazza, L. and Reali, O. (eds) (1985) *Firenze: per una urbanistica della qualità*, Venice: Marsilio.

Canny, A. (2002) 'Flexible labour? The growth of student employment in the UK', *Journal of Education and Work*, 15: 277–301.

Capel, H. (1977) *Capitalismo y morfología urbana en España*, 2nd edn, Barcelona: Los Libros de la Frontera.

Capponi, P. (1992) *Upstairs in the Crazy House: The Life of a Psychiatric Survivor*, Toronto: Viking Press.

Cardwell, D. (2003) 'Mr. Fix-It, meet urban decay', *New York Times*, 3 April: A18.

Carpenter, J. and Lees, L. (1995) 'Gentrification in New York, London and Paris: an international comparison', *International Journal of Urban and Regional Research*, 19(2): 286–303.

Carson, L. (2003) 'Demand rises for housing support: backlog leads panel to close waiting list for section 8 vouchers', *The Baltimore Sun*, 26 October: 1B.

Castells, M. (1981) *Crisis urbana y cambio social*, México DF: Siglo Veintiuno Editores.

Castells, M. (1983) *The City and The Grass Roots*, London: Edward Arnold.

Castells, M. (1996) *The Rise of the Network Society*, Oxford: Blackwell.

Caulfield, J. (1989) 'Gentrification and desire', *Canadian Review of Sociology and Anthropology*, 26(4): 617–32.

Caulfield, J. (1994) *City Form and Everyday Life, Toronto's Gentrification and Critical Social Practice*, Toronto: University of Toronto Press.

Cederna, A. (1956) *I vandali in casa*, Bari: Laterza.

Cederna, A. (1965) *Mirabilia urbis, cronache romane 1957–1965*, Turin: Einaudi.

References

Cederna, A. (1979) *Mussolini urbanista. Lo sventramento di Roma negli anni del consenso*, Bari: Laterza.

Ceppi, M. and Garzena, B. (1975) 'I caratteri dello sviluppo metropolitano a Torino', in P. Ceri (ed.) *Casa città e struttura sociale*, Rome: Editori Riuniti, pp. 65–118.

Ceri, P. (1975) *Casa città e struttura sociale*, Rome: Editori Riuniti.

Cervellati, P.-L. (1978) 'Il progetto della consevazione', in F. Cialdini and P. Falini (eds) *I centri storici*, Milan: Mazzotta, pp. 119–32.

Chatterton, P. (1999) 'University students and city centres – the formation of exclusive geographies. The case of Bristol, UK', *Geoforum*, 30: 117–33.

Chatterton, P. (2000) 'The cultural role of universities in the community: revisiting the university-community debate', *Environment and Planning A*, 17: 685–99.

Chatterton, P. (2002) *Urban Nightscapes: Youth Cultures, Pleasure Spaces and Corporate Power*, London: Routledge.

Chatterton, P. and Hollands, R. (2002) 'Theorising urban playscapes: producing, regulating and consuming youthful nightlife city spaces', *Urban Studies*, 39: 95–116.

Chrisafis, A. (2000) 'Two square miles of housing hell', *The Guardian*, 24 October.

Cialdini, F. and Falini, P. (1978) *I centri storici; politica urbanistica e programmi di intervento pubblico: Bergamo, Bologna, Brescia, Como, Gubbio, Pesaro, Vicenza*, Milan: Mazzotta.

City of Dallas, Economic Development Department (2001) *Annual Report Reinventment Zone Number One: State-Thomas Tax Increment Financing District*, Dallas, TX: City of Dallas.

City of Toronto Planning Board (CTPB) (1976) 'South Parkdale: trends and planning goals', *City of Toronto Planning Board*, Toronto: City of Toronto.

City of Toronto Urban Development Services (CTUDS) (1997) 'Ward 2 revitalization proposals: draft for discussion', *City of Toronto Urban Development Services*, Toronto: City of Toronto.

City of Toronto Urban Development Services (CTUDS) (1999a) 'Parkdale conflict resolution: final report', *City of Toronto Urban Development Services*, Toronto: City of Toronto.

City of Toronto Urban Development Services (CTUDS) (1999b) 'Parkdale Conflict resolution: unit size and amenity area evaluation', *City of Toronto Urban Development Services*, Toronto: City of Toronto.

Clark D. (2000) 'World urban development: processes and patterns at the end of the twentieth century', *Geography*, 85(1): 15–23.

Clark, E. (1987) *The rent gap and urban change: case studies in Malmö 1860–1985*, Lund: Lund University Press.

Clark, E. (1992) 'On blindness, centrepieces and complementarity in gentrification theory', *Transactions of the Institute of British Geographers*, 17: 358–62.

Clark, E. (1995) 'The rent gap re-examined', *Urban Studies*, 32: 1489–503.

Clark, E. (2004) 'Rent rhythm in the flamenco of urban change', in Tom Mels (ed.) *Rhythms of Nature, Place and Landscape*, Aldershot: Ashgate.

Clemente, C. and Innocenti, P. (1999) 'L'idea di città nei piani di Firenze da Detti a Vittorini', Bollettino del dipartimento di urbanistica e di pianificazione del territorio, Università degli studi di Firenze, n. 1–2, pp. 42–6.

Cole, I., Hickman, P. and Reeve, K. (2003) *The Leeds Housing Market: Perceptions of Change*, Sheffield: CRESR Sheffield Hallam University.

Collins J. (1995) *Architecture of Excess: Cultural Life in the Information Age*, New York: Routledge.

Collinson, P. (2001) 'Buy-to-let misery for students' neighbours', *The Guardian*, 5 May.

Community Builders (2002) 'Our HOPE VI Projects', *The Community Builders Incorporated*, available online at: http://www.communitybuilders.org/what-we-do/hopevi_projects.htm.

Comoli, V., Defabiani, V. and Roggero, C. (1980) 'Centro storico di Torino: città quadrata analisi storiche per il riconoscimento delle tipologie', edilizie in A. Abriani, pp. 314–23.

Comune, Di Torino-Ires (1980) *Una strategia territoriale per il recupero delle abitazioni obsolete a Torino*, Milan: Franco Angeli.

Cooper, C. and Morpeth, N. (1998) 'The impact of tourism on residential experience in central-eastern Europe: the development of a new legitimation crisis in the Czech Republic', *Urban Studies*, 35(12): 2253–75.

Cottell, C. (2001) 'Poor students opt to stay put', *The Guardian*, 30 September.

Cotter, Holland (2002) 'The Lower East Side: where witty meets gritty', *New York Times*, 15 November: B29, B32.

Court, J. (2000) 'From 999 to 1001 Queen Street: a consistently vital resource,' in E. Hudson (ed.) *The Provinicial Asylum in Toronto: Reflections on Social and Architectural History*, Toronto: Toronto Region Architectural Conservancy, pp. 183–98.

Crang, M. (1994) 'On the heritage trail: maps of and journeys to olde Englande', *Environment and Planning D: Society and Space*, 12: 341–55.

Crawford, L. (2001) 'Guggenheim, Bilbao and the "hot banana"', *Financial Times*, 4 September.

Crewe L. (1999), 'Geographies of retailing and consumption, progress report', *Progress in Human Geography*, 24(2): 275–90.

Criekingen, M. van and Decroly, J.-M. (2003) 'Revisiting the diversity of gentrification: Neighbourhood renewal processes in Brussels and Montreal', *Urban Studies*, 40(12): 2451–68.

Crilley, D. (1993) 'Architecture as advertising: constructing the image of redevelopment', in G. Kearns and C. Philo (eds) *Selling Places: The City as Cultural Capital, Past and Present*, Oxford: Pergamon Press.

→ Cross, M. and Moore, R. (2002) *Globalization and the New City: Migrants, Minorities and Urban Transformations in Comparative Perspective*, London: Palgrave.

Crosta, P. L. (1975) 'Il riuso della città: un'area di conflitto intercapitalistico', in P. Ceri (ed.) *Casa città e struttura sociale*, Rome: Editori Riuniti, pp. 219–56.

Curtis, P. (2003) 'Vice-chancellors trade accusations over top-up fees', *The Guardian*, 24 November.

Cybriwsky, R (1998) *Tokyo: the Shogun's City at the Twenty-first Century*, Chichester: John Wiley & Sons.

Cybriwsky, R., Ley, D. and Western, J. (1986) 'The political and social construction of revitalized neighborhoods: Society Hill, Philadelphia, and False Creek, Vancouver', in N. Smith and P. Williams (eds) *Gentrification of the City*, London: Unwin Hyman, pp. 92–120.

Dalmasso, E. (1970): *Milano capitale economica d'Italia*, Milan: Franco Angeli.

Daly, M. (1992) *Sydney Boom, Sydney Bust*, Sydney: Allen and Unwin.

Dangschat, J. S. (1988) 'Gentrification: der Wandel innenstadtnaher Wohnviertel', in J. Friedrichs (ed.) *Soziologische Stadtforschung*, Opladen: Leske and Budrich, pp. 272–94.

References

Dangschat, J. S. (1990) 'Geld ist nicht (mehr) alles – Gentrification als räumliche Segregation nach horizontalen Ungleichheiten', in J. Blasius and J. S. Dangschat (eds) *Gentrification – die Aufwertung innenstadtnaher Wohnviertel*, Frankfurt and New York: Campus, pp. 69–94.

Dangschat, J. S. and Friedrichs, J. (1988) *Gentrification in der inneren Stadt von Hamburg. Eine empirische Untersuchung des Wandels von drei Wohnviertel*, Hamburg: Gesellschaft für Sozialwissenschaftliche Stadtforschung.

Dansereau, F., Germain, A. and Eveillard, C. (1997) 'Social mix: old utopias, comtemporary experience and challenges', *Canadian Journal of Urban Research*, 6: 1–23.

Davis, Mike (1992) 'Fortress Los Angeles: the militarization of urban space', in M. Sorkin (ed.) *Variations on a Theme Park: The New American City and the End of Public Space*, New York: Hill and Wang, pp. 154–80.

Dear, M. (1992) 'Understanding and overcoming the NIMBY syndrome', *Journal of The American Planning Association*, 58(3), Summer.

Dear, M. and Taylor, S. M. (1982) *Not On Our Street: Community Attitudes to Mental Health Care*, London: Pion.

Dear, M. and Wolch, J. (1987) *Landscapes of Despair: From Deinstitutionalization to Homelessness*, Princeton: Princeton University Press.

Dear, M. and Wolch, J. (1993) 'Homelessness', in L. Bourne and D. Ley (eds) *The Changing Social Geography of Canadian Cities*, Montreal: McGill-Queens University Press, pp. 298–308.

Del Rio, V. 'Em busca do tempo perdido. O renascimento dos centros urbanos'. Online. Available: http://www.vitruvius.com.br/arquitextos/arq000/esp028.asp, 10/10/2003.

Dematteis, G. (1973) 'Le località centrali nella geografiaz urbana di Torino', Istituto di Geografia Economica, Università di Torino.

Department of Education and Skills (2003) *The Future of Higher Education*, London: HMSO.

Department of Human Services, Victoria (2003) 'New rooming house projects tackle inner city homelessness', press release, August.

Department of Sustainability and Environment, Victoria (2003) 'Port Phillip Change and Gentrification', Research and Analysis Branch, June.

DeSena, J. N. (1990) *Protecting One's Turf: Social Strategies for Maintaining Urban Neighborhoods* Lanham, MD: University Press of America

De Sousa, C. (2002) 'Brownfield redevelopment in Toronto: an examination of past trends and future prospects', *Land Use Policy*, 19: 297–309.

Díaz, M. A. (1989) 'Hacia un modelo de diferenciación residencial urbana en España', *Estudios Territoriales*, 31: 115–33.

Diehl, D. (1999) 'Historic Williamsburgh: Brooklyn bound', *Sunday Daily News*, Lifeline Section, 20 June: 1–3.

Dieser, H. (1996) 'Restitution: Wie funktioniert sie und was bewirkt sie?', in H. Häußermann and R. Neef (eds) *Stadtentwicklung in Ostdeutschland*, Opladen: Leske and Budrich.

Dingsdale, A. (1999) 'Budapest's built environment in transition', *GeoJournal*, 49(1): 63–78.

Diputación Foral de Bizkaia (2001) 'Bilbao, la Transformación de una ciudad', Bilbao. Online. Available: http//www.bilbao-city.net/ (17 January 2002).

Dorling, D. and Rees, P. (2003) 'A nation still dividing: the British census and social polarisation 1971–2001', *Environment and Planning A*, 35: 1287–313.

Douglas, M. J. (1997) 'A change of system: housing system transformation and neighbourhood change in Budapest', Netherlands Geographical Studies 222, Faculteit Ruimtelijke Wetenschappen, Universiteit of Utrecht.

Draaisma J. (2003) Personal Communication, Amsterdam, 8 July 2003.

Drbohlav, D. and Sýkora, L. (1997) 'Gateway cities in the process of regional integration in Central and Eastern Europe: the case of Prague', in *Migration, Free Trade and Regional Integration in Central and Eastern Europe*, Vienna: Verlag Österreich, pp. 215–37.

Dundar, O. (2003) 'Kentsel dönüşüm politikaları üzerine kavramsal bir tartışma', TMMOB Şehir Plancıları Odası Kentsel Dönüşüm Sempozyumu, 11–13 June 2003, Istanbul: YTU Press, pp. 159–72.

Dunn, T. (1974) 'Absentee owners let 85-year-old house decay', *Parkdale Citizen*, February.

Dutton, P. (1998) 'Gentrification in Leeds', papers in Community Studies 13, Bradford: Bradford College.

Dutton, P. (2002) 'Patterns and processes of "studentification" in Leeds', *Regional Review*, 12: 14–16.

Dutton, P. (2003) 'Leeds calling: the influence of London on the gentrification of regional cities', *Urban Studies*, 40.

Dynes, S. (1974) 'The spatial and social implications of whitepainting', unpublished research paper, Department of Geography, University of Toronto, Toronto.

Engels, B. (1994) 'Capital flows, redlining and gentrification: the pattern of mortgage lending and social change in Glebe, Sydney, 1960–1984', *International Journal of Urban and Regional Research*, 18(4): 28–58.

Engels, B. (1999) 'Property ownership, tenure and displacement: in search of the process of gentrification', *Environment and Planning A*, 31: 1473–95.

Enlil, Z. M. (2000) 'Bir sınıfsal proje olarak eski kent merkezlerinin ve tarihi konut dokusunun yeniden ele geçirilmesi: Yeniden işlevlendirme ve soylulaştırma', *Domus*, 8: 46–9.

Ergun, N. (forthcoming) 'Gentrification in Istanbul, Turkey', *Cities*.

Eskinasi, M. (1995) 'Changing housing policy and its consequences: the Prague case', *Housing Studies*, 10(4): 533–48.

Esteban, M. (2000) *Bilbao, luces y sombras del titanio. El proceso de regeneración urbana del Bilbao metropolitano*, Bilbao: Servicio Editorial Universidad del País Vasco.

Eustat (Instituto Vasco de Estadistica) (1999) *Del barrio a la comunidad. censos y padrones de población y viviendas*, 1986, 1991 y 1996, Vitoria.

Fainstein, S., Gordon, I. and Harloe, M. (eds) (1992) *Divided Cities: New York and London in the Contemporary World*, Oxford: Blackwell.

Falk, W. (1994) *Städtische Quartiere und Aufwertung: Wo ist Gentrification möglich?* Basel, Boston, MA and Berlin: Birkhäuser.

Fanelli, G. (1990) *Firenze*, Bari: Laterza.

Farrar, M. (1996) 'Black communities and processes of exclusion', in G. Haughton and C. Williams (eds) *Corporate City? Partnership, Participation and Partition in Urban Development in Leeds*, Aldershot: Ashgate.

Featherstone, M. (ed) (1990) *Global Culture*, London: Sage.

Feldman, M. (2000a) 'Gentrification and social stratification in Tallinn: strategies for local governance', SOCO Project Paper No. 86. Vienna: Institute für die Wissenschaften vom Menschen.

Feldman, M. (2000b) 'Urban waterfront regeneration and local governance in Tallinn', *Europe-Asia Studies*, 52(5): 829–50.

References

Fernandez Durán, R. (1999) 'Globalización, territorio y población. El impacto de la "europeización" – mundialización sobre el espacio español'. Online. Avalaible: http://habitat.aq.upm.es/gtp/ (16 May 2001).

Ferras, R. (1976) 'Barcelone, croissance d'une métropole', Université de Lille III, Service de reproduction des theses, Lille.

FFIEC (Financial Institutions Examination Council) (Annual) *Home Mortgage Disclosure Act, Loan Application Register Data on CD-ROM*. Washington, DC: Federal Financial Institutions Examination Council.

Filion, P. (1991) 'The gentrification–social structure dialectic: a Toronto case study', *International Journal of Urban and Regional Research*, 15(4): 553–74.

Filion, P. (1999) 'Rupture or continuity? Modern and postmodern planning in Toronto', *International Journal of Urban and Regional Research*, 23(3): 421–44.

Fincher, R. and Jacobs, J. M. (eds) (1998) *Cities of Difference*, New York: Guilford Press.

Firenze 2010 (2003) 'Piano strategico per l'area metropolitana fiorentina', Comune network, Florence.

Fitzgerald, S. (1987) *Rising Damp: Sydney 1870–90*, Melbourne: Oxford University Press.

Fitzgerald, S. and Keating, C. (1991) *Millers Point: The Urban Village*, Sydney: Hale and Iremonger.

Florida, R. (2001) 'The geography of Bohemia'. Online. Available: http://www.heinz.cmu.edu/~florida/ (25 June 2002).

Florida, R. (2003) *The Rise of the Creative Class: and How It's Transforming Work, Leisure, Community and Everyday Life*, New York: Basic Books.

Forrest, R., Kennet, P. and Izuhara, M. (2003) 'Home ownership and economic change in Japan', *Housing Studies*, 18: 277–93.

Franz, P. (2000) 'Soziale Ungleichheit und Stadtentwicklung in ostdeutschen Städte', in A. Harth, G. Scheller and W. Tessin (eds) *Stadt und soziale Ungleichheit*, Opladen: Leske und Budrich.

Friedrich, K. (2000) 'Gentrifizierung. Theoretische Ansätze und Anwendung auf Städte in den neuen Ländern', *Geografische Rundschau*, 52(7–8): 34–9.

Friedrichs, J. (2002) 'Globalization, urban restructuring and employment prospects', in M. Cross and R. Moore (eds) *Globalization and the New City: Migrants, Minorities and Urban Transformations in Comparative Perspective*, London: Palgrave, pp. 119–32.

Friedrichs, J. and Kecskes, R. (eds) (1996) *Gentrification. Theorie und Forschungs-ergebnisse*, Opladen: Leske and Budrich.

Frost, L. (1992) 'Suburbia and inner cities', in A. Rutherford (ed.) *Populous Place: Australian Cities and Towns*, Sydney: Dangaroo Press.

Frúgoli Júnior, H. (2000) *Centralidade em São Paulo: trajetórias, conflitos e negociações na metrópole*, São Paulo: Cortez and Editora da Universidade de São Paulo.

Fujitsuka, Y. (1990) 'Spatial changes in the central area of Kyoto city: analysis of renewal buildings', *The Human Geography*, 42: 466–76.

Fujitsuka, Y. (1992) 'Burgeoning of gentrification in Nishijin, Kyoto', *The Human Geography*, 44: 495–506.

Fujitsuka, Y. (1994) 'Gentrification: a review of research in western countries and future research on Japanese Cities', *The Human Geography*, 46: 496–514.

Fulford, R. (2002) 'The cool cycle: the ecology of the hip urban neighbourhood', *enRoute Magazine* (Air Canada in-flight magazine), April 2002.

Gabriel J. (1998) *Whitewash: Racialized Politics and the Media*, London: Routledge.

Gale, D. E. (1978) 'Middle class resettlement in older urban neighborhoods: the evidence and implications', *American Planning Association Journal*, July: 293–304.

Gale, D. E. (1980) 'Neighborhood resettlement: Washington, D.C.', in S. B. Laska and D. Spain (eds) *Back to the City: Issues in Neighborhood Renovation*, New York: Pergamon Press.

Gambi, L. (1973) 'Da città ad area metropolitana', in *Storia d'Italia*, V, *I documenti*, Turin: Einaudi, pp. 367–424.

Gandhi L. (1998) *Postcolonial Theory: A Critical Introduction*, Sydney: Allen and Unwin.

Gans, H. (1982 [1962]) *Urban Villagers. Group and Class in the life of Italian Americans*, New York: The Free Press.

Garzena, B. P. (1996) 'Torino, segregazione e mobilità intra-urbana', in R. Curto e Barbano (ed.) *La casa scambiata*, Turin: Stige.

Gdaniec, C. (2000) 'Cultural industries, information technology and the regeneration of post-industrial urban landscapes. Poblenou in Barcelona – a virtual city?', *GeoJournal*, 50: 379–87.

Gelder, K. and Jacobs, J. M. (1998) *Uncanny Australia: Sacredness and Identity in a Postcolonial Nation*, Melbourne: Melbourne University Press.

Gelezeau V. (1997) 'Renewal for moon villages in Seoul: rebuilding the city and socio-spatial segregation', *Espace Geographique*, 26: 1–11.

Geolytics, Inc. (2003) *Neighborhood Change Database, Short Form Release, National Version*, East Brunswick, NJ: Geolytics.

Ghanbari-Parsa, A. R. and Moatazed-Keivani, R. (1999) 'Development of real estate markets in Central Europe: the case of Prague, Warsaw, and Budapest', *Environment and Planning A* 31, 8: 1383–99.

Ghirardo, D. (1996) *Architecture after Modernism*, London: Thames and Hudson.

Gibson, M. S. and Langstaff, M. J. (1982) *An Introduction to Urban Renewal*, London: Hutchinson Publishing Group.

Giddens, A. (1990) *The Consequences of Modernity*, Cambridge: Polity Press.

Gilmore, R. W. (2002) 'Fatal couplings of power and difference: notes on racism and geography', *Professional Geographer*, 54(1): 15–24.

Glass, R. (1963) *Introduction to London: Aspects of Change*, London: Centre for Urban Studies and MacGibbon and Kee.

Glass, R. (1964) 'Introduction: aspects of change', in Centre for Urban Studies (ed.) *London: Aspects of Change*, London: MacGibbon and Kee.

Gómez, M. V. (1998) 'Reflective images: the case of urban regeneration in Glasgow and Bilbao', *International Journal of Urban and Regional Research*, 22(1): 106–21.

Gómez, M. V. and González, S. (2001) 'A reply to Beatriz Plaza's "The Guggenheim-Bilbao Museum effect"', *International Journal of Urban and Regional Research*, 25(4): 898–900.

Gould, P. R. (1999) 'Do foraminifera assemblages exist – at least in the Persian Gulf?', in P. Gould, *Becoming a Geographer*, Syracuse, NY: Syracuse University Press, pp. 289–99.

Gouldner, A. (1979) *The Future of Intellectuals and the Rise of the New Class*, London: Macmillan.

Grady, J. (1996) 'The Scope of Visual Sociology', *Visual Sociology*, 11(2): 1024.

Graham, B., Ashworth, G. J. and Tunbridge, J. E. (2000) *A Geography of Heritage: Power, Culture and Economy*, London: Arnold.

References

Graham, S. and Marvin, S. (2001) *Splintering Urbanism: Networked Infrastructures, Technological Mobilities and the Urban Condition*, London: Routledge.

Grieco, L., Hills, W. and Modic, R. (2001) 'In the aftermath of riots, cincy law sparked controversy', *Dayton Daily News*, 22 April: 1A.

Griffin, L. (2002) 'Dallas's state–thomas neighborhood: a study in development contrasts', *The Dallas Morning News*, 4 December.

Hackworth, J. (2001) 'Inner-city real estate investment, gentrification, and economic recession in New York City', *Environment and Planning A*, 33: 863–80.

Hackworth, J. (2002a) Obstacles to expanding the scale of anti-gentrification activism: the case of public housing in the US', unpublished manuscript, Toronto: Department of Geography, University of Toronto.

Hackworth, J. (2002b) 'Postrecession gentrification in New York City', *Urban Affairs Review*, 37(6): 815–43.

Hackworth, J. and Smith, N. (2001) 'The changing state of gentrification', *Tijdschrift voor Economische en Sociale Geografie*, 92(4): 464–77.

Hage, G. (1998) *White Nation: Fantasies of White Supremacy in a Multicultural Society*, Sydney: Pluto Press.

Hall, G. B. and Joseph, A. (1988) 'Group home location and host neighborhood attributes: an ecological analysis', *Professional Geographer*, 40(3): 297–306.

Hall, T. and Hubbard, P. (eds) (1998) *The Entrepreneurial City*, Chichester: John Wiley & Sons.

Hamilton W. L. (2000) 'Vision of greener pastures revinvent the Lower East Side', *New York Times*, 6 January: F1, F7.

Hammel, D. J. (1999a) 'Re-establishing the rent gap: an alternative view of capitalised land rent', *Urban Studies*, 36: 1283–93.

Hammel, D. J. (1999b) 'Gentrification and land rent: a historical view of the rent gap in Minneapolis', *Urban Geography*, 20(2): 116–45.

Hammel, D. J. and Elvin, K. W. (1996) 'A model for identifying gentrified areas with census data' *Urban Geography*, 17(3): 248–68.

Hamnett, C. (1973) 'Improvement grants as an indicator of gentrification in inner London', *Area*, 5(4): 252–61.

Hamnett, C. (1991) 'The blind men and the elephant: the explanation of gentrification', *Transactions of the Institute of British Geographers*, 16(2): 173–89.

Hamnett, C. (1992) 'Gentrification or lemmings? A response to Neil Smith', *Transactions of the Institute of British Geographers*, 17: 116–19.

Hamnett, C. (1994a) 'Social polarisation in global cities: theory and evidence', *Urban Studies*, 31: 401–24.

Hamnett, C. (1994b) 'Socio-economic change in London: professionalisation or polarisation', *Built Environment*, 20: 192–204.

Hamnett, C. (2000) 'Gentrification, postindustrialism, and industrial and occupational restructuring in global cities', in G. Bridge and S. Watson (eds) *A Companion to the City*, Oxford: Blackwell, pp. 331–41.

Hamnett, C. (2002) 'Gentrification and the middle-class remaking of Inner London', paper presented to the Conference on Upward Neighbourhood Trajectories: Gentrification in a New Century, Glasgow, Scotland, September.

Hamnett, C. (2003a) 'Gentrification and the middle-class remaking of Inner London, 1961–2001', *Urban Studies*, 40(12): 2401–26.

Hamnett, C. (2003b) *Unequal City: London in the Global Arena*, London: Routledge.

Hamnett, C. and Randolph, W. (1986) 'Tenurial transformation and the flat break-up market in London: the British condo experience', in N. Smith and P. Williams (eds) *Gentrification of the City*, London: Unwin Hyman, pp. 121–52.

Hamnett, C. and Williams, P. R. (1980) 'Social change in London a study of gentrification', *Urban Affairs Quarterly*, 15: 469–87.

Hannerz, U. (1996) *Transnational Connections: Culture, People, Places*, London: Comedia.

Harland K (2001) 'Commuting to Leeds: social and gender divides', *The Regional Review*, 11: 13–14.

Harris, R. (1987) 'A social movement in urban politics: a reinterpretation of urban reform in Canada', *International Journal of Urban and Regional Research*, 11: 363–81.

Harris, R. (1993) 'Social mix, housing tenure, and community development', in J. Miron (ed.) *House, Home and Community: Progress in Housing Canadians 1945–1986*, Montreal: McGill-Queens University Press, pp. 308–19.

Harris, R. (2000) 'Housing' in T. Bunting and P. Filion (eds) *Canadian Cities in Transition*, 2nd edn, Oxford: Oxford University Press, pp. 380–403.

Harris, P. and McVeigh, T. (2002) 'Student takeover alarms cities', *The Observer*, 21 July.

Harth, A., Herlyn, U. and Scheller, G. (1998) *Segregation in ostdeutschen Städten. Eine empirische Studie*, Opladen: Leske and Budrich.

Harth, A., Herlyn, U. and Scheller, G. (1996) 'Ostdeutsche Städte auf Gentrificationkurs? Empirische Befunde zur "gespaltenen" Gentrification in Magdeburg', in J. Friedrichs und R. Kecskes (eds) *Gentrification. Theorie und Forschungsergebnisse*, Opladen: Leske and Budrich, pp. 167–91.

Harvey, D. (1982) *The Limits to Capital*, Oxford, Blackwell.

Harvey, D. (1989a) 'From managerialism to entrepreneurialism: the transformation of urban governance in late capitalism', *Geografiska Annaler*, 71B(1): 3–17.

Harvey, D. (1989b) *Condição pós-moderna*, São Paulo: Loyola.

Harvey, D. (1990) 'Between space and time: reflections on the geographical imagination', *Annals, Association of American Geographers*, 80: 418–34.

Harvey, D. (1993) 'Social justice, postmodernism and the city', *International Journal of Urban and Regional Research*, 16: 588–601.

Harvey, D. (2000) *Spaces of Hope*, Berkeley, CA: University of California Press.

Hasson, S. and Ley, D. (1994) *Neighbourhood Organizations and the Welfare State*, Toronto: University of Toronto Press.

Häußermann, H. (1983) 'Amerikanisierung der deutschen Städte? Einige Bedingungen der Stadtentwicklung in den USA im Vergleich zur Bundesrepublik in Bezug auf das Wohnen', in V. Roscher (ed.) *Beiträge zur Planung, Politik und Ökonomie eines alltäglichen Lebensbereiches*, Hamburg: Christians Verlag.

Häußermann, H. and Kappahn, A. (2000) *Berlin – Von der geteilten zur gespaltenen Stadt?*, Opladen: Leske and Budrich.

Häußermann, H. and Siebel, W. (1991) 'Berlin bleibt nicht Berlin', *Leviathan*, 19(3): 353–71.

Häußermann, H., Holm, A. and Zunzer, D. (2002) *Stadterneuerung in der Berliner Republik. Modernisierung in Berlin-Prenzlauer Berg*, Opladen: Leske and Budrich.

Hayashi, T. (1995) 'An analysis of gentrification in Nada ward, Kobe city', unpublished MPhil thesis, Nihon University.

References

Hays, C. (2003) 'For Wal-Mart, New Orleans is hardly the big easy', *New York Times*, 27 April, BU1, BU11.

Hegedüs, J. and Tosics, I. (1991) 'Gentrification in Eastern Europe: the case of Budapest', in J. van Weesep and S. Musterd (eds) *Urban Housing for the Better-Off: Gentrification in Europe*.Utrecht: Stedelijke Netwerken, pp. 124–36.

Helbrecht, I. (1996) 'Die Wiederkehr der Innenstädte. Zur Rolle von Kultur, Kapital und Konsum in der Gentrification', *Geographische Zeitschrift* 84: 1–15.

Hellman, P. (2002) 'Over the river, no longer fringe', *New York Times*, 24 October, D1, D5.

Herlyn, U. and Hunger, B. (eds) (1994) *Ostdeutsche Wohnmilieus im Wandel. Eine Untersuchung ausgewählter Stadtgebiete als sozialplanerischer Beitrag zur Stadterneuerung*, Basel, Boston, MA and Berlin: Birkhäuser Verlag.

Hewison, R. (1987) *The Heritage Industry: Britain in a Climate of Decline*, London: Methuen.

Hiebert, D. (1995) 'The social geography of Toronto in 1931: a study of residential differentiation and social structure', *Journal of Historical Geography*, 21(1): 55–74.

Higher Education Funding Council For England (2002). Online. Available: http://www.hefce.ac.uk/news/hefce/2002/fund0203.htm (10 May 2002).

Higher Education Statistics Agency. (2002). Online. Available: http://www.hesa.ac.uk/holisdocs/home.htm (10 May 2002).

Hobsbawn, E.(1985) *A era dos extremos: o breve século XX: 1914–1991*, São Paulo, Companhia das Letras.

Hobsbawm, E. and Ranger, T. (eds) (1983) *The Invention of Tradition*, Cambridge: Cambridge University Press.

Holm, A. (1999) 'Ausgangsbedingungen und Dimensionen städtischen Wandels – ein Stadtspaziergang durch Berlin-Prenzlauer Berg', in M. Schulz und O. Gewand (ed.) *Märkte und Strukturen im Wandel*, VI. Konferenz Amsterdam–Berlin, Berlin: Berliner Geographische Arbeiten.

Holm, A. (2000) 'Neue Eigentümer und veränderte Investitionsstrategien – zur Ökonomie der Stadterneuerung in Berlin', in J. van der Ven and J. van der Weiden (eds) *Berlin im Umbruch*, Beiträge der VII. Konferenz Amsterdam–Berlin, Amsterdam: AME.

Holm, A. und Zunzer, D. (2000) 'Prenzlauer Berg im Wandel Stadterneuerung und sozialräumliche Veränderungen in Sanierungsgebieten', *Gesellschaft für Regionalforschung*, Seminarbericht 42.

Horvath, R. and Engels B. (1985) 'The residential restructuring of inner Sydney', in I. Burnley and J. Forrest (eds) *Living In Cities: Urbanism and Society in Metropolitan Australia*, Sydney: Allen and Unwin.

House of Commons (2001) Houses in Multiple Occupation (Registration Scheme) Bill. Online. Available: http://www.parliament.the-staionery-office.co.uk/pa/cm200001/cmbills/097/2001097 (12 September 2003).

Howe, R. (1994) 'Inner suburbs: from slums to gentrification', in L. Johnson (ed.) *Suburban Dreaming*, Victoria: Deakin University Press, pp. 141–59.

Indovina, F. (2001) 'Economia locale e internazionle nella rivalorizzazione delle città, Bollettino del dipartimento di urbanistica e di pianificazione del territorio', Università degli studi di Firenze, n. 1–2: 9–13.

Indovina, F. and Savino, M. (1997) 'Vantaggi dell'integrazione tra città storica e città moderna', in Acts of the International Conference, 'La ciutat historica dins la ciutat', Universitat de Girona, pp. 125–58.

Insolera, I. (1980) *Roma; Le città nella storia d'Italia*, Bari: Laterza.

Isin, E. (1998) 'Governing Toronto without government: liberalism and neoliberalism', *Studies in Political Economy*, 56: 169–91.

Islam, T. (2003a) 'Istanbul'da Soylulaştırma: Galata Örnegi' (Gentrification in Istanbul: the case of Galata), unpublished MS thesis, Yildiz Technical University.

Islam, T. (2003b) 'Galata'da soylulaştırma: Soylulaştırıcıların demografik ve kültürel özellikleri üzerine bir çalışma', TMMOB Şehir Plancıları Odası Kentsel Dönüşüm Sempozyumu, 11–13 June 2003, Istanbul: YTU Press, pp. 159–72.

Islam, T. (forthcoming) 'Gentrification in Fener and Balat', International 14th Urban Design and Implementations Symposium, 28–30 May 2003, Istanbul: MSU.

Jackson, P. (1989) *Maps of Meaning: An Introduction to Cultural Geography*, London: Unwin Hyman.

Jackson, P. (1991) 'Mapping meanings: a cultural critique of locality studies', *Environment and Planning A*, 23: 215–28.

Jackson, P. (1995) 'Manufacturing meanings: culture, capital and urban change', in A. Rogers and S. Vertovec (eds) *The Urban Context: Ethnicity, Social Networks and Situational Analysis*, Oxford: Berg.

Jackson, P. (1999) 'Commodity cultures: the traffic in things', *Transactions of the Institute of British Geographers*, 24: 95–108.

Jacobs, J. M.(1992a) *The Death and Life of Great American Cities*, New York: Vintage.

Jacobs, J. M. (1992b) 'Cultures of the past and urban transformation: the Spitalfields Market Redevelopment in East London', in K. Anderson and F. Gale (eds) *Inventing Places: Studies In Cultural Geography*, Melbourne: Longman Cheshire.

Jacobs, J. M. (1993) 'The city unbound: qualitative approaches to the city', *Urban Studies*, 30(4/5): 827–48.

Jacobs, J. M. (1996) *Edge of Empire: Postcolonialism and the City*, London: Routledge.

Jager, M. (1986) 'Class definition and the aesthetics of gentrification: Victoriana in Melbourne', in N. Smith and P. Williams (eds) *Gentrification of the City*, Australia: Allen and Unwin, pp. 78–91.

Jenks, C. (1981) *The Language of Post-Modern Architecture*, New York: Rozzoli.

Jones, G. A. and Varley, A. (1999) 'The reconquest of the historic center: urban conservation and gentrification in Puebla, Mexico', *Environment and Planning A*, 31: 1547–66.

Joseph, A. and Hall, G. B. (1985) 'The locational concentration of group homes in Toronto', *Professional Geographer*, 37(2): 143–54.

Kährik, A. (2002) 'Changing social divisions in the housing market of Tallinn, Estonia', *Housing, Theory and Society*, 19(1): 48–56.

Kährik, A., Kõre, J, Hendrikson, M. and Allsaar, I. (2003) 'From a state controlled to a *laissez faire* housing system: local government and housing in Estonia', in M. Lux, (ed.) *Housing Policy: An End or a New Beginning?*, Budapest: Local Government and Public Reform Initiative, Open Society Institute, pp. 183–242.

Katz, Cindi (2001) *Vagabond Capitalism and the Necessity of Social Reproduction*, Oxford: Blackwell.

Kawabata, M. (1996) 'Toshin tonyagai "Muromachi" niokeru kisei', in T. Iguchi (ed.) *Kiseikanwa to Chiikikeizai: Kyotoshi to Shuuhentiiki no Doukou*, Tokyo: Zeimu Keiri Kyoukai.

Kearns, G. and Philo, C. (eds) (1993) *Selling Places: The City as Cultural Capital, Past and Present*, Oxford: Pergamon Press.

Keating, C. (1991) *Surrey Hills*, Sydney: Hale and Iremonger.

References

Keating, L. (2001) *Atlanta: Race, Class, and Urban Expansion*, Philadelphia, PA: Temple University Press.

Keil, R. (2000) 'Governance restructuring in Los Angeles and Toronto: amalgamation or secession?', *International Journal of Urban and Regional Research*, 24(4): 758–81.

Keil, R. (2002) '"Common-sense" neoliberalism: progressive conservative urbanism in Toronto, Canada', *Antipode*, 34(3): 578–601.

Kendig, H. (1979) *New Life for Old Suburbs: Post-war Land Use and Housing in the Australian City*, Sydney: Allen and Unwin.

Kennedy, M. and Leonard, P. (2001) 'Dealing with neighbourhood change: a primer on gentrification and policy choice', discussion paper prepared for the Brookings Institution Center on Urban and Metropolitan Policy.

Kenyon, E. L. (1997) 'Seasonal sub-communities: the impact of student households on residential communities', *British Journal of Sociology*, 48: 286–301.

Keyder, C. (1999a) 'The setting', in C. Keyder (ed.) *Istanbul: Between the Global and the Local*, Maryland: Rowman & Littlefield.

Keyder, C. (1999b) 'The housing market from informal to global', in C. Keyder (ed.) *Istanbul: Between the Global and the Local*, Maryland: Rowman & Littlefield.

Keyder, C. (1999c) 'A tale of two neighborhoods', in C. Keyder (ed.) *Istanbul: Between the Global and the Local*, Maryland: Rowman & Littlefield.

Kich, Z. (2000) *Report on Housing in Poland*. Online. Available: http://www.habitants.de/ archiv/cities_for_all/housing_rights/poland1.htm.

Kim, K. (1997) 'Problems and prospects of urban preservation; a case study of Kahoedong-district in Seoul', *Municipal Problems*, 88: 43–62.

King, A. D. (ed.) (1991) *Culture, Globalization and the World System*, London: Macmillan.

Kipfer, S. and Keil, R. (2002) 'Toronto Inc? Planning the competitive city in the new Toronto', *Antipode*, 34(2): 227–64.

Kloosterman, R. C. and Leun, J. P. (1999) 'Just for starters: commercial gentrification by immigrant entrepreneurs in Amsterdam and Rotterdam neighborhoods', *Housing Studies*, 14(5): 659–77.

Kohen, J. L. (2000) 'First and last people: Aboriginal Sydney', in J. Connell (ed.) *Sydney: The Emergence of a World City*, Oxford University Press.

Kok, H. and Kovács, Z. (1999) 'The process of suburbanization in the agglomeration of Budapest', *Netherlands Journal of Housing and the Built Environment*, 14(2): 119–41.

Kopstein, K. 'USAID assistance program to Poland in local government and housing sector reform – a history and assessment from 1990 – 2000', The United States Agency for International Development, 16 April 2000.

Korte, G. (2001) 'Council tries to untangle its own genesis probe', *The Cincinnati Enquirer*, 19 September.

Kovács, Z. (1994) 'A city at the crossroads: social and economic transformation in Budapest', *Urban Studies*, 31(7): 1081–96.

Kovács, Z. (1998) 'Ghettoization or gentrification? Post-socialist scenarios for Budapest', *Netherlands Journal of Housing and the Built Environment*, 13(1): 63–81.

Kovács, Z. and Wiessner, R. (1999) 'Stadt- und Wohnungsmarktentwiclung in Budapest. Zur Entwicklung der inner städtischen Wohnquartiere im Transformationsprozess', Beiträge zur Regionalen Geographie 48, Leipzig: Institut für Länderkunde.

Krase, J. (1982) *Self and Community in the City*, Washington, DC: University Press of America.

Krase, J. (1993) 'Traces of Home', *Places: A Quarterly Journal of Environmental Design*, 8(4): 46–55.

Krase, J. (1997) 'Polish and Italian vernacular landscapes in Brooklyn', *Polish American Studies*, LIV(1): 9–31 (Spring).

Krase, J. (1999)'The present/future of Little Italies', *Brooklyn Journal of Social Semiotics*, Spring. Online. Available: http://www.brooklynsoc.org/semiotics/index.html.

Krätke, S. (1991) 'Berlin: Umbau zur neuen Metropole', *Leviathan*, 19(3): 327–52.

Ladányi, J. (1997) 'Social and ethnic residential segregation in Budapest', in Z. Kovács and R. Wiessner (eds) *Processe und Perspektiven der Stadtentwicklung in Ostmitteleuropa*, Passau: LIS Verlag, pp. 83–96.

Ladányi, J. and Szelényi, I. (1998) 'Class, ethnicity and urban restructuring in post-communist Hungary', in G. Enyedi (ed.) *Social Change and Urban Restructuring in Central Europe*, Budapest: Akadémiai Kiadó, pp. 67–86.

Lake, R. W. (2002) 'Bring back big government', *International Journal of Urban and Regional Research*, 26 (4): 815–22.

Lambert, C. and Boddy, M. (2002) 'Transforming the city: post-recession gentrification and re-urbanization', paper presented to the Conference on Upward Neighborhood Trajectories: Gentrification in a New Century, Glasgow, Scotland, September.

Laska, S. and Spain, D. (eds) (1980) *Back to the City: Issues in Neighbourhood Renovation*, Oxford: Pergamon Press.

Latham, A. (1999) 'Powers of engagement: on being engaged, being different, and urban life', *Area*, 31(2): 161–8 .

Lauria, M. and Knopp, L. (1985) 'Towards an analysis of the role of gay communities in the urban renaissance', *Urban Geographer*, 6: 152–69.

Law, C. M. (1992) 'Urban tourism and its contribution to economic regeneration', *Urban Studies*, 29(3/4): 599–618.

Laycock, M. and Myrvold, B. (1991) *Parkdale in Pictures: Its Development to 1889*, Toronto: Toronto Public Library Board, Local History Handbook No. 7.

Layton, J. (2000) *Homelessness: The Making and Unmaking of a Crisis*, Toronto: Penguin.

Lazare, D. (2001) 'Cincinnati and the X-Factor', *Columbia Journalism Review,* July/August (4).

Leeds Economy Handbook (2002), Leeds: Leeds City Council.

Lees, L. (1994a) 'Rethinking gentrification: beyond the positions of economics or culture', *Progress in Human Geography*, 18(2): 137–50.

Lees, L (1994b) 'Gentrification in London and New York: an atlantic gap?', *Housing Studies*, 9: 199–217.

Lees, L. (1996) 'In pursuit of difference: representations of gentrification', *Environment and Planning A*, 28: 453–70.

Lees, L. (1999) 'The weaving of gentrification discourse and the boundaries of the gentrification community', *Environment and Planning D*, 17: 127–32.

Lees, L. (2000) 'A reappraisal of gentrification: towards a "geography of gentrification"', *Progress in Human Geography*, 24(3): 389–408.

Lees, L. (2002a) 'Rematerializing geography: the "new" urban geography', *Progress in Human Geography*, 26: 109–20.

Lees, L. (2002b) 'Urban geography: the "death" of the city', in A. Rogers and H. Viles (eds) *The Student's Companion to Geography*, 2nd edn, Oxford: Blackwell.

Lees, L. (2003a) 'Policy re(turns): gentrification research and urban policy – urban policy and gentrification research', *Environment and Planning A*, 35: 571–74.

References

Lees, L. (2003b) 'Super-gentrification: the case of Brooklyn Heights, New York City', *Urban Studies*, 40(12): 2487–510.

Lees, L. (2003c) 'Visions of "urban renaissance": the urban task force report and the urban white paper', in R. Imrie and M. Raco (eds) *Urban Renaissance? New Labour, Community and Urban Policy*, Bristol: Policy Press, pp. 66–82.

Lees, L. and Bondi, L. (1995) 'De/gentrification and economic recession: the case of New York City', *Urban Geography*, 16: 234–53.

Lees, L. and Demeritt, D. (1998) 'Envisioning the livable city: the interplay of "Sin City" and "Sim City" in Vancouver's planning discourse', *Urban Geography*, 19: 332–59.

Lefebvre, Henri (1996) *Writings on Cities*, translated and edited by Eleonore Kofman and Elizabeth Lebas, Oxford: Blackwell.

Leland, J. (2003) 'A new Harlem gentry in search of its latte', *The New York Times*, 8 August: F1, F6, F7.

Lemon, J. (1993) 'Social planning and the welfare state', in L. Bourne and D. Ley (eds) *The Changing Social Geography of Canadian Cities*, Montreal: McGill-Queens University Press, pp. 267–80.

Leontidou, L. (1990a) *Cities of Silence. Working Class and Urban Space in Athens and Pireus, 1909–1940*, Athens: Themelio.

Leontidou, L. (1990b) *The Mediterranean City in Transition, Social Change and Urban Development*, Cambridge: Cambridge University Press.

Lévi-Strauss, C. (1973) *Tristes Tropiques.* Translated from French by John and Doreen Weightman, London: Jonathan Cape Limited.

Ley, D. (1980) 'Liberal ideology and the postindustrial city', *Canadian Geographer*, 25: 238–58.

Ley, D. (1981) 'Inner city revitalisation in Canada: a Vancouver case study', *Canadian Geographer*, 25: 124–48.

Ley, D. (1986) 'Alternative explanations for inner-city gentrification', *Annals of the Association of American Geographers*, 76: 521–35.

Ley, D. (1994) 'Gentrification and the politics of the new middle class', *Environment and Planning D*, 12: 53–74.

Ley, D. (1996) *The New Middle Class and the Remaking of the Central City*, London: Oxford University Press.

Ley, D. (2002) 'Artists, aestheticization and the field of gentrification', paper presented to the Conference on Upward Neighborhood Trajectories: Gentrification in a New Century, Glasgow, Scotland, September.

Ley, D. (2003) 'Artists, aestheticisation and the field of gentrification', *Urban Studies*, 40(12): 2527–44.

Ley, D. and Mills, C. (1986) 'Gentrification and reform politics in Montreal, 1982', *Cahiers de Geographie du Québec*, 30: 419–27.

Ley, D. and Mills, C. (1993) 'Can there be a postmodernism of resistance in the urban landscape?', in P. Knox (ed.) *The Restless Urban Landscape*, New Brunswick, NJ: Prentice Hall, pp. 255–78.

Ley, D., Tutchener, J. and Cunningham, G. (2002) 'Immigration, polarization, or gentrification? Accounting for changing house prices and dwelling values in gateway cities', *Urban Geography*, 23(8): 703–27.

Logan, W. (1985) *The Gentrification of Inner Melbourne: A Political Geography of Inner City Housing*, St Lucia, Queensland: University of Queensland Press.

Logan, J. and Molotch, H. (1987) *Urban Fortunes: The Political Economy of Place*, Berkeley and Los Angeles, CA: University of California Press.

Lowenthal, D. (1985) *The Past is a Foreign Country*, Cambridge: Cambridge University Press.

Lozanovksa, M. (1994) 'Abjection and architecture: the migrant house in multicultural Australia', in L. Johnson (ed.) *Suburban Dreaming*, Victoria: Deakin University Press.

Lund Hansen, A., Andersen, H. T. and Clark, E. (2001) 'Creative Copenhagen: globalization, urban governance and social change', *European Planning Studies*, 9: 851–69.

Lyons, M. (1996) 'Employment, feminisation and gentrification in London, 1981–1993', *Environment and Planning A*, 28: 341–56.

Lyons, T. (1998) 'The Parkdale rebellion', *Eye Magazine*, 29 October.

Lyons, T. (2000) 'Gentrification war: a case study of how residents associations kill rooming houses', *Eye Magazine*, 13 July.

Machiya Club (2002) 'The Kyo-Machiya Match-Maker System – and how to apply'. Online. Available: http://www.machiya.or.jp/index-e.html (20 September 2002).

Marcuse, P. (1986) 'Abandonment, gentrification and displacement: the linkages in New York City', in N. Smith and P. Williams (eds) *Gentrification of the City*, London: Allen and Unwin, pp. 153–77.

Marcuse, P. (1989) 'Gentrification, homelessness and the work process: housing markets and labour markets in the quartered city', *Housing Studies*, 4(3): 211–20.

Marcuse, P. and van Kempen, R. (eds) (2000) *Globalizing Cities: A New Spatial Order?*, Oxford: Blackwell.

Marinho de Azevedo, R. (1994) 'Será o novo Pelourinho um engano?', *Revista do Patrimônio Histórico e Artístico Nacional*, 23: 134.

Marrero, I. (2003) 'Del Manchester catalán al SoHo Barcelonés? La renovación del barrio del Poblenou en Barcelona y la cuestión de la vivienda', paper given at the fifth Coloquio Internacional de Geocrítica Barcelona, May 2003. Online. Available: http://www.ub.es/geocrit/sn/vmarer.htm (27 May 2003).

Marshall, J. (1982) *Madness: An Indictment of the Mental Health Care System in Ontario*, Toronto: Ontario Public Service Employees Union.

Martínez Monje, P. M. and Vicario, L. (1995) 'Déclin industriel et polarisation socio-spatiale: le cas de Bilbao', *Espace-Populations-Sociétés*, 3: 349–68.

Martínez Rigol, S. (2001) 'El retorn al centre de la ciutat. La reestructuració del Raval entre la renovació i la gentrificació', unpublished MPhil thesis, Universitat de Barcelona.

Martinotti, G. (1993) *Metropoli, La nuova morphologie della città*, Bologna: Il Mulino.

Massey, D. (2004) 'Geographies of responsibility', *Geografiska Annaler B*, 86: 5–18.

McCarthy, M. (2003) 'Growing army of undergraduates transforms run-down urban areas for better and worse', *The Independent*, 6 September.

McDowell, L. (1997) 'The new service class: employment, gender and housing decisions among London bankers in the 1990s', *Environment and Planning A*, 29: 2061–78.

McLoughlin, J. B. (1992) *Shaping Melbourne's Future? Town Planning, the State and Civil Society*, Cambridge: Cambridge University Press.

McNeill, D. (2000) 'McGuggenisation? National identity and globalisation in the Basque country', *Political Geography*, 19: 473–94.

McNeill, D. and While, A. (2001) 'The new urban economies', in R. Paddison (ed.) *Handbook of Urban Studies*, London: Sage Publications.

References

Merrett, S. (1979) 'L'imborghesimento delle aree urbane', in M. Folin (ed.) *Tecniche e politiche del problema della casa in Europa: la Gran Bretagna*, Padua: Marsilio Editori, pp. 140–50. 'Gentrification', in *Housing and Class in Britain*, a second volume of papers at the political Economy of Housing Workshop of the Conference of the Socialist Economists, London.

Merrifield, A. and Swyngedouw, E. (eds) (1997) *The Urbanization of Injustice*, New York: New York University Press.

Merton, R. K. (1957) *Social Theory and Social Structure*, Glencoe: Free Press.

Mickler, S. (1991) 'The battle for Goonininup', *Arena*, 96: 69–88.

Midgley, C. (2002) 'Hell of residence', *The Times*, 4 December.

Mieterberatung und Stadtforshung (1998) 'Privatmodernisierungen in Prenzlauer Berg 1998', unpublished, Berlin.

Mieterberatung und TOPOS Stadtforschung (1995) 'Privatmodernisierungen in Prenzlauer Berg', unpublished, Berlin.

Mills, C. (1988) '"Life on the upslope": the postmodern landscape of gentrification', *Environment and Planning D: Society and Space*, 6: 169–89.

Mills, C. (1993) 'Myths and meanings of gentrification', in J. S. Duncan and D. Ley (eds) *Place/Culture/Representation*, London: Routledge, pp.149–70.

Mimura, H., Kanki K. and Kobayashi, F. (1993) 'Urban conservation and landscape management: the Kyoto case', in G. S. Golany, K. Hanaki and O. Koike (eds) *Japanese Urban Environment*, New York: Pergamon.

Mincey, D. (2001) 'Reacting to rage', *Black Athlete*, 20 April.

Ministerio de Fomento (2003) *Boletín Estadístico*, 33(10).

Mitchell, D. (1997) 'The annihilation of space by law: the roots and implications of anti-homeless laws in the United States', *Antipode*, 29(3): 303–35.

Molotch, H. (1976) 'The city as a growth machine: toward a political economy of place', *American Journal of Sociology*, 82(2): 303–32.

Monclús, F. J. (2000) 'Barcelona's planning strategies: from "Paris of the South" to the "Capital of West Mediterranean"', *GeoJournal*, 51: 57–63.

Motta, L. (2000) 'A apropriação do patrimônio urbano: do estético-estilístico nacional ao consumo visual global', in A. Arantes (ed.) *O espaço da diferença*, Campinas: Editora Papirus.

Moulaert, F., Rodríguez, A. and Swyngedouw, E. (eds) (2003) *The Globalized City. Economic Restructuring and Social Polarization in European Cities*, Oxford: Oxford University Press.

Muecke, S. (1992) *Textual Spaces: Aboriginality and Cultural Studies*, Sydney: University of NSW Press.

Munt, I. (1987) 'Economic restructuring, culture, and gentrification: a case study in Battersea, London', *Environment and Planning A*, 19: 1175–97.

Murphy, P. and Watson, S. (1997) *Surface City: Sydney at the Millennium*, Australia: Pluto Press.

Musterd, S. and van Weesep, J. (1991) 'European gentrification or gentrification in Europe?', in S. Musterd, and J. van Weesep (eds) *Urban Housing for the Better-Off: Gentrification in Europe*, Utrecht: Stedelijke Netwerken, pp. 11–16.

Nanba, T. (2000) 'Gentrification of prewar inner city housing in Japan', *Bulletin of Nagoya College*, 38: 109–23.

Narita, K. (1987) *Daitoshi Suitai Chiku no Saisei: Jumin to Kinou no Tayouka to Fukugouka wo mezashite*, Tokyo: Taimeidou.

Narita, K. (1995) *Tenkanki no Toshi to Toshiken*, Kyoto: Chijinshobou.

Narita, K. (1999) 'Daitoshi suitai chiku no saisei: Jiba tositeno daitoshi inner area', in M. Okuda (ed.) *Urban Sociology (Sociology in Japan 4)*, Tokyo: University of Tokyo Press.

National Coalition for the Homeless/National Law Center on Homelessness and Poverty (2002) *Illegal to be Homeless: The Criminalization of Homelessness in the United States*, Washington, DC: NCH/NLCHP.

National Low-Income Housing Coalition (2001) *Out of Reach*, report. Online. Available: http://www.nlihc.org (accessed April 2002).

Nello, O. (2000) 'Las areas metropolitanas', in A. G. Olcina and J. Gómez Mendoza (eds) *Geografía de España*, Barcelona: Ariel, pp. 275–98.

Newman, K. (2003) 'Shaping urban and neighborhood revitalization in Newark: markets, politics, and public policy', manuscript under review at *Annals of the American Academy of Political and Social Science*.

North, M. and Christie, S. (1997) 'The de-industrialisation of Chippendale: industrial heritage in the post-industrial city', DUAP, Heritage Assistance Plan.

Noworol, A. and Serafin, R. (1998) 'Krakow towards a sustainable urban life', paper given at Economic Commission for Europe (ECE) workshop 'Encouraging Local Initiatives Towards Sustainable Consumption Patterns', 2–4 February, Vienna, Geneva: United Nations.

Oliveira, M. N. de (2000) 'Avenida Paulista: a produção de uma paisagem de poder', in A. Arantes (ed.) *O espaço da diferença*, Campinas: Editora Papirus.

Olivera, A. and Abellan, A. (1997) 'Las características de la población', in R. Puyol (ed.) *Dinamica de la Población en España. Cambios demográficos en el ultimo cuarto del siglo XX*, Madrid: Sinesis, pp. 311–56.

Oncu, A. (1997) 'The myth of the "ideal home" travels across cultural borders to Istanbul', in A. Oncu and P. Weyland (eds) *Space, Culture and Power: New Identities in Globalizing Cities*, London: Zed Books.

Osborne, K. (2000) 'Council let genesis slide, 2 members say', *Cincinnati Post*, 16 February.

Ozdemir, D. (2002) 'The distribution of foreign direct investments in the service sector in Istanbul', *Cities*, 19(4): 249–59.

Padovani, L. (1996) 'Italy' in P. Balcin (ed.) *Housing Policy in Europe*, London: Routledge, pp. 188–209.

Papageorgiou-Venetas, A. (2002) 'A future for Athens', *Ekistics*, 415–17: 209–19.

Peck, J. and Tickell, A. (2002) 'Neoliberalizing space', *Antipode*, 34(3): 380–404.

Peressini, T. and McDonald, L. (2000) 'Urban homelessness in Canada', in T. Bunting and P. Filion (eds) *Canadian Cities in Transition*, 2nd edn, Oxford: Oxford University Press, pp. 525–43.

Petsimeris, P. (1990) 'La mobilité intra-urbaine comme la dimmension cachée de la ségrégation urbaine', *Géographie Sociale*, 11: 112–39.

Petsimeris, P. (1991) 'Torino: lo spazio sociale intra-metropolitano nell'era della deurbanizzazione', in P. Petsimeris (ed.) *Le trasformazioni sociali dello spazio urbano*, Bologna: Pàtron, pp. 163–88.

Petsimeris, P. (1994) 'La mobilità residenziale nello spazio intra-urbano di Torino, 1951–1991', *Storia Urbana*, 66: 145–68.

Petsimeris, P. (1998) 'Urban decline and the new social and ethnic divisions in the core cities of the Italian industrial triangle', *Urban Studies*, 35(3): 449–66.

References

Philip, M. (2000) 'Researchers fear segregating rich from poor will bring the ghetto to Canada', *The Globe and Mail*, 5 August.

Phillips, M. (1993) 'Rural gentrification and the processes of class colonisation', *Journal of Rural Studies*, 9(2): 123–40.

Piccinato, G. (1978) 'La questione del centro storico', in F. Cialdini and P. Falini (eds) *I centri storici*, Milan: Mazzotta, pp. 15–35.

Pikionis, D. (1985) (in Greek) *D. Pikioni's Texts*, Athens: Editions of the Cultural Foundation of the National Bank.

Pinho, O. de A. (1996) 'Descentrando o pelô', MA thesis, Department of Anthropology, UNICAMP.

Plaza, B. (2000) 'Evaluating the influence of a large cultural artifact in the attraction of tourism. The Guggenheim Museum Bilbao case', *Urban Affairs Review*, 36: 264–74.

Podmore, J. (1998) '(Re)Reading the "loft living" habitus in Montreal's inner city', *International Journal of Urban and Regional Research*, 22: 283–302.

Pogrebin, R. (2002) 'Way uptown, the west is being won. It's wild', *New York Times*, 23 August: B1, B4.

Potenza, S. (1975) 'Alcune ipotesi sul modello di risanamento del centro storico di Venezia in relazione alla legge speciale', in P. Ceri (ed.) *Casa città e struttura sociale*, Rome: Editori Riuniti, pp. 257–78.

Powell, A. J. (1967) 'Redevelopment in a metropolitan region context', in P. Troy (ed.) *Urban Redevelopment in Australia*, Canberra: Australian National University.

Pratolini, V. (1980) *Le quartier*, Paris: Albin Michel.

Pred, A. (1977) *City-Systems in Advanced Economies*, London: Hutchinson.

Proença, L. R. (2001) 'Espaço público e política dos lugares: usos do patrimônio cultural na invenção contemporânea do Recife antigo', PhD dissertation in Social Sciences, IFCH, UNICAMP.

Proença, L. R. (2002) 'Contra-uos e espaço público: notas sobre a construção social dos lugares na "Manguetown"', *Revista Brasileira de Ciências Sociais*, 17(49): 115–34.

Prosser, J. and Schwartz, D. (1998) 'Photographs within the sociological research process', in J. Prosser (ed.) *Image-based Research: A Sourcebook for Qualitative Researchers*, London: Falmer Press, pp. 115–29.

Psomopoulos, P. (1977) 'Guiding the growth of metropolitan Athens', *Ekistics*, 262: 120–33.

Qiu, J. (2002) 'Consideration of "gentrification" in contemporary Chinese urban renewal', *Tropical Geography*, 22: 125–9.

Rapport, A. (1995) 'Review of Herzfeld', *Man*, 1(3): 645–6.

Rayner, M. (1997) *Rooting Democracy: Growing the Society we Want*, Melbourne: Allen and Unwin.

Rebizant, P. *et al.* (1976) 'New from old: a pilot study of housing rehabilitation and neighbourhood change', unpublished paper, Faculty of Environmental Studies, York University, Toronto.

Redfern, P. (1997a) 'A new look at gentrification: 1 gentrification and domestic technologies', *Environment and Planning A*, 29: 1275–96.

Redfern, P. (1997b) 'A new look at gentrification: 2 a model of gentrification', *Environment and Planning A*, 29: 1335–54.

Reimann, B. (2000) *Städtische Wohnquartiere*, Opladen: Leske and Budrich.

Reynolds, H. (1996) *Frontier: Reports From the Edge of White Settlement*, Sydney: Allen and Unwin.

Rieger, J. H. (1996) 'Photographing social change', *Visual Sociology*, 11: 5–49.

Rink, D. (1997) 'Zur Segregation in Ostdeutschen Großstädten', in S. Kabisch, A. Kindeler and D. Rink (eds) *Sozial-Atlas der Stadt Leipzig,* Leipzig-Halle: UFZ.

Ritzer, G. (1993) *The McDonaldization of Society*, Thousand Oaks, CA: Pine Forge Press.

Robinson, F. and Shaw, K. (2003) 'The last chance for community-led regeneration in England? A review of the new deal for communities', paper presented to the conference of the International Network for Urban Research and Action, Trebnitz.

Robson, G. and Butler, T. (2001) 'Coming to terms with London: middle class communities in a global city', *International Journal of Urban and Regional Research*, 24: 70–86.

Rodríguez, A. and Martínez, E. (2001) 'Del declive a la revitalización: oportunidades y límites de las nuevas políticas urbanas en Bilbao', *Ciudad y Territorio/Estudios Territoriales*, 33(129): 441–59.

Rodríguez, A., Martínez, E. and Guenaga, G. (2001) 'Uneven redevelopment. New urban policies and socio-spatial fragmentation in metropolitan Bilbao', *European Urban and Regional Studies*, 8(2): 161–78.

Rodríguez, V., Puga, D. and Vázquez, C. (2002) 'Bases para un estudio de la gentrificación en Madrid', *Boletín de la Real Sociedad Geográfica*, 137/138: 273–310.

Rofe, M. (2003) '"I want to be global": theorising the gentrifying class as an emergent elite global community', *Urban Studies*, 40(12): 2511–27.

Rolnik, R. (1997) *A cidade e a lei. Legislação, política urbana e territórios na cidade de São Paulo*, São Paulo: Studio Nobel.

Rosaldo, R. (1989) 'Imperial nostalgia', *Representations*, Spring, 26: 107–21.

Rose, D. (1984) 'Rethinking gentrification: beyond the uneven development of Marxist urban theory', *Environment and Planning D: Society and Space*, 1: 47–74.

Rose, D. (1989) 'A feminist perspective of employment restructuring and gentrification: the case of Montreal', in J. Wolch and M. Dear (eds) *The Power of Geography: How Territory Shapes Social Life*, Boston, MA: Unwin Hyman, pp. 118–38.

Rose, D. (1996) 'Economic restructuring and the diversification of gentrification in the 1980s: a view from a marginal metropolis', in J. Caulfield and L. Peake (eds) *City Lives and City Forms: Critical Research and Canadian Urbanism*, Toronto: University of Toronto Press, pp. 131–72.

Rose, D. (2003) 'The uneasy cohabitation of gentrification and "social mix?" A case study of residents of infill condominiums in Montreal', unpublished manuscript.

Rose, D. and Le Bourdais, C. (1986) 'The changing conditions of female single parenthood in Montréal's inner city and suburban neighborhoods', *Urban Resources*, 3(2): 45–52.

Rose, D. and Villeneuve, P. with Colgan, F. (1988) 'Women workers and the inner city: labour force restructuring and neighbourhood change in Montréal, 1971–1981', in C. Andrew and B. Milroy (eds) *Life Spaces: Gender, Household, Employment*, Vancouver: University of British Columbia Press, pp. 31–64.

Rossi, P. (1955) *Why Families Move: A Study in the Social Psychology of Urban Residential Mobility*, New York: Free Press.

Rubino, S. (1992) As fachadas da história. As origens, a criação e os trabalhos do Serviço do Patrimônio Histórico e Artístico Nacional (SPHAN) 1936–1968, MA thesis, Department of Anthropology, UNICAMP.

Rugg, J., Rhodes, D. and Jones, A. (2000) *The Nature and Impact of Student Demand*, York: York Publishing Services.

Ruoppila, S. (1998) 'The changing urban landscape of Tallinn', *The Finish Journal of Urban Studies (Yhteiskuntasuunnittelu)*, 36(3): 36–43.

References

Ruoppila, S. (2002) 'Elamute arendusprojektid: paiknemine ja tingimused Tallinas / Location and conditions of residential real estate development in Tallin, 1995–2002', *Maja – Estonian Architectural Review*, 4: 20–5.

Ruoppila, S. and Kährik, A. (2003) 'Socio-economic residential differentiation in post-socialist Tallinn', *Journal of Housing and the Built Environment*, 18(1): 49–73.

Said, E. (1978) *Orientalism: Western Conceptions of the Orient*, London: Penguin.

Sargatal, M. A. (2001) 'Gentrificación e inmigración en los centros históricos: el caso del barrio del Raval en Barcelona', *Scripta Nova*, 94(6). Online. Available: http://www.ub.es/geocrit/sn-94–66.htm (29 May 2003).

SAS (1999) 'Sozialstudie äußere Neustadt', unpublished, Dresden.

Sassen, S. (1991) *The Global City: New York, London, Tokyo*, Princeton, NJ: Princeton University Press.

Sassen, S. (1998) *Globalisation and its Discontents*, New York: New Press.

Sassen, S. (2000a) *The Global City: New York, London, Tokyo*, 2nd edn, Princeton, NJ: Princeton University Press.

Sassen, S. (2000b) *Cities in a World Economy*, 2nd edn, Thousand Oaks, CA: Pine Forge Press.

Sassen, S. (2000c) 'Analytic borderlands: economy and culture in the global city', in G. Bridge and S. Watson (eds) *A Companion to the City*, Oxford: Blackwell, pp. 168–80.

Sayer, A. (1992) *Method in Social Science: A Realist Approach*, London: Routledge.

Sayer, A. (2000) *Realism and Social Science*, London: Sage.

Sayer, A. (2001) 'For a critical cultural political economy', *Antipode*, 33: 687–708.

Secchi, B. (1984) *Il racconto urbanistico; la politica della casa e delterritorio in Italia*, Turin: Einaudi.

Sennett, R. (1990) *The Conscience of the Eye: The Design and Social Life of Cities*, London: Faber and Faber.

Sennett, R. (1994) *Flesh and Stone: The Body and the City in Western Civilization*, London: Faber and Faber.

Sennett, R. (1998) *The Corrosion of Character: The Personal Consequences of Work in the New Capitalism*, London: W. W. Norton.

Seronde-Babonaux, A.-M. (1980) *De l'urbs à la ville, Rome, croissance d'une capitale*, Aix-en-Provence: Édisud.

Seth, S., Gandhi, L. and Dutton, M. (1998) 'Postcolonial studies: a beginning', *Postcolonial Studies*, 1(1) 7–11.

Shaw, B. J. and Jones, R. (eds) (1997) *Contested Urban Heritage: Voices from the Periphery*, Sydney: Ashgate.

Shaw, K. (2002) 'Culture, economics and evolution in gentrification', *Just Policy*, 28: 42–50.

Shaw, W. S. (2000) 'Ways of whiteness: Harlemising Sydney's aboriginal redfern', *Australian Geographical Studies*, 38(3): 291–305.

Shaw, W. S. (2001) 'Ways of whiteness: negotiated settlement agendas in (post)colonial Inner Sydney', unpublished PhD thesis, University of Melbourne.

Sheppard, E. and Barnes, T. (1990) *The Capitalist Space Economy: Geographical Analysis after Ricardo, Marx and Sraffa*, London: Unwin Hyman.

Short, J. R. (1996) *The Urban Order: An Introduction to Cities, Culture and Power*, Oxford: Blackwell.

Sibley, D. (1995) *Geographies of Exclusion*, London: Routledge.

Simmel, G. (1903) 'The metropolis and mental life', in P. Kasinitz (ed.) 1995, *Metropolis: Centre and Symbol of Our Times*, New York: New York University Press.

Simmel, G. (1957) 'Fashion', *American Journal of Sociology*, 62(6): 541–58.

Simmel, G. (1973) 'Roma, Firenze e Venezia', in M. Cacciari (ed.) *Metropolis*, Rome: Officina Edizioni, Roma, pp. 188–97.

Simmons, H. (1990) *Unbalanced: Mental Health Policy in Ontario, 1930–1989*, Toronto: Wall and Thompson.

Slater, T. (2002) 'Looking at the "North American City" through the lens of gentrification discourse', *Urban Geography*, 23(1): 131–53.

Slater, T. (2003) 'Municipally-managed gentrification in South Parkdale, Toronto', *The Canadian Geographer*, (48)3: 303–25.

Slater, T. (2004, forthcoming) 'North American gentrification? Revanchist and emancipatory perspectives explored', *Environment and Planning A*, 36: 1191–1213.

Smith, D. P. (2002a) 'Processes of "studentification": cultural differentiation and spatial awareness in the "student ghetto"', paper presented to Upward Neighbourhood Trajectories: Gentrification in a New Century Conference, Glasgow.

Smith, D. P. (2002b) 'Patterns and processes of "studentification" in Leeds', *Regional Review*, 11: 17–19.

Smith, D. P. (2002c) 'Rural gatekeepers: closing and opening up "access" to greentrified Pennine rurality', *Social and Cultural Geography*, 3: 445–61.

Smith, D. P. and Phillips, D. (2001) 'Socio-cultural representations of gentrified Pennine rurality', *Journal of Rural Studies*, 17: 457–69.

Smith, H. (2003) 'Planning, policy and polarisation in Vancouver's downtown Eastside', *Tijdschrift voor Economische en Sociale Geografie*, 94(4): 496–509.

Smith, M. P. (1999) 'Transnationalism and the city', in R. A. Beauregard and S. Body-Gendrot (eds) *The Urban Moment*, Thousand Oaks, CA: Sage Publications, pp. 119–39.

Smith, N. (1979) 'Toward a theory of gentrification: a back to the city movement of capital, not people', *Journal of the American Planning Association*, 45(4): 583–48.

Smith, N. (1986) 'Gentrification, the frontier, and the restructuring of urban space', in N. Smith and P. Williams (eds) *Gentrification and the City*, Boston: Allen and Unwin.

Smith, N. (1987) 'Of yuppies and housing: gentrification, social restructuring and the urban dream', *Environment and Planning D: Society and Space* 5 (2): 151–72.

Smith, N. (1992a) 'New city, new frontier: the Lower East Side as wild, wild west', in M. Sorkin (ed.) *Variations on a Theme Park: The New American City and the End of Public Space*, New York: Hill and Wang, pp. 61–93.

Smith, N. (1992b) 'Blind man's buff, or Hamnett's philosophical individualism in search of gentrification', *Transactions of the Institute of British Geographers*, 17: 110–15.

Smith, N. (1995) *The New Urban Frontier: Gentrification and the Revanchist City*, London: Routledge.

Smith, N. (1997) 'Social justice and the new American urbanism: the revanchist city', in A. Merrifield and E. Swyngedouw (eds) *The Urbanization of Injustice*, New York: New York University Press, pp. 117–36.

Smith, N. (2002) 'New globalism, new urbanism: gentrification as global urban strategy', *Antipode*, 34(3): 428–50.

Smith, N. and DeFilippis, J. (1999) 'The reassertion of economics: 1990s gentrification in the Lower East Side', *International Journal of Urban and Regional Research* 23: 638–53.

References

Smith, N. and Derksen, J. (2002) 'Urban regeneration: gentrification as global urban strategy', in R. Shier (ed.) *Stan Douglas: Every Block on 100 West Hastings*, Vancouver: Contemporary Art Gallery, pp. 62–95.

Smith, N. and Williams, P. (1986a) 'Alternatives to orthodoxy: invitation to debate', in N. Smith and P. Williams (eds) *Gentrification of the City*, London: Allen and Unwin, pp. 1–12.

Smith, N. and Williams, P. (eds) (1986b) *Gentrification of the City*, Boston, MA: Allen & Unwin.

Soja, E.W. (2000) *Postmetropolis: Critical Studies of Cities and Regions*, Oxford: Blackwell.

Sommers, J. and Blomley, N. (2002) 'The worst block in Vancouver', in R. Shier (ed.) *Stan Douglas: Every Block on 100 West Hastings*, Vancouver: Contemporary Art Gallery, pp. 18–61.

Sonobe, M. (2001) *Contemporary Metropolitan Society: Dual City?*, Tokyo: Toshindo.

Spivak, G. (1985) 'Can the subaltern speak? Speculations on widow sacrifice', *Wedge*, 7(8): Winter/Spring, 120–30.

Spivak, G. (1987) *In Other Worlds: Essays in Cultural Politics*, New York: Methuen.

Spivak, G. (1990) *The Post-Colonial Critic: Interviews, Strategies, Dialogues*, edited by Sarah Harasym, New York: Routledge.

Staeheli, L. A., Kodras, J. E. and Flint, C. (eds) (1997) 'State devolution in America: implications for a diverse society', *Urban Affairs Annual Reviews*, 48, Thousand Oaks, CA: Sage Publications.

State Institute of Statistics Prime Ministry Republic of Turkey (1983) *1980 Census of Population*, Ankara: State Institute of Statistics Prime Ministry Republic of Turkey.

Stilwell, F. (1993) *Reshaping Australia: Urban Problems and Policies*, Australia: Pluto Press.

Stoecker, R. and Vakil, A. (2000) 'States, cultures and community organising: two tales of two neighborhoods', *Journal of Urban Affairs*, 22(4): 439–58.

Stretton, H. (1989) *Ideas for Australian Cities*, 3rd edn, Sydney: Transit Australia.

Suchar, C. (1992) 'Icons and images of gentrification: the changed material culture of an urban community', in R. Hutchinson (ed.) *Gentrification and Urban Change: Research in Urban Sociology*, vol. 2, Greenwich, CT: JAI Press, pp. 165–92.

Sudjic, D. (2002) 'Can Liverpool be the Bilbao of the north?', *The Observer*, 15 December.

Sýkora, L. (1996) 'Economic and social restructuring and gentrification in Prague', *Acta Facultatis Rerum Naturalium Universitatis Comenianae, Geographica*, 37: 71–81.

Sýkora, L. (1999) 'Changes in the internal spatial structure of post-communist Prague', *GeoJournal*, 49(1): 79–89.

Sýkora, L. (2003) 'Between the state and the market: local government and housing in the Czech Republic', in M. Lux (ed.) *Housing Policy: An End or a New Beginning?* Budapest: Local Government and Public Reform Initiative, Open Society Institute, pp. 47–116.

Sýkora, L. and Šimoníčková, I. (1994) 'From totalitarian urban managerialism to a liberalized real estate market: Prague's transformations in the early 1990s', in M. Barlow, P. Dostál and M. Hampl (eds) *Development and Administration of Prague*, Amsterdam: Instituut voor Sociale Geografie, Universiteit van Amsterdam, pp. 47–72.

Takagi, K. (1994) 'Restructuring of urban space and emergence of new subculture', *Municipal Problems*, 85: 89–98.

Takagi, K. (1996) 'Transformation of social structure in the urban center redevelopment area; a case study on residents in Tokyo waterfront district', *Municipal Problems*, 87: 99–109.

Takahashi, Y. (1992) *Daitoshi Shakai no Restructuring: Tokyo no Inner City Mondai*, Tokyo: Nihonhyoronsha.

Taylor, K. (1994) 'Things we want to keep: discovering Australia's cultural heritage', in D. Hedon, J. Hooton and D. Horne (eds) *The Abundant Culture: Meaning and Significance in Everyday Australia*, Australia: Allen and Unwin.

Temelová, J. and Hrychová, H. (2003) 'Globalisation, eyes and urban space: visual perceptions of globalising Prague', in 'Urbanism and Globalisation', proceedings of 2nd EuroConference The European City in Transition, Weimar: Bauhaus University.

Thomas, N. (1994) *Colonialism's Culture: Anthropology, Travel and Government*, Cambridge: Polity Press.

Thrift, N. (1987) 'The geography of late twentieth-century class formation', in N. Thrift and P. Williams (eds) *Class and Space*, Andover: Routledge and Kegan Paul.

Thrift, N. and Glennie, P. (1993) 'Historical geographies of urban life and modern consumption', in G. Kearns and C. Philo (eds) *Selling Places: The City as Cultural Capital, Past and Present*, Oxford: Pergamon.

Thrift, N. and Walling, D. (2000) 'Geography in the United Kingdom 1996–2000', *The Geographical Journal*, 166(2): 96–124.

Tickell, A. (1996) 'Taking the initiative: the Leeds financial centre', in G. Haughton and C. Williams (eds) *Corporate City? Partnership, Participation and Partition in Urban Development in Leeds*, Aldershot: Ashgate.

Tickell, A. (1993) *The Role of Leeds and the Regional Financial System*, Leeds: University of Leeds.

TOPOS Stadtforschung (2001) 'Einkommens- und Armutsbericht Berlin 2000', unpublished, Berlin.

TOPOS Stadtforschung (1999) Privatmodernisierungen in den nördlichen Altbauquartieren von Prenzlauer Berg', unpublished, Berlin.

Tosi, A. (1993) *Immigrati e senza casa; i problemi, i progetti, le politiche*, Milan: Angeli Franco.

Treen, C. (1976) 'The process of suburban development in North Leeds 1870–1914', in F. M. L. Thompson (ed.) *The Rise of Suburbia*, Oxford: Pavilion.

Tsiomis, Y. (1985) *Athènes affaire européenne*, Athens: Ministère de la Culture.

Tsoulouvis, L. (1998) 'Planning, the urban system and new forms of inequality in Greek cities', *Progress in Planning*, 50(1): 1–74.

Ueno K., Iwabu, R., Okuno, O., Okano, M. and Yoshino, S. (1991) 'Construction of apartment house in a city central area and its influence on living and community: on the case of a traditional industrial area (Joson in Kyoto city)', *Scientific Reports of the Kyoto Prefectural University: Natural Science and Living Science*, 40: 85–96.

UNESCO, 'Étude sur la réhabilitation des quartiers de Balat et Fener à Istanbul 1998', UNESCO-Commission Européenne-Municipalité de Fatih.

Urry, J. (1990) *The Tourist Gaze*, London: Sage.

USAID (2000) The United States Agency for International Development, Mission to Poland in Local Government and Housing Sector Reform – A History and Assessment from 1990–2000, Washington, DC: The United States Agency for International Development.

Uzun, C. N. (2001) *Gentrification in Istanbul: A Diagnostic Study*, Utrecht: KNAG.

References

Van Criekingen, M. and Decroly J. (2003) 'Revisiting the diversity of gentrification: neighbourhood renewal processes in Brussels and Montreal', *Urban Studies*, 40(12): 2451–68.

Van Weesep, J. (1994) 'Gentrification as a research frontier', *Progress in Human Geography*, 18: 74–83.

Vázquez, C. (1996) 'Espacio urbano y segregación social. Procesos y políticas en el casco histórico de Madrid', unpublished MPhil thesis, Universidad Autónoma de Madrid.

Vicario, L. and Martínez Monje, P. M. (2003) 'Another "Guggenheim effect?" The generation of a potentially gentrifiable neighbourhood in Bilbao', *Urban Studies*, 40(12): 2383–400.

Vidotto, V. (2001) *Roma contemporanea*, Bari: Editori Laterza.

Vigdor, J. (2002) 'Does gentrification harm the poor?', *Brookings-Wharton Papers on Urban Affairs*, 2002: 113–73. Online. Available: http://www.pubpol.duke.edu/people/faculty/vigdor/index.html.

Waitt, G. and McGuirk, P. M. (1996) 'Marking time: tourism and heritage representation at Millers Point, Sydney', *Australian Geographer*, 27(1): 11–30.

Waldron, Jeremy (1991) 'Homelessness and the issue of freedom', *UCLA Law Review*, 39: 295–324.

Walks, R. A. (2001) 'The social ecology of the post-Fordist/global city? Economic restructuring and socio-spatial polarisation in the Toronto urban region', *Urban Studies*, 38(3): 407–48.

Ward, P. M. (1993) 'The Latin American inner city: differences of degree or of kind?', *Environment and Planning A*, 25: 1131–60.

Warde, A. (1991) 'Gentrification as consumption: issues of class and gender', *Environment and Planning D*, 9: 223–32.

Ware, C. (1994) *Greenwich Village 1920–30*, Berkeley, CA: University of California Press.

Wassenhoven, L. (1984) 'Greece', in M. Wynn (ed.) *Planning and Urban Growth in Southern Europe*, London: Mansell, pp. 5–36.

Wasserman, R. (1984) 'Re-inventing the new world: Cooper and Alencar', *Comparative Literature*, 36(2): Spring, 130–45.

Wasserman, R. (1994) *Exotic Nations: Literature and Cultural Identity in the United States and Brazil, 1830–1930*, Ithaca: Cornell University Press.

Weiske, C. (1996) 'Gentrification and incumbent upgrading in erfurt', in J. Friedrich and R. Kecskes (eds) *Gentrification; Theorie und Forschungsergebnisse*, Opladen: Leske and Budrich, pp. 193–226.

Whitzman, C. (2003) 'The dreams attached to places: from suburb, to slum, to urban village in a Toronto neighbourhood 1875–2002', unpublished PhD dissertation, Department of Geography, McMaster University.

Williams, P. (1984) 'Gentrification in Britain and Europe', in J. Palen and B. London (eds) *Gentrification, Displacement and Neighbourhood Revitalization*, Albany, NY: State University of New York Press.

Williams, S. (2000) 'Rehabilitation not gentrification', *Unesco Sources* 10146989, 119: 22. Online, Available Academic Search Premier.

Wirth, L. (1938) 'Urbanism as a way of life', *American Journal of Sociology*, XLIV(1): 1–26.

Wright, P. (1997) 'The ghosting of the inner-city', in L. Mcdowell (ed.) *Undoing Place?: A Geographical Reader*, London and New York: Arnold.

Wyly, E. K. and Hammel, D. J. (1998) 'Modeling the context and contingencies of gentrification', *Journal of Urban Affairs*, 20: 303–24.

Wyly, E. K. and Hammel, D. J. (1999) 'Islands of decay in seas of renewal: housing policy and the resurgence of gentrification', *Housing Policy Debate*, 10(4): 711–71.

Wyly, E. K. and Hammel, D. J. (2000) 'Capital's metropolis: Chicago and the transformation of American housing policy', *Geografiska Annaler*, 82B(4): 181–206.

Wynne, D. and O'Conner, J. (1998) 'Consumption and the postmodern city', *Urban Studies*, 35: 841–64.

Yabe, N. (2003) 'Population recovery in inner Tokyo in the late 1990s: a questionnaire survey in Minato ward', *The Human Geography*, 55: 277–92.

Young, I. M. (1990) *Justice and the Politics of Difference*, Princeton, NJ: Princeton University Press.

Yuan, L. L. and Yuan, B. (1998) 'Singapore no hozon niyoru toshi saikaihatsu', *Urban Housing Studies*, 21: 2–8.

Zevi, B. (1997) *Storia e controstoria dell'architettura in Italia*, Rome: Newton & Compton.

Zivas, D. A. (1988) 'Protection and revival in Plaka, Athens: a program at work', *Ekistics*, 333: 329–36.

Zukin, S. (1982) *Loft Living: Culture and Capital in Urban Change*, Baltimore: Johns Hopkins University Press.

Zukin, S. (1986) 'Gentrification: culture and capital in the urban core', *Annual Review of Sociology*, 13: 129–37.

Zukin, S. (1991) *Landscapes of Power: From Detroit to Disney World*, Berkeley, Los Angeles, CA and Oxford: University of California Press.

Zukin, S. (1995) *The Cultures of Cities*, Cambridge, MA: Blackwell.

Zukin, S. (2000) 'Paisagens do século XXI: notas sobre a mudança social e do espaço urbano', in A. Arantes (ed.) *O espaço da diferença*, Campinas: Editora Papirus.

Index

Page references: in bold type refer to main references within the sequence; italicised refer to illustrations; followed by n refer to endnotes; followed by t refer to tables.

Index